Denver's Lakeside Amusement Park

Timberline Books
Stephen J. Leonard and Thomas J. Noel, editors

The Beast
  Benjamin Barr Lindsey with Harvey J. O'Higgins

Colorado's Japanese Americans
  Bill Hosokawa

Colorado Women: A History
  Gail M. Beaton

Denver: An Archaeological History
  Sarah M. Nelson, K. Lynn Berry, Richard F. Carrillo, Bonnie L. Clark, Lori E. Rhodes, and Dean Saitta

Denver's Lakeside Amusement Park: From the White City Beautiful to a Century of Fun
  David Forsyth

Dr. Charles David Spivak: A Jewish Immigrant and the American Tuberculosis Movement
  Jeanne E. Abrams

Enduring Legacies: Ethnic Histories and Cultures of Colorado
  edited by Arturo J. Aldama, Elisa Facio, Daryl Maeda, and Reiland Rabaka

The Gospel of Progressivism: Moral Reform and Labor War in Colorado, 1900–1930
  R. Todd Laugen

Helen Ring Robinson: Colorado Senator and Suffragist
  Pat Pascoe

Ores to Metals: The Rocky Mountain Smelting Industry
  James E. Fell, Jr.

Season of Terror: The Espinosas in Central Colorado, March–October 1863
  Charles F. Price

A Tenderfoot in Colorado
  R. B. Townshend

The Trail of Gold and Silver: Mining in Colorado, 1859–2009
  Duane A. Smith

Denver's Lakeside Amusement Park

From the White City Beautiful
to a Century of Fun

David Forsyth

With a foreword by Thomas J. Noel

UNIVERSITY PRESS OF COLORADO
Boulder

© 2016 by University Press of Colorado

Published by University Press of Colorado
5589 Arapahoe Avenue, Suite 206C
Boulder, Colorado 80303

All rights reserved

 The University Press of Colorado is a proud member of
The Association of American University Presses.

The University Press of Colorado is a cooperative publishing enterprise supported, in part, by Adams State University, Colorado State University, Fort Lewis College, Metropolitan State University of Denver, Regis University, University of Colorado, University of Northern Colorado, Utah State University, and Western State Colorado University.

ISBN: 978-1-60732-430-0 (pbk)
ISBN: 978-1-60732-431-7 (ebook)

Library of Congress Cataloging-in-Publication Data
Names: Forsyth, David, 1977– author
Title: Denver's Lakeside Amusement Park : from the white city beautiful to a century of fun / by David Forsyth.
Description: Boulder : University Press of Colorado, 2016. | Series: Timberline books | Includes bibliographical references.
Identifiers: LCCN 2015025155 | ISBN 9781607324300 (pbk.) | ISBN 9781607324317 (ebook)
Subjects: LCSH: Lakeside Amusement Park (Denver, Colo.)—History. | Denver (Colo.)—Social life and customs.
Classification: LCC GV1853.3.C62 L354 2016 | DDC 791.06/878883—dc23
LC record available at http://lccn.loc.gov/2015025155

Cover photo credits: author's collection (top left, top right), Karl Gehring, Denver Post/Getty Images (center right), author's collection (bottom right), Sarah Bales (bottom left).

For Laffing Sal and everyone else who
has laughed their way through Lakeside.

Contents

List of Illustrations	ix
Foreword	
Thomas J. Noel	xiii
Acknowledgments	xix
INTRODUCTION: In Search of Blooming Gardens	3
1. Lakeside, an Amusement Enterprise	23
2. Just Take a Trip Out to Jolly Lakeside	39
3. Lakeside, the White City Beautiful	67
4. Keeping Lakeside's Bright Lights Shining	89
5. Benjamin Krasner and Lakeside's New Setup	105
6. Lakeside Speedway and the Roaring Bugs of Speed	131
7. The Wild Chipmunk versus the Mouse	147
8. The Stockers Take over at Lakeside Speedway	167
9. Lakeside Amusement Park, Public Nuisance?	191
10. Lakeside, the Most Entertaining City in America	209
CONCLUSION: A Century of Fun at Lakeside Amusement Park	225
Notes	241
Bibliography	277
Index	289

Illustrations

2.1. Lakeside's Builders | 56
2.2. Lakeside Amusement Park from Sheridan Boulevard | 56
2.3. The Tower and Casino from inside the park, with the bandstand in the front left corner | 57
2.4. The Tower, Casino, and Swimming Pool. The Music Plaza is next to the lake | 57
2.5. The Casino balcony . . . | 58
2.6. . . . and its fine china | 58
2.7. The train station for the Lakeshore Railway, with the lake in the background | 59
2.8. The Natatorium (Swimming Pool) | 59
2.9. Tower of Jewels, a "pillar of fire at night" | 60
2.10. Social area of Lakeside, with the Boat House, El Patio Ballroom, and Skating Rink | 60

2.11. El Patio Ballroom and Skating Rink | 61

2.12. El Patio Ballroom at night | 61

2.13. Amusement area of Lakeside from the lake | 62

2.14. Shoot-the-Chutes, with the Airship and concession stands in the background | 62

2.15. Shoot-the-Chutes, with entrance to the Velvet Coaster and Scenic Railway to the right | 63

2.16. Entrance to the Scenic Railway and Velvet Coaster | 63

2.17. Lakeside's short-lived Tickler ride | 64

2.18. Amusement area at night | 64

2.19 and 2.20. Lakeside's photo studio demonstrated the park's elite nature with its private train car prop and car prop | 65

2.21. Buttons from various events at Lakeside, 1908–13 | 66

2.22. Lakeside's Staride, 1910s | 66

5.1. Interior of El Patio Ballroom, 1927 | 122

5.2. The wilder Derby coaster, 1912 | 122

5.3. Menu from the Plantation restaurant, 1926 | 123

5.4. Joe Mann's Orchestra in the Jail restaurant . . . | 123

5.5. . . . and its tin cups | 124

5.6. Program from Lakeside's greyhound track, 1927 | 124

5.7. Aerial view of Lakeside in the late 1920s, with the greyhound track | 125

5.8. Benjamin Krasner | 125

5.9. Lakeside from Sheridan Boulevard, with a Denver Tramway car passing in front | 126

5.10. College Inn in the Casino | 127

5.11. One of the steam engines outside the train station, 1970s | 127

5.12. Lakeside's old auto entrance on Sheridan Boulevard | 128

5.13. Lakeside's popular Tumble Bug ride | 128

5.14. Stainless steel rocket ship cars on Lakeside's original Circle Swing ride | 129

5.15. Denver Tramway ad for Lakeside's 1947 season | 129

8.1. Aerial view of Lakeside in 2007 shows the shopping mall and the Speedway | 184

8.2. Denver Dry store at Lakeside Mall | 184

8.3. Milo Lane's TV Repair Shop at Lakeside Mall | 185

8.4. Midget drivers Lloyd Axel in car 5 and Burt McNeese in car 55 racing at the Speedway, 1947 | 186

8.5. Based on the number of his photographs handed out, midget driver Johnny Tolan was the most popular driver among women at the Speedway | 186

8.6. Wreck between stock cars driven by Al Taft (17) and Larry Martell (41) at the Speedway, 1958 | 187

8.7. The 1967 Powder Puff Club at Lakeside | 187

8.8. Original merry-go-round in Lakeside's Kiddies Playland | 188

8.9. Lakeside's Fun House, 1940s | 188

8.10. Opening day of the Dragon coaster, built on the site of the Fun House, 1986 | 189

8.11. Poster advertising Lakeside's centennial season, 2008 | 189

8.12. Lakeside owner Rhoda Krasner with her daughter, Brenda Fishman, 2011 | 190

Foreword

Thomas J. Noel

We hope you enjoy this latest addition to the University Press of Colorado's Timberline Series of the best new and reprinted books on the Highest State. The Timberline Series also aspires to break new ground with significant works on neglected aspects of Colorado's past and present.

Residents and visitors have long enjoyed having two amusement parks to visit every summer. While Elitch's, Denver's oldest and largest amusement park, has been immortalized in several books, booklets, and dissertations, its great rival, Lakeside Amusement Park, has not been chronicled until now. In this lively work, Colorado historian David Forsyth tells Lakeside's story well. He does an especially notable job of tying Lakeside to the City Beautiful movement, which transformed Denver from an ordinary, dusty, drab western city into a tree-shaded, park-filled Paris on the South Platte.

Denver beer baron Adolph Zang spearheaded a group of local businessmen who in 1908 founded Lakeside as an elite summer playground wrapped around a 37-acre lake. Zang's use of more permanent brick and wood structures, rather than the temporary plaster of Paris and hemp fiber used for construction at the 1893 Chicago World's Fair and in many amusement parks, helped set Lakeside apart. It was built to last—and it has. To escape Denver's stricter liquor laws and other restrictions, the beer-minded Zang saw to it that the separate town of Lakeside was incorporated to govern the park and a few adjacent properties. Unlike every other US amusement park, Lakeside occupied its own town, set its own rules, and even had its own police force. This tiny town, with a 2010 population of eight, has a few small homes occupied mostly by employees of what is not only an amusement park but one of Colorado's smallest municipalities.

Zang and other Lakeside investors had hoped the land surrounding the park would become prime residential turf. Instead, working-class housing and low-end commercial businesses popped up. Denver's elite did not want to live next to a noisy, proletarian amusement park, with all its riffraff. Not until Lakeside Mall opened in 1954 did any of the town prove to be valuable real estate.

As it developed a more working-class character, Lakeside strove to build and maintain a wholesome reputation. Its "Girly, Girly Show" was called that not because it was risqué but because it appealed mostly to women. After first using traveling companies, Lakeside set up its own stock company in 1911 for summer theater and even staged symphony orchestra concerts. The bathing beach at the lake prescribed separate areas for men and women. Such measures were touted as proof that this amusement park was a tony, respectable resort.

Nevertheless, Forsyth notes that tackier entertainment slowly crept in, including the human fly climbing Lakeside's Tower and a 1920s Flapper Lane to attract girls who dressed in the Jazz Age style. Lakeside also hosted Alligator Joe and his reptiles, bullfights (but stressed that bulls were not killed at the end), and nightly naval battles on the lake that rattled sleeping neighbors.

After Adolph Zang's death, Lakeside struggled financially until Benjamin Krasner, a longtime park employee and Denver businessman, bought it in 1935. Krasner had come to Denver from the East Coast in 1917 to operate a Lakeside concession and had risen to manager of all concessions by 1931. He upgraded the park considerably by bringing in big-time bands such as Duke Ellington, Paul Whiteman, and Glenn Miller. Gene Amole, a local favorite newspaper columnist and radio personality, broadcast these big-band performances live from Lakeside's El Patio Ballroom on station KYMR. For Denver's children, Krasner offered free days complete with free ice cream.

Krasner greatly improved Lakeside during the Great Depression and World War II years, when many parks around the country struggled and even closed. He ventured as far as Europe in search of new rides. To give the entire park a facelift, Krasner hired architect Richard Crowther, later famous for his pioneering solar energy designs. Crowther transformed the park into an outstanding Art Deco–style venue, probably the best Art Deco campus in Colorado. Crowther outlined buildings in sinuous neon with rainbow-hued tubes. Even the new curvilinear, glass block ticket booths featured neon that often mirrored the style of the ride being ticketed.

Crowther's impressive Art Deco remodeling in the 1940s eliminated most of the original Neoclassical design of architect Edwin H. Moorman, who drew heavily from the City Beautiful movement. Much of the Decoesque style still characterizes Lakeside, although the Tower of Jewels never graduated from its Victorian exuberance. This 150-foot-high tower, one of the few remnants of the park's City Beautiful era, shimmers to this day with lights visible for miles.

Lakeside still boasts one of the country's longest miniature railroads, a tiny but ridable miniature Denver and Rio Grande train and a miniature Moffat [Railroad] Tunnel. The park installed its most famous ride, the Cyclone roller coaster, in 1940. This was Colorado's champion roller coaster for decades and a national favorite. By 1986, Lakeside boasted three roller coasters to accommodate the timid, the less timid, and the daring. While the original Satellite ride is long gone from Disneyland, things change slowly at Lakeside, which still hangs on to one of the few surviving Satellite rides from 1958 where anyone can "be a pilot."

Speed demons fancied Lakeside's Speedway, one of Colorado's most popular, from its 1938 opening until it ran out of gas in 1988. That Speedway, Forsyth concludes, "served as the most visible symbol of Lakeside Amusement Park's transformation from elite resort to working-class playground."

Lakeside has defied the odds as well as history to survive for more than a century as a small, family-owned and operated park. The hero of the Lakeside saga is Benjamin Krasner. According to his daughter (and Lakeside's current owner) Rhoda Krasner, her father gloried in a "long and delighted infatuation with Lakeside, a child's magic world." Every summer day he strolled the grounds checking on his beloved trains and rides. He died in 1965, but his only child, Rhoda, who had worked at the park since she was a child, carried on. Rhoda's daughter Brenda, a physician, also helps manage the park with help from her own little girl—the fourth generation of Krasners to be involved.

As owner, Rhoda Krasner has had to deal with many changes. Construction of I-70 in the 1960s brought a major highway alongside the park. Yet apparently the freeway traffic did not stop to dance. Ballroom dancing faded in popularity, and Lakeside closed its ballroom in 1972. The Lakeside Mall opened in 1954 and was demolished in 2008. Four years later a Walmart opened on the site.

Following a roller coaster accident and a fatal fire in the town's lone bar, Lakeside was branded a public nuisance in 1973. A Jefferson County grand jury report listed sixty-five violations of building, fire, and electrical safety codes. The tremendous problems cited by the grand jury would have shut down a less determined owner than Rhoda Krasner, but after a year of repairs and renovations, the park received high praise from the county that had condemned it a year earlier.

Today, Lakeside is a trip back more than a century in time. Although the Gayway Inn is now the Eatway Inn, it still has the grand marble back bar Benjamin Krasner rescued from Denver's Union Station. The signature Tower of Jewels, the merry-go-round, and the miniature train survive from 1908. For the park's 2008 centennial, Rhoda Krasner installed a new attraction for its collection of rides, a 140-foot drop tower called Zoom.

In an age of corporate mega-parks, Lakeside survives as one of America's few small, family-owned amusement parks. Forsyth contends that the Krasners' flexibility and willingness to innovate explain Lakeside's success. In 1938, for example, when most amusement parks were still relying on streetcars to bring visitors to them, Lakeside converted its baseball field to a 7,000-car paved parking lot.

Strong, smart, long-term family ownership has also favored Lakeside. After founder Adolph Zang died, his brother-in-law and nephew devoted themselves to keeping Lakeside open. In 1935 the Krasner family began their long, devoted ownership. Thanks to them, on warm summer nights Lakeside crackles with excitement, romance, and mechanical adventures.

David Forsyth takes Lakeside's story beyond a simple amusement park history and connects the story to larger themes in urban and social history. The park's history, he argues, offers a unique perspective on Denver's growth over more than a century. Issues Denver and other large cities dealt with during that time, including civic beautification, economic development, social changes, and war, influenced Lakeside as much as they did the city. This book began as his exhaustively researched doctoral dissertation at the University of Colorado Boulder. Forsyth, who has worked in the museum field in Colorado for several years, has published articles on popular culture in *Colorado Heritage* and *International Bowling Industry* and has spoken to numerous groups on topics ranging from the history of prostitution to Denver's amusement parks. I had my eyes opened to Lakeside's venerable marvels on a tour David led of this underappreciated wonderland. I believe you, too, will find this book an eye-opener.

THOMAS J. NOEL is co-editor of the Timberline Series of the University Press of Colorado, with Stephen J. Leonard.

Acknowledgments

Although it sometimes feels like a lifetime ago, this book began as my doctoral dissertation at the University of Colorado Boulder in 2008, the same year Lakeside Amusement Park celebrated its 100th anniversary. Through a sometimes long and difficult process, my dissertation committee of Thomas Zeiler, Ralph Mann, Robert Ferry, Robert Schulzinger, and Paul Beale provided valuable guidance and support. My friend and former professor at the University of Colorado Denver, Jim Whiteside, generously read each chapter, helping me refine arguments and correct mistakes. Rebecca Hunt at the University of Colorado Denver, Lauren Rabinovitz at the University of Iowa, and Susan Rugh of Brigham Young University reviewed later drafts of the book, and their comments helped immensely. I thank Jessica d'Arbonne, Darrin Pratt, Laura Furney, and Beth Svinarich from the University Press of Colorado for their help and guidance in getting this book published and Cheryl Carnahan for doing a wonderful job of editing the manuscript.

Another friend and CU Denver professor Tom Noel and his friend, Denver city auditor Dennis Gallagher, helped me get in touch with people who contributed valuable information to my research and writing. And there were many people whose names I never knew but who heard I was working on this book and took the time to share memories and stories of Lakeside, all of which were fascinating. Some of the most fun I had while working on this book was interviewing people connected with Lakeside. Adolph Zang's granddaughter Betty Arnold not only confirmed many of the rumors about Lakeside's construction but also helped me connect all of the Zang family members who were involved with the park during its early years. Frank and Joyce Jamison, who I have known for many years, gave me great information about the park's ballroom and Lakeside Speedway. Gina Quackenbush and the members of the Colorado Carousel Club also worked hard to get me in touch with people who knew much interesting information about Lakeside. The men and women who raced at the Speedway were incredibly fun to talk with. A group of the drivers meet every Thursday to have breakfast and talk about racing, and they were my best sources of information on the Speedway. Every driver I talked with made valuable contributions, but I would especially like to thank Wayne Arner, Leroy Byers, and Sonny Coleman, all of whom took a lot of time to talk with me and introduce me to other drivers. I would also like to thank Sheri Thurman Graham, who let me interrupt a Saturday morning of working on a car to talk with me about the Speedway's Powder Puff Drivers.

I started out claiming that my weekly visits to Lakeside were "research trips," but they quickly became a part of the summer, made even more fun when friends accompanied me. I would especially like to thank Jerrod (J) Brito, Howie Conklin, Alan and Maggie Demers, Trevyn Slusser, and Savannah Weitzel (who helped me choose the photos for this book) for their willingness to join me at Lakeside so often. My friends Ed Lewandowski, Jim Prochaska, and Michel Tritt were also steadfast in their encouragement as I worked on this book. I am also very grateful to Lakeside's owner, Rhoda Krasner, and her daughter, Brenda, for their friendship over the last few years and for the graduation party they hosted for me at Lakeside in August 2013.

Finally, I would like to thank my family for their continued love and support over the years.

Denver's Lakeside Amusement Park

Introduction

In Search of Blooming Gardens

On a warm July day in 2008, Denver city auditor Dennis Gallagher, in the role of Mayor Robert Speer, arrived at Lakeside Amusement Park to help kick off the official celebration of the park's 100th anniversary. Reaching that milestone made the park a unique survivor, but the celebration was for more than the park. It was also for the Zangs and Krasners, whose passion and dedication had kept Lakeside alive; for a small town that had survived against great odds; for a Speedway that had become nationally famous; and for the second shopping mall built in Denver. In a way, the celebration was also for Denver, whose growth, economic ups and downs, and City Beautiful program played important roles in Lakeside's development and survival.[1]

Between 1895 and 1910, developers built nearly 5,000 amusement parks in the United States. Most major cities had at least one park, but with Lakeside Amusement Park's opening in 1908, Denver had four in operation, while memories of a recently closed fifth remained fresh. In their search for rest and relaxation in a crowded, dirty city, Denver's residents eagerly latched on to anything that resembled a park, including amusement parks. Civic leaders had often neglected civic beautification during Denver's rapid growth in the late 1800s, but under the leadership of Mayor Robert Speer, who took office in 1904, Denver set out to become an embodiment of the City Beautiful movement that swept the United States in the early part of the twentieth century. Speer was not the first politician to attempt to beautify Denver, but prior efforts were haphazard and half-hearted at best. What made Speer different from the mayors before him was that he had spent years building up his political base, and he came into office with enormous power.[2]

As Speer was taking his first steps toward realizing his vision for Denver in 1907, brewer Adolph Zang revealed his plans for Lakeside Amusement Park. Zang had spent years building a reputation as a generous and successful businessman working in his father's Denver brewery, almost certainly guaranteeing the success of nearly any project he decided to undertake. The fact that Zang decided to build an amusement park was not at all strange as many brewers, both before and after him, did the same, providing ready markets for their product in amusement parks full of thirsty visitors. Zang, however, had excellent timing on his side when he decided to build his park. With a design inspired by the City Beautiful movement, Lakeside came into being just as Denver's first City Beautiful projects were getting under way.

The ideas of both the City Beautiful and the amusement park owed their existence to Chicago's Columbian Exposition, which an estimated 27 million people from around the world visited between May 1 and October 30, 1893. Honoring the 400th anniversary of Christopher Columbus's voyage, the Exposition was one of the biggest events the United States and even the world had ever seen. Visitors urged relatives, who had often never left the towns in which they lived, to find the time and money to see the Exposition, where they could, among other things, behold exciting new mechanical wonders and people from foreign lands, sample new foods, and ride the Ferris wheel. One of those visitors was Robert Speer, a rising figure in Denver politics, who found inspiration for the beautiful city he dreamed Denver could become. Adolph Zang may have also been a visitor to the Exposition, where Carl Lammers, whose company was the exclusive bottling agent for Zang Beer, had an exhibit and won a prize for the best bottled beer. If he was there, the Exposition may have been where Zang found inspiration for the amusement park he would one day build. The sheer number of marvels visitors could experience at the Exposition was impressive and exhausting, but just as stirring was the environment created by architect Daniel Burnham and landscape architect Frederick Law Olmsted Sr. The focal point was the Court of Honor, a set of similarly designed and constructed buildings around a central plaza, all of which implied "authority and imperialism . . . cultural stature, power, permanence, order, and unity." Judith Adams, in her book on the American amusement park industry, writes that the Exposition and its architecture were, in large part, designed to assure Americans that the country's national stature was "nearing preeminence."[3]

Between 1876 and 1916, organizers held international expositions in Philadelphia (to honor the nation's centennial), Chicago, New Orleans, Atlanta, Nashville, Omaha, Buffalo (at which President William McKinley was assassinated), St. Louis, Portland, Seattle, San Francisco, and San Diego. Nearly 100 million people of all classes visited these fairs, but the Columbian Exposition seemed to have had the greatest impact on American culture. Nearly everyone involved in the Exposition, from planners to visitors, viewed the Great White City of the Exposition as heavenly, clean, orderly, and safe—essentially, everything American cities were supposed to be striving to become. The classically styled buildings of the Court of Honor—grouped around the central lagoon, decorated with impressive sculptural pieces and murals, and all of similar height and design—proved that architecture could bring order out of chaos. Paths and gardens throughout the space gave the grounds a sense of unity while also allowing each building to have its own character within the general guidelines put forth by Exposition organizers. The people who designed and built the Exposition, according to historian David Burg, managed to achieve the often contradictory result of "unity, diversity, and cooperation."[4]

The Black City of Chicago (and, by extension, any major city in America), meanwhile, was chaotic, dark, dirty, and violent, everything people wanted to avoid. Large cities, like Denver, had often grown rapidly and with little concern for aesthetics, especially as they battled for survival amid competition from other cities and against difficult economic conditions. With no sanitation systems in place, trash and waste were dumped in the streets and rivers, making them dirty and disease-ridden. Critics also argued that, with little or no open space for relaxation and recreation, cities were dangerous to mental and spiritual health as well. But the Exposition, writes Erik Larson, taught people to see that cities did not have to be dark, soiled, and unsafe places; they had the potential to be beautiful, a lesson Denver's future leaders and Lakeside's builders learned well.[5]

While some historians argue that the idea behind the City Beautiful movement existed before the fair, no one doubts the architectural influence the Exposition had on it. William Stead is often credited with launching the City Beautiful movement and urban planning with the publication of his book *If Christ Came to Chicago*, in which he argued that American cities could be equal to the great cities of Europe if people allowed designers to do their jobs. Interested civic leaders turned to Daniel Burnham, architect of the Exposition, for advice. Between 1902 and 1909, he completed City Beautiful plans for Washington, DC, Cleveland, San Francisco, and Chicago in the United States and Manila and Baguio in the Philippines. The designs focused on creating a livable urban environment, with healthy and agreeable conditions and abundant recreational facilities. While critics argued that Burnham's choice to use classically styled buildings killed budding American architecture styles, supporters countered that the buildings were only championing the uniformity that marked the Exposition's architecture. A key element of City Beautiful planning, Burnham argued, was that "urban dignity and order . . . must be obtained through impressive and interrelated groupings of buildings," and the classical style lent itself to such a plan. By improving the appearance of a city through unity and introducing public art through sculpture and murals, the proponents of City Beautiful hoped to create a morally uplifting and healthier environment in which people could live and work.[6]

To emphasize moral uplift, the Exposition's organizers wanted the central Court of Honor to remain dignified, free from what they considered the more vulgar devices, amusements, and people that often marked such gatherings. To house the "vulgar amusements" such as freak shows, recreated foreign villages, and rides such as the Ferris wheel, organizers created the Midway Plaisance, which became one of the most popular areas of the Exposition. At the Philadelphia Centennial Exposition seventeen years earlier, fair officials sought to keep the fair pure by convincing city leaders to condemn and burn many of the "honky-tonk amusements" built just outside the fairgrounds. By the time of the 1904 St. Louis World's Fair, organizers incorporated the Midway into the main exposition grounds, signifying that promoters had acknowledged and even embraced the popular amusements the public desired. The amusement park, write historians Gary Cross and

John Walton, simply moved the Midway's attractions to a permanent location. Paul Boyton's Sea Lion Park, which opened on Coney Island in 1895, set off the amusement park boom in the United States. Sea Lion was followed by Steeplechase in 1897, Luna (which replaced the failed Sea Lion) in 1903, and Dreamland in 1904, making Coney Island the most famous amusement area in the United States. Each of these parks constantly tried to outdo the others with more beautiful grounds and bigger attractions and rides, but all were built on long traditions in public amusement.[7]

William F. Mangels was a successful amusement ride manufacturer in the early 1900s whose inventions included the device that created the galloping motion for carousel horses and the Whip and the Tickler rides (both of which were at Lakeside). In his 1952 book *The Outdoor Amusement Industry*, Mangels wrote that "public amusement is as old as recorded history," with permanent amusement centers and beer gardens built just outside many large Europeans cities as early as the 1600s. These amusement centers offered acrobatic acts, zoos, bowling, shooting, athletic displays, games, puppet shows, and animal fights. As early as the 1790s, some of the parks offered balloon ascensions and parachute drops, both of which were still standard features in American amusement parks, including Lakeside, in the late 1890s and early 1900s. Artificial illumination was another important aspect of these early parks, and Mangels wrote that some of the large pleasure gardens had as many as 20,000 oil-fed lamps illuminating their grounds at night; one park went so far as to proclaim that its 60,000 lamps turned night into day. In the mid-1700s, fireworks displays, another source of illumination still found in modern amusement parks, first appeared. Another important development came in 1728 when Vauxhall Gardens in England charged the first admission fee to enter its grounds in addition to offering a season ticket.[8]

European-style pleasure parks found their way to the United States where, according to Mangels, they built more on the tradition of public picnic grounds than on that of beer gardens. Entertainment at picnic grounds was often limited to "athletic games, song festivals, target shooting, bowling, dancing, and the consumption of beer and other refreshments," while a few had simple swings or hand-operated merry-go-rounds. One of the best-known early American resorts was Jones's Woods in New York City, which had several unique attractions, including tents that housed pictorial shows in which "wooden figures moved creakily through mechanical plays." Another prominent park was Parker's Grove (later Ohio Grove), located about twenty miles from Cincinnati, which included many shaded picnic spots, a dance hall, swings, and a mule-powered merry-go-round. In 1886 it was converted into an amusement park, and one of its biggest attractions at the turn of the twentieth century was an automobile ride over an oval course. Owners of similar pleasure grounds throughout the United States converted them into true amusement parks as the park boom took off in the late nineteenth and early twentieth centuries. Glen Echo Park in Maryland started as a national Chautauqua settlement in 1883; six years later it was converted into a trolley park, then reorganized as a modern amusement park in 1911. Riverview Park in Chicago started as a picnic grove in 1879 before becoming an amusement park in 1904, with regular stagings of common amusement park attractions, including the *Battle of the Monitor and Merrimac*, *Sinking of the Titanic*, and *Creation*. Thomas Jenkins Kenny established Kennywood in Pennsylvania, which became one of the best-known amusement parks in the United States, as a picnic grove in 1818. Eighty years later the Mellon family of Pittsburgh leased the property and converted it into a trolley park. Also prominent among these early gardens and picnic groves later converted to amusement parks, Mangels wrote, was Lakeside's longtime rival, Denver's Elitch Gardens.[9]

While these early gardens were popular, it was at Paul Boyton's Sea Lion Park on Coney Island, Mangels said, that "the modern amusement park originated." Among the park's attractions were forty sea lions trained to juggle balls and do other tricks, water races, the first large-scale Shoot-the-Chutes in the country, an old mill water ride, and caged live wolves. What set Boyton's Sea Lion Park apart from picnic groves and beer gardens of the time was the fence around it and the admission fee, designed to keep undesirable customers out of the park, visitors had to pay to get through the gates. The fee did not make the park exclusive, however, as John Kasson, in his book on Coney Island, argues that amusement parks actually helped break down class barriers, if only temporarily. With people from all walks of life careening into each other on the Human Whirlpool at Steeplechase or sharing their fear and excitement on a roller coaster at any of the parks, it hardly mattered who made more money or did what job. The parks also helped break down barriers between men and women as they clung to and smashed into each other and often saw more of each other exposed than polite society found decent. Such behavior was frowned upon outside the parks, but as long as it took place within the safe and controlled confines of an amusement park's gates, it was deemed acceptable by most.[10]

Amusement parks burst on the scene just as American society was beginning a rapid change, with flourishing mass culture, expanding urban populations, and increased leisure time. People were leaving farms and small towns for big cities, transforming the United States from a largely rural, agricultural country to one dominated by industry. The middle class began its rise and was dominated by two groups: one represented professional workers such as doctors and lawyers, while the other represented business, labor, and agriculture. Arguing that newly wealthy industrialists had little concern for their workers, progressive reformers battled to make the eight-hour day, half-day Saturdays, and free Sundays standard for many jobs, giving workers leisure time to enjoy as they saw fit. At the same time, social and moral leaders softened their opposition to partaking in games and other amusement activities on Sundays, allowing those who had Sundays off a chance to enjoy themselves without dire moral implications.[11]

With more leisure time, people flocked to amusement parks because they "provided the city's residents with enclosed playgrounds isolated and insulated from the demands of everyday life." In his book *Going Out*, David Nasaw writes that amusement parks transformed cities from places people wanted to escape in summer months to places people actually wanted to visit. Although air jets might blow off a man's hat or raise a woman's skirt or rides might throw men, women, and children into one jumbled pile, it was okay as long as they were inside the beautifully landscaped and decorated park whose admission fee kept it free from troublemakers.[12]

The rides inside the parks were intriguing as well because they often mimicked the new modes of transportation to which people were adapting. Roller coasters, for instance, were simply modified streetcars that provided a sensation of speed and danger, and Ferris wheels simulated speed and flight. In a sense, writes Judith Adams, amusement park rides allowed customers to "test themselves against the machines . . . that dominated daily urban life." Riders were able to experience risk and danger under safe conditions, and the social release of the parks and the experiences within them provided an escape from drab and dreary city life.[13]

Amusement parks quickly swept across the United States, providing entertainment and fun for the millions of customers who passed through their gates. *Billboard* magazine began in 1894 as a publication devoted to outdoor advertising, but it soon expanded to include sections devoted to theater, radio, movies, circuses, fairs, and amusement parks. From the early 1900s to the early 1960s, its pages were filled with the stories of these parks. Some of them lasted only a season or at best a few years, driven out of business by bigger and stronger competitors or owners unwilling to invest money to keep the parks viable. Changing economic conditions, such as the eventual closure of streetcar lines (which were responsible for building and operating many parks) and the Great Depression, wiped out hundreds of them. The advent of the theme park in the 1950s, with the opening of Disneyland, further isolated the parks that still survived. Despite it all, however, parks quickly captured the American imagination, becoming places of both fun and fear. Freddy "Boom Boom" Cannon informed listeners in his 1962 song "Palisades Park," which celebrated the famous New Jersey park of the same name, that they would "never know how great a kiss can feel / when you stop at the top of a Ferris wheel" as his heart went "up like a rocket ship / down like a roller coaster / back like a loop-the-loop / and around like a merry-go-round." In *Pinocchio*, Walt Disney's 1940 movie, Pinocchio and the other boys are taken to the amusement park Pleasure Island and literally turn into jackasses after overindulging in unlimited freedom and fun. Even the rise of theme parks and the threat they posed to traditional amusement parks played out in popular culture. In the 1977 movie *Rollercoaster*, a deranged man blows up a series of theme park rides, including a roller coaster, while blackmailing theme park owners to prevent further attacks. In a part of the story written but not filmed, the man is revealed to have been seeking revenge on the corporate-owned parks that were driving his parents' family-owned park out of business.[14]

In March 1907, workers employed by Denver brewer Adolph Zang's Lakeside Realty and Amusement Company began clearing 57 of the 160 acres of land the company owned at Forty-Sixth Avenue and Sheridan Boulevard in the new Jefferson County town of Lakeside, across the county line from Denver. Six months later, the workers had laid out the grounds around what was then called Sylvan Lake and started construction on several buildings in what would be Lakeside Amusement Park, the Denver area's newest amusement park (the park was never officially named White City, as is sometimes claimed; that was only a nickname). At the same time, a construction crew in Denver was working to complete the new Municipal Auditorium at Fourteenth and Curtis Streets, one part of Mayor Robert Speer's newly instituted City Beautiful program. Both the amusement park and the auditorium were essential to Speer's effort to make Denver into a model of the City Beautiful ideal.[15]

Denver's residents had sought amusement long before Adolph Zang conceived of the idea of Lakeside. In the city's earlier days, rowdier crowds patronized saloons, gambling halls, and brothels in large numbers, but as the city became more settled in the 1880s many residents wanted cleaner entertainment options. Real estate investor John Brisbane Walker attempted to create such an option with River Front Park, located between Fifteenth and Nineteenth Streets along the Platte River, which opened on July 4, 1887. The park included beautifully landscaped grounds, a race track and baseball diamonds, a boating course on the Platte, and a permanent three-story exhibit hall that resembled an elaborate castle. Winter activities at the park included the Denver Toboggan Club's slides, some of which stretched for 1,000 feet and were traveled by sleds that reportedly reached speeds of 180 miles per hour. When Walker's business interests shifted to New York in 1890, he offered to sell River Front Park to Denver for $1 million. The city refused, arguing that the lack of convenient access to the grounds and poor air quality in the area made the land unsuitable for a city park; Walker eventually sold the land to the Union Pacific Railroad for $1.2 million.[16]

Walker's operation was simply ahead of its time, as Denver's leadership was not especially interested in creating a hospitable environment for such ventures. Robert W. Speer, the leader who *would* be interested, arrived in Denver in 1878, a twenty-two-year-old tuberculosis victim seeking a cure for the disease. After his arrival, Speer went to work for Cyrus H. McLaughlin, a prominent Denver real estate developer. Speer rose to the top of McLaughlin's company and then founded his own, R. W. Speer and Company. Fellow developers liked Speer and his cheerful attitude, and he formed close relationships with many of them, which came in handy when he entered politics. In 1880, voters chose Speer as Denver's city clerk. Five years later he was appointed postmaster by President Grover Cleveland, and six years after that Governor John Routt appointed Speer as the lone Democrat on Denver's three-member Fire and Police Board; Speer was soon the board's president. By 1901 he was head of the Denver Board of Public Works. In many ways Speer was the typical boss who characterized much of the era's politics, and people who did business with the city learned "it was wise to donate cash to the 'Speer Club.'"[17]

In 1902, Colorado voters approved an amendment to the state constitution that created the City and County of Denver and gave the city home rule. Two years later, voters (helped by an estimated 10,000 fraudulent votes) elected Speer mayor and approved a new city charter he had heavily promoted. The new charter included the legal framework for civic beautification and created a three-member Art Commission (made up of an architect, an artist, and a sculptor, with the mayor as an ex-officio member). Speer used the Art Commission, headed by Henry Read, an English artist who had come to Colorado for his health, as a planning office to help promote civic beautification. Financing for the major beautification projects Speer had in mind was made possible by another charter provision that created four different park districts (South Denver, East Denver, Highland, and Montclair), each with the ability to acquire and improve land, levy assessments, and issue bonds with voter approval. Speer finally had the political power to act on his twenty-year-old dream to turn Denver into the City Beautiful.[18]

During Speer's three terms in office, city crews graded and paved more than 300 miles of streets and installed sandstone sidewalks and granite curbs (and cleaned them every night), and millions of dollars went into building storm and sanitary sewers. Decorative streetlamps replaced the seven 150-foot-high arc light towers that had lit the city since 1883, and many of downtown Denver's streets and buildings were covered with decorative lights, leading some to argue that Denver rivaled Paris as the City of Light. In 1908 the city opened a municipal bathhouse at Twentieth and Curtis Streets, and more than 150,000 people bathed there during its first year. Speer's "proudest accomplishment" during his first term, however, was the $650,000, 12,000-seat Municipal Auditorium, completed just in time for Denver to host the Democratic National Convention in July 1908. The auditorium hosted free Sunday afternoon and evening concerts; and thousands flocked to it on other days for operas, gospel revivals, auto shows, and Boy Scout exhibitions. The Municipal Auditorium put Denver, which was desperately trying to win national notice, "on the map as a convention and cultural center," according to historians Tom Noel and Barbara Norgren.[19]

Speer's greatest love, however, was Denver's park system. In planning for Central Park, New York City's mayor, Ambrose Kingsland, argued that the city's public places were not in keeping with its character and that New York needed a grand public park to provide visible proof of its stature. More than fifty years later, Robert Speer would say the same thing about Denver. As Jerome Smiley wrote in his 1901 history of Denver, the city was "an object lesson of what faith, courage, and energy have done in converting a remote frontier town, that had to fight for its right to live, into a great and growing metropolis." According to Smiley, the city had a beautiful environment, notable architecture, and a healthy climate, but it was also sorely lacking in some areas, such as parks, that would make it a truly world-class city. Smiley argued that "Denver's noble surroundings should inspire a high exaltation of municipal life."[20]

Mayor Joseph C. Bates had first called for Denver to acquire parkland in 1872, but it was not until 1881, under Mayor Richard Sopris, that the state legislature allowed Denver to buy 320 acres of school land, at a reduced price, for use as a park. The land became City Park. By 1901 Denver had twelve established parks covering 436 acres. City Park was the best developed, with a lake, a buggy racing track, a small zoo, and the newly built Museum of Natural History. Congress Park was second-largest, with 40 acres, followed by the smaller Washington, Park Avenue, Lincoln, Highland, Jefferson, Platt, Curtis, Dunham, Chaffee, and Fuller Parks. Noel and Norgren write that "fledgling parks and shabby attractions did not make Denver a beautiful or distinguished city," but with a budget of only $67,000 in 1900, the Parks Department could do little. Smiley wrote that, except for the improved areas, Denver's parks were "weed-grown or barren areas," failing to make the city beautiful or distinguished while also failing to provide restful escapes for residents. The improved areas were marvels, however, and Smiley wrote that the "application of intelligent landscape engineering, creation of artificial lakes, and lawn, tree, and flower cultures" had turned them into "blooming gardens." Denver's location in a favored setting among numerous resources and opportunities meant that it should be "an example, a standard, for other American municipalities."[21]

With the park system so slow to take hold in Denver, residents seeking rest and relaxation often turned to any land that resembled a park, including the city's cemeteries. Cemetery monuments were widely recognized as a reliable source of public sculpture by the 1870s, and when Riverside Cemetery opened in 1876 downstream from Denver along the Platte, its founders were intent on creating a fitting setting for the fine monuments they knew would soon come. Planners laid out Riverside in a grid of avenues, drives, and walks; and the property was graded and planted with trees and shrubs in an effort to copy "the landscape or park plan" popularized by Frederick Law Olmsted. The founders of Fairmount Cemetery, which opened southeast of Denver in 1890, expanded on the concept and invested $30,000 in a stone chapel, gateway lodge, water system, graded streets, and a professional arborist to care for the many trees and shrubs inside the cemetery. Throughout the 1890s Riverside and Fairmount were rivals, and each attempted to gain an advantage over the other "through the greater beauty of their landscape and the higher artistic merit of their sculpture." The competition gave Denver two large, beautifully decorated parks outside the city, and it was not uncommon for families to take a carriage or a streetcar to either cemetery on a Sunday afternoon, where they would walk the grounds admiring the magnificent headstones and other structures and enjoy a picnic lunch.[22]

Riverside and Fairmount were not enough to fill the city's recreation needs, however, and in his 1880 history of Denver, William B. Vickers wrote that "Denver, it must be confessed, is sadly deficient in places of legitimate amusement." Within the next fifteen years, the opening of several summer resorts and amusement parks helped correct that deficiency. The first such park in Denver (as well as Lakeside's longest-lasting competitor) was Elitch Gardens, which John and Mary Elitch, operators of the Elitch Palace Dining Room on Arapahoe Street in Denver, opened to the public on May 1, 1890. In 1888 John Elitch had purchased the old Chilcott farm in the Highlands, northwest of Denver, believing he and Mary could save money by growing their own produce for their restaurant. The farm increasingly reminded the Elitches of the time they had spent at San Francisco's popular Woodward Gardens, and in 1889 John proposed turning the farm into a similar park, with gardens, a zoo, and a theater. Like Woodward, the Elitches' new venture did not tolerate "rough company" or sell liquor. The May 2, 1890, issue of the *Denver Republican* called Elitch's a "great institution" and said that "from this time forth people intent upon recreation of a legitimate kind will go to Elitch's Gardens" (a pronouncement seemingly forgotten when Lakeside opened nearly twenty years later). The beautiful gardens, which earned Elitch's praise for the next century, were lauded as magnificent additions to Denver. The first zoo animals arrived at the farm when both P. T. Barnum, a friend of the family, and *Denver Post* owner Harry Tammen, also the new owner of the Sells-Floto Circus, gave Mary Elitch baby circus animals. Most impressive, though, was the "elegant theater," a fixture at Elitch's until the 1980s.[23]

Thomas Edison's Vitascope, an early film projector, was installed at Elitch's in 1896 and became the first amusement park–type attraction there; Elitch's added additional attractions with increasing rapidity after that. In 1897 Ivy Baldwin, a local daredevil, began doing balloon ascensions at the park. In 1899 the Elitches added a penny arcade and constructed a building that housed a reenactment of the battle between the Monitor and Merrimac, a popular attraction at amusement parks across the country. In 1900 a miniature train joined the list of attractions, followed by a Toboggan Coaster in 1904 and the first permanent carousel in 1906.[24]

The second summer resort to open in Denver was Manhattan Beach on the shore of Sloan's Lake, south of Elitch's. Manhattan Beach, which replaced an earlier resort with the same name at Sloan's Lake, opened on June 13, 1891, and is often credited as the first amusement park in the West. The *Denver Times* asserted that the opening of the park, bathing beach, and menagerie gave the city "one of the most beautiful resorts in the country." Like Elitch's, Manhattan Beach featured a zoo, the stars of which were male and female hippopotamuses. Also like Elitch's, Manhattan Beach had beautiful gardens and a theater. The *Denver Times* singled out the fountain in Sloan's Lake as the new park's most unique feature. The center jet on the fountain shot water 100 feet into the air, while the three jets surrounding it reached 75 feet. A system of colored lights at the base of the fountain allowed it to "rise in many colors," producing "one of the prettiest spectacles imaginable."[25]

The restaurant, hotel, bowling alley, and gymnasium rounded out the buildings at the new Manhattan Beach. The boathouse held canoes, rowboats, barges, and a steamboat named the *City of Denver*, and a grandstand beside the lake allowed spectators to watch aquatic events. The park soon added a dance pavilion and roller skating rink. In 1892 Mary Elitch Long took over as manager of the Manhattan Beach theater, a position she held for nearly twenty years. Ivy Baldwin also started doing his balloon ascension act at Manhattan Beach, in addition to continuing at Elitch's. Manhattan Beach was also the site of the first amusement park fatality in Denver. In 1891 Roger the elephant became spooked by either the balloon ascension at the park or the crowd who had rushed to watch it. He trampled six-year-old

George W. Eaton, who had been riding on Roger and fell off when he stood up to watch the balloon.[26]

Over the next ten years, management continued adding to Manhattan Beach's amusement devices, although in a somewhat strange move they tore down the roller coaster in 1902, depriving the park of what was by then a fairly standard amusement park attraction. Another major change at Manhattan Beach for the 1902 season involved admission fees, which that year dropped from a quarter to just ten cents in an effort to "cater to the vast multitude instead of the chosen few," allowing "the masses an opportunity to spend a day away from the care and anxiety of labor, amid such surroundings as are conducive to health and pleasure." Speaking to the *Denver Times* about the new admission fee policy, the park's managers, Hellbrun and Mayer, were careful to point out that they did not allow the sale of liquor in the park and that they were determined that propriety would prevail and nothing would be allowed that would offend the sensibilities of women and children. Hellbrun and Mayer also revealed to the *Times* that they had a powerful weapon at their disposal to maintain order: a giant searchlight, another common feature at amusement parks, was in operation atop the park's observation tower. While the rays from the light reminded people all over Denver that the park existed, it also allowed management to shine light into every corner of the park "so as to insure against any infraction of the rules laid down governing the general conduct of the place."[27]

Lights, from searchlights to smaller bulbs on strings, were an important feature of any amusement park, and Manhattan Beach was the first amusement park in Denver to adopt elaborate lighting schemes. Throughout the park's grounds visitors found arches with rows of colored lights, which made for a "magnificent illuminated promenade." Although management continually remodeled and expanded Manhattan Beach between 1891 and 1904, disaster struck in 1909 when a fire destroyed it. The next year, new management quickly rebuilt the park (renamed Luna) with many of the same attractions but with two notable additions: a movie theater and a new roller coaster. The Aero Coaster, designed by Denverites Harry L. Weber, Theodore Nollenberger, and W. W. McFarland, consisted of a 60-foot conical tower, 120 feet around at the base, with track running around the cone. But Luna Park was never as popular as Manhattan Beach, and customers soon lost interest in it. By the outbreak of World War I, it had essentially been abandoned.[28]

The third amusement park built in Denver, and perhaps the one most significant to the future relationship between Denver and Lakeside Amusement Park, was Arlington Park, which opened in 1892. The men behind Arlington were Denver postmaster John Corcoran, businessman Henry W. Michael, and Police Commissioner Robert W. Speer. The thirty-acre park along the banks of Cherry Creek, between Pennsylvania and Downing Streets, encompassed land known as Arlington Grove, which the *Colorado Sun* called "one of the nicest groves in the vicinity." The *Rocky Mountain News* wrote that, based on an interview with Speer, the plans for the park's "adornment are beautiful." The ground, according to the newspaper, was very uneven, but the park's builders handled this by dredging the creek to straighten it and using the dirt from the dredging operation to level the ground. They also built a half-mile-long lake with an island at the north end of the park.[29]

Aside from the tennis courts, baseball field, and theater, the biggest attraction was a show titled *The Last Days of Pompeii*. A fifty-two-foot-high canvas depicting Mt. Vesuvius was set up on the far side of the lake, with various buildings in front of it, including a temple and a palace. Openings in the stage allowed smoke and flames to shoot up through the set, each series of events controlled electronically. To create the illusion of lava flowing down the sides of Vesuvius, a red light was set up behind the canvas; holes cut through the material allowed it to shine through, while a man moved the light around behind the screen to control the lava flow. The *Denver Republican* found the show an impressive sight, but Mr. Wiley, general manager of the park, said it was "the easiest thing in the world . . . when you know how [to do it]."[30]

As popular as the Fall of Pompeii and other pyrotechnic shows were, new managers completely remodeled the park in 1897. A new Shoot-the-Chutes, which ended in the lake, gave the park its new name, Chutes Park. A favorite show on the chutes during the 1899 season was Professor W. H. Barnes and his diving elk, which would alternately slide down or dive off the chute. Denver's first scenic railway, which depicted the route to the Klondike, was also at Chutes Park. In 1898 the *Denver Times* told the story of William McFarland, a ticket broker who rode the scenic railway, essentially an early roller coaster, at Chutes Park. According to the *Times*, McFarland and his fellow passengers were "more or less sober" when they got on the ride, but McFarland declared afterward that he would not ride it again "for the prettiest $500 bill in the world." The ride up the incline was pleasant, but for him the fun stopped after that. He was so afraid that he missed seeing the tunnel the car went through, and he was never quite certain if he was "going to Heaven or the other place." When he finally found himself on firm ground again, he had to agree with a friend who called the scenic railway "the road of the Lost Soul." Ten years later, when Lakeside opened with its own scenic railway, the ride was much more popular and acceptable and considered much tamer.[31]

In addition to these two major changes, the new management company also added a professional bicycle track around the lake, taking advantage of the bicycling boom sweeping the nation, and they redesigned the football, baseball, and tennis areas. A palace of illusions, a shooting gallery, burro rides, flying horses, mazes, and a haunted swing rounded out the new attractions under construction at Arlington for the 1898 season. According to the *Rocky Mountain News*, everything at the new Chutes Park would be "run in a strictly first-class manner" as management attempted to make the park both entertaining and educational.[32]

Unfortunately, the joy surrounding the new Chutes Park was short-lived. On the night of January 21, 1901, a fire broke out in the engine room of the scenic railway. Firemen told the *Denver Times* they believed tramps had started the blaze, and, within an hour of the first alarm at 11:00 p.m., the park was in ashes. According to the *Times*, nearby residents "rejoiced" as the park burned because they had grown weary of the "noises emanating from it and the objectionable characters it drew there." By the following summer, portions of the park had been rebuilt, but on June 4, 1902, another fire raged through it. The park never reopened, and in 1903 the remains were torn down. The city of Denver pushed Third Avenue through the grounds, and Speer and the other owners divided the land into building lots. In the 1920s Alamo Placita Park was built on the site, with flower beds occupying the filled-in lake.[33]

The glee Arlington Park's neighbors felt as the park burned in 1901 proved that the park's owners had misjudged the way some Denverites would accept their creation. The amusement park itself covered 30 acres, but the Arlington Park Land and Improvement Company owned 120 acres. The 90 acres of land not occupied by the park were sold as residential lots beginning in 1890, although anyone building a house had to observe certain restrictions. Houses had to cost at least $2,000, an effort by Speer and his partners to control the class of people living there. The rules also forbade the construction of bars and the selling of liquor in the area for five years. Speer and his associates firmly believed the kind of amusement park they built would be a welcome addition to the upscale neighborhood they were creating, but neighbors enthusiastically watching the park burn proved that people did not consider a noisy amusement park a good neighbor. The Arlington Park Company's success at controlling the land around the park doomed the park. Lakeside's owners hoped they would be more successful when they built their park fifteen years later.[34]

The last Denver-area amusement park built before Lakeside was Tuileries Park, located in Englewood at the end of South Broadway, between Floyd and Hampden. The site had once been Orchard Park, a popular beer garden in the 1890s. Financed by a group of men from Cripple Creek, Tuileries was patterned after Coney Island in Kansas City and managed by William Simpson, also of Kansas City. In the months before Tuileries opened on July 29, 1906, the owners spent at least $140,000 on construction at the 35-acre site. According to the *Denver Republican*, the park was "the most beautiful natural park in the state" and had "all the familiar amusements," including a lake, roller rink, baseball diamond, and miniature railroad. The newspaper thought the dance pavilion was the largest west of Chicago and deemed the aerodrome, where balloonists and aerialists performed, impressive. The *Republican* reported that management intended to take special care that women and children found no cause for offense at the park, banning liquor sales and making sure the grounds were "amply policed." The July 4, 1901, celebration at Tuileries was an impressive sight as Manager William Gillpatrick hosted five motorcycle races, a baseball game between the Tuileries team and another, a race between two cowboys hoping to win a wife, dancing, and fireworks. Labor Day at the park featured a corn roast at which 10,000 ears of corn, grown on the park grounds, were roasted and given away for free. Although initially popular, increasingly poor attendance forced Tuileries to close in 1912.[35]

Each of these amusement parks stood out as a showplace in a city filled with undeveloped, weed-strewn public parks. The success of Riverside and Fairmount Cemeteries as parks proved that Denver residents were willing to accept recreation areas not traditionally thought of as parks. Like Riverside's and Fairmount's developers, the owners of Denver's early amusement parks invested huge amounts of money in each of them to make them attractive and popular showplaces. Newspapers praised Elitch's gardens and statuary, Manhattan Beach's lighting, and Arlington Park's pyrotechnic displays. Visitors found beautiful gardens, educational attractions, and fine theater performances, all important features of Denver's City Beautiful program. In a city starved for space for recreation and relaxation, the appearance of large, beautiful parks was a welcome sight that received a great deal of notice in the press.

And yet, city officials rarely took notice of the first four parks when they opened. At Elitch's opening ceremony on May 1, 1890, Denver mayor Wolf Londoner attended to help show what the newspapers called proper appreciation for the event. The mayor, "in his usual happy vein," greeted friends in the crowd before speaking of his pride in both the gardens and public-spirited citizens such as John Elitch. Mayor Londoner declared that Elitch Gardens was the best advertisement Denver could hope to have to show how far it had come since its founding in 1859. Only at Lakeside's opening eighteen years later would listeners hear similar sentiments expressed, but that was at a ceremony on a scale far above that of Elitch's relatively simple opening. No official government delegations attended the openings of Manhattan Beach, Arlington Park, or Tuileries, and it fell to the newspapers to promote the new amusement parks. Articles proclaimed each park a welcome and beneficial addition to Denver, unmatched by anything before it. Reporters praised each park's beautiful flowers, paths, fountains, lakes, and picnic areas as unlike anything that came before them (probably true, given Denver's lack of such beauty). Newspapers also stressed each park's purity, with articles stating that liquor sales were not permitted, rowdy children were tolerated only on certain days or during certain times, and powerful searchlights could penetrate every corner of dark parks at night.[36]

As mayor, Robert Speer wanted his city's parks to be as beautiful as Riverside and Fairmount Cemeteries and to offer as much amusement as did Elitch's, Manhattan Beach, Arlington Park, and Tuileries. As such, he had a much broader vision of what could constitute City Beautiful than did many of his contemporaries. Absent from Denver's parks were the infamous "Keep off the Grass" signs that marked New York's Central Park. Denver's residents were allowed (and even encouraged) to walk on the grass and play in the fountains, and one of Speer's more controversial decisions when it came to Denver's parks was to allow couples to spoon in them. Denver, according to the *Rocky Mountain News*, was in need of more people in the early 1900s, and "if love-making in the parks will help it along, why then they can do all the love-making in the parks they want to." Speer liked parks for the practical reason that landscaped park areas could provide flood control (floods were often problems in early Denver) and firebreaks. More philosophically, however, Speer and other Progressive-era thinkers believed "an improved environment would uplift the entire urban population."[37]

Speer's favorite park project during his time as mayor was Civic Center Park, which he envisioned as comparable to the Court of Honor at the Columbian Exposition, with architecturally similar government buildings surrounding a central plaza. Speer believed that, if his plan was followed, Civic Center Park would beautify Denver while also making government more efficient, as all city, county, and state offices would be in one area. While Civic Center Park received much of Speer's attention, he was just as interested in building or completing other parks throughout Denver. George Kessler, who had worked with landscape architect Frederick Law Olmsted, developed the city's park and parkway plan, which proposed a network of parkways that radiated from Civic Center Park and connected all of Denver's parks by road. Included in the plan were three parks near the future site of Lakeside Amusement Park: Sloan's Lake, Berkeley, and Inspiration Point.[38]

With Robert Speer in office, the timing could not have been better for Lakeside Amusement Park and its builders. All of the trends that marked the amusement industry were found at Lakeside in one form or another, yet it managed to be a very unique park. Lakeside, for example, was surrounded by a fence that protected it from unwanted customers, but it was further protected by occupying its own town, something no other park could claim. Having the park located in its own town gave its builders and owners enormous control over the rules and regulations that impacted the park and what happened around it, especially in its early years. Lakeside's close relationship with Denver during the City Beautiful movement was another important difference between it and other parks. Critics blasted the many parks that tried to claim they were part of the City Beautiful movement, arguing that the very nature of amusement parks was in opposition to the values of City Beautiful. But Lakeside and Denver's City Beautiful program were so closely linked that the city's changing economic and political climate had far-reaching consequences for the park's survival. Other observers argued that amusement parks did nothing to educate or uplift, charges Lakeside's owners might have taken issue with as they tried to do both with their park. Lakeside, through its owners' smart business sense, also demonstrated exceptional skill at surviving changing times, an extremely important factor in the park's long life. The park was, and is, an excellent mirror of the world around it, and Lakeside's various owners have demonstrated a remarkable ability to adapt the park to those changing conditions. Unlike thousands of other amusement parks, by being unique, Lakeside Amusement Park has not only survived but thrived.[39]

Of the nearly 5,000 amusement parks built in the United States between 1895 and 1920, only 100 still survived in 2008. Twenty-eight of them had survived long enough to celebrate their centennials. This is the story of how Lakeside Amusement Park, a park like no other, became one of those twenty-eight parks.[40]

CHAPTER 1

Lakeside, an Amusement Enterprise

Michele Bogart argues that amusement parks, specifically designed to incite a "riotous, carnival atmosphere," were completely at odds with the ideas of order and stability City Beautiful supporters sought. Filled with "wild rides and bizarre amusements," the very things the Columbian Exposition's planners confined to the Midway, amusement parks, according to Bogart, presented a "bizarre theater context that would shock viewers by temporarily situating them in a fantastic, disorienting environment—one quite alien to the aesthetic ideals envisioned by City Beautiful advocates." Although he was writing eighty-five years earlier, Jerome Smiley expressed many of the same opinions about Denver's amusement parks. Smiley declared that Manhattan Beach "strains a point to be entitled to its name," though he grudgingly admitted that it was in fact located on a beach on the shore of Sloan's Lake. The lake, Smiley wrote, did the best it could toward "justifying the name its associate bears." Arlington Park (then called Chutes Park) came in for even heavier criticism from Smiley; he said it was designed for "those who enjoy spectacular things, and have a fondness for 'roller coasters';

a playground for grown-up boys and girls." Only Elitch's escaped criticism in Smiley's history, largely because of its theater, which was conducted "upon a high plane" and made the park a "worthily popular place of summer amusements." Fortunately for Lakeside and its builders, Robert Speer disagreed with anyone who said that an amusement park and a beautiful city could not coexist, and he went out of his way to make sure Lakeside Amusement Park was included in his vision.[1]

Lakeside Amusement Park was the creation of Adolph Zang. Adolph's father, Philip Zang, came to Denver in 1869 from Louisville, Kentucky, where he owned a brewery. His first wife refused to come west with him, and after their divorce she and their son, Adolph, moved to Chicago where she could receive better medical care for the goiter that plagued her throughout her life. In Denver, Zang founded the Philip Zang Brewing Company, and soon, according to his great-granddaughter Betty Arnold, nearly every German family in Denver had at least one member employed at the brewery. Zang also started grubstaking miners, taking parts of their claims as repayment, which heavily involved the family in mining over the next fifty years and eventually led to the creation of a bank that would play a large part in Lakeside's early years. In 1870 Philip Zang married Anna Buck, who ran a dairy farm in the Westwood section of Denver with her two grown children from her first marriage, William and Elizabeth. In 1884 Elizabeth married Peter Friederich, a clerk in a real estate company. After his marriage, Friederich went to work for the Zang Brewery, eventually becoming assistant general manager and city manager. Peter and Elizabeth had one son, Phillip, before she died in 1894. William Buck also went to work for the Zang Brewery, and he and the Friederichs were important figures in Lakeside's development.[2]

After he completed the eighth grade, Adolph Zang's mother took him to Heidelberg, Germany, to attend college. His father had been trying for some time to convince his son to move to Denver, and after his marriage in 1881, Adolph told his new wife, Minnie, that they could go to Colorado on their honeymoon to see what it was like. Impressed by what they saw, the couple decided to stay in Colorado, and Adolph took an active role in his father's brewery. In 1895, four years before his death, Philip retired and sold his brewery to an English syndicate, but Adolph stayed on to manage it for the new owners. Betty Arnold recalled her grandfather Adolph as a very smart businessman. He formalized and expanded his father's grubstaking business, which in 1905 led to the creation of the German American Trust Company (the bank dropped German from its name during World War I and then became the American National Bank in 1924), headquartered on Seventeenth Street across from the Daniels and Fisher department store. Zang hired Godfrey Schirmer, an experienced insurance and investment executive, as president of the bank. Schirmer later became the first secretary of Lakeside and his niece, Patricia Campion, married Peter Friederich's son, Phillip. Adolph Zang also built a number of hotels and bars throughout the state that served as outlets for Zang Beer. Among the best-known and most popular of his early beer outlets was the Oxford Hotel, built in 1890 at the corner of Seventeenth and Wazee Streets near Union Station.[3]

On March 20, 1907, Adolph Zang, Peter Friederich, Godfrey Schirmer, John A. Keefe, and Albert Lewin incorporated the Lakeside Realty and Amusement Company with a capital stock of $250,000 (2,500 shares worth $100 apiece). The new company became public knowledge on April 18, 1907, when the *Colorado Transcript* announced that Zang had incorporated the Lakeside Amusement Company, "an amusement enterprise of considerable interest." The newspaper was certain that Zang planned to build a large beer garden at Sylvan Lake in the Berkeley area of Jefferson County, although no official announcement had been made. The *Transcript* assured readers that whatever venture the new company undertook, it would "be on a large scale, as the company is capitalized at $200,000." A week later, with the announcement of the founding of the town of Lakeside, the intention became much clearer.[4]

On April 24, the Lakeside Realty and Amusement Company filed a plat with the State of Colorado for a new town it planned to incorporate in Jefferson County. Although the petition was signed by all forty-four residents of what would become the new town, the law still required a vote of the residents for approval. In August 1907 the *Colorado Transcript* reported that a number of Denver men were among those residents and had "built handsome and comfortable homes in the new settlement." Prominent among them was Marvin Adams, head waiter at The Famous, a Denver restaurant, and the *Transcript* noted that it was "very probable" that he would be elected the first mayor of Lakeside if the town was incorporated. Notice of an election in Berkeley Precinct Number Twenty-Three of Jefferson County finally went out on October 21, 1907, followed by the election on November 12. Forty-one of forty-two people voted in favor of incorporation and selected John

P. Yaeger, Marvin Adams and his wife, Kate, Hugh O'Connell, and Elmer Allen as commissioners of the new town of Lakeside. In another election on December 10, Marvin Adams was elected mayor and police judge. Kate Adams, Ernest Allen, Hugh O'Connell, Chester Wenquist, and John Fashi were chosen as trustees. The *Transcript* reported that Mayor Adams, whose grandson was the first baby born in Lakeside, had great hopes for the new town and predicted that the baby would one day be mayor when Lakeside was a great city.[5]

By the time the incorporation election took place, Zang's Lakeside Realty and Amusement Company was several months into construction on the Denver area's newest attraction, Lakeside Amusement Park. Zang's primary reason for locating his park outside Denver was to avoid the city's blue laws that prohibited the sale of liquor on Sundays, but the decision also set Lakeside apart from other amusement parks in the country, none of which could claim to occupy their own town. Lakeside was essentially a company town from the beginning, and the *Colorado Transcript* reported that "a large majority of the residents are interested directly or indirectly in the Lakeside Amusement Company." Newspapers immediately started making sure the public was aware that Lakeside would be a well-run and orderly resort thanks to the town. In August 1907 the *Transcript* predicted that when the new government of Lakeside was eventually formed, it would "insist upon the best of conduct" at the park but would "guard against the admission of puritanical ideas."[6]

In December the *Transcript* reported that a town jail was under construction (the two-cell block, essentially a steel cube, was located under the park's ballroom), and Mayor Adams gave "it out cold that any person refusing to comply with the laws of the land and the ordinances of Lakeside may bank on getting what's coming to him." According to the *Transcript*, the town's officials were "determined to take the bull by the horns" from the get-go in handling troublemakers. Admitting that it would be impossible to eliminate all menaces, the newspaper was pleased that the park's owners and the town's officials planned to deal with them "promptly and emphatically" to guarantee that Lakeside was a "place where the most fastidious man may take his wife and children in perfect safety." After taking office, Adams and the trustees quickly organized a police force, appointing Albert Ezekiel as the first town marshal. Ezekiel resigned in March 1908 and was replaced by

John Lindsey, who was chief of police in Lakeside for many years. The first deputy marshal was Chas Snyder, and when Mayor Adams presented him with his badge in February 1908 he told him to "use it, but not abuse it."[7]

While the existence of a town dedicated solely to the park was exceptional enough, Lakeside's design also suggested that it would be different from typical amusement parks. Most of Coney Island's amusement park structures, as well as the White City at the Columbian Exposition, were built of staff, a mixture of powdered gypsum, alumina, glycerine, dextrine, and fibers. It created a cheap material that was easy to work with and could be molded into fantastic shapes, but it also decayed quickly, sometimes within months. Staff's low cost was the primary reason it was first used at the Columbian Exposition and Coney Island. Its rapid decay worked very well at amusement parks, which demanded constant change and innovation. Park operators saw little need to invest in expensive permanent structures that would have to be frequently remodeled. Using staff, amusement park designers could mold elaborate shapes and create fantastical structures that would have been incredibly time-consuming and costly, if not impossible, to build from sturdier materials. Staff's impermanence was a good thing, as it was easy to tear down an entire building at the end of one season and have a completely new and often more elaborate structure ready by the start of the next. Coney Island's parks were prime examples of this. John Kasson wrote that at Luna Park, for example, builder Frederic Thompson "threw off all sense of restraint to indulge in an orgy of ebullient forms, bright colors, and sumptuous ornament." Luna's and rival Dreamland's structures were awe-inspiring and created a "colorful holiday world" that crumbled in a short time.[8]

The architectural style of most amusement parks, Kasson wrote, was about as far away from the White City as possible: the Exposition was about discipline, while amusement parks were about release. Lakeside, however, broke with the typical Coney Island style as its buildings, even small columned towers with no purpose other than being decorative, were built from brick and wood and were meant to last. Like Luna and Dreamland, Lakeside had a tower, but its style was more subdued and relied on lighting to create elaborate and dazzling effects. The Tower of Jewels also doubled as Lakeside's main entrance. At Steeplechase on Coney Island, guests entered through massive plaster arches that depicted clowns and masks, while at Dreamland they entered through the outspread wings of a sculpture titled

Creation. Even rival Elitch's went through a succession of entrance gates, from a log structure in the 1890s to an elaborate Victorian-style gate in the 1910s to a futuristic-looking metal structure in the 1960s. David Nasaw writes that such entryways helped assure visitors that they would be safe inside the park's walls, but at Lakeside it was if the owners were saying that its reputation was the only assurance visitors needed to know they were safe inside its beautiful grounds.[9]

In breaking with other amusement parks of the era and spending money on long-lasting brick and wood structures, Lakeside's owners were attempting to demonstrate that the park, with its permanent structures and rides, was something different in the amusement business. Lakeside's architecture was understated but elegant, with similarly styled buildings clustered around the lake and the roofline of the Tower of Jewels mimicked in smaller towers and structures throughout the grounds. The Columbian Exposition's designers might not have approved of everything offered at Lakeside, but the unity found in the style of the Casino, Swimming Pool building, Skating Rink, Ballroom, and row of concessions along the Chutes pool was far more in keeping with the City Beautiful style than with Coney Island.

On September 1, 1907, the *Denver Republican* reported that Edwin H. Moorman, the park's architect, had finished his design and was ready to commence construction of the buildings; over the next several months, crews built fifteen structures at the new park. The most prominent was the Casino and attached Tower of Jewels, the park's main entrance. The Tower was 30 feet square and 150 feet high, with an observation deck at the top from which visitors could "see the surrounding county for a radius of many miles." On top of the Tower was an 18,000 candle power searchlight, said to be the largest and brightest in the United States, which had been atop the Ferris wheel at the 1904 World's Fair in St. Louis. Moorman's design encircled the Tower with lights and called for an elaborate lighting design on its walls. In fact, the *Republican* reported, Harry Weber, the park's chief electrician, was hard at work making sure all of the buildings and grounds were beautifully (and brightly) lit by 100,000 lightbulbs.[10]

Lighting at the park was one of the most impressive things about it as far as most observers were concerned. In one article headlined "Lakeside Park Will Be a Maze of Lights," the *Colorado Transcript* reported that it was "the intention of Lakeside management to make the grounds the best illuminated in the country outside of New York City." The rays of the searchlight on the Tower would "sweep the city and foothills" every night of the season. Five thousand lights were going on the walls of the Tower of Jewels and another 5,000 into the Casino building. Walker strung another 4,000 to 5,000 lights on the Shoot-the-Chutes tower and slide, all in addition to the 20,000 lights in clusters on poles around the lake. The 100,000 lights in the park, said General Manager Albert Lewin, did not include any arc lights management might decide to use in the park. The *Transcript* hinted at both beauty and safety when it declared "there will be few dark spots on the grounds." On May 26, 1908, four days before the park's grand opening, Lewin ordered all of the lights turned on for the first time in a final test. The *Transcript* reported that the "spectacle was grand indeed" and that management was giving the people of Colorado what it had promised, namely "the greatest and finest amusement park ever attempted West of Chicago." The *Denver Republican* also reported that Lewin had successfully tested the motors on all of the park's rides during the week prior to the light test.[11]

While the focus on lighting certainly fit with Mayor Speer's City Beautiful program, it also tied into the continually emphasized idea that Lakeside would be a safe and orderly amusement park. With few, if any, dark corners at Lakeside, management was creating a space in which anyone interested in improper conduct could find no place to hide. The first line of defense for any amusement park against improper conduct, however, was a fence that kept non-paying customers out. Lakeside's planners were sure to build a fence that fit the park's image, surrounding the park on three sides with 7,500 feet of rustic fence the *Denver Republican* referred to as very picturesque. The lake served as a natural barrier on the fourth side. The 8-foot-high fence was a combination of slabs and trees, and Lewin had workers plant spreading vines alongside it to further hide the park from the view of non-paying customers.[12]

Attached to the Tower was the 190-foot by 100-foot Casino, whose first chief steward was Walter C. Ivers. Inside the park the Casino was three stories, with the lower floor exposed on the lake side, but from the Sheridan Boulevard side only two stories showed. The lower floor housed the rathskeller "designed after the old German style," kitchen, ice cellar, and storage rooms, with the overhanging roof supported by elaborate plaster columns. The second level held two dining rooms; one was enclosed for winter dining, as the original plans called for the Casino to be open year-round. The main dining room was open and allowed guests to look out on the lake and enjoy the "mountain breezes, cooled by 'the Snows five thousand summers old'" while eating off of fine china with "Lakeside Casino" printed on it. The third level held a rooftop garden and a small theater. Brightly lit plazas stretched out on either side of the Tower and Casino. Inside the park they provided space for the public to promenade under, while outside, along Sheridan Boulevard, they provided covered automobile parking for automobile-owning customers.[13]

The other buildings on the grounds included a rustic Boat House, Skating Rink, indoor Swimming Pool, boarding area for the Velvet Coaster, the Third Degree fun house, the El Patio Ballroom, and the train station for the miniature railroad. The train station and its clock tower were modeled after Denver's first Union Station, which had burned down in 1895. The ballroom covered 15,000 square feet of floor space, and a number of local, national, and international bands played there during the years it was in operation. The park also included a Music Plaza with bandstand, where Dante's Italian Band, led by Dante Forcellato, played daily. The Natatorium, where the 50- by 125-foot Swimming Pool was located, sat beside the Casino. It was decorated inside with murals of nymphs and cherubs and included a filter system that created a sensation similar to a waterfall hitting the water. In later years the park gave out spare-tire covers that urged people to "Swim in Drinking Water" at Lakeside Park. The Boat House, which cost $10,000, included 160 feet of pier. Three naphtha launches, which used naphtha as fuel for the motors, and a number of smaller boats were available for use on the lake, where customers also found a diving tower and a bathing beach.[14]

While construction proceeded on the park, the town of Lakeside proceeded with establishing itself as a functioning municipality. One of the most important early pieces of business Lakeside's leaders took up came in February 1908 when Kate Adams presented a bill granting the Denver Tramway Company a right-of-way and franchise. With the Tramway Company rushing to build a new line to the park, it needed the town's permission to actually build and operate a streetcar line in Lakeside. Present at the meeting where the bill was initially introduced was George Ribbet, an official with the Denver Tramway Company. The final vote on the proposal was delayed until the town's leaders could more fully inform residents on what it involved. Officials posted notices of the proposal throughout the town of Lakeside and two weeks later, on March 12, 1908, it was adopted unanimously. At Lakeside, Tramway trains would deliver guests right to the park's front gate, a far different situation than Denver's other amusement parks had faced.[15]

Many streetcar companies throughout the United States built amusement parks, known as trolley parks, on large tracts of company-owned land at the end of their lines in an effort to convince customers to pay the full fare to ride to the end of the lines and to increase ridership in the evenings and on weekends. Denver never had trolley parks, which meant the owners of the city's amusement parks had to convince the streetcar companies to build lines to their parks. Unfortunately, Denver's park owners found, that was not always easy. By the 1890s there were dozens of streetcar companies operating in Denver, but the two largest were the Denver City Railway Company and the Denver Tramway Company, the latter of which was still trying to perfect its electric railway. Denver Tramway eventually took over all the other companies and operated its system until June 1950. Jerome Smiley wrote in 1901 that no city had a "more comprehensive and efficient transportation system" than Denver and that the system deserved credit for keeping Denver from having anything like a "'tenement house district' . . . that blight common to so many large cities." Denver's streetcar system allowed people to spread out over a large area rather than being housed "tier upon tier in congested localities," as was the case, Smiley believed, in many large cities.[16]

However, Denver's spread-out development made it hard for residents who did not have private transportation to get to the city's amusement parks. Elitch's was two miles from the nearest streetcar station when it opened on May 1, 1890, forcing John Elitch to hire horse-drawn trolleys that ran at regular intervals between the station and the park. The West End Electric Car Company eventually built a horse-drawn line directly to the park, but it did not begin operating until the spring of 1891. The new line also allowed streetcars to stop at Manhattan Beach, much to the delight of that park's owners. By 1892, when Elitch's took over management of Manhattan Beach, the streetcar companies were forcing people who wanted to visit both parks, which were only a few miles apart, to pay two fares. The *Denver Republican* found this practice unfair, considering that people had to pay only one fare to reach "all sorts and kinds of entertainments of an ephemeral and transient nature" in other parts of Denver and that this situation was detrimental to the financial outlook of the "high class of attractions." The Denver Tramway Company finally extended an electric line to Elitch's in 1899, nine years after the park opened. Arlington Park and Tuileries were more fortunate. Robert Speer, who was rising through the ranks of Denver politics, may have used his political influence to get several electric streetcar companies to run special lines to Arlington Park when it opened in 1892. After it became Chutes Park in 1898, the Denver Tramway Company ran special cars to the park from Fifteenth and Arapahoe Streets every fifteen minutes. At Tuileries, the Englewood car of the Denver Tramway system already ran to the beer garden that had previously occupied the site.[17]

Unlike Denver's other amusement parks, Lakeside's owners never had to worry about how people would get to their park. As construction at Lakeside neared completion in 1908, the *Denver Republican* proudly pointed out that the Denver Tramway Company was rushing to finish its streetcar line to the park well in advance of opening day. The Denver Tramway Company was a private venture, but it was also one of the most powerful companies in the city, with close connections to city government. The fact that it was rushing to complete a line to Lakeside before the park opened rather than many years after the fact was a significant indicator of how important the new park was to Denver. The West Forty-Fourth Avenue line was the direct line to Lakeside, and a spur allowed it to drop riders at the park's front gates. All of the Berkeley, Golden, Arvada, and Leyden streetcar lines also ran to the park once the new track was in place. Return passengers waited for a streetcar to pick them up at a station nearer to Forty-Fourth Avenue, which ran along the south side of the park property. Promotional material claimed that passengers boarding a Tramway car in downtown Denver would be dropped off at Lakeside twenty minutes later. The Denver Tramway Company, a source of pride for the city of Denver, was doing its part to make sure customers got to Lakeside, not only on opening day but every day of the season thereafter.[18]

While nearly every amusement park in the country eagerly sought a streetcar line, Lakeside's owners broke with tradition in another way by including automobile parking in their plans for the park. When Lakeside opened in 1908, the automobile was still, for the most part, a plaything of the rich. In 1906, for example, Colorado mining millionaire Eben Smith paid $4,320 for a Packard Touring Car, nearly twice the amount Robert Speer wanted people to spend on homes built around Arlington Park fifteen years earlier. As late as 1915, five years after Henry Ford introduced the Model T, the *Denver Automobile Directory* read like a Who's Who of Denver, with names such as Boettcher, Bonfils, and Evans appearing in it repeatedly, and they drove Packards and Pierce-Arrows. Denver's population was well over 200,000 people in 1915, but only 5,154 cars were registered in the city during the first half of that year. In 1908, the year Lakeside opened, the forty car dealerships in Denver sold a total of 1,550 cars; if the owners of every one of those cars showed up on opening day at Lakeside, they would not come close to filling it to capacity. But the fact that Lakeside's builders included space for automobile parking from the earliest stages clearly demonstrated which segment of society they were hoping to attract. Other amusement parks, such as San Francisco's Playland at the Beach, which opened more than a decade after Lakeside, struggled with space for car parking and often encouraged patrons to use alternate means of transportation, such as streetcars and buses.[19]

With transportation to the park secured, in April 1908 Lakeside held another election in which Mayor Adams and the six trustees were reelected without opposition. In the same election, voters also had to decide if the town of Lakeside would become "anti-saloon territory." Local option supporters had managed to get that question on ballots in several cities in Colorado, and its passage in Lakeside, a town that existed solely to house a beer baron's amusement park, would have been a major victory for prohibitionists. Lakeside's voters defeated the measure, however, and the town (and park) remained a safe place to have a drink. But prohibitionists were not about to give up that easily, and before long they would make alcohol sales in the park a major issue.[20]

On May 6, 1908, a little more than three weeks before Lakeside Amusement Park's grand opening, the town's board of trustees amended Section 43 of the General Ordinances to state that "no person or corporation shall conduct any roller coaster, scenic railway, or other amusement device of any kind whatsoever, within the Town of Lakeside" without first getting a license for each device. The fee for the license was set at $200 per device per year, and each license was good for twenty years. If a person failed to obtain a license but still operated an amusement device "for which a fee or deposit is charged or made," he or she faced fines ranging from $5 to $100 per offense. It was an interesting law for the council to pass in a company town based around an amusement park. With fifty amusement devices ready to operate on opening day, the town stood to collect $10,000. Lakeside's management may have even supported the fees as a way to fund the town's operation.[21]

Throughout the winter and early spring of 1908, management allowed curious members of the public to visit Lakeside's grounds to watch construction progress, and the *Transcript* estimated that between 10,000 and 15,000 people visited on Sundays during good weather. On Sunday, February 23, 1908, management allowed people to take test rides on the park's unfinished Scenic Railway. The final test run of the day turned to tragedy when a car loaded with sixteen people jumped the tracks and "hurled the occupants" ten feet to the ground below. Five of the riders were seriously injured, and one, forty-six-year-old Francis W. Bray of Denver, suffered a fatal skull fracture, dying from her injuries five days later. Both the *Rocky Mountain News* and Telluride's *Daily Journal* were careful to point out that the Scenic Railway was not finished and lacked guardrails at the time of the accident. Coverage of the accident in Denver's papers was overshadowed by the murder of Father Leo Heinrichs of St. Elizabeth's Catholic Church the same day as the accident, which made for better headlines and filled the pages of the *News* for days afterward. According to newspaper historian Frank Luther Mott, the *Denver Post* in its early years was "sensational in content and treatment," "ran wild in its attacks," and was the "yellowest of the yellow journals," and the publishers of the *Rocky Mountain News* did their best to keep up with it. While Father Leo's murder was definitely a bigger story, the fact that the papers practically ignored the gruesome Scenic Railway accident indicated how invested they were in Lakeside's success.[22]

Park manager Albert Lewin finally closed the construction site to the public on April 26 so workers could spend the next month laying walkways; planting lawns, shrubs, and flowerbeds; and putting the finishing touches on buildings, none of which could be "done to good advantage unless sightseers are temporarily excluded." Even Mother Nature seemed to smile on the park, as the *Transcript* pointed out that of the 875 trees Lewin ordered for the park, only 5 had died and had to be replaced. By May 17, the *Denver Republican* reported, "great strides" had been made in "the beautification of the grounds" in the few weeks the park had been closed to the public. The newspaper asserted that even those who had closely watched the progress made in the months before April 26 would be "delightfully surprised" by what they saw when the grounds reopened to the public.[23]

Ignoring Lakeside Amusement Park's competitors, the *Denver Republican* wrote that nothing like the park had ever been planned or attempted in Denver and praised it as the first non-winter entertainment venue "in keeping with the demands of its cosmopolitan and thoroughly discriminating population." Lakeside would truly be the park of all the people, the newspaper declared, and it was large enough for all classes, though "the park will be so carefully conducted that the most conservative pleasure-seeker will find nothing offensive and no undesirable elements will be catered to." The entire family, proclaimed the *Republican*, would be able to find something to do at Lakeside. Of particular importance was the fact that even the minor concessions, which normally operated in "tents or improvised shacks," were located in beautiful, permanent buildings. The *Republican* wrote that "the best has been none too good for the Lakeside constructionists" who were "courageous business men," and the park was "a striking demonstration of their faith in Denver's future."[24]

The park of all the people was divided into three sections. Once through the Tower and down the Grand Stairway, visitors found themselves in the area known as Central Park. Other than the merry-go-round and the entrance to the miniature railroad, no rides were located in that area. The Casino building opened onto this area, and the Music Plaza was in Central Park as well. Garden areas included plentiful benches, each with "Denver" and "Lakeside Park" stamped into the metal legs. To the right of Central Park, when facing the lake, was the social area where the ballroom, Boat House, and Skating Rink were located. To the left of Central Park was the amusement area.[25]

Lakeside's first visitors could choose from "fifty different forms of amusement, a half-hundred sources of entertainment." The miniature railroad, known as the Lakeshore Railway, encircled the entire thirty-seven acres of the lake and was reportedly the longest in the United States. It took 93,000 pounds of rails from the Pueblo Steel Works to lay the track, and the train was pulled by the steam locomotive from the 1904 St. Louis World's Fair. The Velvet Coaster, which ran along the southern edge of the lake, cost $23,000 and was described as a "decided novelty in the roller coaster line" because it combined the Foster coaster from White City Amusement Park in Chicago with a figure-eight design. W. H. Labb, the park's general contractor, designed and built the 3,600-foot ride. As its name implied, the Velvet Coaster was far tamer than modern coasters, with fairly gentle rises and dips, but for the time it was a thrilling piece of equipment. The park also included a mile-long Scenic Railway designed by LaMarcus A. Thompson, the ride's inventor. Scenic railways were essentially roller coasters over which Thompson built dark tunnels "in which he arranged pretty scenery, startling grottos, and historical tableaus." Before entering the tunnels, the ride's cars tripped a switch that flooded them with light. According to ride manufacturer William Mangels, Thompson Scenic Railways were "regarded as the leading amusement ride" at parks and expositions for many years.[26]

To their left, as visitors entered the park through the Tower, across from the Swimming Pool was the Shoot-the-Chutes. Rather than have the boats splash down into the lake, Labb and his crew constructed a separate lagoon for the ride. Spectators could stand around the lagoon or on a bridge over it and watch as boats full of people were towed to the top of the Chutes tower and then released to hurtle down a ramp into the pool. For a brief moment before beginning their descent, riders on the Chutes had a spectacular view of the park grounds and beyond. The Chutes divided the amusement section of the park into Avenue A and Avenue B. Along Avenue A were the concessions, which included a movie theater, shooting school, box ball alley, the airship, touring cars, the "flying lady," balloon ascension platform, photography studio, the Ferris wheel, and the haunted swing. Avenue B included the Devil's Palace, Third Degree, pony and burro track, train depot, and access to the other rides. The picnic grounds and free swings were accessible from either avenue, which dead-ended at them. Near the entrance to the Velvet Coaster and the Scenic Railway was the Third Degree, the park's first fun house. Third Degrees were found in several other amusement parks around the country, but no description of the interior appears to have survived. From photographs of the buildings, visitors ascended steep ramps to get inside and, after going through the attraction, walked out the back on flat platforms.[27]

Lakeside's merry-go-round was built by the C. W. Parker Company of Leavenworth, Kansas. By the time Lakeside was under construction, merry-go-rounds had become expensive pieces of machinery because of the highly skilled engineering techniques, mechanical construction, elaborately carved figures, and bright illumination that went into them, in addition to the large carrying capacities they required. William Mangels wrote that, despite the great cost, "no amusement resort, county fair or park of any magnitude ever lacks the always popular merry-go-round." In addition to the standard horses, the Lakeside merry-go-round included lions, rabbits, pigs, goats, dogs, gazelles, jaguars, and monkeys. Figures other than horses became popular additions to merry-go-rounds in the late nineteenth and early twentieth centuries, largely because operators thought the innovative figures would draw more business, but the opposite proved to be true. Proper young ladies rode horses, not pigs or monkeys, and many children were frightened by the strange animals and refused to go near them. The carousel may have been one of Lakeside's few missteps as it embraced the City Beautiful ideal, yet it managed to survive every change made to the park.[28]

Another misstep was the Tickler. The first Tickler, invented by William Mangels, was installed at Luna Park on Coney Island in 1906. Its inventor wrote that it was the first ride specifically designed to "jostle, jolt and jounce its riders about in their seats." The ride was built on a large platform that sloped downward, and a course defined by posts and rails covered the platform. Cars full of riders were drawn to the top of the platform and then released. The rubber-ringed cars bounced off the posts and rails as they descended through the course, and "at the end of the journey, the five passengers were usually scrambled together so hopelessly that attendants had to help them disembark." Although the ride cost $6,000 to install, Mangels wrote that the novelty soon wore off, though that was not the problem at Lakeside. Instead, when riders began to suffer broken bones, management removed the ride. As permissive as Mayor Speer's definition of City Beautiful could be, broken bones had no place in his vision.[29]

The baby incubators, another common amusement park attraction, were located in a quiet corner of the park near the Grand Stairway that led down from the Tower. Dr. Martin Couney, a German-born and trained physician, had exhibited premature babies in incubators at amusement parks and fairs around the country, where he charged a twenty-five-cent admission fee to see the babies and gave a lecture about his practices, which included taking their pulse with a gold pocket watch the size of a baseball and passing a gold wedding ring over a baby's fist and arm. The admission fee went to pay for the costs associated with caring for the babies. In addition to Dr. Couney, the staff at Lakeside included two other doctors and three pediatric nurses. An amusement park might have seemed like a strange place to house premature babies in incubators, but Couney had long struggled to get doctors and hospitals to accept his ideas. By placing the incubators in amusement parks, where people congregated and expected to see the strange or shocking, Couney hoped to gain widespread public acceptance of his new device. Before he died in 1950, Couney estimated that he saved 6,500 of the 8,000 preemies under his care. The most famous of the Lakeside babies was Rosemary Fouts, who weighed twenty-eight ounces when she was born on May 24, 1913. By the end of the summer she weighed three pounds, one ounce. Visitors to Lakeside that year cheered every advance Rosemary made and worried, along with her mother, Carrie, over setbacks, such as when one of the other incubator babies died. Even after Rosemary left the park, the public kept track of her until she was eight years old, at which time she disappeared from public view.[30]

By the end of May 1908, Lakeside Amusement Park was ready for its debut. The buildings were up, the attractions were installed, and the Tramway line was complete. The newspapers did their part, busily promoting Lakeside as the greatest addition yet to Denver's amusement places. Lakeside's builders designed and constructed a beautiful amusement park that was easily compatible with the City Beautiful architectural style and decided to operate the park in a manner that allowed Mayor Robert Speer to readily embrace it as part of his City Beautiful program for Denver. It was time for Lakeside Amusement Park to officially open to the public.

CHAPTER 2

Just Take a Trip Out to Jolly Lakeside

In his 1908 song "Just Take a Trip Out to Lakeside," Elmore Lee picked up on many of the things that made Lakeside a valuable City Beautiful asset. It was a "nice trolley ride / out to jolly Lakeside," where the "sights there are pretty / it's Denver's White City / with myriads of lights all aglow." Opening day, May 30, 1908, found the "White City . . . complete. Its walks are gravelled [*sic*]; its shrubbery and trees set out; its benches in place; its police force adequate; its fountain playing; its lights all connected." Mayors Marvin Adams of Lakeside and John Vivian of Arvada were on the platform set up outside the Tower, along with the managers and owners and their families. In his welcoming speech, Mayor Adams said Lakeside was surely the handsomest town in Colorado that day, in addition to being the gem of all the cities encircling Denver. After proclaiming that the "spirit that undertook the enterprise" of Lakeside was the same as that which moved the "the men who first sought gold in our mountains," Adams went on to say that Lakeside would be a favorite destination for men and women worn down by the strain of business, for tourists in search of health, and for "all class[es] of men, women, and children who need recreation and rest." Adams further predicted that the tens of thousands of people who would find their way to Lakeside would "go away felling [sic] stronger and better qualified to resume the business of life." City Beautiful supporters, park planners, and progressive thinkers could not have better expressed what they hoped parks such as Lakeside would do for the people.[1]

After Adams finished his speech, Denver mayor Robert Speer, from his City Hall office in downtown Denver, pushed a button on his desk and, as a crowd of 50,000 watched, the Tower gates swung open. Gertrude Zang, the daughter of owner Adolph Zang, smashed a bottle of champagne against the Tower wall, and to the sounds of Dante's Italian Band playing "The Star Spangled Banner" and the newly composed "White City March" (written in honor of the park), the first paying customers entered Lakeside. Fittingly for the most marvelous event in Denver up to then, "Not a serious accident happened to mar the day. There was not the slightest display of rowdyism nor intoxication. No complaints were received of pickpockets and not a single arrest was made." The park's opening attracted statewide attention. The *Fort Collins Weekly Courier* informed its readers that the park, with its "wealth of varied attractions," added greatly to Denver's sources of entertainment and reflected credit on the state in the mind of every visitor who saw it.[2]

"Lakeside," the *Republican* wrote, "is the place!" The newspaper advised that it was worth multiple visits to the park just to watch "the whole glittering, moving, fascinating show," but doing only that would deprive visitors of enjoying the park's numerous other attractions. Once again, as was often the case with early coverage of the park, Lakeside earned special praise for its lighting design. The lights on poles around the lake were not single lights, the *Republican* reported, but clusters of them, leaving little of the miniature railroad's route along the lakeshore in darkness. The Scenic Railway and Velvet Coaster were "like serpents of fire" stretching along the lake, and the Tower of Jewels was a "pillar of captive fire" topped off by the massive searchlight. The view of the fully lit park from the observation deck on top of the Tower, according to the newspaper, was "one not soon forgotten."[3]

Once a visitor was sufficiently recovered from the awe-inspiring sight of the lights, there were the rides for "jarring, scaring, whirling, mystifying, transporting, and otherwise entertaining." Every ride, according to the *Republican*, was well patronized on opening day, and at 11:15 that night there were still seventy people in line for one more trip down the Chutes. The *Republican* estimated that a young man could take his "most particular friend" to Lakeside; after an afternoon and evening of swimming, roller skating, dancing, fishing, boat rides, dinner, visiting the concessions, and tackling the "dozens of hilarious other attractions," he would come away about twelve dollars poorer. While it would certainly make for a wonderful and inexpensive evening for the couple, the newspaper cautioned that no person could crowd all of those activities "into one afternoon and evening and still survive."[4]

Those who did try to cram all the activities into one day or who met with unfortunate accidents found that they did not have to leave the park to seek medical attention. In early July, park visitor Frank Sedlemeyer was on the lake in a rowboat when a storm arose. Upon reaching the shore, Sedlemeyer stepped out of his boat into the water and grabbed a light pole for support, creating a complete circuit for the electricity. A bystander had to administer several blows with a plank to knock Sedlemeyer free from the pole, after which he was quickly taken to the park hospital. From 1915 to 1929 the hospital was under the direction of Dr. Kate Walker Beall, who became a doctor late in life. After graduating from the Homeopathic Medical College of Missouri in 1899, Kate joined her daughter's medical practice, but in 1913, after the death of her husband, she moved to Denver. She opened her office in a house at Forty-Fifth Avenue and Zenobia Street, which was near Lakeside, and soon became the physician on duty at the park. She remained there until her death in 1929 at age seventy-eight, treating sick stomachs and minor cuts and scrapes. After his accident at the lake, Sedlemeyer spent three days recovering in the hospital, and the *Transcript* reported that he spoke "in the highest terms of the care given him by the Lakeside officials."[5]

With dozens of amusements, the jail beneath the park's ballroom, and the hospital in full operation, Lakeside's management had seemingly met every need customers could conceivably have. They had planned so well that only two minor incidents marred the otherwise perfect opening day. Management at the café and rathskeller had underestimated the size of the expected crowd and ran out of bread and beer at 5:00 in the afternoon, sending workers scrambling to neighborhood stores to buy sandwich-making supplies to feed the rest of the hungry people at the park. The other difficulty came when ticket sellers "found themselves embarrassed by the prosperity of the Denver people" who paid in paper money and silver dollars instead of nickels and dimes. Admission to the park was ten cents, and each ride ticket cost an additional ten cents, which left the ticket sellers frantically searching for small coins after running out partway through the day. Overall, however, opening day was a huge success.[6]

In fact, aside from a few arrests for public intoxication, only one serious criminal event intruded on Lakeside's first summer. Near the end of June, three men—Hugh Cline, Clarence Harris, and Edward Dixon—were arrested on charges of highway robbery and larceny for being part of a pickpocket ring operating at the park. The men, who the newspapers identified as morphine addicts, were arrested by Lakeside's sheriff John Lindsey in the act of robbing several streetcar passengers and the streetcar's conductor, Henry Hogen, on the outskirts of town. The police estimated that the gang had stolen about $1,500 in one day of working the park, including a large diamond belonging to a tourist from New York. The men refused to name the ringleaders of the gang and were in jail awaiting trial when the *Colorado Transcript* reported the incident on June 25, 1908. The newspaper noted that "a number of prominent persons of Denver" had notified Lindsey of their losses, emphasizing the elite nature of Lakeside's visitors when it opened. The newspaper also attempted to do damage control by assuring readers that the quick arrests demonstrated the efficiency and skill of Lakeside's police force, proving there was "no amusement enterprise in the country of the magnitude of Lakeside that is so free from the operation of criminals."[7]

As hard as Lakeside's management worked, Denver officials worked just as hard to make sure everyone knew the value they placed on the park and to make sure it was a success. In 1908 Denver was set to host the Democratic National Convention. It was the first major convention held at Speer's new 12,000-seat Municipal Auditorium, and the city went all out in an effort to make sure delegates had a true Colorado experience. Activities for the delegates included performances by Apache Indians, who demonstrated their war whoops, and an excursion to the old mining towns in Gilpin County, where delegates rode open cars on the Gilpin Tramway, which had once hauled tons of ore from the county's mines. Planners went so far as to truck in snow from the mountains so the delegates could have a snowball fight in July. City Beautiful Denver and the White City came together on June 27, 1908, when Mayor Speer and Denver Fire and Police Board president Earl Hewitt hosted a dinner for 200 convention delegates on the Casino balcony, praised for many years after for the stunning views of the mountains and Colorado sunsets the location offered. The *Colorado Transcript* reported that several prominent Democrats, including National Committee chairman Thomas Taggert of Indiana, were in attendance at the dinner, the first of many times Denver officials led convention visitors to Lakeside.[8]

Lakeside's management was thrilled to have the Democrats or any other convention visitors at the park, and it proved an especially popular destination for them that first summer. Cecil R. Connor, Lakeside's press agent, was happy to escort groups through the park, especially if there was a chance such tours would result in good publicity. Two weeks before the Democrats were at the park, the Denver Press Club and the Writer's Club (an organization of women who wrote for Denver newspapers and magazines) attended a luncheon hosted by the park. After dining and listening to speeches by Albert Lewin and other park officials, the 200 people in attendance toured the grounds and enjoyed the rides. The *Transcript* reported that if they missed seeing anything, "it was not from any fault of the gentlemanly press agent or the Lakeside management," who were hoping that the writers would spread the word about what a wonderful place Lakeside was. The park also hosted the annual picnic for the Denver-area Woodmen of the World camps that summer, which included drills by degree teams, sawing and chopping contests, and baseball games. All proceeds from ticket sales during the picnic went to the building fund of the Golden camp, which was in charge of the event.[9]

As Lakeside's first season neared its end, the park hosted a "monster barbecue" on Labor Day with 35,000 people in attendance. Newspapers proclaimed it was the largest crowd that had ever paid admission to an amusement park in the West. The official close of the first season came with a three-day Corn Festival from October 2 to 4, to which the entire state was invited. Throughout the festival, described as being like Mardi Gras, the park was decorated with arches and rows of ears of corn, corn stalks, pumpkins, and "other field products." For the first night of the festival, workers hung thousands of Japanese lanterns throughout the park grounds, and management put on a "spectacular" fireworks display over the lake. On the second night of the festival "mirth and frolic" reigned, as the park hosted a masquerade carnival. Management awarded $500 in prizes to the most creative costumes, and attendees paraded through the grounds in their costumes before taking part in an evening of dancing in the El Patio Ballroom. Newspapers reported that thousands of horns and ticklers were handed out to guests, and "tons of confetti" was tossed about. On the final night of the event, every person in attendance at the park walked away with a souvenir of the festival. The "most unique affair in the history of Denver summer amusements" was a fitting end to the first summer at Denver's most unique amusement park.[10]

During its first season, Lakeside Amusement Park also received its first write-up in *Billboard* in June 1908, a month after the park opened. According to Julian Helber, the magazine's Denver correspondent, the park's first season was starting with a "buzz and [a] whir." Sunday attendance was averaging 15,000 people, Helber wrote, while the daily attendance was "in proportion" to that amount, although he did not put a number on it. All of the rides were "crowded to capacity limits," and the most popular outdoor attraction was the Dante Band. Helber spotlighted the lighting at the park, writing that "the gorgeous illumination of Lakeside is the admiration of every one of Denver's citizens." No article detailing Lakeside's construction appeared in the magazine prior to opening day, and no other article about the first season appeared throughout the rest of 1908. In fact, Lakeside had to wait until July 1909 before the park received a full write-up in the magazine. That year, *Billboard* reported that Denver was "claiming to have the largest and most modern outdoor amusement resort" between Chicago and the Pacific. The park was "exceptionally well supplied with riding devices," though no rides had apparently been added from the year before, based on the list that appeared in the article. *Billboard* did point out one of the many things that set Lakeside apart from other amusement parks of the time when it mentioned that all of the concessions (which included rides at the time) were "permanently housed in attractive buildings."[11]

Throughout the rest of the 1909 season, *Billboard* continued to sing the praises of Frank Burt, who had replaced Albert Lewin as general manager of Lakeside that year (Lewin became general manager of rival Luna Park before later opening his own outdoor market in Denver). On July 24 the magazine reported that Burt had "transformed things" so that all rides and concessions were doing great business. The next month *Billboard* reported that Burt, who had "the reputation of doing things," had changed the course of the "pay streak" at the park by eliminating shortcuts and keeping people on the newly laid-out paved paths, thereby ensuring that the crowds had to circle the concession stands and thus greatly improving business at the stands. In September, as the park prepared to close for the season, *Billboard* reported that it had been a good summer for Lakeside and that Burt was planning a number of changes for the next season, including an expanded theater.[12]

Lakeside news was conspicuously absent from Denver's newspapers during the summer of 1909, possibly because of serious issues troubling the park and the town that might have threatened its City Beautiful reputation. One issue involved trouble at the Lakeside Realty and Amusement Company. The *Transcript* reported on April 29, 1909, that a "serious disruption among the stockholders" had been troubling the company for several months. The disruption most likely concerned a May 25, 1908, vote by the directors to increase the company's capital stock to $350,000. The vote was not unanimous, and the dispute found its way into the town's election process when trustee John P. Yaeger ran for mayor on the Citizens ticket against Republican Marvin Adams, who had sided with the stockholders in favor of the increase. Adams's entire Republican ticket, including his wife, Kate, the town recorder, went down to defeat. Adams immediately threatened to dispute the election results in court, charging that there were irregularities in the filing of the Citizens ticket and that coercion had been used in the election itself. A justice of the peace swore Yaeger and the rest of the Citizens ticket into office, but Adams and the Republicans refused to give up their offices, leaving the "smallest town in Jefferson county" with "more town officials than any of her sisters." Adams lost the lawsuit and by August had left Lakeside for Denver, where he opened his own bar.[13]

The stockholders dispute and election controversy were minor compared with a much bigger problem Lakeside Amusement Park faced that year as the Anti-Saloon League, stinging from the defeat of its anti-drinking measure in Lakeside the year before, seemed to be out to get the park's owners and managers. A number of people had alleged that the park had been illegally selling liquor on Sundays ever since it opened in 1908. In July 1908 the *Transcript* editorialized that the park was in full compliance with the law and that "but for the free advertising of over jealous prohibs, few visitors to the White City would know that liquor is sold there at all." The agitators, who the *Transcript* identified as "Denver busybodies," needed to "turn their attention to some of the disreputable joints at home" rather than go after Lakeside, in the opinion of the paper's editors.[14]

In 1909 allegations were still flying, and Jefferson County district attorney W. M. Morgan instructed Deputy District Attorney John Livesay (who would soon buy Marvin Adams's old house and move to Lakeside) to investigate. Livesay's interpretation of the Sunday closing law, which Morgan initially agreed with, was that it applied only to saloons, not hotels, restaurants, or cafés, which included Lakeside. However, E. E. McLaughlin, president of the Colorado Anti-Saloon League, wanted Lakeside punished. Morgan, according to the *Transcript*, continually pushed Livesay to investigate the park, apparently at McLaughlin's insistence. The point of contention was the rathskeller, the restaurant on the lower level of the Casino. Morgan and Livesay told Frank Burt, who had just taken over as manager of the park when the investigation began, that dividing the restaurant in half with a partition and keeping part of it closed on Sundays would solve the problem. Within a day Burt had the partition built, but Morgan, at the insistence of McLaughlin, continued to press Livesay to take further action against Lakeside. Livesay firmly believed no one at the park was committing any crimes and refused to investigate further unless Morgan told him who was making the complaints. Instead, Morgan fired Livesay on July 1, 1909.[15]

On July 26 Sheriff Heater of Jefferson County arrested Adolph Zang, his brewery associate T. A. Fredericks, John Keefe, Godfrey Schirmer, and several others for violating the liquor laws. It fell to the *Fort Collins Weekly Courier* to report on the arrests, in an article headlined "Millionaires Are Taken by Sheriff." Although the *Transcript* covered the liquor cases in detail, it did not print any stories on the arrest of Zang and the others. At the beginning of August, the editors of the *Transcript* argued that the prosecution was starting to resemble a persecution, particularly when it resulted in the arrest of men such as Zang. The newspaper again pointed out that Morgan had ruled the park in compliance with the law just a few weeks earlier. By making changes at the rathskeller, which Morgan approved, management had proven it was willing to do whatever necessary to keep the park, a "rival institution to the finest hotels" in Colorado, in compliance with the law. The police were unmoved by the newspaper's arguments and, based on complaints signed by people who said they had been served liquor on Sundays, began arresting everyone from servers at the park to directors of the company.[16]

In addition to the four company directors, nine waiters (the seven listed in the newspaper were G. C. Matthews, Fred Marks, E. P. Fritz, Red Dragoo, Harry

Furlong, Ira Neice, and Hugh Doherty) and new general manager Frank Burt were eventually arrested. On August 10, 1909, Judge Ben Snyder presided over the third trial involving a member of the Lakeside group arrested for violating the law. In a surprise move, the judge dismissed all fourteen cases when it was revealed that the complaining witness, Professor J. W. Hazard, had left the state. An angry Judge Snyder charged Hazard with the court costs for the day, and the fourteen Lakeside defendants "immediately began to talk of damage suits as balm for their feelings over what they claim is persecution." The business community in nearby Golden also began to express concern over what it believed was the unnecessary expense of the ongoing investigation and prosecution. Less than a week after the Hazard complaint was dismissed, the directors of the Lakeside Company made good on their threat and instructed the company's lawyer, J. W. Barnes, to file a $100,000 lawsuit against Hazard for false arrest, defamation of character, and malicious annoyance, among other things. The *Transcript* fully supported the suit, arguing that the ongoing investigation had become "a fine example of legal buffoonery" and that it was time to stop harassing Lakeside, which was operated by some of the richest and most influential men in the state of Colorado.[17]

When Adolph Zang went on trial in November 1909 on charges relating to a new complaint filed by Isaac Hines of Arvada, it was revealed that nearly all of the prosecution's witnesses were employees of the Anti-Saloon League, hired for the sole purpose of obtaining evidence against Lakeside. The hired witnesses included Frank Greene, the center for the University of Denver football team, who under cross-examination by J. W. Barnes "fumbled his testimony worse than he was ever known to fumble a pigskin," according to the *Transcript*. Another witness testified that he had never tasted liquor in his life but could distinguish whiskey, beer, or wine "at a reasonable distance." After the witnesses finished testifying, Barnes tried to get the case against Zang dismissed, arguing that the park's majority owner had nothing to do with the daily operation of the rathskeller. The judge refused and turned the case over to the jury, which promptly convicted Zang.[18]

Five days later, on November 22, 1909, the defendants decided that they could not win and that they were tired of the ongoing cases. Under a plea agreement, the remaining thirteen defendants entered a plea of *nolo contendre*. Barnes asked the judge to overturn Zang's conviction from the week before and grant him a new trial. With the request granted, Zang entered the same plea, and all of the defendants agreed to pay all costs associated with the case. Judge McCall informed the defendants that the plea essentially meant they were guilty and that he could impose fines, sentence them to jail, or both; but as long as they promised not to serve liquor in any manner at Lakeside on Sundays, he would not impose any punishment. Godfrey Schirmer, who was secretary and treasurer of the Lakeside Realty and Amusement Company as well as president of the German American Trust Company, was particularly concerned about pleading guilty and the effect it would have on his reputation and his bank. Judge McCall took special care to assure him that as long as the park remained dry on Sundays, the matter was finished. With the plea deal in place, management at the park was free to put the issue behind them and look forward to 1910.[19]

No coverage of the liquor issues at Lakeside appeared in Denver newspapers. The city was heavily invested in Lakeside's reputation as a major part of its City Beautiful program, and any controversy touching the park seemed off-limits. Speer's realism when it came to strict interpretation of City Beautiful ideals may also have played a part in the lack of coverage. Just as Speer approved of spooning in the parks, he did not necessarily look down on alcohol consumption. While Speer and his partners had forbidden bars or liquor sales in the neighborhood around Arlington Park in 1890, Speer was also Denver's police commissioner at the time, and he took no action against prostitution, gambling, or saloons while in that position, considering organized vice a fact of life. As mayor, Speer argued that vice simply needed to be kept confined and regulated. Henry Buchtel, a Methodist teetotaler who served as chancellor of the University of Denver, was elected governor of Colorado in 1906 and agreed with Speer, saying that "sinners existed as well as saints" and that Denver was better off with well-policed vice districts. Yet some of Speer's City Beautiful programs were in fact designed to cut down on alcohol consumption. Many temperance advocates argued that people drank to "wet their whistles" and that the installation of public drinking fountains, one of Speer's many projects, would allow them to do so while avoiding saloons and alcohol. Speer halfheartedly cracked down on saloons beginning in 1910, after temperance advocates grew increasingly louder in their calls for prohibition, fearing that if he did not do something to regulate saloons, those advocates would force Denver to go dry. In any other city, Speer's acceptance of alcohol would have conflicted with the City

Beautiful movement's objectives. In Denver, however, the independent Speer established his own objectives. Well-policed and regulated, Lakeside was the perfect location for the sale and consumption of alcohol.[20]

The *Colorado Transcript*, in its coverage of the alcohol investigation, increasingly took the position that it was a witch hunt and completely unjustified. In urging Jefferson County residents to think critically about the case and what was happening to the park and its employees, the newspaper first stated that employment at the park supported over 400 families, making it the largest employer in the county and one of the biggest taxpayers as well. The park was "the beauty spot of the West," "the favorite spot of the society of the state," and was "pointed out to visitors from East and West as the show place of the Rocky Mountain region." The *Transcript* went on to point out that the Jefferson County district attorney himself had ruled that the Casino was operated just like the finest hotels in the state, and the newspaper argued that it was no different from the Brown Palace or the Zang-owned Oxford in Denver, the Hotel Colorado in Glenwood Springs, or the Antlers in Colorado Springs. All of these institutions did "more to advertise this state than anything else one can find," and anyone interested in the social and commercial advancement of Jefferson County and all of Colorado knew that to be the case, according to the newspaper. The heated reaction clearly showed the importance people attached to Lakeside Amusement Park just one year after it had opened to the public. The case also demonstrated that as long as Denver was linking itself to the park and promoting it as part of the City Beautiful movement, Jefferson County was happy to have Denver be a part of it. But when it came to something unpleasant like the Denver-based Anti-Saloon League interfering in the county's business, many in Jefferson County were more than happy to tell the Denver intruders to mind their own business and worry about problems in their own town.[21]

As the liquor issue worked its way through the courts, the Cook's, Bartender's, and Waiter's Union, backed by the Denver Trades and Labor Assembly, tried to force Lakeside to close on Sundays. The fight had been brewing ever since the park opened the year before, but it reached new heights when the larger Denver group advised management that it did not consider the park to be union as long as non-union employees worked there. Nothing ever came of the proposed boycott of Lakeside, and management paid little attention to the Sunday closing demand. The *Transcript* sympathized with the park, writing that management at Lakeside seemed to be "having its share of trouble lately." The trouble continued near the end of the 1909 season when J. F. White, the editor of the *Arvada Enterprise*, who the *Colorado Transcript* referred to as "Brother White," complained that it was a great injustice to his close friend Mrs. Anna Guth that the White City was allowed to operate without interference while Jefferson County police, in the past, had continually raided and eventually closed Guth's pleasure resort. Her Northwestern Park, located near Lakeside's neighboring town Mountain View, was in fact an illegal gambling and liquor establishment, and Jefferson County police had arrested Guth numerous times when her resort was known as Pete's Place. Throughout 1907, Guth repeatedly claimed she would close her resort and leave the county, but she continued to bribe Mountain View officials so she could stay in business. Jefferson County officials had finally succeeded in driving her from the county in 1909, but many, including White of the *Enterprise*, continued to fight for her. The editors of the *Transcript* found it "pathetic" that White dared to compare Guth's resort to Lakeside, "the greatest amusement park West of Chicago," sarcastically writing, "it is to weep." White's first attack on Lakeside failed, but he was not done trying to make trouble for the park.[22]

Despite all the trouble, the park did have a good 1909 season. The feature attraction on opening day was a "moving picture spectacle" that depicted General Phil Sheridan's ride to the front during the Civil War, in addition to baseball, boating, dancing, and "fun unrestrained at every amusement abode," according to the *Rocky Mountain News*. More than 30,000 people crowded the park on opening day, and the newspaper reported that, just as the year before, not a single thing happened to darken the celebration. General Manager Frank Burt told the *News* that the moment he saw Lakeside for the first time he wanted to make the park, which was "different in every respect from others, with a high standard of honesty in giving the public its money's worth," one of the most important in the country. Burt argued that Lakeside would do more to "spread the fame" of Denver than anything else could and asked for the cooperation of every man, woman, and child in "making Denver talked about all over the country because of the attractiveness of one of her parks." The *Rocky Mountain News* reported that Denver seemed half-mad for outdoor entertainment after the long winter and that many were anxious to enjoy the "fresh air of Colorado's beauty spot" at Lakeside.[23]

The biggest events at Lakeside that year came at the end of the summer. On the final Children's Day near the end of August, Miss Naomi Alfrey, the Lady of the Lake, directed the children in the play *The Brownies in Fairyland*. The *Transcript* reported that the play was sure to be a success, largely because "practically every child of talent in Denver has been secured to take part." After the children's play, the park hosted three Venetian nights in late August and early September to help wind down the regular season. The festivities included an illuminated boat parade on the lake, aquatic sports, and other activities. Workers spent two weeks constructing barges for the parade, and it took a dozen electricians to create the controls and wiring for the event. The *Transcript* reported that the new illuminations for the Venetian nights turned Lakeside into a "bewitching fairyland" and that the whole show would "go down into history as one of the most beautiful and thrilling spectacles ever seen at an amusement park in this country." With even more elaborate lighting and beautiful scenery, the show fit perfectly with Lakeside's City Beautiful image.[24]

The other big events at the end of the season were more civic-minded in nature as Lakeside's owners and managers sought to show that the park was a good neighbor. On Labor Day the park hosted its second annual free barbecue, which the *Transcript* described as "extensive." Management planned for 50,000 people to attend, 15,000 more than the year before, all of whom would enter the park and eat for free between noon and 8:00 p.m. The newspaper urged readers to try the barbecue for themselves, writing "you have our permission." Far more extensive than the barbecue, however, and more heavily promoted was Good Roads Day at the park, which took place on September 11, 1909. For a number of years boosters had been trying to build a road between Denver and Golden. Finally, in April 1909, the state legislature passed a bill appropriating money for the new road, but to the dismay of its supporters, the legislature approved only $5,000, not the $20,000 for which they had hoped. The commission in charge of the road (made up of the governor of Colorado, the mayor of Denver, and the Jefferson County commissioners) chose Jefferson Avenue, or North Golden Road, as the route while supporters tried to raise enough money to pay for its construction.[25]

After months of fundraising, the boulevard committee's road fund was still $1,400 short of its goal when Lakeside's management stepped in. First, they agreed to build a half-mile section of the road at their own expense. Next, they turned operation of the park over to the boulevard committee for one day. The committee raised the gate admission to twenty-five cents for September 11, and all proceeds from admissions and concessions went to the road fund. Management also put large blocks of tickets to the park on sale at various locations around Denver and Jefferson County, with all proceeds again going to the road fund. The *Transcript* cheered the park, writing that it proposed to do more than "simply wishing it well" to help get the road built. While the park was in fact proving itself a good neighbor, management was also motivated by the fact that a road between Denver and Golden would provide better access to the park for people from both towns. The *Transcript* strongly urged its readers to patronize Lakeside on Good Roads Day because success that day meant "the boulevard between Golden and Denver [would be built], it means starting work immediately, and it means an absolute guarantee that it will be finished." Despite the newspaper's pleas, however, attendance at the event was not as great as expected or hoped, and when it was over the road fund was still $400 short. Still, the newspaper praised the park's management for working so hard on the project. Regardless of the shortfall, work started on the boulevard the next year and continued until the state took over both construction and maintenance in 1911. But as late as February 1911, Lakeside's owners were still willing to raise money to complete the project.[26]

The next civic event was Farmer's Day, essentially a county fair, held at Lakeside two weeks later on September 25, 1909. Only Jefferson County residents were allowed to enter exhibits, and the *Transcript* viewed the event as "the greatest opportunity the county has ever had to advertise its agricultural and horticultural resources." The event's organizers went out of their way to also encourage farm wives to enter baked goods, canned goods, and textile work. Management held the fair inside the Casino building, keeping it safe from any bad weather that might strike. In addition to hosting Farmer's Day, the park also put up $1,000 in prize money for various competitions. Ten dollars in gold went to Dorothy Thomas, voted winner of the baby contest, though it was a tough decision as the *Transcript* reported that the judges were "well nigh floored when it came to choosing from such an array of handsome and well behaved" children. Admission to the grounds was free on Farmer's Day, which allowed thousands of people to "get an idea of what our county soil will produce." It also allowed anyone who had yet to visit the park to see it for free, with the hope that they would come back as paying guests the next summer. As an added bonus and to further promote the beauty of Lakeside, management turned on all the lights on the evening of Farmer's Day.[27]

Its organizers viewed Farmer's Day as a test case to see if a county fair would work in Jefferson County; if successful, they intended to put one on every year. An estimated 10,000 people entered the gates that day, and promoters sold $750 worth of stock in the Jefferson County Fair Association. The day was so successful, and the fair organizers felt so confident, that they went ahead with their plans and in early 1910 signed a contract with the Lakeside Realty and Amusement Company to hold the annual county fair there every year. The fair association even paid for improvements to the park, including livestock stalls and a dirt track solely for their use. The new contract once again brought condemnation of Lakeside from the editor of the *Arvada Enterprise*, J. F. White, who argued that the political machine of Jefferson County first used its influence to take the county fair away from Arvada and give it to Golden. Then, when organizers discovered that Golden lacked a suitable location for the fair, they moved it to Lakeside. White objected to holding the fair at the amusement park because liquor sales were allowed there, a somewhat laughable reason given his earlier defense of Anna Guth's pleasure resort. The editors of the *Transcript* referred to White as one of the "disagreeable grouches" who had kept the face of his hammer "well polished by use on the White City." In addition to condemning "Brother White," the *Transcript* also attacked his newspaper, which they said was published entirely in Denver while claiming to be a Jefferson County publication. In the end, the *Transcript*'s editors wrote, White's criticism had little impact. Lakeside hosted the county fair for the next two years, and White's failure to unseat the amusement park as host seemingly silenced his vendetta against it.[28]

After a spectacular first season, Lakeside Amusement Park certainly experienced its share of growing pains during the 1909 season. The local newspapers followed a pattern established when the Scenic Railway accident occurred in 1908, keeping quiet about unpleasant events at Lakeside, such as the arrest of Adolph Zang and the other park directors and employees. When it became impossible to ignore the situation that brought about the arrests, the *Transcript* jumped to the park's defense, reminding readers how magnificent the park was and what an important institution it was for Denver and all of Colorado. Despite the rocky start, Lakeside's management continued to offer high-class entertainment throughout the summer and hosted three events at the end of the summer designed to show how civic-minded the park was. To help keep Lakeside fresh for the next season, in November 1909 park manager Frank Burt and Samuel W. Gumpertz (one of the most famous amusement park managers in the country) of Dreamland on Coney Island sailed to Europe together to look for new attractions.[29]

As the amusement park successfully established itself, the town of Lakeside worked just as hard to prove that it was a growing and thriving community. Before leaving town in 1909, Mayor Marvin Adams played the role of civic booster almost nonstop, urging many of his relatives and fellow employees at The Famous to move to Lakeside. The *Transcript* proudly announced each new resident's arrival, as when Doctor Burgesser, formerly of Joplin, Missouri, came in late 1908. When a policeman named Sweeney moved his family to the town in December 1908, the *Transcript* reported that the only problem with his arrival was that it gave the Democrats in Lakeside four more votes. Each new house constructed or addition to an existing house was further cause for celebration. When Mayor Adams finished an addition to his house, the newspaper reported that he intended to dedicate it in "good old Missouri style" and invited all Jefferson County residents to the party. After one visit, Mayor Daniel Sutton of Englewood praised the architectural style of Lakeside's homes, especially the Southern California bungalow style of Mayor Adams's house, and told the *Transcript* he intended to promote that style in Englewood. Another visitor, Mayor Louis Cohen of Fairplay, came to observe Lakeside's administration policies, many of which he intended to copy, though he still thought he had "the best town." The *Transcript* responded that everyone was entitled to their opinions but suggested that Cohen "had another think coming." By the summer of 1910, the town's population had boomed to 103 people. Both Joseph Moore, skate man, and William Conklin, machinist, worked at the park's skating rink; Anna, Lillie, and Mable Gustafson and Flora Lindstrom worked as cashiers; and Charles Reiss was the park's bookkeeper. Interestingly, two large gypsy families, the Adamses and the Buffaloes, took up residence in Lakeside that year as well, although whether they worked at the park is unclear from census or park records.[30]

The *Transcript* also made sure to cover the many social functions taking place in Lakeside. In August 1908 Mayor Adams's sister, Blanche Roberts, was the bride at the first wedding held in the town. The newspaper reported that the already pretty Adams home was "profusely decorated in white and pink" and that Blanche and her new husband, Albert McCabe, received many "handsome and costly" gifts after the ceremony. Kate Adams hosted the first Thanksgiving dinner in Lakeside, in November 1908, and the first Christmas celebration the following month. She also founded a Lakeside chapter of the Moonstone Thimble Club, which undertook charitable work. Albert Lewin addressed one of the first meetings of the club in January 1909, after which he and Marvin Adams took the women on a tour of the amusement park, making them, the *Transcript* reported, Lakeside's first visitors in 1909. New Year's Day 1909 was another big celebration, with the *Transcript* writing that Lakeside city jailer Dad Clow had a "hog killing time" and that after a few drinks Mayor Adams was seen "skipping around with the agility of a college athlete."[31]

Just as the town of Lakeside worked toward becoming an established city during its first two years of existence, Lakeside Amusement Park did everything right to become an established part of Denver's City Beautiful movement. In January 1908, four months before Lakeside opened, the *Colorado Transcript* referred to it as "largest and most pretentious park in the West." During its first two seasons, Lakeside did its best to live up to that reputation. As 1909 ended, Denver took the next step toward linking the park to the City Beautiful movement. That year, Mayor Speer proposed that Denver begin publishing a free weekly magazine, arguing that the public had a right to know what city government was doing. Speer also said that "official articles on our Auditorium, Street Lighting, method of Street Cleaning, Museum, Free distribution of trees, Sunday concerts, Parks, Boulevards, etc., would be copied in Municipal Journals and prove valuable as an advertising medium" for the city of Denver. Furthermore, Speer wanted to use the new magazine, which he called a "good news journal," to counter critics from the *Rocky Mountain News*, the *Denver Post*, and especially the *Denver Express*, founded by Edward W. Scripps in 1906. Scripps, who would buy the *Rocky Mountain News* in 1926, called for clean government in Denver, something he felt was impossible to achieve under Speer. By the time Lakeside's 1910 season got under way, the new magazine, *Denver Municipal Facts*, would make it abundantly clear that Speer considered Lakeside Amusement Park an important and welcome part of his City Beautiful program.[32]

Lakeside's builders. *(Author's Collection)*

Lakeside Amusement Park from Sheridan Boulevard. The covered parking area is to the right of the Tower. *(Author's Collection)*

The Tower and Casino from inside the park, with the bandstand in the front left corner. *(Author's Collection)*

The Tower, Casino, and Swimming Pool *(left to right)*. The Music Plaza is next to the lake. *(Author's Collection)*

The Casino balcony . . . *(DPL Western History, X-27402)*

. . . and its fine china. *(Author's Collection)*

The train station for the Lakeshore Railway, with the lake in the background. *(Author's Collection)*

The Natatorium (Swimming Pool). *(Author's Collection)*

Tower of Jewels, a "pillar of fire at night." *(Author's Collection)*

Social area of Lakeside, with the Boat House at left, El Patio Ballroom in the center, and the Skating Rink on the right. *(Author's Collection)*

El Patio Ballroom (*left*) and Skating Rink (*right*). *(Author's Collection)*

El Patio Ballroom at night. *(DPL Western History, X-27627)*

Amusement area of Lakeside from the lake. The Velvet Coaster and Scenic Railway are on the right. *(Author's Collection)*

Shoot-the-Chutes, with the Airship and concession stands in the background. *(Author's Collection)*

Shoot-the-Chutes, with entrance to the Velvet Coaster and Scenic Railway to the right. *(Author's Collection)*

Entrance to the Scenic Railway and Velvet Coaster. *(Author's Collection)*

Lakeside's short-lived Tickler ride. *(Author's Collection)*

Amusement area at night. *(Author's Collection)*

Lakeside's photo studio demonstrated the park's elite nature with its private train car prop (*above*) and car prop (*below*). (*Author's Collection*)

Buttons from various events at Lakeside, 1908–13. *(Author's Collection)*

Lakeside's Staride, 1910s. *(DPL Western History, X-27604)*

CHAPTER 3

Lakeside, the White City Beautiful

The strongest period of the unique relationship between the White City of Lakeside and the City Beautiful of Denver was from 1908 to 1912. During that time, Denver officials proudly showed the park to Democratic National Convention delegates, real estate executives, and convention visitors and continually promoted it in the city-published magazine *Municipal Facts*, while Lakeside's management did its best to live up to Mayor Robert Speer's City Beautiful ideals by keeping Lakeside a clean, safe, fun (but not too fun), educational, and well-managed amusement park. After 1912, however, the two drifted apart. Political factors convinced Speer, always a shrewd politician, not to seek a third term as mayor, putting an end to his City Beautiful program for the time being. At the same time, Lakeside's owners and managers realized that in order to survive, the park needed to appeal to a broader customer base than it had previously.

Denver Municipal Facts, the new magazine published by the city of Denver to highlight Mayor Speer's accomplishments in civic beautification, became the primary link between Denver and Lakeside Amusement Park after 1909.

Between 1909 and 1914 the magazine featured Lakeside twenty-five times, while Elitch's was mentioned fifteen times, Manhattan Beach eleven times, and Tuileries three times. Lakeside's first major appearance in *Municipal Facts* was on January 8, 1910, when a picture of the park graced the cover. The next appearance was in the July 30, 1910, issue, when it was stated that Lakeside used enough electric current each night during the summer to power any city in the state except Denver. The fact that lighting was such an important part of Denver's City Beautiful program made Lakeside's lighting scheme a desirable and noteworthy accomplishment. In fact, the article went on to say, visitors asserted that few other amusement parks in the United States "compare in beauty with Lakeside by night." Just three months later, as the city prepared to open Inspiration Point Park north of Lakeside, *Municipal Facts* proclaimed that the "brilliant spectacle" of the combined lights of Denver and Lakeside made for a breathtaking view from the new park.[1]

During the week of July 17, 1911, the National Association of Real Estate Exchanges held its annual convention in Denver, and city officials and local real estate leaders did everything they could to convince the attendees that Denver was not only the "most hospitable city in the world" but also rapidly becoming a world-class city. The hosts treated delegates to a fireworks show at City Park, automobile tours through the city, excursions to the Continental Divide, and a trip to Colorado Springs to see Pikes Peak and the Garden of the Gods. Officials also arranged for an evening barbecue at Lakeside, with the park in "gala attire" for the event and every attraction free to delegates. *Municipal Facts* declared that visitors would "never forget the wonderful pictures of nature that will pass before their view in a fleeting panorama as the shades of night descend over the purple foothills and snow-capped mountain peaks" as they explored the fine amusement park. Lakeside clearly played a big part in the image civic leaders wanted visitors to have of Denver.[2]

The strongest article linking Lakeside to Denver and the City Beautiful movement appeared in the July 6, 1912, issue of *Municipal Facts*. Proclaiming that Lakeside was recognized as one of the most beautiful summer resorts in the city and was one of the main reasons tourists visited Denver, the article stated that "to witness such a resort in the Far West is a revelation and surprise to every stranger." The brilliant illumination, mountain and foothill views, and sunset dinners on the Casino balcony combined to create Lakeside's immense beauty. In addition, the park was easily accessible by streetcar or automobile over improved city streets and boulevards, the article went on to say, reminders of some of the other civic improvements brought about through Mayor Speer's many projects. Lakeside, the article seemed to say, was a perfect poster child for everything Speer and City Beautiful supporters were trying to do: it was beautiful, it provided relaxation and recreation, and, best of all, it was easy for visitors to get there whatever their chosen mode of transportation.[3]

Lakeside's presence was proof of Denver's growing national prominence, or so city leaders and promoters argued through articles such as the July 6, 1912, *Municipal Facts* piece. After singing the park's praises, the article stressed that Adolph Zang and his "patriotic associates" built Lakeside, which should be the pride of every Coloradoan, out of "a spirit of civic betterment and improvement rather than hope of big financial gains." The fact that Denver men financed and built the park without using outside money was another source of pride to the author of the article and further proof that many people, not the least of whom were Zang and his associates, had a strong belief in Denver's bright future. The park's owners, the article concluded, were happy to have Lakeside simply "add to the glory of the municipality and to supply one more vital reason that Denver is the best residence city in the United States." Adolph Zang, according to his granddaughter Betty Arnold, was a kind and generous man, known for taking neighborhood children to circuses and Fourth of July events and happily handing out quarters on Halloween, but he intended for Lakeside to be profitable. *Municipal Facts'* claim that Zang and his associates built Lakeside out of a spirit of civic betterment and improvement without concern for profit, while beneficial to the park's image, also showed the lengths to which Denver officials went to promote the park as a unique addition to the city.[4]

The July 6 article also mentioned Elitch's, Manhattan Beach, and Tuileries, but in nowhere near the glowing terms it used to describe Lakeside. Elitch's, according to the article, catered only to the "better classes" of people in Denver, and from the park's beginning John and Mary Elitch wanted only good, clean entertainment. However, rather than focus on the amusement attractions at Elitch's, the article emphasized the park's famous theater and the number of well-known stars it attracted, as well as the weekly symphony concerts. The park's beautiful gardens and the fact that Elitch's was the only amusement park in the country managed by a woman were also mentioned.

Municipal Facts singled out Manhattan Beach for its beauty and for the fact that, despite "vicissitudes usually attendant upon resorts of this character," management had succeeded in rejuvenating the park and making it a popular place once again. While the article also declared that Tuileries was a beautiful resort, the greatest attraction there was the motordrome, where "speed demons" raced over the one-third-mile board track. Tuileries was a nice park, the article said, but it catered to the masses with "liberal entertainment." Lakeside and Elitch's were obviously at the top of Denver's amusement attractions, based on the article in *Municipal Facts*, but Lakeside in 1912 was just a step above Elitch's. In a city-published magazine dedicated to promoting Mayor Speer's accomplishments in civic improvement, the article left readers with the distinct impression that there was no better advertisement for Denver's City Beautiful goals than Lakeside Amusement Park.[5]

In exchange for Denver's support, Lakeside's owners did their best to promote themselves as part of City Beautiful as well. In their 1910 brochure, they wrote that it was a delight and a surprise for tourists to experience Lakeside, and "to find such a summer park in the 'Wild and Wooly West' is a distinct revelation to the 'tenderfoot.'" With the beauty of its surroundings, the size of its grounds, and the park's general attractiveness, the brochure proclaimed, there was "no prettier public playground than the resort in the shadows of the foothills, where blow the breezes from the Rockies, cooled by 'the snows five thousand summer[s] old'"—a line that appeared in numerous brochures, advertisements, and newspaper articles. In its 1910 brochure, the Denver Convention League pointed to all of Denver's amusement parks as proof of Denver's status as an up-and-coming city but wrote that Lakeside offered visitors a chance to see "all of the sights that a 'White City' has to offer."[6]

Amusement parks throughout the country offered visitors as many sights as did Lakeside, but in no other major city pursuing City Beautiful programs was an amusement park adopted as a major component of those programs. In San Francisco, amusement parks had never truly taken hold, in part because the city was destroyed by fire in 1906 at the height of the amusement park craze, and afterward residents worried more about rebuilding their homes and businesses than they did about building amusement parks. When the situation stabilized in the late 1910s and early 1920s, John Friedle and Arthur Loof partnered to combine their separate operations at

Ocean Beach, which became Playland at the Beach in 1921. The city of San Francisco assisted Loof and Friedle by widening and paving the road leading to the park and by extending the existing concrete esplanade on the beach all the way to the park, but that was all. By the 1920s there were streetcar lines leading to the park, so there was no need for the streetcar companies to rush to build new ones. Playland, the *San Francisco Chronicle* made clear, was something for everyone to enjoy but was a purely private enterprise that only came about when private developers felt financially secure enough to build it. The City Beautiful movement was on the downward side of its popularity in 1921, but there is no indication it would have played a role in Playland even had it been otherwise.[7]

Chicago's most popular amusement park, Riverview, opened in 1904 along an existing streetcar line. There was little hope of Chicago adopting the park as part of its City Beautiful movement, especially after 1912, when the city's building inspectors condemned the park's two-week-old observation tower, called the Eye-Full Tower, because they did not believe the elevators were safe. However, the city did not entirely object to the park. In a move reminiscent of Robert Speer's official visits to Lakeside, Chicago mayor William "Big Bill" Thompson began hosting annual Schoolkid Days in 1920, where he distributed free passes to the park to Chicago's public school students. Women's groups complained that closing the schools for a day only corrupted the children, but Thompson unsuccessfully defended the program, arguing that he gave copies of the US Constitution and biographies of George Washington and Abraham Lincoln to the children. He ended up canceling the visits. Mayor Thompson also prevented Riverview from becoming a battleground for the Capone and O'Banion gangs, who enjoyed attacking each other's speakeasies near the park. As popular as the park was, speakeasies and gangsters hardly fit with the City Beautiful image.[8]

Cleveland's Euclid Beach was one of that city's earliest parks, opening in 1895. In 1901 it was purchased by the Humphrey family and was known after that as a "Sunday School" operation because the family did not permit alcohol in the park, refused to tolerate rowdy behavior, and did not allow any suggestive or gruesome attractions. Like Lakeside, the park employed its own police force to make sure customers followed the rules although, unlike Lakeside, the police force did not have the power of a city behind it. While Euclid Beach stood the best chance of any of Cleveland's parks of being connected to the City Beautiful movement, it never happened. Rival Luna Park, which opened in 1903, served beer and catered to European immigrants, and suggestive attractions drew continual criticism from Cleveland's religious leaders, who called the park a "School of Vice." Luna's management loved the publicity the criticism generated, but the park's public image made it impossible to link it to City Beautiful ideals if anyone had wanted to do so.[9]

Lakeside was clearly unique in its very close relationship to Denver and its City Beautiful movement, and both sides worked hard to maintain that connection for as long as possible. As one sign of that hard work, the *Transcript* reported in October 1909 that big changes were in the works for the park's 1910 season. The biggest change was at the Casino, where management spent $45,000 to convert the interior restaurant on the second floor into a much larger theater. The park's original theater had boomed during 1909 under the direction of Walter Clarke Bellows, Elitch's Theater's longtime manager, and management decided a bigger space was in order. Finished in ivory and old gold and steam-heated, the theater provided space for traveling companies to produce musical comedies and light operas. Management decided against keeping a stock company at the theater, arguing that it was "more in keeping with Denver's metropolitan importance" to engage "quality . . . companies" from the East. The managers stressed that they would not allow any vaudeville acts to perform there. To make up for the lost restaurant space, management expanded and enclosed the popular balcony restaurant with movable glass walls and connected it to the theater with arched doorways. *Billboard* predicted that, with the changes, the 1910 season "bids fair to be the most profitable" one yet for the park.[10]

While the *Colorado Transcript* and *Billboard* reported that work on the new Casino Theater was progressing nicely, Scripps's *Denver Express* painted a very different picture. Near the end of March 1910, work on the theater came to a halt when a fight broke out on the job site between members of the Independent Brotherhood of Structural Ironworkers and the International Structural Ironworkers no. 24. Members of the latter reported that Lakeside management had promised to use all union men for work at the theater and argued that, because the Independent Brotherhood was not a union, the job should have gone to them. When the men were unable to convince Lakeside's management, they went to the park on March 25 and confronted both management and the men working there in an attempt to get the job. When the Independent Brotherhood refused to leave, a fight broke out. Lakeside police responded to the disturbance, and witnesses reported to the *Express* that Chief John Lindsey was so badly beaten that he had to be rushed to St. Luke's Hospital in Denver. The rest of the Lakeside police force found themselves helpless in the face of the overwhelming number of ironworkers and had no choice but to let the fight wear itself out. Doing their best to maintain the park's City Beautiful image, no other Denver newspapers reported the disruption.[11]

The fight created such a delay in construction on the new theater space that the victorious Independent Brotherhood workers had to rush to get it done in time for the 1910 season. They barely made it, with the *Colorado Transcript* reporting on May 26, 1910, just two days before opening day, that the theater was finally done. The newspaper declared the 1,700-seat theater "one of the prettiest and most comfortable playhouses in the West." Allan K. Foster, credited with having more successes on the New York stage than any other director, was in charge. The well-known actors he brought with him included Lothe Kendell, Beth Tate, Alice Clifton, Georgia Harvey, Lew Kelly, Toney Hart, Arthur Dean, Carl Kaynor, Allen Carter, and "Bud" Ross. The *Transcript* reported that backing these actors, "all of whom have won enviable reputations with the larger Eastern companies," was a chorus of twenty-five women and fifteen men. The newspaper assured its readers that they would see elaborate costumes and magnificent sets at each production. Ticket prices ranged from twenty-five cents for the balcony to seventy-five cents for the best seats. As promised, the plays staged at the theater that summer were mostly musical comedies, which, the *Transcript* repeatedly reminded its readers, were popular with New York audiences. They included *The Promoters* and *Not Yet but Soon* by Ward and Vokes, *Chinese Honeymoon*, *Evangeline*, *When Reuben Comes to Town*, *Jack and the Beanstalk*, and *Piff Poff Pouf*. The plays were not as serious as those produced at Elitch's Theater, which the Denver Convention League described as "high class summer theater," but Lakeside's visitors found the productions enjoyable, and attendance was good.[12]

Lakeside's new theater was not the only change for 1910, as management installed a new attraction, the Creation. An attraction with the same name at Coney Island's Dreamland was described as a "quasireligious show . . . that recreated the first chapter of Genesis five times a day." The same production at Riverview Park in Chicago, also copied from Dreamland, used eighty-five feet of moving scenery, live organ and choir performances, and "appropriate sound effects." In addition to the Creation, a new athletic field and grandstand, which surrounded a half-mile racetrack and baseball diamond, appeared on the southeast corner of the Lakeside property. The new baseball field at Lakeside was very much in keeping with the park's elite nature at the time. According to Steven Reiss in *City Games*, early sportswriters promoted the "cultural fiction" that baseball encouraged social integration by giving people from all walks of life the chance to socialize at the ball field. In reality, it was white-collar workers who had the time and money to play the sport and attend the games. Early ballparks were often located in suburban areas, where land was cheaper than in the core part of town; because of their great distance from the city center, they were not easily accessible to blue-collar workers. It was not until the 1920s, when Lakeside was shifting to a more working-class amusement park, that working-class people began attending baseball games in considerable numbers. Despite Lakeside's easy accessibility, which promoters frequently mentioned, the ball field was still in keeping with the park's elite image. The changes, said the *Transcript*, transformed Lakeside "into an even more elaborate amusement resort."[13]

Billboard's prediction that 1910 would be a good season seemed like a safe bet, and it did, in fact, get off to a good start. On July 16, 1910, the magazine reported that the Fourth of July crowd was the biggest the park had seen since opening day in 1908. The new theater, where a five-week run of Gilbert and Sullivan comic operas was playing, was doing "tremendous business," while Don Philippina and his band drew big crowds to the park's ballroom. A week later, on July 23, *Billboard* reported that Lakeside was "enjoying a big patronage daily" and that the Casino, "known as the Girly Girly Show" since few men were interested in attending the plays, was putting on clever comic operas. The Skating Rink, dance hall, Shoot-the-Chutes, roller coaster, and other attractions were also doing a "great business."[14]

Just two weeks later, however, the situation had taken a dramatic turn. On August 13 *Billboard* reported that business at Lakeside was "disappointing," and Frank Burt went so far as to cancel a two-week engagement of the American Band, which was supposed to have started on August 14. The disappointing crowds did not prevent Denver from hosting an afternoon picnic and concert at Lakeside for the thousands of people who attended the city's first Railroad Day, held to honor the importance of the railroads in Colorado. Both Mayor Speer and Governor John Shafroth, a powerful Progressive, addressed the gathering. By the time the park closed in September, *Billboard* reported that the season had been "very good" but that Burt was looking forward to putting the 1910 season behind him and getting ready for 1911 by looking to the big amusement parks in the East for ideas on what to do at Lakeside the next year. It must have seemed like a bad omen, however, when on May 13, just before the park opened for the 1911 season, Adolph Zang's brother-in-law and park co-founder and vice president, Peter Friederich, died suddenly of a stroke at age forty-nine. His funeral, under the direction of Denver Saloonkeeper's Union no. 1, took place four days after his death. Peter's son Phillip inherited his father's share of Lakeside, continuing the Friederich association with the park.[15]

Despite the disappointing 1910 season and the bumpy start to 1911, Lakeside was still so prominent that Governor Shafroth attended the season opener on May 28, 1911. After a brief speech, the governor signaled the park band, seated on the Casino balcony, to begin playing, marking the official opening. According to the *Rocky Mountain News*, 15,000 people passed through the park's gates on opening day. In June, the park and Denver hosted a three-day Chamber of Commerce Carnival under the direction of the Greater Colorado Fair and Parade Committee, which organizers expected 75,000 people to attend. To entertain the large crowds descending on the park, Frank Burt had a number of "new and novel" attractions in store, including the first appearance of the famous Alligator Joe and his reptile collection.[16]

Based on *Billboard*'s coverage, the theater once again was the most popular attraction at Lakeside in 1911. In a bold move, Burt dropped the admission fee to the theater. Reserved seats were still available for a price, but Burt's new policy was to "give the public a fine show for nothing." Although the move seemed to go against the park's elite character, it actually fit City Beautiful values by bringing culture to the masses. A month into the 1911 season, the theater was "proving a good drawing card." While Lakeside's managers initially rejected the idea of keeping a stock company at the theater in favor of bringing in what they considered higher-class shows from New York, by 1911 they decided to use a combination of local and out-of-town performers. Management formed the Lakeside Stock Company, but at its head was a visiting actress, the famed Beulah Poynter. According to *Billboard*, the "charming little actress" wrote, staged, and produced all the plays she acted in, and the quality of her work won her a large following of admirers. The 1911 theater season at Lakeside opened on June 3 with Poynter starring in *The Bishop's Carriage*. *Billboard* reported that the selection of that play started the season with a big hit and that Poynter was a "decided hit with the Denver public." After the end of Poynter's run at the theater, on June 24, the Lakeside Stock Company finished out the season with plays of its own choosing.[17]

In a further effort to avoid another disappointing season, Burt turned to Cecil Connor, the "hustling" representative for Western Resources Publicity Service (and former Lakeside press agent), to take over advertising for Lakeside. Although *Billboard* reported that Connor was "making matters hum" at the park, management also decided to experiment with using word of mouth to draw customers. In July the park hosted a three-day picnic for the Colorado Boosters. Attendance the last night of the gathering filled the park to capacity, but more important, according to *Billboard*, was the advertising the park received for hosting the event. Lakeside closed out the 1911 season by hosting a White Dress Parade for girls under age sixteen. Participants were judged on the beauty and attractiveness of their white costumes, as well as their grace, neatness, and charming personality. The first-place winner, crowned queen, received a diamond ring. Overall, *Billboard* reported, the year had been "fairly profitable."[18]

While the 1911 season ended well for Lakeside, the year did not. On November 14, 1911, about two months after Lakeside closed for the season, a fire broke out at the park. The blaze destroyed the Scenic Railway and the Velvet Coaster before the Lakeside Fire Department, assisted by a fire company from Denver, could extinguish it. The fact that Denver willingly sent one of its own fire companies to battle a blaze at Lakeside, where heat from the flames was so intense that it melted a fire hose 100 feet away, spoke a great deal about how devoted the city was to the amusement park. Lakeside's owners assured the public that they would repair the damage in time for the 1912 season. The physical damage to the park was significant, but much more significant to Lakeside's future were less visible changes as the relationship between Lakeside and Denver's City Beautiful started to unravel.[19]

By the time of the fire, Denver's citizens were becoming increasingly weary of the perceived corruption of the Speer administration. Frederick Bonfils of the *Denver Post* wrote in one of his columns that Speer would be remembered "as the most inefficient and corrupt mayor Denver ever had, as the stuffed prophet." The *Rocky Mountain News* jumped on the anti-Speer bandwagon while pointing out that the *Post* had once supported the mayor. Speer freely admitted that he was a boss politician but maintained that he was a good boss, not the typical corrupt one people associated with the term. Good boss or not, Speer was a smart politician, and he knew he was out of favor at the moment. He wisely decided not to run for a third term, and voters chose reform candidate Henry Arnold as his successor. After one ineffective year as mayor, Arnold was replaced with a commission government. The commission government hired landscape architect Frederick Law Olmsted Jr. to draw up plans for Civic Center Park, other new parks and parkways, and Denver's mountain park system, but City Beautiful languished under the new administrations as they pursued other programs and projects. In 1916 voters abolished commission government in Denver and returned Speer to office as mayor. After his return, he focused his attention on completing Civic Center and further developing the mountain parks. Speer died in office in 1918, and Denver's City Beautiful movement largely died too until Benjamin Stapleton became mayor in 1923.[20]

While Denver's political scene changed, the neighborhoods around Lakeside were also developing in an unexpected way. In 1907 Zang and park manager Albert Lewin had hoped that some of Denver's wealthiest residents would build fine homes on the 103 acres of Lakeside land not occupied by the amusement park, thereby helping to secure the park's elite reputation. When Denver's elite started moving out of the Capitol Hill neighborhood in the 1910s and 1920s, however, they moved to the Denver Country Club and Denver Polo Club neighborhoods, not to Lakeside.

A major stumbling block to realizing their dreams was the fact that Lakeside's owners were limited in the amount of land around the park they actually controlled. To the north and east of the park was Denver, to the west Arvada, and to the south Mountain View and Wheat Ridge. North of Lakeside was Denver's Inspiration Point Park, which meant there was little fear of any development taking place there. But east of the park across Sheridan Boulevard was the Berkeley neighborhood. Devious real estate promoters described Berkeley as an ideal neighborhood for tuberculosis patients, not the upper-class people for whom Zang and others had hoped. Colorado had long been promoted as a healthy place for tuberculosis victims to live, and thousands upon thousands, including Robert Speer, came to Denver for that reason. But by the early 1900s healthy Coloradoans increasingly disliked TB sufferers coming into the state, and a growing number of people willingly took advantage of them. Jerome Smiley expressed the opinion held by many Denverites, writing that greedy innkeepers and transportation workers had falsely promoted Colorado's climate as more beneficial to TB sufferers than it actually was. Smiley argued that the state's healthy residents had the right to protect themselves against disease carriers, writing that "the question as to whether the natural right of the healthy to retain health and be protected so far as may be against its impairment, is or is not one that should receive preference." In 1908, the same year Lakeside opened, Colorado banned indigent sick people from entering the state and considered making consumptives wear bells around their necks. Unscrupulous employers loved TB sufferers because they were willing to work for very little money, and cheating real estate agents preyed on their desperation to sell them false hope in neighborhoods such as Berkeley and Highlands.[21]

The other towns around the park similarly developed into working-class enclaves. The town of Wheat Ridge had Colorado's first Grange hall and a Lutheran sanitarium by the end of the nineteenth century, in addition to a number of wheat farms, which gave the town its name. In the 1920s developers such as George Olinger, owner of a Denver funeral home chain, transformed the town into a place of affordable suburban homes featuring six-room houses for $2,000. The town of Arvada was an agricultural hub starting down the path to becoming a working-class suburb at the time Lakeside opened. Mountain View, a small town south of the park, was also filled with working-class homes. By the 1920s, Lakeside was surrounded on all sides by working-class neighbors, and the only homes ever built in Lakeside were those Marvin Adams and other early residents built along Sheridan Boulevard.[22]

Streetcar lines had defined the way Denver and its suburbs developed. If a new development was not near an existing line, developers either built one of their own or convinced an existing company to extend a line, giving Denver an extensive street railway system by the early 1900s. This system, Smiley wrote, allowed "men of moderate means" to buy houses in "pleasant places away from the business center." The "thousands of pretty dwellings and of suburban cottages" found on the outskirts of Denver and its neighboring towns allowed workers to live among trees and grass and flowers rather than crowded into tenements, as they surely would have been in other cities. This development for "prudent citizens even of limited means" was to the "great good of each and the common benefit and pleasure of all." While Smiley acknowledged the economic value of these homes, through increased property values and higher tax receipts, he wrote that the emotional and health benefits were far greater and helped make Denver an outstanding place among US cities. But, as Smiley pointed out, pretty dwellings and suburban cottages were not occupied by Denver's wealthy.[23]

The rise of working-class neighborhoods around Lakeside Amusement Park gradually changed the park's customer base, and the younger, less affluent people who increasingly constituted the park's visitors desired an escape from life's cares instead of the moral uplift City Beautiful–era customers had sought. To replace the destroyed Velvet Coaster, management hired the father and son team of Josiah and Fred Pearce to build a Derby Racing Coaster at a cost of $125,000. The massive 3,800-foot-long coaster, which opened in time for the 1912 season, wrapped around the roller skating rink and ballroom and was a far more thrilling ride than anything the park had seen. Unlike most of the other concessions, which the park itself owned, the Pearces owned and operated the Derby for a number of years before Lakeside bought the ride from them. The Derby Racing Coaster marked the first time an amusement attraction was located in what was previously the social area of the park, a sign of what was to come as Lakeside shed its City Beautiful image.[24]

While construction of the Derby showed that the park was moving toward more thrilling and typical amusement devices, advertising for the park took on a more carefree tone as well. The 1912 Western League Baseball schedule, published by Lakeside, still largely used the conservative advertising style employed by the park in previous years. Short sayings at the bottom of each page reminded baseball fans that, after the final out of a game, there was still time to enjoy a sunset dinner on the Casino balcony or that a man could "make a hit / with your Lady Fair / if you take her often / to Lakeside Park!" But other sayings urged baseball fans to "sacrifice your worries on Lakeside's Altar of Pleasure. Life is worth living and, remember, 'You'll be a long time Dead.'" The schedule also listed Lakeside's 1912 attractions, which included non–City Beautiful attractions such as man-eating sharks and a motordrome.[25]

Management also finally gave in and turned the theater over to a full stock company in 1912. The Fealy-Durkin Stock Company opened the 1912 season in June and continued its run at Lakeside's theater for the next several years. One of the principals, Maude Fealy, was a longtime Denver stage presence and had been involved with the Elitch's theater for many years before moving to the Orpheum Theater in Denver. For the move to Lakeside she partnered with her second husband, James Durkin. The featured actress for the 1912 season was Ann Sutherland, referred to in programs as "America's greatest star." *Billboard* reported that the theater, under the management of Fealy-Durkin, would be one of Lakeside's feature attractions for 1912. The change that took place in the type of plays produced at the theater under Fealy-Durkin's direction was another sign that Lakeside and Denver's City Beautiful were growing apart, as the plays took on a more fanciful air, ranging from serious to outright comical. One of the biggest productions that year was *Samson*, which promoters cautioned was not the well-known biblical story patrons might have expected but instead the story of a rich man whose wife was forced to marry him to save her parents from bankruptcy. The other plays in 1912 included *A Colonial Girl*, a love story set during the American Revolution; *The Lily*, described in the program as "one of America's strongest plays," starring Ann Sutherland; and *The Sign of the Cross*, which was set "in Rome during the time of Nero during the persecution of the Christians, and shows their wonderful belief in their Maker and their sacrifice for Him who creates all things." One theater-goer noted on the front of her program for the July 14 performance of *Fifty Miles from Boston* that the production was "so-so." As Lakeside's management sought to appeal to its new, broader customer base, the odd mixture of shows, from comical to religious, was far from the high-class New York shows it had once booked.[26]

Band concerts were another big draw for the 1912 season, and management booked the Boston Marine Band, Creatore, Earent Williams, and the sixty-piece Na Vassar Ladies Band, among others. A free circus roamed the grounds that summer, and Alligator Joe and his reptiles made a well-publicized return to Lakeside. The centerpiece of Alligator Joe's exhibit was a live manatee shipped in from Florida; it took twenty men to unload the crate when it arrived in June 1912. Alligator Joe and his crew constructed a large tank for the animal, which many hoped would be the first to survive so far north of its natural home. *Billboard* reported that if the sea cow survived the season, it would be sent back to Florida at the end of the summer, though the magazine never followed up on the story. The *Rocky Mountain News* did report at the end of May that Alligator Joe's wife had disappeared with the couple's young daughter and about $2,000 in cash. Alligator Joe, whose real name was William Frazee, speculated that his wife enjoyed the liveliness of the amusement season but could not handle the off-season when the couple resided in the Florida Everglades. On a happier note, *Billboard* noted, Lakeside added two new amusement attractions that year. One was a fairly typical amusement park ride, a Tunnel of Love. *Billboard* described the other, the Waltz Trip, as a new innovation but did not elaborate on what it involved.[27]

In yet another change, Lakeside did manage to go dry in 1912. At the beginning of the season, the five bartenders who worked the park went out on strike under the orders of the Cook's, Waiter's, and Bartender's Union. Earlier in the year the park announced that it would be fair to the union, but J. A. Conkle, president of the Denver Trades and Labor Assembly, unexpectedly ordered the bartenders out on strike without giving a reason. The cooks and waiters also went out, effectively shutting down the park's restaurant as well. While the representatives of the three unions went after Conkle, the park announced that the "drouth" of beer would continue all summer. Crowds on opening day could find no prepared food in the park, so concessionaire J. W. Miller opened the rathskeller and, with his assistants, cooked as best he could. The strike was a big blow to sales of Zang Beer at Lakeside.[28]

As the 1912 season came to an end, another big change rocked Lakeside. Although insurance had covered most of the cost of rebuilding after the fire that destroyed the Velvet Coaster in 1911, the price of that insurance increased dramatically. Adolph Zang decided that he could no longer afford it and made the difficult decision to sell the park. In February 1913 William Buck (Zang's step-brother), John Keefe, Arnold Bloedt, Frank Kirchoff (one of the original builders), and Phillip Friederich (Zang's step-nephew) incorporated the Colorado Realty and Amusement Company in Wyoming to take over ownership of the park. The capital stock of the new company was $200,000, divided into 2,000 shares at $100 apiece. All officers of the new company had been officers and directors of Lakeside Realty and Amusement, but gone from active roles were three of the most important and prominent men from the original company—Zang, Schirmer, and Lewin. Friederich became general manager of the park, and according to *Billboard*, the park performed exceptionally well under his leadership. Although Adolph Zang was no longer in the picture, the Zang family was still a presence at the park, as all members of the family had free passes. Betty Arnold recalled spending many happy days there as a child with her father, cousins, and other relatives. The family often took a picnic lunch to eat on the picnic grounds or dined at the park's restaurant, which Arnold remembers as "wonderful."[29]

Only two articles on Lakeside appeared in *Municipal Facts* in 1913, both dealing with Denver hosting the German-American Bundes Turnfest. The group built a large grandstand west of Lakeside's baseball field to host athletic events. It fell to the *Denver Post* to announce that management planned to stage genuine bullfights on the Lakeside athletic field that year. Management built a new 5,000-seat arena for the fights, which the newspaper stressed would have all the excitement of ordinary bullfights but none of the violence, as the bulls' lives would be spared. The program also featured comedy bullfights in which bulls tossed heavily padded matadors about. Among the matadors appearing at Lakeside were Ostobina Acosta, Roberto H. Horano, R. C. Burbank, Antonio Rivas, Jose Avila, and Jose Rodriguis; according to the *Post* the men made quite a sight as they paraded through Denver in their gold- and silver-trimmed costumes. The fact that the show's manager was Harry Burlew, a private detective, not always the most reputable profession in the public's opinion, may have added to its unsavory nature and kept it from the pages of *Municipal Facts*.[30]

The 1913 season at the Casino Theater featured Fealy-Durkin–produced plays such as Cecily Hamilton's *Just to Be Married*, which the *Denver Post* referred to as a "caustic comedy." On the same page, the *Post* promoted society and children's matinees at Elitch's of "famous" plays such as *Sauce for the Goose* and James A. Heine's *Shore Acres*. The *Denver Republican* described Fealy-Durkin's production of George Cohan's *Get Rich Quick Wallingford* as being "as breezy as a trip on the launch, as noisy as the terrifying derby, as exhilarating as a shoot down the chutes." In other words, the play was a perfect fit for a theater at an amusement park. But more in keeping with City Beautiful ideals, Lakeside's theater also produced a series of twelve concerts of pieces by famed composers such as Wagner, Tchaikovsky, and Schubert. The pieces were performed by the Cavallo Symphony Orchestra under the direction of Raffaelo Cavallo, who happened to be Maude Fealy's step-father, and the programs for each concert included biographies of the composers and descriptions of how each piece was composed. One attendee noted on her program that the concerts were "delightful." The concerts were a rarity, however, as the plays took on a more popular and entertaining tone to keep customers returning.[31]

The customers did keep returning to the park, but with each passing year the changes at Lakeside seemed to come more rapidly. In preparing for the 1913 season, Lakeside advertised in *Billboard* that it was looking for new rides and novel shows but that any new concessions needed to be clean. With five-year contracts on concessions ready to expire, manager Frank Burt promised excellent locations to new concessions, as long as they had "the right kind of goods to deliver." Management clearly was taking the park in a new direction by 1913, but it was attempting to do so within the confines of the City Beautiful image the park had worked hard to project and maintain. The next year, management added monoplanes to the aerial swing and a star-shaped Ferris wheel–style ride called the Staride. The eighty-foot-high ride, possibly the only one ever built, was constructed entirely of steel, had eight rounded cars, could carry forty-eight passengers at a time, and operated "at a high rate of speed." Management also added William Mangels's latest ride invention, the Whip, in which cars attached to cables by flexible arms swung out at curved ends of the track, simulating the snap of a whip. In 1915 park president Frank Kirchhoff announced that the park would feature forty-five days of motorcycle racing and that the theater would remain open the entire fifteen-week season because of increased attendance (in one day that summer, the Denver Tramway reported that it carried 12,000 people to Lakeside alone). While not in keeping with the City Beautiful image, the new thrills enabled Lakeside to stay in business.[32]

Its customers loved the new Lakeside, and in 1914 they composed a song to honor the park, its attractions, and employees. The Old Mill, under the command of Mr. Riffle, sent its riders through a dream fairyland. Mr. Miller made sure visitors got through the House of Troubles, all 1,001 of them, "with many a laugh and joyous shout," while Eddie Kline at the Whip made sure everyone who rode it had a laugh. Mr. Pomeroy and Marion at the Staride safely loaded passengers in the cars "and up you go clear out of sight" until the lights on the ride seemed to meet the stars in the sky. Mr. Branson at the Derby ensured that each passenger enjoyed a "wonderful trip" on the coaster, while those seeking tamer adventures could visit Betty and Jean at the merry-go-round or Mr. Bush on the miniature train. Mr. Knoth at the Fun House "will be at your side" to make sure even the most fearful would be brave enough to get through it, and Johnny Miller oversaw the bumper cars, so everyone, the song urged, should "Shoot the Chutes at Lakeside, do!"[33]

Denver's City Beautiful proponents were not as fond of the changing park, and an article in the May 23, 1914, issue of *Municipal Facts* showed how distasteful those changes were to them. Only one new attraction at the park, a working model of the Panama Canal, reflected City Beautiful values in that it was educational and demonstrated US prominence in the world. The model, which *Municipal Facts* called "the most noteworthy one," was under the direction of Captain Ernest Ruhl, who had helped build the real canal. The other new attractions were less ideal. A new minstrel show featured "coontown melodies vieing with the strumming on banjo and guitar," while the Lakeside Museum (probably located in the Casino) housed prehistoric and antediluvian exhibits. *Municipal Facts* called these two "extremes in the gamut" of what Lakeside offered to please all tastes, but the attraction that most differed from past offerings was the new Tango Lair, which replaced the rathskeller on the lower level of the Casino building. The featured act was Little Miss Dong Fung Gu and her "nimble" husband, "liliputian Chinese tango dancers" from Chicago. A picture of the Derby, which completely overshadowed the park's onetime social area, was the main feature of the article. This was the last major article about Lakeside to appear in *Municipal Facts*. The magazine mentioned Lakeside only once more that year, when it hosted an afternoon of entertainment for the Elks' Convention, held in Denver in July 1914. After 1914, no articles on Lakeside appeared in *Municipal Facts*.[34]

Municipal Facts barely concealed its distaste for what was happening at Lakeside, but the *Rocky Mountain News* seemed generally pleased. Like *Municipal Facts*, it mentioned the plantation show and the Lakeside Museum but referred to them as "preferred attractions." The newspaper reported that one of the feature attractions at the park that summer was a painting of Christ and that the most "interesting and timely" of the attractions was the working model of the Panama Canal, which management unveiled just as the USS *Denver* became the first American ship to pass through the canal. The *News* stressed that any children left at the children's playground were always under the care of a trained nurse and that the new bathing beach introduced that year was an "ideal feature." Where the *Municipal Facts* article featured a picture of the Derby coaster, showing how it dominated the park, the *News* article featured pictures of the Tower of Jewels and Olympian Way, the walkway lined with sculptures that ran along the west side of the Chutes pond. While the city of Denver seemed to have written Lakeside off as part of the City Beautiful movement, the Denver newspaper, which had always been somewhat reluctant in its coverage, appeared unwilling to dismiss the link to City Beautiful.[35]

By 1914, political and economic factors were severely straining the Lakeside–City Beautiful relationship, and an old social movement put further pressure on the Zang family. The Anti-Saloon League never stopped trying to get every town in Colorado, including Lakeside, to go dry, and in 1914 the reformers managed to get statewide prohibition on the ballot. Theater programs at Lakeside that year, where the plays included *The Maverick* and *The Lure*, featured ads for beer and ads stating that President Woodrow Wilson opposed statewide prohibition. When the election finally came in November, Denver voters overwhelmingly rejected the measure, but their opposition was not enough to overcome the support it enjoyed outside the city. Denver tried to block the law from taking effect there, arguing that it had the right to permit liquor sales within city limits, but prohibitionists disagreed. On January 1, 1916, the state of Colorado went dry, three years before national Prohibition. Patrons at the Heidelburg Café in downtown Denver sang "Last Night Was the End of the World" on New Year's Eve 1915.[36]

Prohibition hit Denver's breweries hard. The Coors Brewery in Golden produced malted milk and near beer and relied heavily on its ceramics division to carry the business. The Zang Brewing Company was less fortunate. Zang attempted to make ice cream and near beer, but its efforts met with failure, and before the year was out the brewery closed its doors. Although Adolph Zang had not been associated with the brewery since 1913 (the same year he sold Lakeside), its demise surely was a blow to him. He turned his attention to his mining properties and in September went to inspect the Vindicator Mine in Goldfield, Colorado, just outside Cripple Creek. While at the mine, he suffered a hemorrhage and needed immediate medical care. Though he was seriously ill and flat on his back when he arrived in Denver, the nurse with him later recalled that he gave a wonderful tour of the city between Union Station and the Zang Mansion at 709 Clarkson Street. On September 28, 1916, the sixty-year-old Zang died at his home in Denver from the hemorrhage and complications from diabetes.[37]

Adolph Zang's death seemed to signal the end of the City Beautiful era at Lakeside. At the theater that year, the programs were filled with simple jokes and cautioned that theater-goers should not tip theater employees, as acceptance of gratuities was grounds for instant dismissal. Productions that year included *M'lle Modiste*, an opera comedy in two acts, produced by Ira Hardy's New York Musical Comedy Company and starring Dorothy Maynard; and *The Spring Maid*, an operetta. One of the biggest productions was the musical comedy *Sweethearts* by Victor Herbert. Though the *Rocky Mountain News* found the performance "pleasing," it cautioned that the singers needed to better gauge the acoustics of a people-packed auditorium and that the orchestra needed to be strengthened. Gone, though, were the days of fine and popular New York productions and concerts of works by great composers, as the park's working-class customers seemed to have little interest in theatrical offerings. They did, however, have interest in one of the other marvels Lakeside offered that summer. To officially kick off the season on May 27, the park hired Harry Gardiner, better known as the "Human Fly," to climb the walls of the Tower at 4:00 and 9:30 p.m. Gardiner had started climbing buildings in 1905 and during his lifetime ascended over 700 of them. The *Rocky Mountain News* referred to Gardiner's visit to Lakeside as "an unusual free spectacular attraction," sure to please what the paper expected to be the record-breaking crowd in attendance when the park opened that day. As entertaining as the Human Fly might have been, it was also a showy spectacle, something the park had avoided in the past.[38]

An even more vivid sign of the break was the way newspapers reported on Lakeside beginning in 1916. When the body of William A. Taylor was discovered at the park in June 1910, the *Colorado Transcript* reported it in a small six-line story headlined "Death amidst Gayety" and never followed up on the case. Six years later, in July 1916, when thirty-year-old W. B. Mills of Iowa and nineteen-year-old Emma Dye of Denver drowned in the lake after their boat capsized, a bold headline in the *Transcript* screamed "Two Are Drowned in White City Lake." The four-paragraph article pointed out that Mills met Dye in Denver while attending the Locomotive Firemen and Engineers Convention. The boat the two rented at the park was found at closing time on the evening of June 30, but not until the next afternoon did a passenger on the miniature railroad spot their bodies in the lake. The article ended with the suggestive line that, according to the clerk at the hotel where Mills was staying, "Mills often spoke of his wife in Iowa." Far from keeping any death or scandal at Lakeside quiet, as Denver newspapers had done since the accident on the Scenic Railway in 1908, by 1916 such incidents were trumpeted in large headlines. That same year, neighbors filed the first noise complaint against Lakeside. The *Transcript* wrote that residents near the park were making "vigorous protests" because of the noise from a naval battle that took place at 11:00 each night, and they petitioned authorities to "abate the nuisance." The complaints were reminiscent of those voiced by the neighbors of Arlington Park as they happily watched it burn in 1901.[39]

During its City Beautiful period, Lakeside Amusement Park did exactly what modern observers say no amusement park could do—it remained decent and respectable. The park's builders and managers purposely attempted to attract a certain class of customer, as the planned automobile parking and repeated cautions that Lakeside was for conservative amusement seekers demonstrated. The people of Denver perceived Lakeside and rival Elitch's in terms of decency and respectability. By the 1960s they saw Elitch's as the more elite and conservative park, while Lakeside was more working class and rowdy. But in describing the parks that way, people noted that their public images had in fact reversed themselves. Denver certainly saw Lakeside as decent and respectable, as numerous articles in *Municipal Facts* and official visits to the park attest, and the city demonstrated distaste for the changes taking place at the park by 1914, as the next-to-last article on the park to appear in *Municipal Facts* made clear. The fact that no other articles about the park were published in *Municipal Facts* is further proof that Denver perceived a definite change in the image of the park by 1914.[40]

Even if Lakeside had not undergone such dramatic changes in the early 1910s, it was unlikely that the relationship between Denver's City Beautiful program and the park would have survived much longer. By the 1920s and 1930s, the City Beautiful movement was beginning to fall out of favor, both architecturally and socially. Critics condemned City Beautiful as a cosmetic fix to far more serious economic, social, and political problems. But for fifty years it had been one of the most prominent social movements in America, and "to unplanned, ugly and crowded cities, it brought order, beauty, and space." By the 1940s, however, few people were followers of City Beautiful. Like all amusement parks, Lakeside needed to stay in step with the times in order to survive, and clinging to the outdated City Beautiful movement was not a good idea. It was time for Lakeside Amusement Park to reinvent itself, but whether it could do so depended on Adolph Zang's family.[41]

CHAPTER 4

Keeping Lakeside's Bright Lights Shining

American amusement parks faced tough times in the late 1910s and early 1920s. With the average age of the typical amusement park customer steadily dropping, the more "youthful crowd... was looking for thrills" instead of the gentler pastimes favored by older customers of the past. Increased automobile ownership, according to Judith Adams, allowed older customers, who wanted a "more select and less outrageously crowded pleasure environment," to travel to parks or beaches that specifically catered to them. Older parks also unintentionally alienated automobile-owning customers with their lack of parking lots. Many parks scrambled to tear down older rides and attractions to create parking lot space, but they were often too late. Inexpensive streetcar fares and reduced entry fees at parks allowed what Gary Cross and John Walton call a more "down-market" crowd to visit the parks with increasing frequency, but a national railroad strike in 1921 and 1922 that included streetcar workers caused a sharp drop in attendance at many locations. Prohibition hurt a number of parks as well, particular those owned by brewers. And three years of poor summer weather in the early 1920s, a fact repeatedly noted by *Billboard* magazine, also hurt attendance at the parks. By the time the Great Depression began in 1929, hundreds of amusement parks had closed their gates.[1]

To avoid joining the ranks of failed amusement parks, Lakeside Amusement Park needed to change. With Denver rapidly moving away from its City Beautiful program, one major supporter of the park was gone. Adolph Zang's death in 1916 was a severe blow to his family and the park, and within a few months of his death, Lakeside was bankrupt. At a sheriff's auction on February 13, 1917, Hibernia Bank and Trust of Denver, which had issued bonds when the Colorado Realty and Amusement Company purchased the park in 1913, bought the million-dollar Coney Island of the West for $42,750.47. The only other bidder was the company's attorney, who offered just $20,000, less than half the bank's bid. The article announcing the sale of the park to Hibernia was the last time coverage of Lakeside Amusement Park appeared in the *Colorado Transcript*. Future coverage of the park appeared only in the *Denver Post* and the *Rocky Mountain News*, newspapers hostile to Mayor Speer and his City Beautiful program.[2]

The Zang family, however, did not give up on Lakeside. Their management team stayed in place, running the park for the bank while trying to arrange financing to redeem the property. The family eventually worked out a deal with American National Bank, headed by former Lakeside secretary Godfrey Schirmer, to borrow $80,000 to pay off the park's debts. In November 1917 the Denver Park and Amusement Company, owned by Frank Kirchoff, William Buck, and Phillip Friederich, became the new owner of Lakeside Amusement Park. In addition, John Keefe and Arnold Bloedt, also connected to the previous two ownership companies, served as directors of the new company but were not listed as owners. The capital stock of the new company was $100,000, divided into 10,000 shares at $10 apiece. Only one change took place in the team that had managed the park for so many years. Beginning in 1912, when he secured an appointment as director general of concessions and admissions for the 1915 Panama-Pacific International Exposition in San Francisco, Lakeside manager Frank Burt had been dividing his time between Denver in the summer and San Francisco in the winter. Shortly after Lakeside was sold to the Denver Park and Amusement Company, Burt left to become resident director of Seal Beach in California.[3]

After repurchasing Lakeside in 1917, its owners could have looked to the Panama-Pacific Exposition for ideas on how to reinvent the park. The exposition's architects maintained some of the traditions that had marked previous fairs, such as buildings grouped around central courts, a wall around the grounds, and an admission fee, but they also broke with tradition in several important ways. One was in the use of color. Unlike the Columbian Exposition's white buildings, which had been the basis for the design of both the City Beautiful movement and Lakeside, the buildings in San Francisco were decorated in blues, browns, reds, and golds. Employee uniforms, banners, signs, and tickets were color-coordinated to match the buildings. The buildings were built from travertine, an artificial stone first used in 1910 in Pennsylvania Station in New York City, not the cheap and impermanent staff of previous fairs. Visitors could watch movies, watch or participate in automobile and motorcycle races, and fly in airplanes. Bakelite plastic, in an endless array of colors, made its debut at the Panama-Pacific Exposition. As a whole, the exposition reflected a vibrancy that made the fairs before it pale in comparison, and it would have been a good place to look for those seeking a new identity for an amusement park.[4]

Lakeside's owners were not alone in their search for a new identity in the 1920s. Denver was also struggling, again desperately wanting to prove that it was a "sophisticated metropolis, not a barren cow town." The mining and agricultural economies that had once dominated the city (and all of Colorado) were declining, and Denver's role as a manufacturing center was also in a downward spiral. Throughout the state, political leaders seemed worn out after years of swift and hard economic development, and many wanted to simply "age gracefully" after frenziedly establishing the state over the previous fifty years. Despite the moral crusading of the Progressive period, Denver was still wracked by vice, as a violent illegal liquor trade and prostitution prospered in the city. Racial violence also rocked the city, as bombs went off in the houses of blacks who moved too close to City Park or other white areas of town. As more blacks, Hispanics, and Catholics moved into central Denver, middle- and upper-class residents fled for new neighborhoods such as Bonnie Brae or Cherry Hills.[5]

Denver's other amusement parks had their share of troubles as well. Both Manhattan Beach and Tuileries closed their gates for the last time before the outbreak of World War I, and Mary Elitch Long's beloved park was in serious financial trouble. Long paid the park's bills whenever she had the money to do so, but more often than not she simply put them aside. Finally, in 1909 she approached John Elitch's old friend, Denver Police magistrate (and future mayor) Benjamin Stapleton, seeking help. Stapleton, in turn, approached several of his friends and political supporters, all prominent Denver businessmen, who provided financial assistance for the troubled park. By 1916, however, they feared that Long had reached a breaking point and, to solve her financial woes, that she might sell the park to their political rival, *Denver Post* and Sells-Floto Circus owner Frederick Bonfils. The businessmen formed a consortium and paid Elitch's bills and back taxes in exchange for stock in the park company, but they had no interest in managing an amusement park. One of the men, Robert Speer, persuaded his longtime friend John Mulvihill to take over management of Elitch's. Within a few months, Mulvihill decided he wanted to buy the park, and after careful consideration Mary Elitch Long agreed to the sale. The sale to Mulvihill, whose family would own Elitch's for the next eighty years, ensured that Elitch's survived, leaving it and Lakeside as Denver's only amusement parks.[6]

Robert Speer was again elected mayor of Denver in 1916 and quickly revived his City Beautiful program after returning to office, but the United States declared war on Germany in April 1917. Focusing on the war effort, Speer established a city-owned bakery and coal company in an effort to prevent profiteers from gouging Denverites as prices of goods soared during the conflict. Speer also established a military training school in Denver. Thousands of men from Denver either volunteered or were drafted to serve during the war, but overall the war had relatively little impact on Denver as people went about their business, which included visiting amusement parks.[7]

As the war in Europe raged, Lakeside's owners took their first steps toward reinventing the park as a working-class destination. With *Denver Municipal Facts* no longer promoting Lakeside after 1914, the park needed a new champion; the *Rocky Mountain News*, which had first taken the role of promoter in 1914, stepped into the void. As Lakeside prepared to open for the 1917 season, the newspaper reported on May 27 that even though the park had indeed experienced a few poor seasons, the "men who have the kept the bright lights of Lakeside shining for nine summers . . . are not quitters." The men had stood by the park through good times and bad and at the end of each meager season had gone "into their pockets" to pay the bills and open again the next summer. In words that could have been taken directly from an issue of *Municipal Facts* just a few years earlier, the *Rocky Mountain News* wrote that the park's managers "deserve the cooperation of the public," as they ran one of the finest amusement parks in the country. The men who owned the park had all their money invested in Denver, and it was only fitting, the newspaper seemed to be saying, to allow them to succeed in their endeavor.[8]

The *News* singled out the theater for special praise, writing that it was "attractive and delightfully cool" and suggesting that the only reason the theater had failed to turn a profit the previous year was because of the large overhead involved in running it. For the 1917 season, management had engaged a new stock company and planned to once again produce musical comedies that were new to Denver audiences. The lead actress that season was Maybelle LaCouvre, whom the *News* described as "decorative and a good singer and dancer" with prominent roles in productions of *Alma, Where Do You Live?* and *The Girl Question* in New York. The lead actor was Frederick Dunham, a Denver native who had long experience in musical theater but had never appeared onstage in Denver. The opening production for the summer was the musical comedy *Bright Eyes*, and the newspaper strongly urged readers to do their part and attend performances because the "economical management" the operators promised would not by itself allow the theater to turn a profit. The newspaper's encouragement failed to increase attendance, however, and the 1917 season was the Casino Theater's last. That same year, Benjamin Krasner, a Russian immigrant from Binghamton, New York, arrived in Denver and secured a concession contract at the park. Krasner had immigrated to the United States with his family at age four, and as a young man in New York he worked as a "train butcher," selling candies and sandwiches. Krasner worked at Lakeside for the next eighteen years, becoming concession manager in 1931 and saving the once-again bankrupt park in 1935.[9]

Lakeside's famous lights did go dark for one night near the end of the 1917 season when a pheasant accidentally touched both the positive and negative electrical wires leading into the State Home west of Arvada, causing a short-circuit. It seemed a fitting end to a difficult summer, and during the off-season the owners set about totally rearranging the park for the 1918 season. The Casino Theater was converted into a restaurant that featured stage shows and dancing, and management added several new but unnamed rides to the park. Surprisingly, given the addition of rides and the other changes, the size of the park actually shrank during the renovations. Nevertheless, H. D. Hardigan, the general manager of the new park company, told *Billboard* that Lakeside would "be conducted on as large a scale as formerly." The changes did seemingly revive interest in the park, with *Billboard* reporting that Lakeside enjoyed good patronage as the 1918 season got under way.[10]

Encouraged by the improved business situation, Lakeside's owners made additional changes to the park in 1919. The aging swings on the once-popular Circle Swing, which swung out over the lake, were replaced with more modern-looking monoplanes. Park manager Phillip Friederich reported to *Billboard* that the addition of the monoplanes more than tripled the amount of money Lakeside had been earning on the Circle Swing. Management also reworked the bathing beach at the park, which had first opened in 1915. The original beach was connected to the Boat House and dock by a long boardwalk, with a sand beach running alongside it. The boardwalk ended at the bathhouse, which had large, sand-covered verandas on which bathers could sun themselves. One section of the beach was reserved for women only. *Billboard* did not report on the exact changes management made to the bathing beach for 1919, but the magazine did say that the beach was new and a curiosity for the Mile High City. By 1920, *Billboard* was reporting that, with all the changes, Lakeside "appeared more beautiful than it has ever been in the past" and that business was so good that summer that the park remained open an extra week to accommodate the crowds. *Billboard* reported that on one particular night at Lakeside, cars from sixteen states were parked there.[11]

After closing at the end of the 1920 season, the "painters, carpenters, decorators, mechanics, engineers, and entertainment specialists" busily prepared for the next season. According to *Billboard*, most of the rides and buildings in the park were repainted the traditional white, which had helped give the park the nickname White City when it first opened. Special attention was given to the grounds, with *Billboard* reporting that they looked "prettier than ever before." Workers also replaced the dance floor in the El Patio Ballroom with a new floor that allowed dancers to move with the grain as they danced, rather than against it. As the park opened for its fourteenth season, *Billboard* declared that Lakeside looked as "spick and span as a brand-new dollar" and predicted that it should enjoy a good summer, publicity very similar to articles in *Municipal Facts* a decade earlier. The 1921 season was in fact a good one, especially at the El Patio Ballroom, which was filled to capacity most nights. The Fountain Room, opened in the former Casino Theater the previous summer, featured Permitt's Male Quartet and the Melvin Anthony

Jazz Orchestra, as well as a mystery show titled "Just for Fun." Management eliminated the separate admission fee at the very popular bathing beach for customers who brought their own suits and towels.[12]

For all the changes, however, the owners still struggled with completely letting go of the park's City Beautiful past. In 1922 *Billboard* reminded readers that Lakeside was perhaps most famous for its "wonderful scenic settings," and the next year the park's owners decided to bring back the sunset dinners in all their glory. J. W. Miller, former manager of the Casino restaurant, arrived at Lakeside several weeks before the season opener and immediately set to work renovating the old space. Attempting to replicate the atmosphere that had once defined the restaurant where guests ate off of fine china with the words "Lakeside Casino" on it, Miller ordered new silverware, dinnerware, and linens for the restaurant. He also enlarged the kitchen and serving spaces. Miller was intent, *Billboard* reported, on making sure the restaurant would "live up to the reputation he established in former years." During the 1922 season, the balcony restaurant was open from 6:00 p.m. until 9:00 p.m., after which time the new Casino garden offered free dancing, music, and entertainment until midnight.[13]

Management also began to stage carnivals that were similar to the elaborate affairs that had been the grand finales of some of Lakeside's early seasons. In 1923 Sekedali (pronounced seek-a-dolly), a midsummer carnival, ran from August 8 to August 14. Opening night featured a costume contest at which $200 in gold was divided among the winners in the fancy dress, comical, and novel categories. The second day was Kiddies' Frolic, with free ride tickets and ice cream handed out to hundreds of children; the day ended with a drawing that included a live pony as first prize. Sekedali also brought several national conventions to Lakeside, including the Fraternal Order of Eagles, the DeMolay Society, and the Sons and Daughters of Liberty. The brightly decorated park and visits by national convention attendees could have been straight from Lakeside's City Beautiful era.[14]

Throughout the 1920s, management also maintained one of the most visible and distinctive elements that had connected Lakeside to the City Beautiful program: its lighting scheme. In 1927 chief electrician John Flohr designed a colorful new lighting arrangement for the Tower of Jewels that was widely praised for its beauty. Two years later Flohr introduced yet another new lighting design for the Tower, and *Billboard* raved that the new scheme "excels all previous efforts . . . in dressing the park with a garb of electrical splendor." The Tower's lights changed yet again in 1931, when the bulbs' colors went to scarlet and blue for the season. Lakeside's owners also spent enormous amounts of money on projects similar to those carried out in the past. Of the $50,000 they spent in 1927 alone, the majority went to remodeling the El Patio Ballroom, where they had new lighting effects and Spanish-style decorations installed. Workers constructed a sound booth near the end of the ballroom to hold the equipment used for radio broadcasts from the park that featured Chief Gonzalez and his El Patians. Other changes for the 1927 season included new cement walkways, a new athletic field, and expanded parking facilities—all projects similar to City Beautiful–era undertakings.[15]

As tightly as the owners clung to some City Beautiful links, the working-class neighborhoods around the park had only continued to grow during the 1920s; and bars and pool halls, inexpensive restaurants, and small shops closed in on Lakeside along Sheridan Boulevard and Forty-Fourth Avenue. Lakeside's owners, with their limited ability to control land around the park, did their best to deal with the new circumstances as, in some areas, they ventured about as far from City Beautiful as possible. In 1920, for example, management leased the park to the Cheyenne-based Yellowstone Pictures, which planned to make six movies a year over the next three years. The movie company quickly remodeled space in the Skating Rink and ballroom into studios, complete with dressing, drying, and cutting rooms and a laboratory. More than $8,000 in electrical equipment was on its way to the park at the time the deal was announced, bringing the total spent on the movie studio conversion to $33,000. Yellowstone would produce only Westerns, according to its manager, Charles Bartlett, and Colorado, Bartlett told the *Rocky Mountain News*, was "ideal for picture work" because of its natural scenery. A series of scandals in the early 1920s had rocked the public's perception of the movie industry, and in an effort to restore its credibility with the public, the industry formed the Motion Picture Producers and Distributors of America in 1922 to self-regulate and police it. But a movie studio inside Lakeside was a major change from the park's elite days. The movie studio fizzled out fairly quickly, but it showed that the owners were taking big, though hesitant, steps toward changing Lakeside's image.[16]

In another big change, a portion of Lakeside was renamed Flapper Lane in honor of the flapper craze of the 1920s. Flappers were post–World War I women who, writes historian Michael E. Parrish, "appeared eager to abandon all social restraints on their behavior by taking to heart the idea that equality meant enjoying the pleasures customarily reserved for men." Flappers were known for their short hair and androgynous dress, and according to popular culture they engaged in too much drinking, smoking, and flirting. The *Estes Park (CO) Trail* described a flapper as "a girl who refuses to use her own or anyone else's brains" and who was "long on bobbed hair, short skirts, arms, neck, back, chatter and jazz" and argued that such women should be banned by constitutional amendment. The *Ouray Herald* printed evangelist Mattie Crawford's opinion that "the little flappers are flapping their souls away."[17]

Flappers and their male friends (sometimes called sheiks or flippers) represented a shocking new cultural phenomenon very different from Lakeside's conservative City Beautiful–era patrons, but the park welcomed them with open arms. On July 18, 1922, the park hosted a contest to name "Denver's premier flapper," which was more in keeping with typical amusement park fare than with the elegance and beauty once associated with Lakeside Amusement Park. More than 40,000 people, almost as big as the crowd that had been at the park on opening day in 1908, were in attendance to help choose the winner from 7,000 contestants. Among the judges were Lieutenant Governor Earl Cooley and famed Denver judge Benjamin Lindsey, prompting Telluride's *Daily Journal* to tease that the contest had political significance. The winner was Marjorie Nichols of Denver, who Denver newspapers called "a decided blonde."[18]

With a trendier crowd coming to the park, Lakeside's owners added several new attractions throughout the 1920s. One of the most popular was the Old Mill, and *Billboard* made sure to point out that Lakeside's was one of the longest in the world. Commonly known as the Tunnel of Love, Old Mill rides featured life-size depictions of fairy tale scenes placed in alcoves along the ride's route that riders saw as they passed by in boats. Replacing the park's original Third Degree fun house were a Hilarity Hall, built by Lakeside consulting engineer E. J. Lauterback, and a House of Troubles. Park management also replaced the monoplanes on the Circle Swing with more stylish seaplanes and purchased the Derby coaster in 1924 from the Pearce family, which had operated the ride since building it in 1912. In 1928 management replaced the twenty-year-old rustic-style boathouse near the ballroom with new and improved boating facilities closer to the center of the park. They also installed a Grant orthophonic Victrola, which played new electrically recorded records rather than the old acoustically recorded versions.[19]

Two new restaurants at Lakeside that opened in the 1920s vividly demonstrated the park's owners' conflicted feelings about its new image. The Jail restaurant opened in the Casino building in 1926, and *Billboard* praised it for "providing a novelty that is filled with endless fun." Staff were dressed as either prisoners or guards, and the walls of the restaurant were painted to look like stone with bars on the windows. Customers were referred to as inmates and were served chicken dinners "prison style" on tin plates while vaudeville and dancing acts performed. Instead of the fine china that once was standard in the Casino, customers who survived their evening of incarceration in the Jail were given souvenir tin cups that proudly stated "Compliments Jail—Lakeside." A jail-themed restaurant was very different from the openness and uplift of the well-designed parks and spaces City Beautiful promoted, but the new restaurant came into being at a time when crime stories were often associated with the working class, the very customers Lakeside needed to attract in order to survive. Lurid stories of crime involving the wealthy were rarely heard, historian Mary Frances Berry writes, because they avoided exposing such things to the public. The park's working-class customers were not offended, however, packing the Jail nightly during the summer.[20]

That same year the Plantation restaurant also opened in the Casino building. The Plantation served what *Billboard* called "real Southern style chicken dinners," and advertisements for the restaurant included a picture of a stereotypical mammy figure cooking at a stove. The name of the restaurant as well as its promotional material were part of an advertising trend in the 1920s that saw companies using images of the South to sell their products, most famously Aunt Jemima pancake mix. To many Americans, the image of the old South was one of a place of leisure and comfort, where people were saved from work and worry by the former slaves who still willingly served their old masters. The mammy, who cooked for her white masters and helped make their lives easier, fit this trend. The purpose for using these fictional images of the old South in advertising, writes historian M. M. Manring, was to create an image of an upper-class lifestyle for consumers who had to go to work every day or who lacked servants to clean their houses. For a moment, they could pretend that a cheerful black woman was making their lives less hectic and more glamorous. The two restaurants were a vivid contrast: one was about as far as possible from the old elite atmosphere of the park, while the other purposely used imagery meant to recreate and sustain that elite atmosphere.[21]

In case anyone missed just how much the image of Lakeside had changed since 1916, the 1925 edition of *Clason's Denver Map Guide* referred to Elitch's as a beautiful picnic ground, while at Lakeside, referred to as Denver's Coney Island, the dance hall (ballroom) and cabaret (formerly the Casino theater) were emphasized rather than the park's beauty. A little more than a decade earlier, these map guides had listed Lakeside as one of the must-see attractions for out-of-town visitors. As Lakeside went about adding more thrilling rides to the park, John Mulvihill was making his own thrilling changes at Elitch's, one of the biggest being construction of the Wildcat roller coaster in 1922. In addition to the Wildcat, perhaps the most notable change Mulvihill made to the park was construction of the legendary Trocadero Ballroom in 1917. Mary Elitch had disapproved of public dancing and never allowed a ballroom in the park while she owned it. For entertainment at the Trocadero, Mulvihill hired Rudolph Ganz and his seventy-five-piece symphony for evening concerts. To make way for a parking lot (one of the few issues with which Lakeside's owners did not have to contend), Mulvihill tore down several of the old zoo buildings at Elitch's. As Elitch's reputation as the more white-collar of Denver's amusement parks grew, the city's more conservative amusement park goers were using their cars to go to Elitch's, not Lakeside, as they had once done.[22]

Still, to all outward appearances, Lakeside was thriving. Behind the scenes, however, financial arrangements revealed that the park was not healthy. In August 1927 the Denver Park and Amusement Company leased twenty-three acres of land northeast of the park to Lusion Gibson Throckmorton, a greyhound racetrack developer. Throckmorton, in turn, leased the land to the Denver Greyhound Racing Association, which banked with Adolph Zang's American National Bank of Denver. In fact, Godfrey Schirmer had been the one who originally suggested that Throckmorton talk to Phillip Friederich about possibly leasing land at the park on which to build a greyhound racetrack. Construction started on the grandstand and track almost immediately after the lease was signed, and Lakeside had one season of greyhound races in 1927. But the next year nine lawsuits were filed against the Denver Park and

Amusement Company, including one by Frank Kirchoff, president of Denver Park and Amusement, on behalf of his lumber company. The suits alleged that the Denver Greyhound Racing Association had defaulted on money owed to the nine companies that filed the lawsuits. The district court ruled in favor of the plaintiffs, who filed nine liens against Lakeside totaling nearly $40,000, and ordered the park property sold to satisfy the debts.[23]

The Denver Park and Amusement Company, with the backing of American National Bank, which still held a $60,000 mortgage on the park, appealed the ruling to the Colorado Supreme Court. Company and bank officials argued that the court erred in allowing the liens to be considered primary obligations because American National's mortgage should have taken precedence. Company officials also argued that Throckmorton's lease to the Denver Greyhound Racing Association was invalid since betting was allowed at the races in violation of state law. With an invalid lease, they said, they were not responsible for any of the greyhound track's debts. As the trial wore on, Frank Kirchoff found himself in the unusual position of testifying for Denver Park and Amusement against his lumber company while also testifying against the park on behalf of his lumber company. The Colorado Supreme Court was unmoved by the new arguments and upheld the lower court's ruling in favor of the nine original plaintiffs, leaving Lakeside's owners with the choice of either paying off the debts or selling the park. As the trial worked its way through the court system, Godfrey Schirmer died on November 15, 1928, at age sixty-five. While Schirmer may have been gone, his bank decided to protect its interest in Lakeside and loaned the owners $100,000 to refinance the bank's mortgage and pay off the debts incurred by constructing the greyhound track. Once again the park survived, but within a few years the big loan would come back to haunt its owners.[24]

For the 1929 season, management ordered new motorboats for the lake as well as modernization of the big launch, both of which, *Billboard* reported, were heavily patronized on opening day. Landscaping changes allowed for a better view of the lake, according to *Billboard*, and the magazine also promoted a new filter system at the Swimming Pool that changed the water three times during each twenty-four-hour period. But there were relatively few changes to the park for the 1929 season, especially given the precarious financial position in which the owners found themselves. The park ended its season less than two months before the stock market crashed that October.

At first, the Great Depression had little impact in Denver except in the financial district, where many of the city's great millionaires saw their fortunes wiped out overnight. Until late 1931 the city seemed safe from the trouble engulfing the East, but when metal prices fell and industry slowed, Denver's economy sank. The Great Depression was brutal to amusement parks, as patronage dried up and owners were unable to pay bills, resulting in hundreds of parks closing their gates. Both Lakeside and Elitch's survived, but they fought hard against each other for every customer.[25]

With finances tight, Lakeside's owners still worked to reinvent the park, but the pace slowed considerably. The new Lindy Loop was a ride that capitalized on Charles Lindbergh's famous solo flight across the Atlantic Ocean in 1927. The ride resembled a modern Tilt-a-Whirl in the way it operated: each car was mounted on crescent-shaped rails and could freely slide from one end of the rails to the other. The ride consisted of eight such cars attached to a circular track that then moved up and down over a series of hills, forcing each car to slide back and forth on the rails. The ride, built by the Herschel-Spillman Company of New York, was a popular attraction at amusement parks across the United States. Lakeside also joined the miniature golf craze sweeping the country in 1930, with a course that stretched from the fun house to the Derby coaster. In addition to rides, one of the chief attractions for families remained the "well-shaded picnic grounds with a beautiful view of the distant mountains."[26]

Popular band leader and Denver resident George Morrison and His Orchestra became the lead performers at the El Patio Ballroom in 1930. At one time Morrison and his band had an exclusive contract with Columbia Records' "race records" division, which attempted to have black bands record popular jazz music to sell to black customers. When Columbia did not renew his contract, Morrison and his band returned to Denver, where they joined with actress Hattie McDaniel to perform in the city's vaudeville theaters. Morrison eventually opened his own club, the Casino, on Welton Street, in Denver's Five Points neighborhood. Lakeside general manager Joseph Moore renamed the group George Morrison and His Rigadooners as a play on the French word *rigodon*, which meant a dance or music for a dance. Morrison and his band played the El Patio for a number of years, but no black customers were allowed inside the park to watch them. As much as the White City may have changed since 1908, only white customers were allowed inside its gates (the same was also true at Elitch's at the time). Among white customers, however, Morrison and the Rigadooners were enormously popular, and customers filled Lakeside's ballroom nightly to hear them perform.[27]

While big bands and flashy attractions kept attendance at Lakeside up, management put on a number of special events to help ensure big crowds during the 1930 season. Every Thursday, children enjoyed free admission to the park and free ice cream, and on occasion Togo the Wonder Dog performed for them. Bob Graf, a comedy diver, was a regular feature at the Swimming Pool, along with pool parties with life-size swimming toys for children. Management also constructed a marble fountain covered with electric lights in the Swimming Pool, which *Billboard* called an "added feature." The biggest draw of the summer, however, was the fireworks show on July 3, which more than 35,000 people attended. During the Forresters of Colorado's annual gathering at the park, an airplane was given away, though *Billboard* did not make it clear whether it was given away by the park or the Forresters. The final celebration of the season was on Labor Day, when more than 30,000 people entered the park. Throughout the summer the weather cooperated, which according to *Billboard* brought record crowds on weekends and allowed the park to stay open two weeks later than usual. Overall, *Billboard* reported, 1930 was indeed an excellent season for Lakeside.[28]

Lakeside enjoyed another successful season in 1931, with more than 650,000 people visiting. During the twelve free days for children, more than 96,000 people entered the park's gates. The biggest draw that year, according to *Billboard*, was the El Patio Ballroom and the big-name bands ballroom manager Roy Easter booked for guest appearances: the Coon-Sanders Orchestra, Jan Garba's Band, Wayne King, George Olson, and Irving Aaronson and His Commanders. *Billboard* declared that these five were among the best-known bands in the country, and their presence in Denver gave Lakeside a huge boost during what was otherwise a bad economic year. When an especially well-known band played the park, Lakeside took out big advertisements in Denver's newspapers, which also gave each of the appearances special coverage. In Depression-era Denver, music was popular, and the low prices at El Patio allowed many people the chance to see and hear famous bands live. The local musicians' union pled with management at both Lakeside and Elitch's to give local bands a chance to play in their ballrooms, but big-name bands drew the customers and continued to play at both parks. To keep the ballrooms busy, Elitch's introduced a one-cent admission fee to the Trocadero with paid park admission, while Lakeside offered a two-for-one ticket at El Patio.[29]

Also in 1930, Phillip Friederich returned to Lakeside as an assistant to park manager Joseph Moore after a five-year absence. *Billboard* was pleased with his return, writing that under Friederich's earlier leadership "Lakeside hummed with activity and bustled with many yearly innovations." Friederich remained with the park over the next four years and may have been behind some of the gimmicks Lakeside used to keep people coming to the park after his return. In 1932 rival Elitch's gave away one free car per week while Lakeside gave away free picnic lunches to every paying customer daily, cash prizes at special events such as the Mardi Gras celebration, and in 1933, free trips to the Century of Progress International Exposition in Chicago. The gimmicks worked, and *Billboard* was able to report at the close of the 1933 season that business at the two parks was not too bad.[30]

Not too bad, unfortunately, was not good enough to cover the $100,000 loan Lakeside's owners had taken out against the park in 1928, and in 1933 American National Bank of Denver demanded full repayment. Lakeside's owners were unable to come up with any of the money and, when the bank foreclosed, it looked as if the park might be forced to close. Bank officials quickly realized that if Lakeside did in fact fail to open in 1933, the odds of ever seeing any money were slim, which led them to get a court order opening the park for the season. Judge Samuel Johnson of Golden appointed Harry Zimmerhackel, a Denver lawyer and former city council member, as receiver; and bankrupt Lakeside opened on schedule for a less than spectacular 1933 season.[31]

Between the end of the 1933 season and the start of 1934's, new general manager Linden K. Haney spent more than $10,000 on improvements at Lakeside. The biggest change was at the Swimming Pool, where a glass-enclosed sunbathing beach was built. Haney also installed new bumper cars at the Skooter attraction and built a penny arcade. Thirty-two teams signed up to play in the park's softball league, and semi-pro baseball teams played at the park's ball field on Saturdays and Sundays. In a significant change from previous years, big-name bands were booked for one-night stands only, filling in gaps between longer engagements by local musicians. Impressed, *Billboard* reported that Lakeside could "easily regain its old-time popularity" with the changes, and halfway through the 1934 season Haney reported that the park had already been visited by double the number of people that had come in all of 1933. Unfortunately, the improved business was not enough, and later that year the bondholders who backed American National Bank's loan to Lakeside grew tired of the bank's management of the park. A bondholders' protection committee, made up of Dr. J. M. Morris, J. Reimer Espy, Karl Koch, August Drumm, and H. L. Luchenback, took over operation of Lakeside, but the park fared no better financially under them than it had under Zimmerhackel.[32]

After more than a decade of reinventing the park, the distinction was clear by the 1930s—Lakeside was for families who wanted to bring picnics with them rather than buy food at the park, while Elitch's and its theater was for the more serious-minded amusement seekers. *Billboard* recognized the change, writing in 1930 that Lakeside, with its "extremely varied amusements diversified in appeal to boys young and old," was very popular with families while the chief attraction at Elitch's was its theater. The men behind the Denver Park and Amusement Company had done their best to remake Lakeside Amusement Park after 1917, but all of them had been involved with the park since its opening in 1908 and were too close to it to make the needed changes. The changes they did make reflected their ambivalence about leaving behind the City Beautiful–era designs and way of operating, which was not what the park needed. What they did accomplish was ultimately not enough to save the park, but their changes were well received, with the series *Life in Denver* calling Lakeside one of the better outside amusement resorts in the Rocky Mountain region. Lakeside also found new support in the pages of the *Rocky Mountain News*, which championed the park as heartily as *Denver Municipal Facts* had a decade earlier. But as the 1934 season ended, Lakeside truly needed a new image more than ever if it was going to survive. Luckily for Lakeside Amusement Park, concession manager Benjamin Krasner had a plan.[33]

CHAPTER 5

Benjamin Krasner and Lakeside's New Setup

Severe economic hardship meant most people had less money to spend on entertainment during the Great Depression. Amusement parks, however, writes David Nasaw, survived the Depression in better shape than most other venues as the parks underwent a retrenchment of their own in the 1920s. Many of the smaller trolley parks were either closed or sold by the streetcar companies that owned them, and those that remained competed with larger parks for customers. The amusement parks that survived into the 1930s saw owners promoting relatively inexpensive activities such as beaches, picnic grounds, and ballrooms and investing less money in new rides and improvements to the grounds. Cleveland's Euclid Beach Park and Pittsburgh's Kennywood, for example, survived the Depression by hosting company picnics and family-oriented events. At Coney Island, the "era of the 'dripper'" began as visitors who were unable to afford to rent a bathhouse at the beach wore dry bathing suits under their clothes on the trip out and the wet suits on the way home. The amusement parks on Coney grew seedier each year as money grew tighter, with some sinking so low as to hold cockroach races, but the crowds still came, ready to enjoy a day of relatively inexpensive entertainment.[1]

In the March 2, 1935, issue of *Billboard*, publicist Ernest Anderson urged amusement park owners to do the exact opposite of what most were doing. Writing of President Franklin D. Roosevelt's plan to pump several billion dollars into the economy through government works projects in an effort to get money circulating again, Anderson said he wanted park owners and managers to adopt a similar policy. Anderson condemned "Mr. Average Park Manager" who refused to spend money on paint, advertising, new rides and concessions, and shows and instead simply threw open the gates to their parks while "muttering feebly, 'Well, boys, she's open!'" He suggested that these park managers were better off closing their parks or calling a junk dealer to haul everything away. Pointing to a handful of park managers who had succeeded in turning their parks around, Anderson praised them for their ability to develop an "Arabian Nights Dream from a city sewer dump" and urged more to follow their examples. If an attraction at a park was not producing, he urged owners to tear it down and replace it with something more attractive to customers. Anderson wanted park owners and managers to be ready for the influx of customers sure to come once the government's money was in circulation.[2]

Lakeside Amusement Park concession manager Benjamin Krasner wanted to spend money on the park, but first he had to buy it. As soon as the 1934 season at Lakeside ended, he entered into negotiations with the bondholders' protective committee that had operated the park that year. Krasner's family and friends who still lived on the East Coast were ready to loan him the money to buy the park, but the negotiations were "considerable," according to *Billboard*, and went on for several months. Finally, on February 23, 1935, Benjamin Krasner became the new owner and general manager of Lakeside after paying a little over $61,000 for the park. Joining Krasner in the new Lakeside Park Company were Albert W. Johnson as general superintendent, Robert R. Mullen in charge of advertising, and park electrician John Flohr. Krasner was president of the new company, and he was assisted by his sister Jennie's husband, Martie Ruttner. The Ruttners and Krasner lived in an apartment in the Casino Theater building for several years after he bought the park. Immediately after completing the purchase, Krasner went to Chicago to meet with executives at the Music Corporation of America

(MCA) to negotiate a new contract to have name bands play at the park during the 1935 season.³

Having big-name bands appear at Lakeside was a vital part of Krasner's plan to remake the park. The introduction of lower-priced records by Decca during the Depression made music a much more popular pastime than it had been, and people of all ages swarmed ballrooms for the chance to hear favorite bands perform live and to dance. For younger people, dancing also provided an opportunity to meet members of the opposite sex. In 1928, for example, nineteen-year-old Ned Stout was injured while riding the Derby coaster at Lakeside. Stout unsuccessfully sued the park, testifying that the only reason he was on the Derby was because he and a friend had met a couple of girls while dancing at El Patio and the girls wanted to ride the coaster. The introduction of Swing and Big Band style music at ballrooms also drew an older crowd, who soon flocked to dance halls, often crowding out the younger people who had once dominated them. Whether it drew the young or the old, booking famous bands to play at Lakeside's ballroom seemed a sure way to increase business.⁴

Breaking with past management, Krasner booked the bands for much earlier in the season, which *Billboard* credited with giving Lakeside's summers a good start. One of Krasner's biggest scores was signing Kay Kyser and his band, who performed at the El Patio Ballroom for several years. Kyser was a major recording star in the late 1930s and early 1940s, recording over 400 songs, appearing in several movies, and hosting a weekly radio show on NBC called *Kay Kyser's Kollege of Musical Knowledge* from 1938 to 1949. Kyser was so popular at Lakeside that his name was permanently painted above the bandstand in the El Patio and was featured prominently on billboards for the park. Another major star who performed at Lakeside was Glenn Miller, an appearance that stung rival Elitch's, whose management desperately wanted the famous musician to perform there. In 1942 Duke Ellington played Lakeside (and hosted a catered dinner for Benjamin and Miriam Krasner on the porch of the ballroom), followed by Denver-born Paul Whiteman and His Orchestra. During the late 1930s and early 1940s, if people wanted to see famous actors, they went to Elitch's theater; for famous musicians, they went to Lakeside's El Patio.⁵

In another big change, Krasner resumed heavy advertising of Lakeside, something *Billboard* noted previous owners had not done for many years.

Krasner coined a new slogan for the park, "Denver Has Gone Lakeside," and hired Derby Sproul and William Robertson to promote it. Large billboards soon appeared alongside roads all over Denver announcing opening day for the season, with one square on each board having nothing but a question mark. The question marks drew considerable attention as people tried to guess what would eventually take their place. On May 26, the day after the park opened for the 1935 season, the new slogan replaced the question marks. Newspaper ads carried the slogan, too, and it was printed on hundreds of spare-tire covers given to visitors at the park on opening day. Picnics remained a popular draw at the park, the largest attracting 27,000 customers, while the *Denver Post* sponsored two picnics that drew 12,000 and 11,000, respectively. The two fireworks displays, on July 3 and August 1, drew upward of 20,000 people each. Krasner also continued the free Children's Days, during which children were admitted to the park for free and given free ice cream. With its low prices and popular offerings Lakeside was a popular escape during hard economic times, but *Billboard* made sure to point out that much of the credit for the successful season belonged to Benjamin Krasner and the changes he was making to the park, headlining its September 21, 1935, article on the season "Lakeside's New Setup by Krasner in Denver Has Big Public Appeal."[6]

Shortly before leaving for Chicago to talk with MCA, Krasner announced that he was planning to spend $12,000 on improvements to the grounds before opening day, the first of many changes the new owner would make. He hired California-based architect Richard Crowther to give Lakeside's grounds an up-to-date look that was more complementary to the new rides than was the park's Exposition-style architecture. In a 1992 interview with Stuart Leuthner of *American Heritage* magazine, Crowther said that while he believed Krasner himself was very conservative, "he understood the amusement business and realized the park needed a new look." It was far easier for Krasner, who had never known Lakeside at the height of its City Beautiful days, to change the park than it had been for previous owners. The only structure off-limits to Crowther's imagination was the Tower of Jewels and the attached Casino. While Crowther wanted to do something new and different with the Tower, Krasner told him it was too much of a landmark and would not allow him to touch it.[7]

Lakeside's new look, created over several years in the late 1930s and early 1940s, was an Art Deco masterpiece. The style, which grew out of the 1925

Paris Exhibition, emerged at a time of growing disillusionment with historically based design, such as the style that marked Lakeside and the City Beautiful, and a strong belief that the new century should have a new style. Art Deco, according to art historians Bevis Hillier and Stephen Escritt, was "self-consciously new." Zig-zag Art Deco, seen, for example, in Radio City Music Hall and the Chrysler Building, consisted of ornate designs and sharp features. Moderne, which heavily influenced automobile designs of the 1930s, was sleeker and smoother and was the version Crowther used at Lakeside. No matter what form it took, though, Art Deco was most "often seen to be at best frivolous, at worst immoral," wrote Hillier and Escritt. Strict modernists dismissed Art Deco as commercially driven and therefore not a true art form, but the style lent itself to new consumer items, from women's jewelry to radios to kitchen appliances. Its popularity in movie set designs in the 1920s and 1930s, where it was used to depict both sinister and industrial settings, introduced it to a much wider audience in the United States than elsewhere. The escapist nature of movies required matching buildings in which to exhibit them, and Art Deco architecture became the norm for those theaters. Advertisements for products as varied as coffee, needles, and shoes also picked up on the Art Deco trend and used images such as skyscrapers, planes, and streamlined trains to promote their products. Soon, products designed in the Art Deco style were appearing in the Sears catalog, which Hillier and Escritt argue "brought modernity to even the most remote parts of America." Art Deco seemingly was made for an amusement park in search of a new, fun image.[8]

To begin, Crowther designed and built new ticket booths for each ride at Lakeside. Crowther took great care in the design of each booth, with the character and style he used "often mirroring the style of the ride itself." True to the Moderne style, the ticket booths were sleek and included curved lines and a great deal of glass. Lighting remained an important part of Crowther's design for Lakeside, but instead of incandescent lights, he used neon and "created sinuous signs and etched his buildings with the rainbow-hued tubes." Crowther also covered the rides with new multicolored fluorescent lights. Each new ticket booth was declared "delightful . . . as sleek and stylized as the Bakelite radios of the era, and not so very much larger." Among the most impressive booths were those for the Hurricane, Cyclone, and Whip. Every time a new ride was added to the park in the years that followed, it received its own ticket booth designed to match the older ones.[9]

Krasner and Crowther decided to move Lakeside's original 1908 Parker merry-go-round into an entirely new building (its third home at the park) rather than remodel the old one. As part of the change, Krasner had all of the animals, which were painted white, stripped and repainted in more lifelike colors. The new building, which was revealed to the public on opening day in May 1942, was not the typical "domed, lattice-worked, curlicued" structure found in most parks, said one article. Covered with purple, pink, and blue neon lights and blue tile, it was described as unique and angular, with a "futuristic charm." Attached to the new Merry-Go-Round Building, which was built on the site of the second building that had housed the ride, was one of the new main ticket booths for the park. Crowther also made changes to the El Patio Ballroom, installing new signage and railings on the front of the building but leaving the exterior of the main structure and the interior, which resembled a Mexican village, relatively untouched. The transformation, wrote Stuart Leuthner in *American Heritage*, produced a "remarkably uniform and pleasing group of High Deco buildings," and even the addition of European rides after World War II did little to alter the park's appearance.[10]

While Crowther was busily giving Lakeside's buildings a new look, Krasner continued to change rides and other attractions. By the beginning of the 1937 season he had spent more than $60,000 on improvements at Lakeside (about $15,000 less than Elitch's spent the same year). The largest project at Lakeside in 1937 was remodeling the rathskeller, then called the Old Heidelburg Room, in the basement of the Casino. The new $25,000 restaurant, called the College Inn, was designed to resemble a softly lighted, Gothic-arched nightclub. The restaurant had a dance floor and served sandwiches and other refreshments but no liquor (though it did later serve Coors beer). In other improvements that year, workers constructed a new roadbed for the miniature railroad (still one of the longest in the world), installed new rails on the Derby coaster, and launched new Dodge and Chris Craft speedboats on the lake. In addition, Krasner had all of the concession stands rebuilt or remodeled and again renovated the Swimming Pool. Overall, *Billboard* reported, business at the park was up by about 30 percent at the end of the 1937 season. National conventions returned to the park when the Elks held their annual gathering there on July 14, 1937, further evidence that Krasner's changes were making the park a popular gathering place once again.[11]

In another smart move, Krasner hosted picnics for Denver-area newspaper and radio stations, which, according to *Billboard*, "resulted in columns of valuable free publicity." Picnics proved such a popular draw that in 1938 Krasner built a $15,000 picnic pavilion, known as Casa Mañana—complete with two kitchens, coffee urns, and free gas ranges—on the southern edge of the park. He also re-landscaped the grounds around the new picnic pavilion and installed outdoor ovens for which the park provided free wood. By 1941, Lakeside was hosting an average of four big picnics a week, sponsored by department stores, fraternal orders, and businesses; it also continued the traditional Labor Day celebration. In addition to the new picnic pavilion, other changes at the park for 1938 included opening the pool for night swimming, as management added new underwater lights and remodeled the men's shower room in black and ivory tile (the women's shower room had been done the year before). Three years later, attendance at the remodeled pool set a new record when 1,873 people paid the thirty-five-cent admission fee to pass through the turnstile. On the lake, crews built a new boat dock, complete with a nautically themed ticket booth and a lighthouse. Workers reconditioned the Fun House, which included installing what would become the park's most infamous resident, Laffing Sal, a 6'10"-tall mannequin that stood on a foot-high pedestal. Her "raucous belly laugh," recorded on 78 RPM records, echoed throughout the park for years as she both greeted visitors to the Fun House and terrified small children, and she remains one of the most asked-about attractions at the park. Another crew worked for two and half months and used 2,000 pounds of paint to repaint the Tower of Jewels, the lone remnant of the park's City Beautiful era; as *Billboard* reported, its "16,000 lights make it visible for miles." At the end of July, *Billboard* reported that the park was "meeting marked success," with all attractions drawing large crowds as Denver enjoyed another good tourist season.[12]

Krasner forged ahead with his remake of Lakeside in 1939, adding a new restaurant on the north side of the Tower called the Gayway Inn. Two of the new restaurant's most notable decorative features were a large, multicolored fluorescent light fixture that ran the length of the ceiling and an ornate back bar Krasner had saved from Denver's Union Station. Krasner told *Billboard* that 1939 was his best year at the park so far and, with every change seemingly leading to increased business, he spent an estimated $95,000 on improvements for 1940. The old baseball field on the southwest side of the park was finally dismantled, giving way to a parking lot that could accommodate 8,000 cars. Krasner also added several new and far more thrilling rides to the park in the late 1930s, including the Eyerly-made Octopus, Loop-O-Plane, Roll-O-Plane, and Rock-O-Plane; a Hurricane ride (which simulated flying an airplane); a Tumble Bug; and stainless steel rocket ship cars on the old Circle Swing ride. The Denver and Rio Grande Railroad continued working on the miniature railroad as well, installing a new block signal and building a new tunnel, said to resemble the Moffat Tunnel. According to *Billboard*, 80 percent of the riders on the miniature railroad were adults. During this period Krasner also created what was called the Sunken Gardens from the pool of the long-gone Shoot-the-Chutes ride.[13]

Lakeside's most thrilling change for 1940, however, was a new roller coaster called the Cyclone. Benjamin Krasner had spent a great deal of time touring amusement parks in the late 1930s as he made his plans for Lakeside, and he was particularly impressed by the Zephyr coaster at Pontchartrain Beach in New Orleans. He contacted Edward Vettel, who had designed the Zephyr and was one of the best roller coaster builders during the 1930s and 1940s, and asked him to design a coaster for his park. The end result was the Cyclone. One reporter later wrote that the Cyclone was the "biggest, scariest, loopiest and queasiest" coaster Vettel had built to that point. Vettel himself said at the time, "I don't know what we'll do with the younger generation. You just can't seem to give them a coaster with dips deep enough nor curves sharp and daring enough to scare them."[14]

The 85-foot-high Cyclone "brought a new level of thrills and excitement" to Lakeside, according to the National Amusement Park Historical Association. Riders left the station and traveled through a dark, 200-foot-long tunnel before emerging to climb the 85 feet to the coaster's first drop, which then sent them on a dizzying 4,300-foot-long route of twists and turns, rises and falls. The coaster's station was designed to fit with the rest of the park's new Art Deco look and was covered with neon lights. Like all the other rides, it was given its own ticket booth, a curvilinear glass block building, where eager riders paid fifteen cents for a ticket. On the platform was an "inverted ziggurat-like" booth for the operator, and for many years customers could ride the Cyclone as many times as they wanted by handing an additional ten cents to the operator in the booth without ever getting out of their seats. Large red levers on the platform operated the train's brakes, and a light-up board above the tunnel entrance showed waiting riders where on the track the previous train was at the moment. The finishing touch to the station was the cast-iron handrail, complete with miniature coaster cars and riders pressed into the design. The Cyclone's grand opening on May 17, 1940, put Lakeside at the top of coaster enthusiasts' lists, both locally and nationally, for many years, with it consistently ranked among the best wooden coasters in the country for decades. One writer later pointed out that it also made Lakeside the winner of the roller coaster wars in Denver for more than two decades, until Elitch's built its Twister roller coaster in 1964.[15]

By 1940, Krasner had started hosting a dizzying number of special events at the park to draw even more customers. In August, a Pageant of Youth, sponsored by the North Denver Civic Association, drew 4,000 people and culminated with the crowning of Miss North Denver. A series of college nights throughout the summer ended on September 4 with the crowning of Miss Colorado Co-Ed. By 1942, *Billboard* noted that the college nights were "well plugged" at all colleges in Colorado and drew many students. The park also hosted several special dances and a free circus that summer. Business was up by 14 percent over the previous year, according to *Billboard*, and Krasner kept the park open an extra week. The special events proved so popular that Krasner continued them for the 1941 and 1942 seasons.[16]

As much as Krasner had changed Lakeside, some old issues from the park's past still lingered. Segregation at the park became a public issue on August 23, 1940, when the *Colorado Statesman*, a black newspaper published in Denver, reported that Mr. and Mrs. Robert Barber, staff members of the *Kansas City Call*, had been prevented from entering Lakeside. The newspaper reported that park officials stated that "Negroes are not allowed in the amusement section, the dance hall, or the Swimming Pool," a common situation in parks throughout the country. Lakeside had been segregated since opening day in 1908, and even though the neighborhoods around the park changed in the 1920s, the ban on black customers remained. Although blacks made up only 2.4 percent of Denver's population in 1920, segregation was seemingly the rule almost everywhere in the city—in pools, theaters, military posts, clubs, and restaurants. In the 1920s the Ku Klux Klan rose to great political power in Denver, claiming Denver mayor Benjamin Stapleton, Colorado governor Clarence Morley, and US senator Rice Means as members. In 1925, at the height of its power, the Klan held one of its rallies at Lakeside, which thousands of members attended.[17]

The lone exception to Lakeside's restricted entrance policy was Frank Buford, a black pit man at Lakeside Speedway, who had a special dispensation to get through the gates. Driver Wayne Arner called Buford a "knowledgeable and important guy," and his presence in the pits was deemed a necessity by many drivers. He worked with several championship winners, including in 1942, 1947, and 1948, before eventually becoming flagman for the Rocky Mountain Midget Racing Association in 1962, "pioneering in an era when blacks in motorsports were more a rarity than today" writes Bill Hill. Bob Campbell remembered that his father, the driver Foster "Foss" Campbell, played a large part in getting permission for Buford to enter the park, essentially forcing management to let him in. Most drivers remembered Buford as the only black employee at Lakeside Amusement Park at the time.[18]

Despite the racially restricted entrance policy, Lakeside had been widely known as a place where black bands were allowed to perform ever since George Morrison and His Rigadooners first appeared there. In fact, in an oral history recorded in the late 1970s, Elitch's owner Jack Gurtler noted, with some distaste, that black bands were allowed to play in the El Patio Ballroom (ignoring the fact that the same was true of the Trocadero at Elitch's). Management apparently saw no contradiction in allowing black bands to play the ballroom while banning blacks from patronizing the park. And blacks were the only group excluded at Lakeside, especially as the neighborhoods around the park became populated with Jewish, Italian, and Russian families. Elitch's remained segregated until 1948, when it finally bowed to public pressure and integrated. Lakeside most likely integrated at about the same time, the lone exception being the Swimming Pool. It remained segregated until the day it closed in the 1960s, not uncommon for amusement park swimming pools.[19]

While Benjamin Krasner was busily turning Lakeside into a popular Art Deco paradise, rival Elitch's was undergoing its own changes. John Mulvihill died in 1930, and his son-in-law, Arnold Gurtler, took over as president and general manager. Gurtler's new slogan for his park was "Come to Elitch Gardens where a quarter can buy a day of dreams!" One of Gurtler's first changes was replacing the solid wood fence around the park with a wire one so the public could see all the fun things to do in the park as they passed by on the street. Gurtler also continued his father-in-law's expansion of Mary

Elitch's famous flower beds. At a time when Lakeside was turning its athletic field into a parking lot, Gurtler revived and expanded John Elitch's original baseball field on the southwest corner of the park grounds to accommodate semi-professional teams, including one sponsored by Elitch's. Like Krasner, Gurtler worked with MCA to get big bands at the Trocadero because they drew the customers. Overall, the competition between Lakeside and Elitch's was usually friendly, in part because they drew different groups of customers, but that was not always the case. In 1954, filming began in Denver on *The Glenn Miller Story*, a movie about the life of the famous bandleader who had grown up and attended college in Colorado. Portions of the movie, starring Jimmy Stewart and June Allison, were filmed at the Trocadero Ballroom at Elitch's, even though Miller never performed there. Miller had, however, played at Lakeside, a fact that remained a sore subject with the Gurtler family more than a decade after the fact.[20]

Throughout every change at Lakeside during this period, Krasner continued to book as many famous bands as he could. Phil Harris, the popular bandleader on *The Jack Benny Program* and star of his own radio show, played the park twice. When Harris returned to Lakeside for a one-night engagement in 1939, two years after his first appearance there, the *Denver Post* reported that the park charged the lowest price it had ever set for a one-night band performance in an effort to allow as many people as possible to see the popular bandleader and radio star. The programs at Lakeside's and Elitch's ballrooms proved so popular that they were broadcast live over the radio. Elitch's program, titled *An Evening at the Troc*, went out live over KOA every Saturday night, while a teenaged Gene Amole, eventually a legend in Denver radio and a widely read columnist for the *Rocky Mountain News*, broadcast from Lakeside's El Patio on station KYMR.[21]

By 1940, Lakeside's new identity as a blue-collar amusement park was secure. More thrilling rides, popular restaurants, and an Art Deco makeover confirmed the park's new image and allowed it to survive during a difficult period when numerous other parks around the country went bankrupt and closed. The customers loved it. As the 1940 season came to an end, Benjamin Krasner promised to continue his remodeling of Lakeside in 1941, but he did so knowing that war might erupt at any time. Many in the amusement park industry wondered how the parks would fare during wartime and if people would still want to visit them. Julian Bamberger, head of Lagoon Resort in Salt Lake City, addressed the issue at the December 1940 meeting of the National Association of Amusement Parks, Pools, and Beaches. He argued that not only would the American public still want to visit amusement parks but that the need for escape would be greater than ever as tensions increased. Bamberger argued that operators "should not let the public down" and that they should "as never before give them the best we can offer," as amusement parks offered a perfect escape from stressful times. War meant that more people were returning to work and earning money but also that they were finding fewer goods to spend that money on, so amusement parks were the ideal places to spend free time and excess money. Bamberger wanted the parks to play a role during the war, and both Lakeside and Elitch's would do their best to follow his advice and assist people "in the gentle art of funmaking."[22]

As the world waited for what would happen next, on February 9, 1941, Benjamin Krasner married Miriam Caplan of Kansas City, Missouri. After their wedding at the BMH Synagogue in Denver, the couple honeymooned in California. They eventually had one child, a daughter named Rhoda. The proud father renamed the lake at the park Lake Rhoda in her honor. The outbreak of war on December 7, 1941, put a stop to normal operations at amusement parks throughout the country. Wartime rationing often made it nearly impossible for parks to keep up with anything but basic maintenance, and adding new rides was extremely difficult. But, at the same time, huge crowds appeared at the parks. In 1943, for example, a record 43 million people visited the amusement parks on Coney Island.[23]

The war had been under way for several months when Lakeside opened for its 1942 season. The previous season had seen business up by 12 percent overall, with the biggest opening week attendance in a decade (up by 20 percent, Krasner told *Billboard*). Even with the war on, park owners hoped for a good 1942 season, and articles in *Billboard* urged park owners to make wartime necessities such as blackouts a game rather than something to fear. At Lakeside, material and labor shortages caused by the war slowed progress on Krasner's ongoing renovations, but he pushed ahead with them as best he could. For the most part, however, the park attempted to operate as normally as possible. Management even advertised in *Billboard* in April 1942 for a new roller coaster operator and a new superintendent who needed to be "experienced, capable of handling help," and able to "take charge of twelve rides." In addition to the new Merry-Go-Round Building unveiled that summer, visitors also found extensive changes in rides, according to *Billboard*, and got to enjoy the debut of the Henry Busse band at the El Patio Ballroom.[24]

The war years were profitable for Lakeside, largely because an influx of military personnel and war workers into the Denver area gave the park a massive new customer base. Prior to the war, Denver's leaders, struggling with the effects of the Depression, realized there was money to be made in the defense industry, and in 1937 the city convinced the army to locate an Air Corps training center in the area by floating $750,000 in bonds to buy the 880-acre Agnes Memorial Sanitarium at East Sixth Avenue and Quebec Street. The city added 960 acres of land to the property, which became Lowry Air Base, and within six years thousands of men were on the base learning aerial techniques. At the same time, the World War I–era Fitzsimmons Army Hospital underwent an extensive renovation. The war buildup was so fast and large that the base was soon inadequate, and in May 1942 construction began on another base, Buckley Field, southeast of Lowry. It opened six weeks later. Other military installations, including the Rocky Mountain Arsenal, the Remington Denver Ordnance Plant, and the Carothers-Clark Egg Dehydration Plant, transformed Denver into a city facing labor shortages, and people looking for work flooded the city. Soldiers also inundated Denver as, in addition to the air bases, they were also stationed and trained at Camp George West in Golden, Fort Logan on the southwest edge of Denver, and the Medical Supply Depot at Thirty-Eighth and York. An estimated 4 million servicemen and women passed through Denver during World War II, and the city tried to be a good host. USO clubs sprang up throughout Denver, private individuals greeted trains and took soldiers out to eat at local restaurants, and firemen convinced motorists headed for the mountains to take along bored soldiers who had nothing else to do for the day.[25]

To both transport the large numbers of new people and ease problems caused by gas and rubber shortages, Denver revived its tramway system, which stopped at Lakeside and Elitch's. By 1943 the number of military personnel in Denver was up dramatically, and *Billboard* wrote that both parks expected "hefty play" for the summer, largely because of their locations on the tramway lines. At Lakeside, management gave between 3,000 and 6,000 tickets to soldiers each week during the war, which allowed free entry to the park and half-price tickets to all rides. Even after the war ended, Krasner continued the policy for the 1946 season, giving 3,000 tickets a week to the local

USO. Elitch's was more generous, admitting every soldier in uniform and allowing them on every ride for free for the duration of the war.[26]

Crowds at Lakeside had their chance to show their disgust with Adolph Hitler when management attached a picture of the German leader to an outside wall of the Fun House and allowed guests to throw baseballs at it. The park, though, tried to stay focused on fun, the eventual end of the war, and the bright future that was sure to follow. The park's slogan for 1942 was "For Fun in '42, Just Make It Lakeside." One advertisement in 1944 stated that "Lakeside looks ahead to the end of the war" and the completion of an improvement program that would make it "the greatest amusement park in the entire West." Sadly, two tragedies less than ten days apart made for a grim start to Denver's 1944 amusement park season. At Lakeside, on June 25 the brakes on the Cyclone coaster failed, and a fully loaded train crashed into another train at the loading platform. Park employees William Haffner and Purlie Douglas grabbed onto the train and tried to stop it when they realized the brakes had failed, but it still managed to travel seventy-five feet past its normal stopping point. Seven people were injured; and eighteen-year-old Bonnie Hicks of Denver, who was in the third car, became frightened, jumped from the train, and struck a support beam, causing a fatal skull fracture.[27]

The accident at Lakeside came just nine days after the worst amusement park tragedy in Denver history had occurred at Elitch Gardens. On June 16, fire broke out in the park's Old Mill ride, and within minutes it was out of control, with smoke billowing 150 feet in the air. Six people became trapped in the ride and died when park employees and firefighters were unable to reach them. Horrified Denverites questioned the safety of the ride and why it had taken so long for anyone at the park to report the fire. The 135-page report from the coroner's inquest blamed the age of the attraction, ignorance, neglect, and carelessness for the tragedy, which happened on the exact site of an attraction destroyed by fire in 1914. Elitch's historian Betty Hull wrote that Arnold Gurtler heard the victims' screams until the day he died.[28]

By the time Lakeside opened for the 1945 season, the war in Europe was over but fighting still raged in the Pacific. The highlight of the last wartime season at Lakeside was an appearance by Tony Pastor and His Orchestra, whose hits included "Let's Do It" and "Paradiddle Joy." According to the *Denver Post*, the "all season clamor" at Lakeside that year had been "we want

Pastor." The end of Pastor's first week at the park coincided with V-J Day, and the *Post* reported that crowds flocked to see the man who once had "a caddy to carry his sax case" (the caddy was bandleader Artie Shaw). With the war over, Pastor's appearance was a sign that the good times at Lakeside were only going to get better. The park managed to host its usual "flashy fireworks display" under the supervision of longtime park electrician John Flohr. Krasner reported that attendance was up 20 percent over the 1944 season.[29]

With wartime rationing coming to an end, Krasner was free to move forward with more remodeling at the park, and he spent $125,000 on landscaping, painting, and other projects in time for the 1946 season. A storm dumped five inches of snow in Denver on opening day that year, but a large crowd bundled up in heavy coats and turned out to watch Krasner turn on the Tower lights and officially open the park for the season on May 19. Two days later, with the snow gone, 24,000 people passed through the gates. The Lakeside that opened on that snowy day in 1946 operated in a very different city than the one it had served before the war began. The city's population boomed as military personnel, who remembered Denver as a friendly town, returned after the war to attend school and start families. One survey reported that as many as 92 percent of the military men stationed in Denver wanted to come back. The influx of newcomers, along with the return of longtime residents, transformed Denver from a "drowsy provincial city into a sprawling metropolis," as the population grew from 322,000 in 1940 to 415,000 in 1950. In 1946 the city issued a record 5,198 building permits, and the fast-growing city needed new leadership with new ideas. The next year, thirty-five-year-old Quigg Newton, who promised to reform City Hall, defeated the seventy-seven-year-old four-term incumbent mayor Benjamin Stapleton. Newton quickly implemented his reform agenda, creating the Career Service Authority, redrawing city council districts, reforming trash collection, and revamping Denver General Hospital. Newton also reorganized the planning office to deal with a "rapidly growing city that lacked a vision for its future."[30]

Much was unclear when it came to Denver's future, including whether the City Beautiful concept had a place in it. By the mid-1940s, the City Beautiful movement had fallen on hard times in Denver, one of the few cities where it still clung to life. Like Lakeside, the once-stately Civic Center Park, the most visible symbol of the City Beautiful movement, was surrounded by less-than-desirable businesses, including "bars, strip joints, and even a mortuary." City planner Maxine Kurtz decided to take on the challenge of cleaning up the park and tried to complete Robert Speer's dream of surrounding it with government offices. In 1955 the new Denver Public Library opened on the southwest side of the park, followed by the Denver Art Museum. Kurtz also encouraged the clustering of new state office buildings on the east side of the park. The work helped reinvent Civic Center as a city gathering place, just as Benjamin Krasner's reinvention of Lakeside once again made it a thriving business.[31]

Just as the old guard in Denver was giving way to new leaders and new ideas, two deaths in the second half of the 1940s marked the final passing of Lakeside's early leadership. On January 8, 1947, longtime park owner and manager Phillip Friederich died in a Fredericksburg, Texas, hospital at age fifty-six from injuries he sustained in a car accident several days earlier. Two-and-a-half years later, on July 7, 1949, his uncle, William Buck, died in Denver at age eighty-nine. The last two founders of Lakeside were gone. Obituaries for both men noted that, among their many other accomplishments, they were instrumental in founding and running the park for many years, even though they had not been associated with it for a long while.[32]

Throughout the rest of the 1940s, Krasner continued making modifications to the park in a never-ending effort to keep it thriving. With the Art Deco makeover largely complete by the end of the war, Krasner focused his efforts on rides and attractions rather than remodeling buildings. The parking lot was paved for the first time, a move *Billboard* said would be "pleasing" to the drivers of the thousands of cars it could hold. Krasner actually had to scale back on the number of picnics and other special events the park hosted as, even with the vastly improved picnic facilities, the park was unable to handle the picnic crowds that descended on it. As a result, Krasner booked only school picnics in an effort to help the schools with their special events. Krasner also removed the Sunken Gardens from the old Shoot-the-Chutes pool in the late 1940s, making it the home for Skoota Boats, newly imported from England. The gas-powered boats were described by the *Denver Post* as "the same idea as the scooter cars—you whiz around the water bumping into other customers." The boats were a novelty in the United States, and the only other ride like it was in New York City. Skoota Boats was the first of several European rides Krasner brought to his park.[33]

By 1949, the pattern at both Lakeside and Elitch's was well-established. Constant innovation along with big-name bands seemed to be the formula by which both parks could survive. Lakeside booked the famous trumpet player Sonny Dunham and pianist Frankie Carle, while Elitch's had Dick Jurgens and Lawrence Welk. Redesigned landscaping, new rides, heavy advertising, and special picnics characterized both parks' business models as they competed for every customer. By the end of the 1940s, they were not just competing against each other. New venues, such as the Denver area's first legal dog track, Mile High Greyhound Park in Commerce City, helped pull customers away from the amusement parks. Arnold Gurtler's son Jack believed business at Elitch's would be down 8 percent to 10 percent for the 1949 season as a result of the track's opening and resorted to placing Day-Glo signs advertising Elitch's on the fronts of Denver's streetcars.[34]

David Nasaw began his book *Going Out* by observing that "they are all gone now," referring to the stately movie theaters, baseball parks, and "amusement parks with their acres of roller coasters, tilt-a-whirls, chutes, and carousels." They had been victims, he writes, of racial problems, seedy reputations, and competition from theme parks. Those that survived, such as Kennywood and Cedar Point, did so because "they were not linked to the central city by mass transit." Yet Lakeside, linked to Denver by streetcar until 1950 and then by bus, did survive. Benjamin Krasner's ability and willingness to adapt Lakeside to changing times and conditions clearly worked well for his amusement park, and it continued to delight and entertain when others built during the same period were no more than distant memories. With Krasner in charge, Lakeside Amusement Park was more than ready for a new decade and some surprising new challenges.[35]

Interior of El Patio Ballroom, 1927. *(DPL Western History, X-27612)*

The wilder Derby coaster, 1912. *(Author's Collection)*

Menu from the Plantation restaurant, 1926. *(Author's Collection)*

Joe Mann's Orchestra in the Jail restaurant . . . *(DPL Western History, X-27619)*

... and its tin cups. *(Author's Collection)*

Program from Lakeside's greyhound track, 1927. *(Author's Collection)*

Aerial view of Lakeside in the late 1920s, with the greyhound track in the lower left corner. *(DPL Western History, X-27622)*

Benjamin Krasner at the park, early 1950s. *(Denver and Rio Grande Western Railroad Photograph Collection, Lakeside Amusement Park, Box 9 FF358, History Colorado, Denver)*

Lakeside from Sheridan Boulevard, with a Denver Tramway car passing in front. The Cyclone coaster is in the center of the picture. *(Author's Collection)*

College Inn in the Casino. *(DPL Western History, X-27607)*

One of the steam engines outside the train station, 1970s. *(Author's Collection)*

Lakeside's old auto entrance on Sheridan Boulevard. The Speedway is visible through the gate. *(DPL, Richard Crowther Collection)*

Lakeside's popular Tumble Bug ride. *(Author's Collection)*

Stainless steel rocket ship cars on Lakeside's original Circle Swing ride. *(Author's Collection)*

Denver Tramway ad for Lakeside's 1947 season. *(Author's Collection)*

CHAPTER 6

Lakeside Speedway and the Roaring Bugs of Speed

The biggest, loudest, and most visible sign of Lakeside Amusement Park's transformation from an elite, City Beautiful park to a working-class park was Lakeside Speedway, a one-fifth-mile oval race track built on the south side of the park in 1938. Within a few weeks of its grand opening, the Speedway became one of the top attractions at Lakeside, consistently drawing 6,000–7,000 customers every Sunday. At the peak of its popularity, after the track became more established, it was not uncommon to find 10,000–11,000 people in the stands on race night. The Speedway, more than anything else, confirmed Lakeside's new working-class reputation; as driver Wayne Arner said, the Speedway was "very blue collar."[1]

The first racecars at Lakeside Speedway were midgets, essentially small replicas of regulation-size racecars with wheel bases of about sixty inches and weighing around 500 pounds (they later increased in weight to close to 1,000 pounds). Midgets first appeared around 1914 in California but were little more than a hobby for the teenagers who built and drove them prior to World War I. When they revived in the 1920s, racing was, according to midget racing historian Jack Fox, "disorganized at best" and did not truly take off until the 1930s when two California midget builders, Ken Brenneman and "Hap" Woodman, convinced the managers of the Santa Ana Municipal Stadium and the Oakland Speedway to allow them to hold races. The early midget races were little more than sideshows sandwiched between the more elaborate motorcycle and large-car races, but despite their shaky start the midgets steadily gained in popularity throughout California. With the sport seemingly operating on a permanent basis near the end of 1933, building the cars became big business and several of the early drivers, including Brenneman, focused on building rather than racing them. In 1934, oilman Earl Gilmore built Gilmore Stadium in Los Angeles and opened it to the midget racers. Having a permanent home secured the sport's popularity in California and allowed it to start its spread across the United States. By 1934 it had reached New York, New Jersey, Ohio, Wisconsin, Missouri, and Illinois, reaching Denver and Hawaii the next year.[2]

Historian Louisa Ward Arps wrote that early automobile owners in Denver frequently raced on makeshift tracks all over the city, as well as up and down Federal Boulevard and South Logan Street. Perhaps the most famous of the early tracks was the one-mile oval-shaped track at Overland Park (originally named Jewell Park when it was built by the Denver Circle Railroad) in southwest Denver. First used for horse races, enthusiasts next tried racing bicycles, but the sand in the track soon put a stop to that. Overland was perfect, however, for motorcycle racing, which became the next big draw there. Car races soon followed, and as cars became more sophisticated, the stunts became zanier. Ivy Baldwin, who had taken part in hot air balloon ascensions at Elitch's and Manhattan Beach, attempted to tie a balloon to a Stanley Steamer before having the car race at top speed around the track. The scheme flopped when Baldwin's gas generator failed on the first day and filled the balloon until it burst on the second day. The famous driver Barney Oldfield, the first man to drive a car at sixty miles per hour, attempted to race an airplane flying above the Overland track but called it off after the plane did one loop and encountered mechanical problems. Oldfield's failed stunt did succeed in bringing airplane demonstrations to Overland; in November 1910, three Wright biplanes visited the park. Pilot Arch Hoxsey flew one of the planes all the way to Lakeside Amusement Park and back.[3]

The last big race at Overland was in July 1925, when the Denver Press Club sponsored a 100-mile race and offered $10,000 in prizes. When Denver (which had bought the park after World War I and turned it into an automobile camp) closed the auto camp in 1930, it also tore up the race track to make way for the golf course that now occupies the site. In Overland's absence, tracks quickly popped up all over the Denver area. One of the biggest was DuPont Speedway in Commerce City, which had a half-mile dirt oval and a five-eighths-mile paved oval track. The School of Mines in Golden had a one-fifth-mile dirt oval track constructed at its stadium in 1938, and another one-fifth-mile dirt track was located near Higley Airport at Twenty-Sixth Avenue and Oneida Street in 1936. By the late 1930s there were tracks as far as away as Akron, Alamosa, Colorado Springs, Glenwood Springs, Greeley, Pueblo, Sterling, and Trinidad.[4]

Billy Betteridge, a pioneer of California midget racing, staged a midget exhibition at DuPont Speedway in Commerce City in 1933, but the first true midget races in Denver took place in 1935 on the old Bundes Turnfest field at Lakeside Amusement Park. The event's organizers scheduled a total of six programs for the summer, with eleven races per program. The first races were on June 19, and the *Rocky Mountain News* reported that they had "the spectators on their toes thruout [sic] the evening," although only ten drivers competed. Lou Erwin, the only local driver, was the crowd favorite; it was the biggest disappointment of the evening when, after doing well in the time trials, he bent a wheel and pulled a tire on his Bugatti-powered car, eliminating him from the remaining races. Pat Cunningham, an experienced midget racer from California, was the odds-on favorite to win the final twenty-lap event after having won the preceding four races. During the final race, however, the chain drive on his car broke, and Bill Werner, driving the Henderson Special, won, followed by Jimmy Robins in second and Salt Lake City driver Spec Hemminger in third. Other drivers at the first race included Chuck Boyer, Cliff Moyer, Swede Williams, Jim Roberts, and Theodore Hemberger.[5]

Drivers ran the second series of races at Lakeside two days later with another local driver, Romey Pedroza, joining the participants. Pedroza's driving career was short-lived, but he went on to greater fame because of his mechanical expertise, especially with Offenhauser engines. Cunningham was again the odds-on favorite to win the final event as he "puffed away nonchalantly on his cigaret [sic] and pushed the throttle to the floorboard" to win four of the ten races. But, as with the first round, during the final twenty-five-lap race his car "sputtered, popped once or twice and called it quits for the night," and he lost to Jimmy Robins. In fact, Robins was the only driver who finished the final race after all the others cars developed disabling engine troubles. The *Rocky Mountain News* excitedly described the midgets as "roaring motor bugs of speed, spitting blue fire in the straight-away and skidding perilously around curves," but with so few competitors, the races failed to hold the public's attention. After running the first two programs, the organizers suspended the races while the drivers revamped the track. A brief article in the *Rocky Mountain News* on July 12, 1935, implied that fans found the Lakeside track boring and assured readers that "for the benefit of cash customers demanding a few more thrills," the new design was far more hazardous. Among other changes, the drivers lengthened the track to accommodate shorter curves and increase "its trickiness." When the races resumed on July 13, five more cars joined the field, including another local driver, Ted Dumbauld, bringing the total to fifteen. The "roaring motor bugs" may have returned in force, but the *News* never reported any results of the races.[6]

At the next week's races, Pat Cunningham remained the favorite to win. The newspaper described him as "heavy footed and fearing nothing" once he was in the cockpit of his car, making him the obvious star among the "nerveless drivers" at Lakeside. The same field of drivers from the week before competed, joined by a few new ones, though the paper failed to include their names. Fans also witnessed the first midget racing accident in Denver history when Ted Dumbauld's Bugatti-powered car flipped over head-first. Dumbauld was not seriously injured, but the wreck eliminated him from the race and gave the victory to Cunningham. On July 19 the *News* reported, with some uncertainty, that the races were expected to return the following week, with seven drivers from Omaha joining. But even the redesigned track failed to hold the public's attention, and Lakeside's first attempt at midget racing proved disappointing. With few cars and drivers, the public seems to have quickly lost interest in the new sport, and newspaper coverage of the races all but disappeared. In fact, baseball and softball games at Lakeside received almost twice as much coverage as the final four midget races.[7]

Two years later, promoters decided to bring midget racing to Denver a second time, with the first races on May 9, 1937, at Merchant's Park, the old baseball field at Center Avenue and Broadway. In its second go-round, the sport proved much more popular than it had two years earlier, in part because a "real promoter," Tom Holden, who had been running big-car races in Kansas, was behind the attempt. The midget track at Merchant's Park was a one-fifth-mile dirt oval, with a 90-degree turn at what was home plate. The new track was popular, but many drivers, including Lloyd Axel and his racing partner, Vic Felt, were disappointed that Merchant's Park only allowed small engines. Seeking a track where they could use bigger and more powerful motors, Axel convinced his friend Benjamin Krasner, the new owner of Lakeside, that the amusement park would be an ideal spot for a second Denver track. Drivers Jerry Brown and Sonny Coleman remembered that Krasner loved racecars, and he was thrilled with the idea of once again having them at his park. As soon as Krasner approved, Axel and his friends built the one-fifth-mile dirt track in "no time at all," and Lakeside Speedway opened on April 24, 1938.[8]

The drivers built the Speedway on the site of the arena built for the German-American Bundes Turnfest in 1913, the same spot at which the 1935 races had taken place. A new, covered grandstand was built on the west side of the new track, which was also the site of the announcer's booth, located above turn four, and the race officials' booth. Krasner made various additions to the grandstands in the years he operated the Speedway, most of them in the same covered style as the original grandstands, with backs on the seats for comfort. In the late 1950s Krasner filled in a small portion of the pits with open-bleacher seating. The original guardrail around the track was initially one rail high, but by 1953 it had three rails on it, supported by wooden posts driven deep into the ground. The flagman's area at the start/finish line (which was hit by cars more than once over the years) was protected by the same type of guardrail, and the track eventually added a green/yellow/red light system at the end of each straightaway to alert drivers to track conditions. The pits were located at the south end of the stands and separated from the track by a board fence. The entrance to the pits from the track was at the end of turn two, while the entrance to the track from the pits was located at the end of the front straight in turn one. The main entrance to the Speedway was on the north end, where the ticket booth and main concession stand were located. There were additional concession stands south of the east stands and in the pits. The car entrance was on the south end of the track. In time, a heavy chain-link fence was installed along the front of the grandstands to protect spectators from flying debris, a common hazard at the races.[9]

The track itself was, as driver Bob Olds called it, "a pain in the ass." At only one-fifth of a mile long, the track was both short and narrow, although not as narrow as some other tracks the same size. The track ran from north to south, with the back straightaway going downhill and the front straightaway going uphill. The north turn of the track was banked and the south turn was flat, which was unusual as most tracks in the country either had two banked or two flat turns. According to Sonny Coleman, legend held that during the track's construction, workers had already dug down to build the south turn and were doing the same on the north turn when they ran into an underground river, preventing them from having two flat turns. To take advantage of the unusual design, cars needed to run high on the north turn and slow down on the south turn (the sight of many accidents, according to Leroy Byers). Very few drivers mastered passing on the south turn, said Coleman, although if a driver could stay alongside the car he wanted to pass while in the south turn, he "had him beat." But according to driver Charlie Gottschalck, for drivers who learned to race at Lakeside, it was an easy track. In fact, many drivers said, learning on Lakeside's challenging track made it easier to race on any other track they might encounter. Gene Pastor was one of the few drivers who remembered Lakeside as anything but difficult, calling it a "fun track." Pastor was only seventeen when he rolled a midget at Lakeside in 1958, well under the minimum driving age of twenty-one. Pastor's father was well aware of the fact that his son was underage, Wayne Arner recalled, but the other drivers were afraid of the elder Pastor so they let his son go ahead and race. Sonny Coleman also remembered the Speedway as a fun but still challenging track.[10]

Lloyd Axel won the opening race in 1938 in front of a crowd of 3,000 people. Because it was better organized and had a bigger field of drivers than in 1935, news of the new track spread rapidly, and the crowds grew larger with each week's races. The popularity of the midget races at Lakeside Speedway with both the park's regular customers and racing fans around the state made Krasner a "staunch supporter" of the sport. One of the earliest advertisements for the Speedway proclaimed that there were "plenty of thrills when these speed-mad drivers race for first place," and customers happily paid the forty-cent admission fee to secure a seat in the stands (admission to the park at the time was only ten cents). Watching the races became a popular Sunday afternoon and evening activity for families, who would attend church in the morning and then spend the rest of the day at Lakeside watching the speed-mad drivers. With the surging popularity of the races, Krasner invested an additional $25,000 in the Speedway in 1939, paving the track for the first time and enlarging the grandstands to hold 5,000 spectators.[11]

On May 14, 1939, the opening day of racing season, a standing-room-only crowd packed the Speedway's grandstands; two weeks later, five of the thirty-seven Offenhauser-powered midgets that existed in the United States appeared at Lakeside, including one owned by Denverite Judd Pickup (the first Offy-powered car in Denver). Spectators were also treated to one of the most remarkable accidents in the sport's short history that summer when driver Bob Vorbeck attempted to pass another car. After hitting one of the hay bales that lined the track, which sent him bouncing back into the car he was trying to pass, Vorbeck's car flipped several times, at one point launching twenty feet into the air, before rolling to a stop. Incredibly, Vorbeck was uninjured. The 1939 season ended with a 100-lap finale on October 1. The American Automobile Association (AAA) became the first sanctioning body for the midget races that year, though the next year the racers voted to form their own club, the Rocky Mountain Midget Racing Association (RMMRA), with Lloyd Axel as the first president.[12]

By July 1938 it was obvious that Lakeside was outdrawing Merchant's Park on Sundays, prompting promoter and flagman Tom Holden to switch the races at Merchant's to Tuesdays, Wednesdays, and Fridays, without success. Finally, in mid-August he halted the races at Merchant's Park and waited for Lakeside's season to end in September, after which he staged eight more races at the old track. Holden struggled to come up with a winning program for Merchant Park's 1939 season, and in September he decided that he simply could not compete with the larger, popular, and more organized Lakeside Speedway. In addition to the quality of the track, Lakeside's location appealed to both drivers and fans. Many of the midget drivers lived in North Denver or the northern suburbs; as Foster Campbell's son Bob said, Lakeside Speedway's location was "convenient." If a car happened to break down during a race, it was easy for drivers to go home and get parts or other supplies. For drivers heading to tracks on either the East or West Coast, Lakeside was almost the only track at which they could get in some race time on their journey. In later years, as Lakeside Speedway's reputation grew, it became a destination rather than simply a stopping point. Drivers coming from the

West Coast made sure to carry canvas to cover their cars as they drove over Loveland Pass to prevent gravel and rocks from damaging them. As driver Gene Pastor remembered, the track was "talked about all over the country."[13]

Most of the drivers who raced at Lakeside believed the Speedway helped carry the amusement park through a number of very tough years in the 1930s and 1940s, with one driver estimating that the park earned between $100,000 and $300,000 per year from the track alone. According to the drivers, Krasner knew how important the Speedway was. Leroy Byers, a well-known midget racing photographer and historian, said Krasner willingly paid appearance money to get big-name drivers to appear at the Speedway. In 1947, for example, the Jimmie James Team appeared at Lakeside for three days, which resulted in a big article in the *Denver Post* promoting the Speedway (and the amusement park). James owned three black midgets, numbered 28, 38, and 48, and hauled them on a matching black trailer; more than sixty years later, other midget drivers vividly remembered the impressive sight of those three cars and their trailer at Lakeside. Out-of-towners drove two of the cars, with prewar midget champion Ernie Gessell driving 48 and Californian Johnnie Parsons driving 38. Denver driver Aaron Woodard was fortunate enough to drive the 28 car. After Gessell and Parsons lost their first races, Woodard got permission from Krasner to set the James cars up to race on the Speedway's difficult track, providing better entertainment for the crowds in the stands.[14]

Lakeside Speedway became the undoing of many drivers who were used to what Gene Pastor called "pretty tracks." Arrogant out-of-town drivers expected to go in, handily defeat local drivers, and win points and prize money, referring to the practice as "picking cherries." As both Wayne Arner and Leroy Byers said, however, the "local drivers suckered them," as the visitors simply could not do things at Lakeside Speedway that they could at other tracks. Local drivers knew, for example, that they needed to slow down on the south turn of the track and stay to the inside. Out-of-town drivers mistakenly believed they could pass the locals by speeding up and staying high on the turn, which resulted in most of them spinning out and allowed the local drivers to pull ahead. Local drivers also knew how to place the weight in their cars to take advantage of the Speedway track, something out-of-state drivers did not learn until they had been at the track for two or three weeks. Locals also knew how to modify the chassis of their cars to handle the track (as Leroy Byers said, Lakeside "didn't take much of a motor, but you had to have a chassis you could handle") and what tires to put on their cars (Avon Junior Formula 1). Tires were the key to racing at Lakeside, according to Sonny Coleman, because the asphalt at the Speedway was different from what drivers at bigger tracks were familiar with, and the position of the sun at different times further altered the consistency of the track as it heated and cooled. Dempsey Wilson, a big-name midget driver, appeared at Lakeside and did poorly until a few locals helped him with some tips on how to set up his car. A few other "smart drivers," as Coleman referred to them, figured it out as well, but they were rare. As late as the 1970s and 1980s, big-name racecar drivers came to Lakeside for the Rocky Mountain Classic as they sought points in their run for the national championships. Almost without exception, they failed at Lakeside, much to the delight of local fans.[15]

Krasner was certainly willing to pay to get famous drivers to the Speedway, but he was even more generous to local drivers. Sonny Coleman, Bob Olds, and Leroy Byers vividly remembered Krasner helping out the local drivers as much as possible, with Coleman saying that if not for Krasner and his generosity, half of the midgets in Denver would never have been able to run for a full season. Krasner went so far as to loan some drivers the money to buy new motors if their cars needed them, and almost without fail, said Coleman, the drivers repaid him. Miles Spickler raced a Kurtis Kraft car that originally had a Drake engine in it, which was essentially a souped-up motorcycle engine. In 1947 he put an Offy engine in the car, but even it soon needed parts to keep running. Anxious to have Spickler and his car at the Speedway, Krasner loaned him the money to make the necessary repairs. Krasner also loaned Lloyd Axel the money to buy a new car (as much as $3,800) based on just a phone call Axel made from California. At the same time, said Wayne Arner, Krasner "never cheated anybody," and when a driver won on race night "Ben paid what he said" the prize money for the night would be. As Bob Olds recalled, Krasner "ran the pay window, he ran the pit gate, he knew what was coming in and going out." Krasner's generosity and honesty earned him enormous respect from the drivers. While Krasner enjoyed the sport and respected the drivers, keeping the cars running and the drivers happy also kept the races competitive, which in turn increased the crowds at the Speedway and the amusement park on Sunday nights.[16]

Many famous drivers passed through Lakeside Speedway in the years it operated (including Al and Bobby Unser), while others who started there went on to great fame and fortune in the sport. But two of the men who dominated the sport at the Speedway became true legends in Denver racing. Lloyd Axel was a Denver native, born in June 1905. Axel's first entry into automobile racing came in 1925 at Ord, Nebraska, when he drove a regulation-size car owned by Vic Felt. Over the next twelve years, Axel won main events at race tracks all over the country, but in 1937 midget driver Burton Spickler let Axel drive his midget at Merchant's Park. Axel fell in love with the "Lilliputian racecars," so much so that he was the leader when the racers defected to Lakeside in 1938. In 1940 Axel partnered with Denver race fan Herman Mapelli, owner of Mapelli Meat Company, who bought an Offy engine for Axel's new car; Axel went on to win the 1940 and 1941 Rocky Mountain Midget Racing Association championships. He also came in second to Louie Unser (of the famous racing family) in the 1941 Pikes Peak Auto Hill Climb. When the 1942 season was cut short by war, Axel sold his two racecars and devoted himself to the war effort while also making sure the RMMRA was ready to resume racing when the war ended.[17]

Axel purchased two new cars for the 1946 season, but he never won another championship. In 1946 he came in second behind Johnny Tolan. Axel traveled for the next two years, and when he returned to Denver in 1950 he formed his own club, the Mile High Racing Association (MHRA), and helped run rival Englewood Speedway, much to the dismay of many longtime Denver racers. After one season the MHRA folded, and Axel largely retired from active racing. Although he died in 1971, he is still remembered as the bad guy of Lakeside Speedway, the consequence of winning so many times.[18]

Johnny Tolan, another Colorado native, "probably did more to put Denver midget racing in front of a national audience than any other single competitor from the Mile High State," writes Bill Hill. Tolan was born in Victor, Colorado, in 1918 and eventually moved with his family to Denver, where he became a football star at St. Francis High School. After graduating, he worked in his father's plumbing business and had no intention of becoming a racing star until he saw his first "big-car" race at DuPont Speedway in Commerce City in 1938. Convinced to try it himself, Tolan decided to start with the midgets. He built his own car and debuted in 1939 at both Lakeside Speedway and Merchant's Park. He won the first race in which he competed, which also happened to be his only win that season. By 1941 Tolan had advanced to driving one of owner Charlie Allen's cars, but during World War II he left racing to join the Marines.[19]

Tolan returned to Denver and Lakeside Speedway in 1946 and went on to win the 1946 and 1947 RMMRA championships. He started the 1948 season with several wins in car number 1, which his 1947 sponsor, Roy Leslie, purchased for him, but he left before the season ended to compete in bigger venues. After forty-three career wins in Denver, he never again won a race in the city, although he returned several times. Tolan moved to racing big cars, competing in three Indianapolis 500s in the 1950s. According to Wayne Arner, Tolan's good looks made him enormously popular among women who attended the races, which happened more frequently when he was racing, and more of his headshots were handed out to them at Lakeside Speedway than those of any other driver.[20]

While drivers like Axel and Tolan helped draw crowds, the sound of the track also helped draw people in. The roar of the engines at the Speedway quickly became one of the most distinctive features of the park. The races at Lakeside Speedway were loud, so much so that they could be heard for miles around the park. Rhoda Krasner remembered hearing the roar of the engines, which she called "powerful and inviting," from her family's home near Sloan's Lake, about twenty blocks south of the park. As one driver said, "The sounds, the smell, everything about it attracted people." The only other sound from Lakeside remembered as vividly as the roar of engines at the Speedway is that of Laffing Sal's laughter reverberating across the lake.[21]

Between twenty-five and thirty cars competed each race night, with twelve to fourteen cars per event, a far better field than the handful of cars and drivers that were there for the first attempt in 1935. Photographer Jerry Miller said the goal was to get through a race without an accident, but the races could be quite dangerous. One of the first major accidents at Lakeside Speedway happened in May 1940 when a wheel came off Lloyd Axel's car and flew into the stands, injuring three people, one seriously. The accident did nothing to diminish the popularity of the races, and on May 4, 1941, the first day of racing that season, over 4,000 people filled the grandstands. The first midget racing fatality in Denver happened that season when, on August 10, Carroll Kelly swerved to miss an accident in front of him and rolled his car several times. His injuries included a fractured skull, crushed chest, and broken shoulder. He died from his injuries the following February. In another accident, driver Vic Schey was fatally injured on July 4, 1942. Both Schey and his brother Buddy Shay (who changed the spelling to help with the pronunciation) were popular drivers at Lakeside. At the time of his fatal accident, Schey and his brother had rigged a midget with a foot throttle on the left to accommodate his broken leg. Buddy was never certain if his brother's foot got tangled in the throttle or if the throttle got stuck, but he crashed the car into the fence, flipped over on the guardrail, and rolled several times. He died from his injuries three days later. The next week's race, held to benefit Vic Schey's family, drew the largest crowd yet at the Speedway, with 7,095 people in the stands.[22]

Another fatality occurred when a driver was ejected from his car as he lost control on one of the track's turns. He survived, only to be run over by the cars behind him as his helpless and horrified wife and children watched from the stands. Sonny Coleman said it was not unusual to lose one or two drivers a year to accidents at Lakeside, in addition to fans receiving minor injuries from flying debris. The advent of safety equipment in the 1950s and 1960s for both fans and drivers helped cut down on injuries. Of particular importance for the drivers were roll bars, which were attached just behind the cockpit on midget cars. The installation of a chain-link fence on the grandstands helped protect fans from flying debris from accidents.[23]

The 1942 racing season opened with the threat that the government would shut down auto racing to save on rubber and gasoline usage during wartime, but over 7,000 people packed the stands at the Speedway each night until the government order came through on July 29. As many drivers left to join the military, the 1942 season witnessed a steadily decreasing number of cars competing in the races, with only eleven in the final 100-lap race on July 29. A record seven cars completed the race. To keep the race track active, Krasner teamed with promoter Johnny Atkins to stage outdoor wrestling and boxing matches, which according to *Billboard* were the first outdoor wrestling matches in Denver in years, but the crowds were disappointingly small. When racing finally resumed on May 22, 1946, over 11,000 people were there, seriously overcrowding the stands and overwhelming police who were trying to direct traffic around the park. People in cars heading to the Speedway eventually gave up on getting any closer to Lakeside, parked their cars wherever they could, and walked—sometimes up to two miles—to the park. After the races were over that night, the crowd ripped down part of the fence around Lakeside to create another exit from the lot. Many people claimed the resulting mess was Denver's first traffic jam.[24]

The overcrowded stands and Denver's first traffic jam demonstrated how deep America's love affair with the car had become by 1946. The affair was slow to start, with only 8,000 cars on the road in 1900. But after the upheaval of the Great Depression of the 1930s and war shortages in the 1940s, interest in cars surged. After sixteen years of struggling to survive, automobile manufacturers found themselves struggling to meet demand. People who had never been able to afford a car prior to 1929 had earned enough money during the war to buy one afterward, and they wanted to join the car culture. By 1950, car companies were producing between 5 million and 6 million cars a year and even at that were barely able to keep up with demand. Everything associated with cars exploded after the war as well—highways, hotels and motels for travelers, gas stations, and racing.[25]

The surging popularity of midget racing led to the creation of the first midget racing circuit in Colorado in 1946 with the opening of tracks in Fort Collins and Colorado Springs, along with the formation of the Colorado Automobile Racing Club. Englewood Speedway, located at West Oxford and Clay Streets, opened the next year, but the RMMRA refused to sanction the track and threatened to fine and suspend any of its members who raced there. Drivers who wanted to race at Englewood formed a new club, the Mile High Racing Association (later known as the Colorado Midget Racing Association), and a number of drivers defected from the RMMRA. Lakeside Speedway remained dominant, however, in part because there was nothing else in town that could compete with it. Denver's only professional sports team was the Denver Bears baseball club, which in 1948 began playing at the new Bears Stadium (later renamed Mile High Stadium). But according to Leroy Byers, a Bears game in the late 1940s might draw 800 or 1,000 spectators (for example, about 125,000 people total attended all the games during the 1947 season), while a race at the Speedway regularly drew several thousand a night. Even the greyhound races at Mile High Greyhound Park, which Elitch's manager Jack Gurtler feared would negatively impact attendance at the amusement parks and which Krasner feared was the one thing that might kill the Speedway, failed to diminish the racing crowds. With no widespread television ownership and no major sports competitors, Lakeside Speedway dominated leisure time in Denver.[26]

A new crop of drivers also helped drive the popularity of the sport. Driver Sonny Coleman, who won the 1950 RMMRA championship at Lakeside, came home from the US Navy after World War II and was unable to find a job right away. He got into racing to "make a few bucks," although he added that racecar drivers were always broke and looking for money. Coleman drove for owner Roy Leslie, taking car 62, which was powered by a Ford V8-60. Drivers typically earned 40 percent of whatever the car won, but because Coleman agreed to stay with the Ford, Leslie gave him 50 percent. He felt comfortable with the Ford and remembered it as a reliable car that never finished worse than fifth in the races. The Ford was not supposed to be as fast as the Offys, although according to Coleman it was fast enough to beat all the Offys some of the time. He had to run it hard to keep up with them, however, and he had a few crashes, the most dramatic of which occurred when the car spun out on freshly laid oil on the track and ended up hitting a telephone pole outside the track. Coleman was not severely injured, fortunately, and when Krasner heard about the accident he called Leslie and apologized profusely. The car was consistent throughout the 1950 season, and it came as somewhat of a surprise when Coleman won the championship that year. A Ford engine had never won a championship at Lakeside until then.[27]

By the late 1940s, the midget racing circuit had grown to include tracks in La Junta, Englewood, Pueblo, and Scottsbluff, Nebraska (though that track lasted only part of one season in the RMMRA). In 1947 Lloyd Axel, who had organized the defection to Lakeside in 1938, led a new group of drivers who broke away from the RMMRA and based themselves at Englewood Speedway, which opened that year. Englewood management found that it was still impossible to compete against the midgets at Lakeside, but they could get big crowds with stock car races. Attendance at Lakeside Speedway was down slightly from the 7,000 that had been common just a few years earlier, but the midget races remained popular and it was not unusual to find 5,000–6,000 people paying fifty cents apiece to sit in the stands at Lakeside on race nights, which moved to Wednesdays and Sundays.[28]

It was obvious by 1950, however, that fans were starting to lose interest in the midgets, as attendance at the races steadily dropped. The mighty RMMRA, which had once reached across Colorado, had only one track left under its control—Lakeside Speedway. Several factors were to blame for the decline. Television ownership became more widespread, camping became popular (especially when people had the ability to put campers on the backs of their trucks), and baseball grew in popularity as well, with the attendance at Bears games climbing steadily, reaching a total of 463,039 for the 1949 season. In addition, young men who had gone off to fight in the war were marrying and starting families, creating new priorities for money formerly spent on entertainment. Drivers Bob Olds and Charlie Gottschalck blamed changes in the midgets for the declining popularity as well. By 1950, according to them, the cars were becoming the same, which made competition between them less exciting. Previously, each builder, owner, and driver imprinted his personality on the cars. Running races three nights a week may have oversaturated the market, in addition to making it expensive for families to attend that many races. Sonny Coleman placed some of the blame for the decline on the midget drivers, saying that they "got too big for their britches," with the RMMRA trying to dictate how Krasner should run the track. The drivers went so far as to try to force him to bring back the AAA as a sanctioning body. Krasner refused, telling the drivers there was not enough money to pay $800 a night to the AAA and that he would either close the track or run only stock cars if they persisted with their demands.[29]

Krasner and the track managers attempted to revive interest in the midgets with a number of changes. They inverted the order of the cars in heat races, with the fastest car starting at the back, but when it came to the feature race the fastest car started on the pole and went on to win the race most of the time. There was a definite lack of action, as the other cars simply fell in line behind the leader and rarely tried to pass. Driver Roy Bowe did a lot of passing on the outside, something Sonny Coleman tried to do in his Ford-powered car as well, much to the surprise of many, but it was not enough to keep spectators interested. The one exception to the follow-the-leader style of racing was the car sponsored by Eddie Bohn's Pig 'n' Whistle restaurant. Made to look like a pig, with a horn that oinked, the car was what Lakeside visitor Frank Jamison called "the joke car." It always came in last, but Bohn's restaurant and hotel received a lot of advertising from the stunt. Attempting to revive interest in the Speedway, Krasner scheduled a stock car race for the program on August 6, 1950. The crowd went wild. The new cars were such a big hit that he added one stock car race to the rest of the scheduled midget programs for the season. Bob Olds remembered thinking that the first night the stock cars ran at Lakeside was "the beginning of the end" for the midgets.[30]

In an effort to boost the midgets for the 1950 season, Krasner hired two West Coast promoters, Bob Ware and Bill Asay, to help publicize the midget races, but the results were not spectacular. Crowds at Lakeside Speedway held steady at 3,000 or 4,000 people a night, down from the average of 5,000–6,000 the year before. The success of the first stock car race in August clearly indicated what direction the Speedway would go in the future. The RMMRA limped through the 1951 season at Lakeside before losing the Speedway, its last track. The "slam bang style of competition" among stock cars had proven more popular than the midget races, and stock car drivers did not demand as big a purse as did midget racers.[31]

Between 1952 and 1958, the RMMRA virtually ceased to exist. With no tracks to race on and little interest in the sport, there was no need for the once-powerful group. Two drivers formed the Denver Midget Racing Club in 1952, running at Englewood Speedway, but after six programs it was done. The Colorado Automobile Racing Club, which sanctioned the stock car races, expanded to promote midgets in 1956, including ten races at Lakeside. The public's declining interest in midget racing was not limited to Lakeside Speedway, however. Its popularity dropped at tracks all over the country, so much so that the sport itself almost ceased to exist. It would have done so, wrote racing fan and historian Allan Brown, if not for the "efforts of obstinate, yet courageous individuals" who kept the sport alive until times got better. In the nearly twenty years that the midgets ruled the Speedway, they not only helped sustain Lakeside Amusement Park, they also helped the Speedway establish a national presence. Nearly every driver who raced at Lakeside Speedway emphasized how important the track was to both Denver and the sport. Sonny Coleman referred to the Speedway as the ultimate race track for midgets in the area, while Leroy Byers called it one of the best midget racing tracks in the country. Like Lakeside Amusement Park, however, Lakeside Speedway needed to adapt to changing times and tastes if it wanted to survive.[32]

CHAPTER 7

The Wild Chipmunk versus the Mouse

Lakeside Amusement Park's last true connection with its City Beautiful days came to an end in 1950 when longtime electrician John Flohr, the only employee who had witnessed firsthand the transformation from elite park to blue-collar park, retired after thirty-nine years. He left just as amusement parks were beginning to experience some of their most turbulent years yet. Desegregation led many white customers to stay away from the parks, which resulted in many of them closing in the 1950s and 1960s. Other customers stayed away from aging parks, concerned over their grimy appearance and the questionable safety of their older rides. The close proximity of older parks to bus and tramway lines also continued to lead some to believe that public transportation allowed rough customers to overrun the parks. It was in this amusement park environment of the 1950s that Disneyland, the nation's first theme park, opened in July 1955. In the biggest challenge yet to the traditional amusement parks that had played an important role in American entertainment, theme parks soon spread across the country. Lakeside Amusement Park, which had proven time and again to be a survivor, was ready for the challenge.[1]

While Benjamin Krasner had never backed away from the challenges of operating an amusement park, the new decade got off to a bumpy start for him. Early in the morning of August 19, 1951, Krasner and his wife, Miriam, were returning home from Lakeside when two men who wanted to rob the park emerged from the shadows. They forced Krasner back into his car at gunpoint and drove the Krasners around for over an hour, apparently unable to find their way to Lakeside. Finally reaching the park, the two men marched the Krasners through the gate to the main office. The group was confronted by night watchman H. M. McGee, whom the robbers relieved of his gun and blackjack and took hostage as well. Once in the park office, one man accompanied Krasner to his office to empty the two safes while the other kept watch over Miriam Krasner and McGee. A second night watchman, Albert W. Stickrod, saw Miriam Krasner sitting in the telephone operator's chair as he made his rounds but, used to seeing the Krasners at the park at all hours, thought nothing of it. He even mistook the sport-shirt–clad robber for Benjamin Krasner. The safes held $5,566 in cash, which the thieves took, and about $1,000 in coins, which they were unable to carry. With the cash in their possession, the two men left Miriam Krasner and McGee in the office with instructions not to call the police and forced Krasner back into his car, which they drove about three and a half miles southeast of the park. After telling Krasner where they would leave his car, they told him to get out and walk. When he was unable to find his car, Krasner woke a nearby resident and called the police. Two men were later tried and convicted for several robberies, including the one at Lakeside, but were never charged with kidnapping the Krasners because of an error made in filing that charge.[2]

The publicity-shy Krasners did not like the attention the incident generated, but the front page of the next day's *Rocky Mountain News* told readers of their ordeal in bold headlines, indicating just how disturbing it was to Denver that a well-respected, prominent member of the business community and his wife, who also ran one of the area's favorite playgrounds, had been kidnapped and robbed in such a daring manner. The crime also sent shockwaves through the amusement park industry, with an article on it appearing in the September 1 issue of *Billboard*. The magazine rarely printed articles involving crimes such as this one, but it did so this time, perhaps meaning it as a warning to other amusement park owners that some criminals might be getting bolder than the common pickpockets who had roamed the parks in the early days.[3]

Other incidents at Lakeside throughout the decade seemingly served as reminders that amusement parks were going through a rough period. On June 18, 1954, twenty-two-year-old Airman Third Class Dan Coleman, who was stationed at Lowry and sometimes worked as a brakeman on the Cyclone, was thrown from one of the coaster's cars. The train had just gone down the first hill and was making a 90-degree turn when Coleman, who was sitting on the back of his seat, was thrown from it. He struck two support posts with such force that all the blood vessels in his body above the waist ruptured, and he died instantly from a fractured skull and a broken spine. Coleman had bragged to friends before getting on the coaster that he liked to ride standing up because he "got more kick out of it that way," and a coroner's jury ruled that he died because he had disobeyed and disregarded safety rules. Eight years later, almost to the day, nineteen-year-old Airman Second Class Barry Lindsey, also stationed at Lowry, died on the Cyclone when he stood up and struck his head against a plank that supported a walkway alongside the track.[4]

Lakeside also faced a lawsuit filed by Flora Hook, wife of Denver City Councilman Irving Hook, which dragged on from 1955 to 1960. Hook claimed she was injured on August 12, 1955, when she was thrown to the floor of a Loop-O-Plane car, allegedly because the ride operator failed to properly fasten the leather strap that was supposed to hold her in her seat. She sought $20,000 in damages. Lakeside's attorneys argued that Hook was injured because she failed to hold on to the metal bar that went across her lap and that there was no evidence to show that the leather strap was not properly fastened. The Denver District Court dismissed the suit, which Hook appealed to the Colorado Supreme Court. That court upheld the dismissal, ruling that amusement park customers who went on thrill rides had to accept responsibility for any injuries they sustained. Justices Albert Franz and Frank Hall dissented, arguing that customers had a right to assume they would not be injured on rides and that the case should have gone to a jury because "negligence could have been inferred."[5]

As difficult as times might have been, Krasner's passion for Lakeside Amusement Park was as strong as ever. By 1950 he had perfected the mix of constant innovation, more thrilling rides, and special gimmicks that kept Lakeside thriving at a time when other parks were dying rapidly. Trains had always been a passion of Krasner's, recalled his daughter, Rhoda, in a 2000 interview, and in his free time he studied timetables and routes, fascinated by the machines. The Lakeshore Railway was his chance to indulge that passion while also making his park stand out. Joining the 1904 World's Fair steam engine in 1950 was a new $25,000 diesel-powered California Zephyr built by Joseph Ruth, a Denver-based diesel equipment manufacturer. The gleaming stainless steel miniature diesel engine, the first of its kind in the country, came complete with air horn, air brakes, and matching stainless steel passenger cars. The stainless steel construction reflected both sunlight and the park's lights at night as it traveled around the lake, and a special device in the engine built up exhaust until the train sounded exactly like a full-size diesel. Over 10,000 people were present for the train's dedication, and the *Denver Post* reported that the new train carried "capacity loads of passengers" the entire first week it ran. Three years later park superintendent Harry Thornsberry and park mechanic Pete Giovanni built a second steam engine, named the Prospector, for Lakeside. The train included six new passenger cars painted yellow and silver; Denver, Rio Grande, and Western Railroad president Judge Wilson McCarthy was the engineer for the first run of the new train. Krasner later renamed the older steam engine Whistling Tom and the new one Puffing Billie after characters from one of his daughter Rhoda's favorite books.[6]

Other new attractions for the 1950 season included the park's first Tilt-a-Whirl and the Rock-O-Plane (made by the same company as the Loop-O-Plane and Roll-O-Plane already at the park). For adult customers Krasner opened the Riviera Club, an "ultra-modern cocktail lounge," on the west side of the El Patio Ballroom, which quickly became a popular gathering place. Becoming less popular was the ballroom itself, where attendance was below expectations even though it boasted appearances by Jimmy Dorsey, Les Brown, Tex Beneke, and other well-known bands. Krasner told *Billboard* in September 1950 that he was considering dropping the park's long-standing name-band policy in favor of a house band. Far more impressive numbers were posted by the picnic business at Lakeside, with a record 17,000 people attending the Gates Rubber Company outing, while picnics hosted by the Denver Public Schools' ROTC, radio station KLZ, the *Denver Post* for back to school in September, and the Colorado Federation of Labor on Labor Day drew at least 10,000 people each. Overall attendance at Lakeside was at least equal to 1949 levels, according to Krasner, but the ride business was down 5 percent as bands, picnics, and midget races brought bigger crowds than the rides.[7]

Krasner aggressively expanded Lakeside's adult offerings in the 1950s, but he also one-upped rival Elitch's when he opened the park's Kiddies Playland in time for the 1951 season. Located on the southern edge of the park, the new amusement area contained "10 safe, new rides for kids." Eventually, it grew to include fourteen rides, most of which were miniature versions of the adult rides at the park, including a child-sized Whip (manufactured by William F. Mangels, creator of the original Whip), a Flying Tigers ride, and a steel version of the Cyclone. Perhaps the most unique ride, however, was the new carousel, installed in 1960. Rather than horses, children got to ride on airplanes, motorcycles, helicopters, fire engines, buses, and cars. Each vehicle was equipped with lights and horns, and when the ride was in full operation it resembled "a Paris traffic jam," according to the *Denver Post*. Scrambling to keep up, Elitch's opened its own KiddieLand the following year. Jack and Budd Gurtler, son of Elitch's owner Arnold Gurtler, began taking a more active role in Elitch's management when they returned from the US Marines in 1945 in preparation for the day when they would eventually be in charge of the park. One of their first major projects was KiddieLand, and at the opening ceremony cowboy star Hopalong Cassidy welcomed a record crowd of children to Elitch's new play area.[8]

Although many people, including Jack Gurtler, characterized the rivalry between Lakeside and Elitch's as friendly, only once did the two parks actually join forces. In 1952 Lakeside and Elitch's served as co-hosts for the summer conference of the National Association of Amusement Parks, Pools, and Beaches (NAAPPB). The Denver gathering, which drew 100 amusement park operators, began at Lakeside on the evening of August 6, where visitors were suitably impressed by the lighting, the lake, and the Art Deco architecture. The next day began with a Western-themed gathering at Elitch's, where the visitors received cowboy hats, ties, and kerchiefs before heading back to Lakeside for a Western-style lunch hosted by Benjamin and Miriam Krasner. After visits to Buffalo Bill's grave and Red Rocks Amphitheater, the day ended with a gala party at Elitch's hosted by the Gurtlers, who had transformed the park into a Western town for the evening. The meeting was a huge success, declared *Billboard*, thanks to the Gurtlers and the Krasners, and it gave the park operators a chance to discuss the problems they faced without convening a formal business meeting.[9]

Krasner's co-hosting of the NAAPPB conference was not the only activity that earned him high praise from the amusement park industry during the 1950s. He had worked tirelessly since 1935 to revive Lakeside and keep it prosperous, but even with all his hard work he still had to deal with the honky-tonks, pawn shops, and pool halls that had been creeping in on the park's borders for decades. While Krasner could not control what happened outside the town of Lakeside, inside the town was different. The large tract of land on the southwest side of the park, where Adolph Zang had hoped to see upper-class homes materialize, was still vacant as the 1950s began. In 1953 Krasner made his biggest and boldest move yet to protect his park, selling the land to a group of investors who wanted to build a shopping mall.

Shopping malls, writes historian James Farrell, were simply a new take on an older retail idea. Shopping centers made up of grouped stores, usually anchored by a grocery store surrounded by a few other shops, had long existed. The first step toward shopping malls came when new shopping centers turned the stores inward to face away from the street. The new strip malls, as they were called, appealed to drivers in the first decades of the 1900s because they allowed them to get in, get the things they needed, and get back on the road quickly. Their success doomed them, however, as "heavy traffic, random placement, and visual chaos" soon led to their falling from favor among selective customers. Community shopping centers, designed to meet the needs of entire suburban neighborhoods, attempted to address those problems and took off in the 1920s and 1930s until the Depression and World War II halted their development. The postwar housing boom and construction of the interstate highway system replaced community shopping centers with regional shopping centers. These centers were usually anchored by at least one major department store, with smaller, sometimes lesser-known stores filling the rest of the space. All the stores were under one roof, and the buildings housing them had a central interior courtyard, were climate controlled, and created a total separation between car and pedestrian movement. The best example of the new design was Southdale Center in Edina, Minnesota, which opened in 1956 and was the country's first fully enclosed shopping mall.[10]

In 1951 developer Gerri Von Frellich and his associates hired Seattle-based Larry Smith and Company to search the Denver area for an ideal community in which to build a shopping center. The company, which had completed similar surveys for Macy's, Gimbel's, the Hudson Company, and several major shopping center developers throughout the country, soon decided that the Lakeside/Arvada/Wheat Ridge area was ideal. The researchers said there were 200,000 people within a ten-mile radius of the area who did not have access to enough local stores to fulfill their needs and who lacked convenient access to downtown Denver shops. Von Frellich and his associates initially wanted to build their mall in Arvada, but after the town rejected the idea, they turned to the neighboring town of Lakeside. In late 1953 Von Frellich and his company, Markets, Inc., entered into negotiations with Benjamin Krasner to buy sixty-two acres of land on the southwest side of Lake Rhoda; the rest of the Lakeside property remained under the control of the amusement park company.[11]

In a happy coincidence for the developers, the state had plans to build a new highway connecting Denver to Golden, which offered easy access to the Lakeside area. In announcing construction of the mall, tentatively named Lakeside Village, Von Frellich told the *Rocky Mountain News* that it would be a "complete duplication in services and products" of what was found in downtown Denver. The $12 million shopping center was reported to be about one-fourth the size of downtown Denver and 40 percent larger than Denver architect Temple Buell's recently completed Cherry Creek Shopping Center. Longtime Denver retailer Denver Dry Goods had already signed a contract to be the anchor store of the new mall; also included in the 400,000-square-foot mall was the largest King Soopers grocery store in the Denver area, the largest Woolworth's in the five-state region, a White's home and automobile supply store, Fashion Bar, Lerner's, Maternity Mode, and Fontius Shoes. The mall also included a three-block-long tunnel used for deliveries underneath it. Meant to keep pedestrians safe from truck traffic at the mall, the tunnel could also double as a fall-out shelter in the event of a nuclear attack.[12]

Denver's newspapers proclaimed the mall the largest between Chicago and the Pacific Coast, and to make sure its readers knew just how immense it was, on August 12, 1956, the *Rocky Mountain News* listed how much material had gone into its construction. In building the mall, workers had used enough steel to build forty-two large US Army tanks, in addition to 6 acres of roofing material, 21,000 acres of glass, and a mile of street curbing. Nearly 958 tons of air-conditioning equipment cooled the building, and there were eleven-and-a-half miles of piping and 12,500 light fixtures. The 4,500 parking spaces around the mall turned out to be insufficient on opening day as the parking lot soon filled to capacity, forcing people to drive the streets around the mall and amusement park looking for places to park. The mall employed 1,600 people, 300 of whom worked at the Denver Dry Goods store alone. An August 9 *Rocky Mountain News* article reported that most mall employees lived in the neighborhoods around the amusement park and were "being hired in shifts to fit their own hours." Financially, Lakeside Mall was a "boon to the economy of northwest Denver and Jefferson County." The mall created a half-mile-long barrier on the west side of Lakeside Amusement Park and, when combined with the Speedway, a half-mile-long barrier along the south side of the park. With Inspiration Point Park on the north side of the Lakeside property, the amusement park was surrounded on three sides, preventing outside businesses from moving any closer. While not the exclusive homes Adolph Zang had once hoped for, the mall was the best Benjamin Krasner could do.[13]

The grand opening of Lakeside Mall took place over a three-day period from August 30 to September 1, 1956; more than 50,000 people, the same number who had helped open the amusement park in 1908, attended the ceremonies. In a scene reminiscent of the park's grand opening, Denver mayor Will Nicholson "praised the 'foresight which made the brilliant new institution possible'"; according to the *Denver Post*, "most of Denver's Who's Who" were seen at the opening, including US representative Byron Rogers of Denver and Jefferson County commissioners Emil Schneider, Walter True, and Clarence Koch. Ten "pretty hostesses" dressed in blue escorted guests through the mall, while each individual store held ribbon-cutting ceremonies and offered prizes and gifts. Entertainment included Ringling Brothers' Bozo the Clown, Al Balater's band, Kent Bailey's Western Band, and the Lakewood Westernairs. Also reminiscent of the park's opening day in 1908, Lakeside police chief Leo Peterson declared the gathering "the most orderly crowd I've ever handled."[14]

Over the next year, more than a dozen new stores moved into the mall, and the shopping center continued its policy of hiring from the surrounding neighborhoods, which meant the "people who serve customers at Lakeside Center are neighbors in the largest sense of the word and they extend their cordial hospitality to their work." The mall was a definite contrast to the bars, pool halls, and small restaurants around the park, but, like the park itself, the mall had to take note of the working-class neighborhood in which it existed. In August 1958 John Barr, president of Montgomery Ward and Company, arrived in Denver to open a new Montgomery Ward's store at Lakeside Mall. The store, the company's first in a shopping mall in the United States, was part of an $84 million expansion the company was undergoing. The store was designed for "the outdoor man, the do-it-yourself fan, and the professional carpenter and mechanic," far different from the customers attracted by Denver Dry Goods, which for many years had served Denver's elite shoppers. About 4,500 people attended Ward's opening ceremony at which Miss Colorado 1958, Cynthia Cullen, cut the ribbon; within the next half hour about 6,500 people had passed through the store. After Montgomery Ward's grand opening came the 1959 opening of Lakeside National Bank, the first bank to receive a national charter since 1937. Special sales lured thousands of customers to the fifth birthday celebration in 1961; the next year the center was declared a "Shopper's Dream" and a "model for shopping centers all over the country and in Canada." It posted annual sales of $30 million.[15]

Thousands of people, from as close as across the street to as far away as Broomfield and Boulder, visited the mall each day. Every time they looked across the parking lot, they were looking at Lakeside Amusement Park. Krasner could not have asked for better advertising, and the amusement park industry recognized that fact. In a September 22, 1956, article headlined "Krasner Spot Extends Run, Garners Biz," *Billboard* reported that the mall's opening had "brought the park more transient traffic and scored good advertising and publicity for the amusement zone." Krasner's gamble in selling Lakeside's undeveloped land to Von Frellich had paid off, insulating the park on its southern and western sides and improving business at the same time. It was a move other amusement parks would undertake in the future, as when Disneyland planners completed the Downtown Disney zone around that park in 2001 and created a similar zone on a much larger scale at Walt Disney World in Florida.[16]

While the mall was under construction, Krasner made sure to keep his amusement park interesting for the new customers it would bring. By 1953, Lakeside's El Patio was "jammed with dancers" eager to hear the Dorsey brothers and Woody Herman, the leading acts that summer. The increasingly popular stock car races at the Speedway brought additional crowds, with *Billboard* informing readers that Krasner and Lakeside were "using stock car and midget racing to good results." Krasner was so happy with the results that he told *Billboard* he planned to bring in additional rides for the 1954 season. However, he did make one major change at the ballroom the next year, switching to a house band after twenty-five years of relying on big-name bands to draw crowds. Krasner hired Eddy Rogers, a former star of the radio favorite *Your Hit Parade*, as its leader. The move proved popular at first, with ballroom manager Lou Clark reporting steady crowds and Krasner telling *Billboard* that house bands might be a good move for struggling ballrooms everywhere. Krasner also introduced family days, convention rates, and group package prices for organizations looking to hold events at Lakeside in 1954 in an effort to stir up more business.[17]

The initial increase brought by a house band at the ballroom soon faded, and the return of name bands in 1955 boosted business at the ballroom, but not to the level it had once enjoyed. Clark suggested to *Billboard* that business was down at ballrooms everywhere, but the coat and tie policy that had always been in place at El Patio (and at Elitch's Trocadero) may have kept some customers away, as Denver was experiencing a hotter than normal summer. Other longtime ballroom visitors suggested that the park's policy of charging those who wanted just to listen to the bands (as opposed to only charging those who wanted to dance, as was the case at Elitch's) was to blame for the downturn. The picnic business was much better. King Soopers rented the entire park for one day and gave tickets to any customer who bought at least $20 worth of goods from its stores, eventually drawing 20,000 people to its event. Not to be outdone, Safeway hosted a picnic of its own but had only 5,000 people attend, while the Star Supermarket chain of Colorado Springs chartered forty buses to bring its customers to the park. The Gates Rubber Company picnic drew 13,000, and the Union Pacific and Public Service Company picnics drew 7,000 each. If nothing else, Krasner could plan on packing his park with picnic customers from Denver's blue-collar industries.[18]

The Cyclone and the miniature railroad were the top rides for the 1955 season, followed by the newly introduced Rotor ride, which was similar to a modern Round-Up. Riders stood along the outside edge of the ride as it started to spin and rise into the air at an angle, relying on centrifugal force to hold them against the walls once the floor retracted. Also introduced that year was a new steel coaster, located next to a stretch of the Cyclone's track, which became one of the most popular and famous coasters at Lakeside. In most parks the coaster was known as a Wild Mouse, but Krasner thought that seemed like a poor name for a coaster in the Rocky Mountains, which, as he had noted on family trips, were teeming with chipmunks. He named Lakeside's version of the ride the Wild Chipmunk. Once cars on the ride reached the top of the ramp, they followed a sharply curved path that gave the impression the car would go over the edge at each turn before descending a series of steep hills; the *Denver Post* described it as a "darting, twisting, dipping ride." Krasner gave architect Richard Crowther complete control over everything from the choice of colors to the placement of lights and benches for the new ride. While *Billboard* praised Krasner for giving Lakeside's customers what they wanted that summer, on the same pages of the magazine was the story of a brand new park that would play a significant role in the future of nearly every amusement park in the world, including Lakeside.[19]

Benjamin Krasner worked hard to make sure Lakeside Amusement Park remained a clean and desirable place, but not all parks were as careful. One California businessman's work-related travel gave him the opportunity to visit amusement parks across the country, and like many others he believed amusement parks in general had become messy, run-down places. A father, he spent numerous afternoons watching his daughters ride the merry-go-round at Griffith Park in Los Angeles. While sitting on a bench watching them, he often thought that an amusement park should have more for families to do together, and so Walt Disney decided to do something about it. Disneyland's grand opening on July 17, 1955, dramatically changed the amusement park industry. Disney's new venture, writes Judith Adams, was "an amusement park different from all other such parks, where there would be none of the dirtiness, sham, deterioration, and menacing atmosphere that dominated all existing amusement enterprises."[20]

In many ways, Disneyland successfully did what Adolph Zang and his associates had already done at Lakeside Amusement Park in 1908. As at Lakeside, Disneyland officials were in charge of security, parking, sanitation, and hundreds of other small details at the park, all designed to create a happy and satisfying visitor experience. The park itself was located behind an earthen wall covered with plants, hiding it from public view. However, the new park also broke with some traditions. After quickly realizing that requiring visitors to pay for each ride tended to bog down customer traffic, Disneyland first introduced ride ticket books and eventually a gate fee that covered all attractions in the park. Disneyland was not near public transportation, so it took long trips in airplanes or cars to get there, thereby weeding out the perceived-to-be-rowdier customers who used public transportation to get to the older amusement parks. The creation of Disneyland also ushered in the era of large-scale corporate ownership of amusement parks. Unlike Lakeside's owners, however, Disney was not able to control land outside his amusement park and was helpless to stop the undesirable businesses that soon crowded in around it, ready to take advantage of the millions of people visiting the park each year. It was a problem to which Disney would not find an answer until he started planning Walt Disney World in Florida, where he gained the kind of control Lakeside had enjoyed since 1908, though on a larger scale.[21]

In the first six months Disneyland was open, more than a million people passed through its gates. In July 1965, ten years after it opened, the park hosted its 50 millionth guest (Lakeside reached the 50 million visitor mark in 1973, sixty-five years after it opened). Disneyland was a huge success, and once competitors started copying the concept, theme parks dominated the amusement park industry from then on. However, the change was not all bad news for the smaller, family-owned parks. Heavy advertising for Disneyland, especially on Walt Disney's weekly television program on ABC, got people interested in visiting their local parks. But unlike most of the traditional amusement parks, Denver's parks soon found Disney practically at their front gates thanks to two new ventures.[22]

In 1957 a group of developers announced their plans to build Magic Mountain, a theme park with a Storybook Lane and a narrow-gauge railroad, west of Denver in Golden. An offering circular for the project stated that it would bring back the Old West of 1858, with an old Western village, cavalry post, and stockade, and would look to the future with a Magic of Industry Exposition area in addition to thrill and educational rides. Denver businessman Walter F. Cobb and sculptor John Calvin Sutton, the men behind Magic Mountain, hired Los Angeles–based Marco Engineering to build the park. Marco was the creation of Cornelius Vanderbilt Wood Jr. (who went by C. V.), who had helped supervise the construction of Disneyland before going on to manage it for six months after it opened in 1955. He left Disneyland to go into the theme park business for himself and hired more than a dozen members of Disney's staff to help him spread the Disneyland concept throughout the

United States. Wood's involvement with Magic Mountain left many with the mistaken impression that Walt Disney himself was involved with the project. Stories about the construction of Magic Mountain soon filled the pages of *Billboard*, letting industry insiders know the project was a significant development in the amusement park business.[23]

A small group of only 2,500 people attended the dedication of Magic Mountain's Cavalry Post and stockade on February 1, 1958. The builders finished the rest of the entrance area to the park in 1959. Marco based the Old West village, named Centennial City, on historic Colorado architectural styles and used the famous Disneyland technique of forced perspective to make the buildings appear taller than they actually were. The Victorian-style train depot, however, was "far more impressive than any depot Jefferson County had yet seen," and the narrow-gauge train was pulled by Denver and Rio Grande Engine no. 420, built in 1889. But despite its grandeur, Magic Mountain was never financially successful. According to Judith Adams, the project was doomed from the start because the backers "collectively lacked any enthusiasm for the amusement business." By 1959 the financial situation had deteriorated to the extent that Cobb stepped down as president when he realized it was no longer a good investment for him. The park went into foreclosure and further construction stopped; the Storybook Village, fairgrounds, Outer Space Ride, and Magic of Industry Exposition were never built. Several people tried to save the property, including New York developer William Zeckendorf and Walter Cobb himself, but in late 1960 the bankrupt Magic Mountain was sold at auction. It successfully reopened in 1971 as Heritage Square but was known as much for its stores and theater as for its amusement devices.[24]

While the *Denver Republican* had praised Lakeside in 1907 as a sorely needed addition to Denver's summer amusement options, by the late 1950s a different attitude seemed to prevail, with Denver newspapers asserting that residents needed more activities that people could enjoy even during the winter. Bowling alleys and swimming pools enjoyed renewed popularity in the 1950s as family-friendly entertainment venues. Bowling in particular had a sleazy reputation by the early 1900s, but a careful marketing campaign in the 1940s and early 1950s that stressed clean, air-conditioned buildings and automatic pinsetters succeeded in making the sport a family-friendly form of entertainment. In late 1958 Walt Disney's lawyer, Loyd Wright Sr., approached him with a proposal for a recreation complex that would include a large bowling alley and a swimming pool. Disney convinced most of his family to invest in the project and several other celebrities as well, including George Burns and Gracie Allen, Jack Benny, Burl Ives, Spike Jones, Art Linkletter, and John Payne. After months of study, the investors decided to locate their project on seven acres of land on South Colorado Boulevard and Kentucky Avenue in the Denver suburb of Glendale. Construction on the new venture, appropriately named Celebrity Lanes, was already under way when Disney, Jack Benny, Spike Jones, and John Payne arrived in Denver on December 14, 1959, for the groundbreaking ceremony. At a reception at the Brown Palace Hotel afterward, Benny joked that although he knew "as much about bowling as Zsa Zsa Gabor does about housekeeping," he was not going to miss the chance to make money on what he was sure would be a successful venture. Disney, in his remarks, promoted the center as a perfect place to fill the recreational needs of adults and children, one of his primary concerns with Disneyland.[25]

The Celebrity Lanes complex featured an eighty-lane bowling alley, Colorado's largest indoor pool (it held 500,000 gallons of water, and Mickey Mouse and Goofy were known to water ski on it behind speedboats), a massive videogame arcade, a slot car track, restaurants, and a health spa. The bowling alley opened in 1960, with other elements of the complex opening over the next year until the swimming pool officially opened in July 1961. The initial investment proved disappointing for the famous investors, leading the Walt Disney Company to buy them out in 1962 and rename the complex Celebrity Sports Center. In 1964 Disney started using Celebrity as a training ground, giving future managers of Walt Disney World experience managing a family resort. Since the only experience they did not gain at Celebrity was in managing a hotel (the original plans for the complex called for a hotel, but it was never built), Disney leased a Hilton hotel in Florida and turned its management over to Disney staff. Disney sold Celebrity to a group of Denver bankers and real estate investors in 1979, and it remained in operation until June 1994, when it succumbed to developers eager for the land and pressure from Glendale residents who came to perceive it as a haven for delinquents. At the height of its popularity, Celebrity drew millions of visitors a year, from regular customers to nationally known sports figures. Lakeside stayed competitive, with Krasner expecting the park to draw between 600,000 and 700,000 visitors during its 1960 season.[26]

Walt Disney was one of the most influential forces in the second half of the twentieth century, providing what LeRoy Ashby calls "the narratives for the postwar American way—sentimental, wholesome, innocent." As his biographer Steven Watts notes, Disney mediated "a host of jarring influences," including "individuality and conformity, corporate institution and small-town values, science and fantasy, consumerism and producerism." When it came to Denver's amusement parks, however, Disney's vision failed to move the city's residents, and Lakeside Amusement Park outlasted both Magic Mountain and Celebrity Sports Center. A reporter for the *Rocky Mountain News* wrote that Lakeside "offers in the original much of the same kind of architecture the late Walt Disney paid untold sums to recreate in his Main Street entry of Disneyland and more recently in Florida." The working-class suburbs that gave Lakeside its customer base dated to the 1920s, which helped insulate the park from the suburban explosion of the 1950s and the new culture that came with it. With a long-established and loyal customer base, Lakeside had stood toe-to-toe with the new giant of the amusement park industry and had actually come out on top in Denver.[27]

Lakeside's victory was largely thanks to Benjamin Krasner, who responded to the Disney challenge by stepping up his efforts to keep Lakeside a thriving venture. With business at the park booming after the mall's opening, Krasner embarked on another expansion, and in February 1958 he filled in fifty feet of Lake Rhoda on the northeast side of the lake. Two new rides filled the space: the Scrambler, which simulated an egg beater by spinning riders past each other, and the Satellite, a German-made rocket-ship ride that allowed riders to control their own craft. Krasner spent $100,000 for the location, installation, and equipping of the Satellite, the first ride of its kind in the United States. In an amusing twist, his purchase of the ride allowed Krasner to one-up Disneyland, which had to settle for getting the second Satellite later that year. Both the Scrambler and the Satellite threatened to unseat the Cyclone as the top attraction in the park, with *Billboard* reporting that the line for the Scrambler formed at 6:00 p.m. and never dwindled until the park closed. Another new attraction at the park that year was a 160-foot by 50-foot dirt track constructed on the edge of the lake, where people could rent miniature gasoline-powered sports cars imported from Germany. The cars, which were completely under the riders' control, were immediately popular. In addition, Krasner replaced the aging bumper cars with twenty new

Auto Skooters, also imported from Germany. The addition of the Scrambler, Satellite, and racecars brought the total number of adult rides at Lakeside to twenty-three. The Cyclone hung on to remain the favorite, however, with the *Rocky Mountain News* referring to it as "the daddy of all roller coasters."[28]

New bands, free acts, and special performances provided entertainment for the growing crowds that descended on the park. In July 1955 Lakeside hosted Countess Agnes Van Rosen's Tournament of Thrills, a three-day series of bullfights with top bullfighters from Mexico. It was the first time since 1913 that bullfights had taken place at Lakeside, and over 4,000 people were in attendance at one performance when a bull knocked down and trampled, but did not seriously injure, matador Rafael Lorrea. An appearance by Gene Holter's Wild Animal Show, which included camel races, Si Otis and his trick mule, Big Babe the performing elephant, and polo games featuring zebras and donkeys, marked the opening of the 1956 season at Lakeside and brought back memories of older animal shows at Manhattan Beach and Arlington Park. The El Patio Ballroom, remodeled and renamed Moonlight Gardens Ballroom in 1956, hosted the world premiere of a new band headed by a former singer with Dick Jurgens's band, Al Galante, who had been a regular at Elitch's Trocadero. In an effort to interest younger people in the ballroom, Krasner also started booking popular recording bands, including the Four Lads (whose hits included "Instanbul" and "Moments to Remember") and the Diamonds (who were a year away from releasing one of their biggest hits, "Little Darlin'"). *Billboard* referred to the competition between Lakeside and Elitch's as "the battle of the bandstands," although Elitch's seemed to have a slight edge as the Trocadero was crowded to near capacity nightly. There was, however, a "definite increase" in the business at Lakeside's Moonlight Gardens once the changes were made, but by 1958 Moonlight Gardens was open only on weekends, and Krasner was back to using a house band.[29]

The *Rocky Mountain News* reported that "Lakeside's entire operation is planned for family fun," and an article in the June 2, 1958, issue of *Billboard* described the way the park had gone after this customer base in the 1950s. School groups held picnics at the park at the end of school years, while industrial, church, and civic groups and service clubs made up the overall picnic traffic through Lakeside. Many groups took advantage of a reduced ride fare policy that allowed them to sell park tickets as fundraisers. Krasner had coupons in more than 300 hotels in the Denver area that allowed free admission to the park, after which customers had to purchase individual ride tickets. The coupons had a place for the hotels to stamp their names, making it appear as if they were the ones paying for their guests to get into the park, which in turn promoted goodwill toward the hotels. Businesses, unions, and numerous other groups provided company days for employees and their families at Lakeside. Public Service Company of Colorado, Denver's power company, for example, continued to hold its annual picnic at Lakeside, drawing thousands of employees and their families to the park. With lower admission costs than Elitch's and ample picnic grounds, Lakeside promoted itself as an inexpensive place for families to escape their cares and worries for a short while.[30]

As the 1950s came to a close, one final mishap served as a reminder of what a difficult decade it had been. On September 13, 1959, two days before Lakeside closed for the season, a car on the Wild Chipmunk carrying two brothers, Don and Jim Christiansen, came to a stop. The ride operator, Don Saxon, an airman from Lowry, pulled the emergency brake to stop the cars coming up behind the stopped car, but the brake failed. Four other cars hit the stopped car, resulting in broken bones and bruises for some of those involved in the accident, though no one was seriously hurt.[31]

The pace of change at Lakeside Amusement Park slowed considerably in the 1960s, a welcome break for Krasner after the frenzied pace he had kept up in the 1940s and 1950s, but he was far from done with the park. As late as 1961, he still had Richard Crowther planning improvements, including new tickets booths for the ballroom and Staride and a new sign for the Satellite. Krasner had tried to keep Lakeside fresh, and Crowther's new designs were no exception as the Staride booth would have featured a gold star very similar to the stars on the Celebrity Sports Center sign, and the Satellite sign would have resembled a rocket and been topped with a large gray plastic globe. The new booths and sign were never built, however. After selling the park's thirty-five-year-old Lindy Loop ride in 1964, Krasner purchased three more new rides from Germany. On the Matterhorn ride, the cars, which resembled bobsleds, traveled a circular path that went up and down, simulating a ride on a bobsled. The *Denver Post* noted that the ride was as impressive for its beauty as for its thrills, with artists hand-painting the exterior of the ride with scenes of sledders, skiers, skaters, and mountaineers. On the ride's interior, blinking lights helped further the impression of moving through snowstorms.

Krasner also added new Skoota boats to the pond that year and a Trabant, where riders sat on a rotating disc as it spun while rising and falling. The new rides, according to the *Post*, were incredibly popular with Lakeside visitors, and the park could handle over 10,000 riders per hour.[32]

Just as a daring robbery had marked the beginning of a demanding era for Lakeside, a second one marked its end. On September 8, 1964, three masked men, armed with guns, entered the park's main offices at 3:15 in the afternoon and emptied the safe and cashier's cage of over $36,000, proceeds from the Labor Day weekend at the park and Speedway. Krasner later told reporters that the robbers came half an hour before an armored car was scheduled to pick up the money and take it to the bank, strong evidence they had been planning the heist for a while. The theft naturally led Denver newspapers to compare it to the 1951 kidnapping and robbery, but Krasner put the robbery behind him and looked forward to 1965. On opening day that year a record crowd turned out, including thousands of high school students who came for the traditional Color Day. The Devil's Joy Ride, a dark ride so named because the attraction was inside a building rather than out in the open, was the new attraction for the summer. According to an advertisement for the ride, it was eighty feet by forty feet, and the exterior was decorated with devils and other grim-looking figures. The installation at Lakeside was the first in the United States and marked the first time since the 1910s that the park had a new dark ride. One of the biggest crowds ever visited the park over Memorial Day weekend that season, and the park was so popular that Krasner returned the ballroom to a nightly schedule instead of weekends only.[33]

By 1965, Lakeside Amusement Park had survived the collapse of the City Beautiful movement, successfully reinvented itself as a working-class amusement park, and bravely faced competition from onetime Disney employees and Walt Disney himself. As the park entered the 1960s, it became a Denver legend. Articles in the *Denver Post* in the 1960s attempted to find the origins of the famous carousel, and Krasner and his brother-in-law, Martie Ruttner, who was helping him run the park, told the newspaper that no records existed as to where the ride came from or when it was installed. Even the park's oldest employees, said the *Post*, remembered it just "being there when they came." Another sentimental article in 1962 profiled the two engineers who ran the trains: K. C. Watkins, seventy-nine, had retired after forty-two years with the Rio Grande Southern and Union Pacific Railroads, while Percy Perkins, seventy-four, had spent forty-eight years with the Burlington, Colorado and Southern, the Denver and Rio Grande Western, the Southern Pacific, and the Los Angeles, San Pedro and Salt Lake Railroads. Krasner had hired them to run the trains because he believed their knowledge was too valuable to lose. But as the 1965 season came to an end, Denver was again changing rapidly, and many wondered if Lakeside Amusement Park still had a place in the big city.[34]

CHAPTER 8

The Stockers Take over at Lakeside Speedway

Tom Wolfe, in his book *The Kandy-Kolored Tangerine-Flake Streamline Baby*, wrote that stock cars were the invention of people whose lives had been "practically invisible" until World War II allowed them to earn the money to build "monuments to their own styles." By the 1960s, stock car racing had replaced baseball as the most popular sport in the South, but for most of what Wolfe called the "educated classes in the country," stock cars were "beneath serious consideration, still the preserve of ratty people with ratty hair and dermatitis." In the essay that gave the book its title, Wolfe described his discovery of the custom car culture of the 1950s and 1960s, which, like stock cars, had spread rapidly after 1945. Regarding the type of kid, as he referred to them, who was so passionate about cars that were meant to be both art and speed machines, Wolfe said they were "not from the levels of society that produce children who write sensitive analytical prose." Yet those kids created something that would quickly become one of the most popular sports in the United States.[1]

Stock cars evolved from the roadsters of an earlier era in automobile racing and were, as the name implies, strictly stock cars: they were equipped as purchased, with no modifications for racing allowed. The stock car division later grew to include modifieds, which allowed for some modifications, especially to the engines, and Late Model, which were cars built especially for racing. All three classes raced at Lakeside Speedway in the nearly forty years that stock cars dominated the track. By the mid-1950s, automotive historian Leon Mandel wrote, automakers in Detroit, led by Ford, had recognized the growing phenomenon and began to specifically build and market cars with drag or stock car racing in mind.[2]

Racing historian Allan Brown places the first stock car race in 1909 with the running of the 22.75-mile Long Island Stock Car Classic, but racing did not become truly popular until the 1930s. In 1934, Oakland Speedway scheduled a 250-mile stock car race, and two years later the American Automobile Association (AAA) sanctioned a 200-mile race in Daytona Beach. The stock cars returned to Oakland Speedway in 1938 with a 500-mile race. By the time the United States entered World War II, organized stock car races had spread to Indiana, Pennsylvania, and Georgia. As it had with the midgets, the war put a stop to stock car racing, but as soon as the war ended and rationing was lifted, drivers began racing once again. Many fans felt the sport was not spreading as rapidly as they had hoped it would, however, and in response, a group of men led by driver and promoter Bill France formed the National Association for Stock Car Auto Racing (NASCAR) in 1947 to promote and sanction stock car races. Within a few years of NASCAR's formation, fans around the country had established several other sanctioning bodies, including the Central State Racing Association, the Midwest Auto Racing Club, and the Automotive Racing Club of America. The AAA, which had sanctioned midget races for years, finally joined the stock car movement in 1950. The first major race for stock cars under the new sanctioning bodies was a 500-mile event at the new one-and-a-quarter-mile Darling Raceway in South Carolina.[3]

In Colorado, a group of drivers organized the Colorado Automobile Racing Club (CARC) in 1946. Their primary goal was to get roadsters, which were gaining in popularity, off the streets and onto tracks, mostly for safety reasons. Prior to CARC's formation, the only place drivers had to race their roadsters was on the streets of Denver. With the club's backing, the first sanctioned roadster races took place at the Jefferson County Fairgrounds' rodeo grounds on Table Mountain in 1946, which was not an ideal location. Seeking a better spot, the group moved the races to the five-eighths-mile track at Brighton Speedway, where spectators soon filled the grandstands to capacity for each race. At Brighton, the CARC started charging a small admission fee to "form a hospital fund" for the drivers, but the club quickly realized that Brighton Speedway lacked adequate protection for spectators. By the end of 1947, they had moved the races to Englewood Speedway, which was attempting to challenge Lakeside Speedway's dominance in midget races.[4]

The quarter-mile asphalt track at Englewood was a challenge to the drivers of large stock cars, which weighed between 1,900 pounds and 2,600 pounds and were meant for longer tracks. But the drivers liked Englewood and decided to modify their cars to work better with the track. With the weight of each car cut down to 1,200 to 1,400 pounds—just slightly heftier than the heaviest midget—and the standard tires replaced with those used on the midgets, drivers found that the Englewood track became manageable. By the opening of the 1948 season the stock cars were, according to an article in *Speed Age* magazine, "approaching the track record times, attendance and payoff records" of the midgets racing at Englewood. On opening day of the 1948 race season, the stock car races outdrew the opening day game of the Denver Bears for the first time, something the midget races had been doing for many years.[5]

As the number of spectators at the races grew each week, the drivers realized that they needed to put on a good show for their fans. For the 1948 season they added clowns, special stunts, and guest appearances; cleaned up the appearance of both the cars and pit crews; and began making appearances at other Denver-area tracks. Their first appearance at Lakeside Speedway was on August 6, 1950. Drivers Morris Musick and Gib Lilly (who were also involved with midget racing) won the first races. Seeing how enormously popular they were in their first outing at the park, Benjamin Krasner immediately added stock cars to the rest of the season's schedule; their enduring popularity made stock cars a regular feature at the Speedway for the 1951 season. The midgets attempted to cling to their dominance, but by the end of the 1951 season stock cars clearly had the upper hand at Lakeside.[6]

Midgets and stock cars shared the track at the Speedway for as long as it operated, and by the 1960s the two groups enjoyed a friendly working relationship, but it had not been easy getting there. For much of the 1950s, many midget drivers felt bitter toward the stock car drivers over what they felt was their shabby treatment by the stockers. In 1952 Lakeside Speedway pulled out as the last remaining track in the Rocky Mountain Midget Racing Association (RMMRA) circuit, leaving the midgets without a sanctioning body. The Denver Midget Racing Club sanctioned the races from 1952 to 1954 but sponsored only one race at Lakeside, in 1953. The AAA returned to Lakeside Speedway in 1953 and 1954, sponsoring three midget shows each of those years, but they were part of a touring midget racing program rather than regular races. Well aware of the midgets' plight, the CARC decided to step in and sanction the midget races at Lakeside beginning in 1956, much to the anger, writes historian Bill Hill, of some of the midget drivers. They blamed the stock car group for nearly driving the midgets out of business in the first place and, falsely fearing that the group was out to control the midgets, they ended up resenting its backing. But according to Hill, many of the stock car supporters had been, and still were, fans of the midgets, and several of the stock car drivers had driven midgets in addition to the bigger cars. The stockers simply wanted to see the smaller cars survive, and the CARC sanctioned the midget programs at Lakeside until the RMMRA was revived in 1958.[7]

The increasing popularity of stock cars at the Speedway was good for business but represented a bit of a sad change for Benjamin Krasner. Krasner was a fan of racing in general, but the midgets, remembers driver Marv Slusser, were his favorite cars. Krasner, however, had repeatedly proven himself a very smart businessman who was more than willing to adapt his amusement park to changing times to keep it viable. The same proved true at the Speedway. Stock cars, said Slusser, were simply a sign of changing times, and Krasner knew his Speedway had to change in order to survive. Krasner made an effort to keep the midgets around, however, moving their races to Saturday nights while giving the stock cars the prime Wednesday and Sunday night spots.[8]

The vehicles themselves accounted for much of the popularity the stock cars enjoyed. By the late 1940s midgets had become expensive to buy and even more expensive to maintain. Stock cars were just the opposite. In the first years they raced, most of the cars at Lakeside (and other tracks) were 1932, 1933, or 1934 Fords with standard V6 engines. As stock car driver Bob Land said, the fact that stocks were cheap to buy meant there were so many of them around that "everybody knew somebody who had one." Land referred to stock cars as the beer while the midgets were the champagne, while Sonny Coleman, who raced both midgets and stock cars at Lakeside, described the stock car drivers as kids who wanted to race but could not get started with the midgets because of a lack of money or other issues. By 1957, forty-eight stock cars were appearing each race night at Lakeside, twenty-four in the A class and twenty-four in the B class (there were about eighty cars at Englewood at the same time). The B cars were not as fast as the A cars (which could reach speeds of up to sixty miles per hour), but having the B class allowed those drivers to both race and get recognition, something they greatly appreciated. There was also what was called a Hooligan race at Lakeside, which was made up of the cars that had not managed to qualify for the B class race. Driver Sheri Thurman Graham, one of the few women drivers at Lakeside, described the twenty-five-lap Hooligan race as essentially a demolition derby in a circle, and one of the regular competitors was a driver called Cowboy Jackson. Graham remembered that Jackson always had impressive-looking cars that did not run well and that he always seemed to lose even the Hooligan. When Jackson finally won a Hooligan one night, everyone in the grandstands rose to their feet to cheer for him.[9]

In addition to their greater number, the stock cars also provided much more action for the fans. Unlike the midget races, all of the stock car races were fully inverted, with the fastest car starting in the last position. The stock car drivers also did a lot more passing than the midgets had done, which was something fans liked to see in races. While the drivers may have been kids, Sonny Coleman said those kids were exceptionally skilled at making their cars handle well on Lakeside's difficult track. Times for the stock cars were also more exciting. Given the follow-the-leader–type racing most midgets were doing by the late 1940s, one car might finish a race only a few hundredths of a second ahead of or behind the next car. When it came to the stock car races, there could be as much as a full second difference between cars, which made a huge difference to the fans who wanted action.[10]

Accidents, which Bob Land blamed on the open style of the wheels on the cars and the tightness of the track, also made the stock car races more thrilling for fans. Stock cars, midget driver Charlie Gottschalck remembered, were very easy to flip, resulting in far more rollovers with them than with the midgets. The increased rollovers resulted in what Sonny Coleman called "wrecks you wouldn't believe," and many jokingly referred to the upside-down stock cars as taxi cabs. Given the diminutive size of the Speedway's track and the relatively large size of the cars, wrecks involved nearly every car, with driver Sheri Thurman Graham saying "when they had a pileup, they really had a pileup." While they did have a higher tendency to roll over, the stock cars were relatively safer than the midgets because of their larger size, enclosed passenger compartments, and safety equipment. As driver Marv Slusser recalled, stock car accidents might hurt the drivers a little bit, but unlike the midget drivers, they were not getting killed in accidents. One program from 1950, while still heavily promoting the midget races, featured a picture of a demolished Essex stock car driver Blu Plemons had managed to lodge between the guardrail and grandstands. Looking at the photo in 2012, Plemons asserted that he had never put a scratch on any of the cars he raced at Lakeside or anywhere else. Plemons's assertion led his fellow drivers to joke that while the car was indeed destroyed, it was true that there was not a single scratch on it.[11]

Stock car drivers were also a far rowdier bunch than those who had driven the midgets, and fist fights frequently broke out between drivers, especially after accidents or between races. Just as more accidents seemed to get the crowds more animated, the fights made things even more exciting. Fights also broke out among the frustrated midget drivers, who were not happy at having been replaced by stock cars. Rarely, however, did the midget drivers get into altercations with the stock car drivers. Sonny Coleman did not remember any animosity between the two groups of drivers, although Bob Campbell vividly recalled one night when someone pulled the spark plug wires off the stock cars in an effort to keep them from running.[12]

The stock car races also brought the first female drivers to Lakeside Speedway. The Powder Puff Girls were typically the wives or girlfriends of the regular drivers, and they usually sold programs and played music between races. Sometime in the mid-1950s the CARC decided to have the women compete in a ten-lap trophy dash. Women drivers were considered somewhat of "a lark" at the time, and most spectators and drivers viewed the first Powder Puff race as simply another part of the entertainment package CARC had been perfecting since 1948. The Powder Puff drivers, however, took their races very seriously, and many proved to be very good at racing. In fact, according to Powder Puff driver Sheri Thurman Graham, some of the men were surprised at how well the women handled the cars; before long the Powder Puff races became a regular feature at Lakeside. It had been a long-standing rule at the Speedway that women were not allowed in the pits, which photographer Jerry Miller referred to as "sacred" space. Even the trophy girls were excluded from the pits, recalled Marv Slusser: after the men ran their races, the trophy girls were escorted into the pits to present the trophies and then taken back out to the stands. The Powder Puffs had two races, fifteen minutes of hot laps and one ten-lap race after the B class cars ran. Prior to their races, the women drivers gathered outside the gates to the pits and were escorted in by a pit hostess. They sometimes had little time to prepare, especially if the car they were going to drive was one of the cars from the B class races, which finished just ahead of them. The one exception to the rule was Krasner's daughter, Rhoda, who sometimes worked the concession stand located in the pits in later years. Women were finally allowed in the pits shortly before the Speedway closed in 1988.[13]

While most of the early Powder Puff racers drove cars that belonged to their husbands or boyfriends, CARC rules did permit women to have their own cars as long as the car was registered with the club. Few took advantage of the opportunity, however, because auto racing was still an expensive sport (Graham called it the most expensive of all the sports with which she was involved), and being able to drive someone else's car made sense financially. Sonny Coleman remembered one woman in particular, Audrey Bolyard, who took racing especially seriously. Bolyard was so serious that she had her own custom-built car for Powder Puff races at Lakeside. Although she only drove for a short while, Bolyard, who came from Kansas, was "one hell of a race driver" according to those who knew her, and she won several championships within the CARC Powder Puff division in her light-purple car at Lakeside. Women who shared cars with their husbands also generally shared all of the equipment that went with racing. Sheri and Don Thurman, for example, shared the helmet the rules required all drivers to wear.[14]

For all the racers, the entire operation was very much a family affair. Pit crews were often made up of fathers, brothers, and male cousins, while mothers, aunts, and female cousins served as pit hostesses and children as trophy boys or girls. In addition to helping on race night, the entire family also helped get the cars, which always needed maintenance, ready during the week. Sheri Thurman Graham said the lives of drivers and their families essentially revolved around the cars. For example, she remembers working on the family's racecar with her father-in-law whenever her husband had to be out of town for work. Each Sunday night of racing began with the drivers and their families arriving at Lakeside early to eat hamburgers (which Graham called the best hamburgers in town) at the park's restaurant before heading to the pits to prepare for the night ahead. The races were also family affairs for the fans, who often spent Sunday afternoons in the amusement park, eagerly awaiting the moment when the Speedway's ticket booth would open so they could buy their tickets for that night's event.[15]

The Powder Puff Club had grown to thirty members by 1968, though only eleven of them actually raced. By 1973 there were twelve drivers. More women would have liked to have raced, according to those who were there, but they did not have their own cars and did not know anyone who would let them drive one of their cars. A number of the owners, according to Graham, were not open to letting women drive their cars. The average age of the female drivers, according to a story in the *Denver Post*, was twenty-six-and-a-half, and they had twenty-eight children among them. In addition to racing, the women appeared in parades, had a booth at the annual Arvada Harvest Festival, and took part in fundraising programs. The Powder Puff drivers met with either Benjamin or Miriam Krasner to plan each week's program.[16]

The Powder Puff drivers, according to Graham, had a smaller percentage of accidents in their races than did the men. She credited this to the lower number of cars in the Powder Puff races and the ten-lap limit but said there were certain women the other drivers were very careful of when they did pass them. The shortened races also made it harder for the women to win if they did not have a good pole position at the start because a driver in the back had to pass all the other drivers in a very short amount of time, at least one per lap and sometimes two, to become the leader. The restrictions on their races were sometimes irritating, and Graham said the Powder Puff drivers could have been competitive if given more of a chance, but no one challenged the situation. One spectator suggested that they could go to a lawyer and sue for the chance to race with the men rather than in a separate class, but so many of the women shared cars with their husbands or boyfriends that it would have been difficult to decide who would get to drive. At the same time, according to Graham, a number of male drivers and owners would have pulled their cars from the races before they let women drive them or would compete alongside them. Throughout the years the Powder Puffs raced at Lakeside, the men kept a tight hold on the races and steadfastly refused to let the women have more time or more races, a situation Graham noted still exists as women try to break into NASCAR. Still, the fans at Lakeside enjoyed watching the women race, and the women thoroughly enjoyed their time on the track.[17]

The Powder Puff drivers, said Graham, raced for the same reasons as the men: they "wanted quick time and to win." The Powder Puff drivers accumulated points throughout the season depending on where they finished in the races, ranging from four points for first place down to one point for fourth place; at the end of the season the driver with the most points became the track Powder Puff champion. Midway through the 1968 season, Graham, who was Rookie of the Year in 1966, was the point leader; she went on to be that year's Powder Puff champion. She detailed her experience driving for the *Denver Post*, remembering that the first time she raced at Lakeside Speedway she was so excited that she ran over her husband's toolbox while driving into her stall at the track. She quickly proved her capacity for racing, however, and managed to beat her husband, Don Thurman, by 0.18 seconds in the time trials driving the 1933 Ford they shared. This happened so frequently, she later said, that members of the pit crews had bets on whether she would out-time her husband. She told reporter Lois Barr that her family was very supportive of her racing career, which to her was the most exciting of the sports she took part in (the list also included bowling, volleyball, and softball). She dismissed accidents as something that just occurred as part of racing, and given the safety equipment drivers were required to wear, she noted that drivers were rarely hurt. Graham told Barr that after one particular accident, the result of the throttle in her car sticking and causing her to hit the wall, she was more worried about the car than she was about herself. She even took part in demolition derbies at both Lakeside and Englewood Speedways, although at Lakeside she competed against men rather than fellow women drivers. She later said she simply loved to race and drive because it "just felt natural" to her.[18]

It was obvious from the tone of the article in the *Denver Post* that, for most people, women racecar drivers at Lakeside were still a novelty in 1968, even though they had been racing as part of the CARC for several years by then. Barr wrote in the *Post*, for example, that Graham's most embarrassing moments racing were splitting her pants while getting into her car one night and pinning a man against the fence in the pits when she entered too quickly.

Of that incident she said, "He probably thought I was a typical woman driver." But it was also obvious that the women took racing very seriously. Graham told Barr that mechanical knowledge was essential to racing and that she had worked on the car with her husband and was capable of changing spark plugs and tires and installing wiring on her own. She also thought racing had made her a much better driver in general because of the faster reflexes and knowledge of what speed could do that racing instilled, and she urged other husbands to let their wives race.[19]

Regardless of whether the men or the Powder Puffs were driving, the bigger cars consistently packed the stands every night during race season just as the midgets had once done, and on holidays the grandstands were often filled with standing-room-only crowds. The crowds, however, were not the same group of people who had come for the midget races. The stock cars, said driver Marv Slusser, attracted a very different group of spectators to Lakeside Speedway; Sonny Coleman described them as "absolutely totally different." Though midget racing was a working-class pastime, those attending them often dressed up for what was a special event, with the men in suits or slacks and dress shirts. In contrast, stock car fans arrived in their work clothes and expected a good show. Coleman began backing off from stock car racing when several particularly rowdy fans threatened to go after his wife and daughter, who were sitting in the stands watching him race. It was one thing for other drivers to fight with him, but when anyone went after his family they had crossed a line, and for him that was enough. Photographer Jerry Miller commented that the stock cars, which brought a very different spirit, essentially resulted in the Speedway being two different tracks depending on whether the midgets or the stock cars were racing.[20]

As difficult as the change from midgets to stock cars might have been for some, by 1953 even *Billboard* had recognized the important role stock cars played in drawing business to Lakeside. In early August the magazine reported that the stock cars were primary among the attractions that "keep the crowd coming back" and that the park used both stock and midget racing to "good results." As stock cars continued to increase in popularity, in 1953 KLZ-TV, the CBS affiliate in Denver, began broadcasting a half hour of the races each Sunday night. The broadcasts introduced a new audience to the races and in the process made Lakeside Speedway bigger and more popular than ever. That same year, Universal Pictures released the movie *Johnny Dark*, starring Tony Curtis and Piper Laurie. In the movie Dark, played by Curtis, is an automobile designer who comes up with a radical new design for a racecar. His employer rejects the design, so Dark, with the help of his boss's granddaughter, played by Laurie, steals it and enters the car in a Canada-to-Mexico race, which he wins. To help promote the movie, Universal urged the Sports Car Club of America and other racecar groups to sponsor Johnny Dark–themed events at their tracks. Although the details of the event have been lost, Lakeside was onboard, hosting a Johnny Dark stock car race at the Speedway in June.[21]

The Johnny Dark race started a new tradition at the Speedway, as Krasner began hosting special appearances by various novelty acts that overflowed the already packed grandstands. Joie Chitwood's Thrill Show played a three-day engagement at the Speedway in July 1955. Chitwood was a very successful racecar driver who competed in seven Indianapolis 500s before giving up driving in 1943 to focus on his stunt driving show, which was reportedly the inspiration for Evel Knievel's act. Over 110,000 people packed Chicago's Soldier Field to see one of his shows in the 1950s. Chitwood's drivers did jumps, rolled cars, raced at high speeds, and performed dozens of other stunts—usually in Chevrolets, which sponsored his show. Bill McGaw's Tournament of Thrills, which was similar to Chitwood's show, appeared at the Speedway in August 1955. Both shows, said *Billboard*, "pulled crowds greater than the usually jammed grandstand for the twice-weekly stock car shows." Two years later Krasner scheduled a "Little 500" race at the Speedway. The 500-lap race went on for nearly five hours, one hour of which was broadcast live on television. The special race drew an additional 4,500 people "into his already jammed" park, according to *Billboard*. The heavy promotion and special events worked amazingly well. One month into the 1958 season, the Speedway ticket booth had already taken in as much money as it had on all the busiest nights the previous year put together, which was impressive given that during the previous year the Speedway had consistently attracted 10,000 customers on race nights.[22]

Beginning in 1955, Krasner realized that he could use the races, which usually started at the end of April or the beginning of May, to get a head start on the summer amusement season. Other than the Speedway, no part of the park was open for business, but it allowed Krasner to report to *Billboard* that his park was open earlier than rival Elitch's while also boosting the total seasonal earnings for the park. The stock cars were "one of the biggest crowd getters" for the park, reported *Billboard* in 1955, and even inclement weather failed to diminish the crowds that packed the grandstands on race nights. The rain did sometimes turn the track into an unsafe mess, and race officials attempted to dry the track as best they could between storms. If it was getting to be too late in the evening, however, they would call off the rest of the night's program, and the Speedway would issue rain checks for the next Sunday. While not ideal for the next week's gate receipts, the rain checks were appreciated by the fans and helped the Speedway earn a reputation that kept them coming back for more.[23]

The 1955 season also proved the wisdom of Krasner's decision to allow KLZ-TV to broadcast the races. Still running thirty minutes long, the program usually aired two or three races plus part of the demolition derby if time allowed. But, wrote *Billboard*, the show rarely, if ever, broadcast the end of the "ear-splitting final event," which left "the video audience wanting more." If seeing the races on television was not enough to convince people to attend in person the next week, failing to see the finish of the final event was, and *Billboard* reported that attendance was up each week following a television broadcast. The broadcasts were simply one more part of Krasner's tireless promotional efforts. Nearly every midget driver who raced at Lakeside remembered how actively Krasner promoted both the amusement park and the midget races, using his connections with the *Denver Post* to make sure both received heavy coverage. He was no less active with the stock car races. By 1956, frequent news stories about, and pictures of, the stock cars were appearing in newspapers; combined with the weekly television shows, they pushed attendance at the Speedway ever higher. The broadcast also introduced the Speedway to people around the country. One fan who had moved to California was shocked when he turned on the broadcast of a race one night only to see the familiar sight of Lakeside Amusement Park in the background. The television broadcast moved to ABC affiliate KBTV in 1957, and Krasner reported to *Billboard* that he was going to keep the Speedway open into September, as the grandstands were still packed on Sunday nights.[24]

Interest in the standard stock cars began to drop a bit in the mid-1960s and into the 1970s, but unlike the midgets, much could be done to help renew their popularity. The Speedway experimented with Figure-8 racing for a short time in the mid-1960s, and the sound of the cars hitting each other as they crossed in the middle of the track area became common. The Speedway also introduced a compact class, made up of Plymouth Valiants, Ford Falcons, and a Corvair, which many thought was more suitable for Lakeside's small track. In the early 1970s the compact cars became the Late Model class, which were cars built specifically for racing. Lakeside made the change official for the 1975 season, when the track announced that Late Models would be based on newer compact bodies such as Pintos, Vegas, Gremlins, and Mustangs. There were no weight restrictions on the new cars, however, as the Speedway did not have a scale with which to weigh them. Some drivers argued that the new cars with their V8 engines were too much for the Speedway's track, that they never should have been allowed on it and ultimately led to its downfall.[25]

The demolition derby was another popular Speedway feature revived in the 1970s to heighten interest in the track. The new demolition derby also revived the Figure-8 configuration, which during regular races had resulted in accidents that damaged expensive cars. During a demolition derby involving junkers, however, those accidents were valuable entertainment, and the last car still running was the winner. As one park employee said, the demolition derby made sure people stayed until the very end because it was fun to see who would emerge victorious. The idea was similar to Benjamin Krasner making sure that the end of the final race was never broadcast over television in the 1950s—it forced people to come to the Speedway and stick around until the entire program was over.[26]

Driver Marv Slusser called the Speedway a "racer's track." Most stock car drivers remember the track in the same terms as midget drivers, with its uphill and downhill straightaways, banked north turn, and flat south turn creating a difficult situation for drivers. Like the midget drivers before them, stock car drivers had to set up their cars differently for Lakeside than they did for other tracks, and the track was the undoing of as many stock car drivers as midgets. Most midget drivers believed anyone who could master the Speedway's track could drive anywhere; stock car drivers Marv Slusser and Blu Plemons believed the same for the stock cars. Sheri Thurman Graham said that, while the track's size and layout made it difficult, "if you found a good groove you could really go." As difficult as the Speedway might have been to drive on, Slusser, Plemons, and Graham all remembered it as a fun track. But the three also drove when the original, smaller stock cars were on the track. The bigger, heavier Late Models offered a very different experience.[27]

The 1988 season marked the fiftieth anniversary of Lakeside Speedway. It would also be its last. To celebrate the anniversary, organizers decided to hold two special midget races, one in May and one in July, in addition to the usual stock car races. Driver Tom Evans won the special fiftieth anniversary midget race on May 7, 1988, while John Eatwell, president of the RMMRA, won the regular midget race that day. Randy Roberts won another midget race on July 16. The midget drivers' second special race, which featured a fifty-lap race in honor of the milestone, was scheduled for July 27. Don Daly, who had raced at Lakeside in 1938, was slated to be there for the event. But before the midgets could run the race, tragedy struck.[28]

On Sunday, July 24, 1988, about 4,000 people were in the stands watching the stock car races when shortly after 10:00 p.m., about halfway through the main event, a Late Model Camaro driven by Gary Burton went out of control on the southwest corner of the track and hit the guardrail. The car flew several feet through the air before hitting one of the track's stoplights, which caused it to spin around and hit the chain-link fence that protected spectators from flying debris. The car itself never hit anyone, but the impact shredded a wooden fence, the pieces of which went flying into the stands. Burton walked away from the accident with only minor injuries, but thirteen spectators were hit by pieces of the wooden fence, and one, Kristy Carlson, a hairstylist at Westminster Mall, was killed.[29]

The accident was not the first or even the most spectacular accident at the Speedway. Debris from cars and accidents, ranging from tires to engine parts, had been flying into the stands for years. Sheri Thurman Graham recalled one night when the engine blew on the car she shared with her husband, Don Thurman, showering fans sitting in the upper levels of the grandstands with parts. Graham also remembered a night when one of the stock cars hit the guardrail and actually drove a short way on the chain-link fence that protected fans. But throughout fifty years of accidents, a fan had never been killed, and for everyone involved with the Speedway, Carlson's death was a horribly shocking event.[30]

Critics immediately charged that the Speedway was in poor condition, which alone had been responsible for the fatal accident. One driver, Bob Denney, told a reporter from the *Rocky Mountain News* that racers had repeatedly asked for improvements to the track and guardrail but that only minimal maintenance was done. Marv Slusser and others said the track was too small to handle the big Late Model cars, which were far different than the earlier, smaller cars that had raced on the track for years. Tim Miles of the CARC told the *News* that the chain-link fence that protected spectators was one of the safest available, while Dick Pachello, president of the CARC, said his club's drivers would not be on the track if they felt it was unsafe. Stock car driver Bob Land speculated that the accident happened because the frequent overlays since 1939 had raised the height of the track significantly, but the guardrail had not been raised a corresponding amount. Still others blamed the wreck on what they termed poor workmanship by the professional maintenance team that, a couple of years earlier, had replaced the husband and wife who had maintained the track for nearly three decades.[31]

Two days after the accident, insurance company investigators and police officials completed their inquiry at the Speedway and released the track in time for the midget races scheduled for July 27. The fifty-lap race, which driver Palmer Crowell from Oregon won, took place in front of a crowd of about 3,000 people and was preceded by a vintage midget exhibition run. The evening's only major accident occurred when two cars leaving the track hit one of the vintage midgets, knocking it over on its side and causing a small fire in the car. A sprint driver who was watching quickly dealt with the fire, and the midget's driver was not seriously injured. For the first race after the fatal accident, it was a successfully uneventful evening. It was also one of the last races held at Lakeside Speedway. For years, many nearby residents had been unhappy with the Speedway because of the noise it generated; some drivers believed neighbors saw the fatal accident as their chance to force Rhoda Krasner to either close the track or close the park.[32]

In talking about Lakeside Speedway, Benjamin Krasner once said "as long as the boys want to run them [racecars], keep it open," but on September 2, 1988, his daughter, Rhoda, made the difficult decision to close the Speedway. Both stock car and midget drivers were stunned by the news. The secretary of the CARC told the *Rocky Mountain News* that the organization was devastated by the loss of the track, while RMMRA officials revealed that they had spent two hours and used every argument they could think of trying to convince Krasner to keep the track open. Jerry Van Dyke, president of the Colorado Motorsports Hall of Fame, remarked that the loss of Lakeside Speedway took away the only remaining paved track in the Denver metro area. In March 1990, nearly two years after the fatal accident, Kristy Carlson's father, Ronald, filed lawsuits against the amusement park, the Speedway, the town of Lakeside, and driver Gary Burton. The defendants settled the lawsuits out of court the following December, but no details of the settlements were released.[33]

Lakeside Speedway had enjoyed a wild ride between 1938, when the first midget racers transformed it from an unused athletic field, and the day it closed in 1988. For many of its longtime fans, the closure was a tragic end to what had been one of the most prominent race tracks in Colorado. But Lakeside Speedway had managed to outlast most of its onetime rivals. Its biggest competitor, Englewood Speedway, for example, had closed in 1979. Of the 8,200 tracks that once existed in the United States, 7,000 were gone by 2002. Most racing activity in the Denver area eventually moved to Colorado National Speedway in Erie and the drag strip at Bandimere Speedway in Morrison. In its day, however, Lakeside Speedway had hosted some of the best drivers Colorado had to offer. Johnny Tolan, who started out as a midget racer at Lakeside, was not the only driver from the track who went on to race in the Indianapolis 500. Jim Malloy was the 1959 and 1960 CARC champion at Lakeside; he went on to race in four 500s and was fatally injured in an accident while preparing to run his fifth. The Colorado Motorsports Hall of Fame is filled with inductees who became stars at Lakeside.[34]

An indication of how important the Speedway was and the role the Krasners played in its success came when Benjamin Krasner and his daughter, Rhoda, were inducted into the Colorado Motorsports Hall of Fame in 2006. Four years later Benjamin Krasner was inducted into the National Sprint Car Hall of Fame for his work as a promoter. In Krasner's biography for the Sprint Car Hall of Fame, Justin Zoch wrote that as an amusement park owner, Krasner knew how to entertain, as he "kept giving the people of Denver all the auto racing they wanted, and they came in droves" while behind the scenes he "worked hard to keep the cars coming to Lakeside." Fans vividly recall driving to the track, waiting for the ticket booth to open, the smell of hotdogs and hamburgers from the concession stands, and the roar of the engines. Each fan had a favorite driver, and the track was small enough that fans could rush down to the pits to shout encouraging words at them while booing the driver who was the "bad boy" of the track for having won most often that season. Decades later fans could recall what number car their favorite driver was in and who sponsored it. Above it all, they could hear the sounds of the amusement park competing with the cars' engines for attention. Memories of Lakeside Speedway are so strong that, even years after its closure, one spectator wrote that anyone near the Speedway late at night could "hear the ghosts, the bark of the 'Flathead,' the zing of the 'Stove bolt 6,' the deep throated rumble of the 'Offy,' the snarl of the 'V8-60,' and faintly from the pit PA system . . . Reed Walker say, 'Ladies and gentlemen, here is the lineup for the main.'" [35]

Aerial view of Lakeside in 2007 shows the shopping mall in the upper right corner and the Speedway to its left. I-70 is in the lower right corner. *(Joel A. Rogers)*

Denver Dry store at Lakeside Mall. *(Author's Collection)*

Milo Lane's TV Repair Shop at Lakeside Mall. *(Author's Collection)*

Midget drivers Lloyd Axel in car 5 and Burt McNeese in car 55 racing at the Speedway, 1947. *(Author's Collection)*

Based on the number of his photographs handed out, midget driver Johnny Tolan was the most popular driver among women at the Speedway. *(Author's Collection)*

Wreck between stock cars driven by Al Taft (17) and Larry Martell (41) at the Speedway, 1958. *(Author's Collection)*

The 1967 Powder Puff Club at Lakeside. *(Sheri Graham Collection)*

Original merry-go-round in Lakeside's Kiddies Playland. *(Author's Collection)*

Lakeside's Fun House, 1940s. *(Author's Collection)*

Opening day of the Dragon coaster, built on the site of the Fun House, 1986.
(Author's Collection)

Poster advertising Lakeside's
centennial season, 2008.
(Author's Collection)

Lakeside owner Rhoda Krasner (*right*) with her daughter, Brenda Fishman (*left*), 2011. *(Karl Gehring,* Denver Post, *Getty Images)*

CHAPTER 9

Lakeside Amusement Park, Public Nuisance?

As theme parks rapidly came to dominate the industry in the 1960s and 1970s, smaller, family-owned parks like Lakeside Amusement Park disappeared more rapidly than ever before. They had been a rarity since the 1930s, when only about 300 still survived. With the advent of theme parks, there were a total of 997 amusement park businesses in the United States in 1963. That number dropped to 466 in 1982 but had risen to 744 five years later; 80.5 percent of those parks were corporate-owned, however, a dramatic change from the early years of the industry. The high costs associated with staying competitive had eliminated most of the family-owned parks, which were often unable to keep up with the constant changes the business required. In Denver, where theme park developers had researched the market and decided it was too isolated for the destination parks they were building, Lakeside and rival Elitch's survived, the two family-owned parks left alone to fulfill the city's summer amusement needs.[1]

The enormous pressure amusement parks faced from larger competitors may not have been an immediate threat to Lakeside, but other issues had the potential to have a powerful impact on the park's future. Denver was in need of room to grow, but a 1974 amendment to the state constitution prevented the city from annexing land to accomplish that. Forced to turn inward, federally funded urban renewal projects created space for the city to grow up rather than out. All across Denver, some of the city's most significant historic buildings fell to the wrecking ball, including the Tabor Grand Opera House and the First National Bank of Denver building. Denver's experiment with urban renewal led to the city's first organized historic preservation movement, but not before many landmark buildings were lost. While urban renewal never made it to the town of Lakeside, some of the ideas and attitudes behind it seemed to do so, nearly to the detriment of Lakeside Amusement Park.[2]

Unlike the owners of most other small parks, Benjamin Krasner was able to keep up with bigger theme parks when it came to spending money to keep Lakeside fresh. By 1965 he had spent thirty years of his life keeping the park competitive with the constant addition of rides and attractions, from new ticket booths to construction of the Cyclone to automobile races at the Speedway. In a 1973 interview, his daughter, Rhoda, said he had worked hard even as a child, resulting in his having had "a restricted childhood," which explained "his long and delighted infatuation with Lakeside, a child's magic world." Krasner was a fixture at the park, walking the grounds every day during the summer in his three-piece suit, making sure the trains (which he was especially passionate about) ran on time, and studying all the other rides. He rarely rode the Cyclone, recalled Rhoda, usually limiting his trips on it to one or two near the end of the season. Before taking his rides, however, he had spent months leaning on the nearby fence watching the coaster and could feel every place that needed work before the next season.[3]

Krasner's hard work and passion had earned him enormous respect from drivers at the Speedway, Denver's business community, and the amusement park industry as a whole. But outside of the amusement park, he preferred to remain in the background. Other than serving on the board of directors of Rose Memorial Hospital, he kept his charitable contributions quiet, letting his "good deeds speak for themselves." As the summer of 1965 wound down, Lakeside Amusement Park was heading toward the conclusion of another successful season, but on August 8, 1965, Benjamin Krasner died at his Denver home at age seventy-eight. Lakeside was suddenly without the leadership of the man who had been a part of the park for nearly fifty years.[4]

A year before his death, Rhoda had graduated from Mills College in California with a liberal arts degree and was planning to attend graduate school. Born several years after her father purchased the park, Rhoda Krasner had grown up with Lakeside, a "world of carousels and chute [sic] the-chutes, midway barkers trying to out shout the belly tickling laugh of the big fat mechanical lady at the Fun House, a world colored by neon lights, buttered yellow popcorn, and pink cotton candy." One of her first jobs in the park, when she was seven, was bagging peanuts while watching elegantly dressed men and women making their way to the El Patio Ballroom. In subsequent years, she worked wherever her father felt she was needed, usually at the popcorn machine or the games. She became close with the year-round staff, and as "an only child, she found a big family among the park employees," wrote a reporter for the *Arvada Citizen Sentinel*. As a child she rarely rode any of the rides, but at her father's request, park employees often left one of the European gas-powered cars from the small racetrack out for her to drive through the park before it opened each day. As a result, the park was "still a novelty" to her whenever she brought friends to it as a child. After her father's death, according to the *Sentinel*, "the land of enchantment with its fun and its heartaches" was her responsibility.[5]

Rhoda Krasner told writer Stuart Leuthner in 1992 that she was naive when it first came to running the park, saying "you had a young daughter and her mother who were very conscientious about running the merry-go-round . . . but we learned." For several years prior to his death, Benjamin Krasner's brother-in-law, Martie Ruttner, had been helping him manage Lakeside, still living with his wife, Jennie, in the apartment over the park's College Inn restaurant that they had once shared with Krasner. After Krasner's death, Ruttner took over as general manager of the park, running it in cooperation with his niece for the next four years. After Ruttner's death in 1969, Rhoda Krasner became general manager. Taking over the park was a "fantastic transition" for her. In a 1973 interview, she said she had to be continually alert to change and flexible enough to accommodate it, and after eight years of running the park, she had learned much but still had more to learn. By the time she said those words, Lakeside had become a hard teacher.[6]

A major highway project, completed in 1966, provided better access to Lakeside, helping to increase the number of visitors. Planning for Interstate 70 had begun with passage of the Federal Highway Act of 1944, which authorized construction of a highway between Denver and the Colorado border with Kansas. Supporters wanted to extend the road past Denver into Utah, receiving permission to do so with passage of the 1956 Interstate Act. The State of Utah initially opposed building the highway west of Denver because it would have to pass through mountainous terrain in eastern Utah, massively increasing the state's share of construction costs. Officials with the Colorado Department of Highways and one of Colorado's US senators, Edwin Johnson, lobbied hard for the proposed route, however, and eventually convinced Utah. With their united support, the US Congress approved the road in October 1956. Construction of the first piece of I-70 through Denver, which ran between Colorado Boulevard and I-25, started in 1961 and was finished three years later. Construction of the second section, which connected I-25 to Sheridan Boulevard, began in 1964, reaching Federal Boulevard in December 1965 and Sheridan in July 1966. The total cost for the second stretch was $4,501,000, high because engineers had to thread the highway past Rocky Mountain Park, Rocky Mountain Lake, between Berkeley Lake and Denver's Willis Case Golf Course, and then past Lakeside Amusement Park. The highway cut off part of Rocky Mountain and Berkeley Lakes, forcing workers to deepen both lakes to keep their water capacities the same. The highway also cut off a small portion of the north end of the Lakeside property, where the greyhound track had once stood. The end result, however, was what the Colorado Department of Transportation referred to as a "gently winding and beautifully landscaped section of I-70," and motorists who exited onto Sheridan found themselves practically at Lakeside's front gate.[7]

With business at Lakeside steady, Count Basie's band played the Moonlight Gardens Ballroom in 1968, one of the last big-name bands to play there before it closed in 1972. Rhoda Krasner said in a 1986 interview that her father had hoped to reinvigorate the ballroom when he redecorated it and changed its name to Moonlight Gardens in 1956, but it was impossible to "revitalize a trend with décor. We might have just prolonged the era a bit." Lakeside's ballroom was not alone; Elitch's tore down its famed Trocadero Ballroom in 1975. Ballroom dancing may have been fading, but as popular as ever were Lakeside's fireworks displays, which the *Rocky Mountain News* in 1971 declared one of the largest shows in the region. The show included aerial and set displays. The most spectacular sets were the American Flag and Niagara Falls, which was suspended from a 1,200-foot-long cable, while the aerial display used a new triple-burst shell made in England, with each burst producing twenty-four displays. Park customers were allowed to see the show for no additional charge, but many hundreds more gathered outside the park each year to view it as well without having to pay admission. It seemed as if all was well at Lakeside, but two seemingly innocuous incidents at the start of the 1972 season triggered a series of events that threatened the park's survival.[8]

Shortly before Lakeside opened for the summer, the Wheat Ridge Fire Protection District, which had long handled fire services for the park, announced that it would not renew fire protection contracts with the park and the town of Lakeside (Rhoda Krasner later hinted that political rancor over the rebuilding of Forty-Fourth Avenue may have played a role in non-renewal of the contract). The neighboring towns of Wheat Ridge and Mountain View, along with Jefferson County, wanted to direct drainage from the road into Lake Rhoda, but Krasner refused, saying the drainage water would kill the lake's fish and make it harder to run the park's speedboats. With no fire protection contract in place for the year, Krasner purchased two fire trucks and asked the Colorado Division of Labor to train Lakeside employees and residents in firefighting techniques, which was ongoing when the park opened in mid-May.[9]

The second incident, an accident on the Cyclone, happened on May 14, 1972. At about 4:30 p.m. that day, a five-car train on the coaster either slowed down or came to a complete stop at a low point on the track and was hit from behind by another train. Four passengers from both trains were taken to Lutheran Hospital. Only one, ten-year-old Juanita Proctor, was kept overnight, with a broken arm. The hospital characterized all the injuries, including Proctor's, as minor, and Krasner told a *Rocky Mountain News* reporter that the ride would not reopen until investigators discovered the cause of the accident. Three days after the roller coaster accident, the *Denver Post* reported that investigators from the Colorado Division of Labor and the Fireman's Fund American Insurance Companies were paying particular attention to the track in an effort to determine if the cause was unavoidable or if the park was in fact at fault. James Underwood, who worked for the Division of Labor, told a reporter from the *Post* that, while the Division of Labor inspected the park each year, its investigators focused on wiring and other issues and relied on the insurance company to inspect the structure of the roller coaster itself. Underwood did tell the *Post* that Lakeside had received more than 100 citations for safety and fire code violations since June the previous year, most of which were a result of improper exits, improper or malfunctioning equipment, overloaded fuse boxes, and occupant loads that were too high. Underwood stressed that park management had done an "excellent job" of correcting the problems and complying with safety orders.[10]

After two weeks of investigation, the cause of the roller coaster accident still eluded the state Division of Labor and insurance company investigators. In the meantime, two other committees had started investigations of their own at Lakeside. The Jefferson County Fire Safety Committee and two members of the Jefferson County Grand Jury's fire committee arrived at the park on May 19 to look into a number of safety concerns. Although the roller coaster accident played a part in prompting the investigation, the committee members were more disturbed by Wheat Ridge's failure to renew the fire protection contract. The two investigative committees produced a confidential report they gave to Jefferson County district attorney Al Herrmann Jr., who in turn told the *Denver Post* that the report might form the basis for a grand jury investigation of the park.[11]

The grand jury investigation began almost immediately after Herrmann received the report and continued through the rest of 1972 and into 1973. While the grand jury investigated, another tragedy took place that put even more pressure on the park and the town. Harry's Club Forty-Four was located at the corner of Forty-Fourth Avenue and Sheridan Boulevard, just inside the Lakeside city limits. On the night of October 20, 1972, fire broke out in the bar, and the five-month-old Lakeside Fire Department arrived on the scene to fight the blaze. The blaze would have been a difficult one even for experienced firefighters, in part because successive remodels of the building had resulted in new walls built over old walls, which trapped the flames between each layer. Lakeside firemen George Thomas (who was also the mayor of Lakeside), Roy Dunn, and Robert Naylin were working inside the bar when an explosion (whether it was the furnace or a backdraft was undecided) rocked the building. Thomas and Dunn were treated for severe burns to their hands, but the blast trapped Naylin, who was also an employee of the bar, in the basement, where he had gone to fight what the men believed was the source of the fire. Naylin died of smoke inhalation before anyone could reach him; it took rescue workers two days to find his body in the debris.[12]

Bar owner Harry Brown filed a lawsuit against both the Lakeside Park Company and the town of Lakeside asking for $131,800 in damages. Brown alleged that one of his employees had called the Lakeside Fire Department to report the fire but after receiving no answer had to go next door to wake up Mayor Thomas (who lived in the house that once belonged to Marvin Adams, Lakeside's first mayor), who alerted the fire department. Brown said it took forty-five minutes for the fire trucks to arrive and that when they did they were unprepared and lacked proper equipment. Brown further stated that the firemen failed to follow proper procedures to save the furniture or other fixtures in the bar and that the town bulldozed what was left of the building after the fire, destroying any remnants. Even before Brown filed his suit, the grand jury added an inquiry into the fatal fire to its ongoing investigation.[13]

Lakeside opened for its sixty-fifth season in 1973, but as a reporter for the *Arvada Citizen Sentinel* wrote at the time, "there was no big you all come party to mark the stately anniversary." Instead, Rhoda Krasner and the park's employees were anxiously awaiting the grand jury's report, which was finally submitted to the Jefferson County district attorney in late June. The highly critical report listed sixty-five violations of building, electrical, and fire safety codes in the covered parking area along Sheridan Boulevard, the administrative offices, the closed ballroom, the Gayway and College Inns, the Fun House, and the Swimming Pool building (which had been used as storage, a machine shop, and the park's maintenance shop since closing in the mid-1960s). The grand jury argued that none of the buildings was paneled with the fire-resistant material required by law, that the wiring in many of them was dangerously antiquated, and that exits from many of the buildings failed to meet current building codes. The report also blasted the training, or lack thereof, of the town's fire department. The grand jury did give Lakeside's rides a "clean bill of health" but urged the district attorney to do everything possible to prevent the public from entering any of the buildings at the park. After receiving the report, Assistant District Attorney Nolan Brown immediately started legal proceedings to close the park. Lakeside Amusement Park, hailed at its 1908 opening as "the greatest and finest amusement park ever attempted West of Chicago" and "the beauty spot of the West," had been pronounced a public nuisance.[14]

Jefferson County officials sent Rhoda Krasner a copy of the draft report in March 1973, and she responded in a letter the following May, noting that the report did not question the safety of the rides at the park, which had been the chief focus of park employees the last few years. She also argued that all of the listed violations were in areas of the park that were generally off-limits to, or only minimally accessible by, the public. She added that Lakeside would establish a program to correct all of the problems listed. In an interview with the *Denver Post* the day after news of the grand jury's findings was made public, Krasner said she was "mystified" by the timing of the report, released just ahead of the park's always busy Fourth of July weekend. She questioned why Jefferson County had not moved to close the park in March, well ahead of the summer season. Krasner emphasized that all the rides were deemed safe by investigators but worried that with the release of the report and its timing, "the damage is done to us, to our reputation." As news of the investigation became public, it set rumors flying about Lakeside. One story held that the park was for sale for $10 million. At a time when Denver's Urban Renewal Authority was busily tearing down old buildings, another rumor held that Krasner intended to tear down all of the park's landmark buildings along Sheridan Boulevard and replace them with condominiums (a rumor her father had also heard from time to time, always chuckling about it). Yet another rumor asserted that she was going to voluntarily close the park. Krasner flatly denied that any of the stories were true, telling the *Denver Post*, "we're staying open as a family amusement park and will run our operation safely and in a clean manner." She was clearly prepared to fight for the park that she had grown up with and that had been a part of her father's life for decades.[15]

Unmoved by Krasner's willingness to establish a corrective program, on July 3 the district attorney filed for temporary and permanent injunctions to keep Lakeside Amusement Park from operating any of its buildings until the danger no longer existed, but he did allow the park to continue to operate its rides. Krasner and other park officials responded swiftly, filing a three-phase plan for improvements and repairs, the first phase of which listed about thirty projects already completed. Dan Fahrney of the Jefferson County district attorney's office told the *Denver Post* that, through its plan, the park had "complied substantially" with the grand jury's recommendations and that the only remaining items to be worked out before Jefferson County accepted the plan were improvements to water supplies and electrical wiring. By the end of July, the plans for water and electrical repairs had been approved by county inspectors rather than Lakeside city officials, and the district attorney filed for a consent decree from the courts that allowed Lakeside to operate as the work progressed. Under the agreement, the primary concern was an ongoing training program in safety and firefighting techniques for park and town personnel. The plan also called for long-term repair programs for the park's buildings, along with demolition of those that could not be brought up to code. The plan did leave room to negotiate if Krasner wanted to save any of the buildings for historic value, a thoughtful inclusion at a time when Denver was regularly demolishing landmarks. Judge Winston Wolvington, in officially signing off on the plan, set May 1, 1974, as the next inspection date for Lakeside, giving the park a little less than a year to correct the problems if it hoped to open for another season. After several tense months, it looked as if Lakeside had survived what had been perhaps the severest threat yet to its survival.[16]

Lakeside finished the rest of its sixty-fifth season quietly. Only the *Arvada Citizen Sentinel* marked the landmark anniversary by conducting a long interview with Rhoda Krasner that went over much of the park's history. A newspaper article typical of those from the park's past appeared in the *Denver Post* in mid-August, telling the story of *Miss Colorado*, a fifty-six-foot-long cruise boat that went into service on Lake Rhoda that summer. The boat, built in 1937, had operated on Denver's City Park Lake for many years and counted Dwight Eisenhower among its many passengers. Denver's Parks Department eventually put the boat in storage, and it fell into disrepair until Don Swanson, who had ridden the boat as a child, bought it and spent a year restoring it before launching it at Lakeside. The boat, which could hold twenty-five passengers, was equipped with a dance floor, stereo system, and restroom facilities. Mindful of the ordeal Lakeside was still going through, the article carefully pointed out that *Miss Colorado* had "complete safety equipment" for the crew and passengers. Over 17,800 people paid thirty-five cents apiece for a ride on *Miss Colorado* that summer, but Swanson grew discouraged by the results of the safety investigation and abandoned the boat at the end of the season. After a very intense season, Lakeside closed for the winter, and workers prepared to both undertake routine maintenance and step up their efforts at the ongoing work necessary to satisfy the three-phase program approved by the courts in preparation for the 1974 season.[17]

Part of the three-phase plan called for the demolition of Lakeside's existing maintenance shop in the old Swimming Pool building and the construction of a new one in a safer location, away from public areas at the park. During the off-season, workers took cars from many of the rides to the pool building to keep them protected from harsh winter weather or for repairs, which also meant that many of the blueprints and manuals for the park's rides were kept there as well.[18]

Paul McWilliams, a maintenance worker at the park, first noticed smoke coming from the Swimming Pool building shortly after 11:00 a.m. on December 11, 1973. By the time he got to the building from Kiddies Playland, where he was working, flames were shooting out of the windows and spreading to the roof of the building. Jack Thompson, a carpenter working inside the building, noticed flames at about the same time McWilliams spotted the smoke. As the fire spread out from the southern end of the building, employees readied one of the town's two fire trucks, but by the time they got it to the scene the blaze was out of control. Fire departments from Denver, Arvada, Wheat Ridge, and Edgewater arrived to help the Lakeside team, but forty-five minutes after the first reports of the fire came in, it was still a raging inferno. At one point, flames from the blaze reached heights of fifty feet to seventy-five feet, and smoke was visible from all over Denver as it billowed hundreds of feet into the air. Firefighters struggled to keep the blaze from spreading to nearby buildings, including the Casino and the Tower, and Denver fire chief Myrle Wise later told a reporter from the *Rocky Mountain News* that, had the conflagration reached the Casino, "we would have lost the whole park." Between 150 and 200 firemen worked for over an hour to put out the fire, which completely destroyed the sixty-five-year-old building. Nearby residents, who at the height of the fire had resorted to spraying their roofs with hoses to prevent sparks from setting their houses on fire, credited the Denver team with saving the park. It was not the first time they had done so. In 1911, when fire destroyed the park's Scenic Railway and Velvet Coaster, Denver had helped to save a part of its City Beautiful.[19]

Firefighters may have ultimately saved Lakeside, but the damage to the park went far beyond the destroyed building. The blueprints, a new drive system, and all but one car for the fifty-nine-year-old Staride were destroyed, rendering the ride inoperable. Cars, parts, and manuals for numerous other rides were lost as well. Also lost in the fire were most of the park's tools, leading one worker to speculate that the fire posed a major setback to the ongoing work aimed at bringing the park up to code and satisfying the plan accepted by Jefferson County just four months earlier. Maintenance supervisor Charles McWilliams told the *Rocky Mountain News*, "This is really going to hurt us."[20]

As firemen and park employees speculated on the cause of the fire, newspaper reporters revisited the grand jury investigation and report, embellishing articles on the blaze that appeared in the *Denver Post* and the *Rocky Mountain News* with details of the settled case. The first paragraph of the story in the *News* read, "Lakeside Amusement Park, branded a public safety hazard last summer by the Jefferson County Grand Jury, Tuesday was hit by a spectacular fire battled by five fire departments," while the *Post* concluded its article by stating "there was disagreement Tuesday over who was responsible for fighting the blaze," a reminder of the criticism Lakeside's fire department had received from the grand jury. The *News* sought out Assistant District Attorney Nolan Brown for comment, but he refused to do so without knowing more facts about the cause of the fire. In the aftermath of the fire, park employees were understandably defensive about their work over the past several months, with park superintendent Lyle Fulkerson telling the *News* that employees were working daily to upgrade the park's buildings to meet the grand jury's recommendations but that it took time to do everything. Paul McWilliams stressed that no flammable liquids were stored in the area where the fire started, while his father, George, said welding equipment in the area had not been used for several days. Bob Quinn, an Arvada fireman who had helped the grand jury investigate Lakeside the year before, came to the park's defense, saying he had personally turned off the electricity to the Swimming Pool part of the building. Investigators eventually determined that the building's aging electrical system was to blame for the fire.[21]

In the aftermath of the fire, park employees quickly pushed forward with the renovation program. A new cement maintenance building went up near the parking lot, satisfying one requirement of the three-phase plan. Jefferson County agreed to one modification of its agreement with the park, allowing Rhoda Krasner to preserve the park's administration building, which included the long-closed Casino Theater, "for its historical value." The original plan was to demolish the building, which for years had helped define the park's entrance, but under the new plan county officials shut off electricity to the building until it could be brought up to code, and park workers installed a one-hour fire wall on the exterior of the building. As another condition to keep the administration building, Krasner also agreed to install a new water main to increase water supply and pressure in the park, in part to be better prepared in the event of any future fires.[22]

Lakeside's Fun House and ballroom were not as fortunate as the administration building. Krasner planned to refurbish the Fun House but chose not to do it in time for the 1974 season, meaning it would remain closed until the necessary repairs there were completed. The ballroom was beyond repair. District Attorney Nolan Brown told the *Denver Post* that the once-elegant building was "the single most important problem" at Lakeside, saying that its age and interior décor posed the most substantial fire risk in the park, with fire officials estimating that a fire would consume the interior of the building in less than a minute. Krasner made the difficult decision to tear down the ballroom to satisfy the requirements of the three-phase plan. By the following May only the skeleton of the building remained, which itself was gone by the time the park opened for the summer. When Krasner walked through the debris of the ballroom as workers demolished it, she found that much of the framing from the building was still stamped with the name of the lumber company Frank Kirchhof, one of Lakeside's original builders and owners, had operated. The town's original jail, located in the basement of the ballroom, was still intact at the time the building was demolished, and workers moved it to another part of the park for storage.[23]

County officials inspected Lakeside Amusement Park as scheduled at the beginning of May 1974 and found that all of the improvements Rhoda Krasner had agreed to make were near completion. Judge Winston Wolvington stated that he found no reason to believe the remaining projects would not be completed by opening day and accordingly signed an order allowing the park to open for the summer. While the order stated that the park "no longer presents a substantial danger," it did allow the district attorney to take action without notifying Lakeside's owner if he determined that anything in the final stage of the renovations created a dangerous situation for customers. Nolan Brown told the *Denver Post* that he gave Rhoda Krasner "an awful lot of credit . . . she did things I didn't believe were possible" and made sure to point out that the condition and safety of Lakeside's rides had never been questioned. To his knowledge, he told the *Post*, "their reputation . . . has always been top."[24]

Lakeside opened on schedule in 1974 and made it through the season without incident. The press coverage of the park was reminiscent of the days before the grand jury investigation and the fire, with the *Rocky Mountain News* singling out the Cyclone for special attention. Writing that the *New York Times* had put the coaster on its Top Ten list that year because of its design and view of the Rocky Mountains, the local newspaper did nothing but sing its praises. The *News* pointed out that accidents on the Cyclone were rare, with most incidents involving blown-off wigs and dropped eyeglasses, ignoring the accident just two years earlier that had triggered the series of investigations that almost brought down the park. Rhoda Krasner rode the Cyclone with reporter Irene Clurman, and as "teenagers . . . squealed in fear" she "calmly" discussed the maintenance the ride required. Saying that it needed constant checking and painting, Krasner told Clurman that workers walked the track once and rode it at least five times each day before opening it to the public, checking for loose bolts and obstructions. Given what the park had just gone through, the emphasis in newspaper coverage that summer was on safety and the measures park employees were taking to guarantee it. But the thrill, Clurman wrote, was still there. At a time when many amusement park attractions that had once thrilled people now seemed tame, the Cyclone "still had them white-knuckling the guardrails, faces frozen in silent shrieks," and based on the number of people waiting in line for their turn each night, she wrote, "the thrill will never be gone."[25]

Behind the scenes, workers spent much of 1974 and the first part of 1975 on the last challenging project that remained to be completed: bringing the Fun House up to code. Originally constructed as a one-story building in the 1920s to replace the park's original Third Degree fun house, it had been enlarged to two floors in the 1930s. The Fun House used an enormous amount of electricity, and its outdated electrical system had been one of the major faults cited in the 1973 grand jury report. Barry Morrison, a reporter with the *Denver Post*, wrote that it would have been easy for Rhoda Krasner to follow in the footsteps of dozens of other amusement parks and tear down the attraction. Instead, the Fun House underwent a complete remodel that allowed it to reopen with Jefferson County's blessing, and Morrison wrote "it's marvelous to have the Fun House back."[26]

Much of what had made the attraction popular in the past was still there: games, a series of oppositely rotating barrels that people had to walk through, a shifting floor, slides from the second floor to the first floor, the spinning saucer, and Laffing Sal, for which workers built a new steel enclosure. The forty air jets located throughout the Fun House that were used to blow up women's skirts were the only feature that disappeared, victims of an era when most women wore pants or shorts instead of skirts. Inside, artist Jerry Childers created what he described as a "total environment," meaning that the design removed people from the outside world as much as possible. For example, Childers repainted the walls of the entryway in fluorescent colors and lit them with alternating red and green spotlights, which seemed to make the walls move as much as did the shifting floor people had to navigate. Childers painted the spinning saucer black and white and installed strobe lights over it, which seemed to make it spin in the opposite direction from which it was actually going. In the slide area, Childers painted psychedelic designs on the walls and installed black lights, which Morrison wrote gave the "gut-gripping drops . . . twice the impact." On the only new ride in the park that year, the Heart Flip, passengers rode in heart-shaped cars suspended from overhead arms they could spin as wildly as they wanted to by turning a wheel inside the passenger compartment. Krasner spent $10,000 alone on the custom lighting for the ride, rides manager Jim Moffett said, "to make it glow as romantically as it should" and to match the still-famous lighting on Lakeside's other rides.[27]

Given the difficult times Lakeside had gone through, Rhoda Krasner would have had good reason to celebrate the park's landmark seventieth anniversary in 1978, a milestone few amusement parks reached, but it passed without any fanfare. Throughout the rest of the 1970s and into the 1980s, safety, history, and the Cyclone were the dominant themes of Lakeside. In a 1979 article, *Denver Post* reporter Rykken Johnson hit on all three when he wrote about a crew of twelve who spent the entire winter tearing down rides and either repairing or rebuilding them. Three of the men were responsible for just the roller coaster, inching their way along the track to give it a "microscopic check" as they searched for loose nuts and bolts. An article in the *Rocky Mountain News* two years earlier also described the inspection, adding that workers could tell if a bolt was loose just by the sound it made when hit with a hammer. John Christian, the park's maintenance director, said the crew spent more time on the coaster than on any other ride and that he himself walked the track at least once a day before the park opened and sometimes twice if he noticed a particular problem. The coaster was special, Christian said, because "it wouldn't be an amusement park without a roller coaster." In 1979 Rhoda Krasner decided to have new red and blue trains built for the Cyclone, for appearance and safety reasons. Unhappy with the boxy design of new commercially made cars, the park hired Denver furniture maker Hans Vichiola to replicate the sleigh-like shape and oak construction of the original trains. Vichiola made only two changes on the new trains: he replaced the steel shields on the front of the cars with a fiberglass copy, which made it easier to change them in the event vibrations from the ride cracked them, and, in a nod to safety, the new cars had a stronger chassis than the originals. The red train debuted in 1979, followed by the blue train in 1980.[28]

The same article in the *Denver Post* also made sure to highlight the extensive training all ride operators at Lakeside received before being allowed to run the rides. The training began about two weeks before the park opened for the summer. In addition to learning how to run the rides, ride operators also had to take classes in park rules and regulations, safety procedures, and ride operation. The final exam consisted of the trainees teaching the trainers to operate all of the park's rides. Given all the positive press Lakeside received after 1974, it was as if Denver's newspapers had gone back to the 1910s and wanted the park to once again succeed by assuring readers that the problems of 1973 were gone and the park was safe. As the 1980s dawned, it seemed as if Lakeside had put the worst well behind it and was comfortably embracing its position as a historic amusement park.[29]

Lakeside was justifiably proud of its history, but that history had always included the necessity to change to keep people interested in the park. That was no less the case in the 1980s. In 1981, for example, most of the rides in the park were given new color schemes: the Round-Up was painted what rides manager Jim Moffett called Pepto Bismol pink, the Whip "grape sherbet," and the cars on the Satellite and Hurricane "a mixed basket of Easter-egg colors." The Cyclone still remained the top attraction, however, and in 1985 the *Rocky Mountain News* assembled a panel of three teenagers to rate Denver's coasters. Lakeside's Cyclone and Wild Chipmunk were rated "semi-awesome," about equal to Elitch's coasters. Lakeside may not have drawn as many people as Elitch's (a 1987 estimate put Elitch's annual visitors at 850,000 and Lakeside's at about half that number, although Rhoda Krasner believed it was higher), but in rides it was proving itself equal to its rival.[30]

Occasionally, however, memories of less happy times returned. In 1982, insurance inspectors wanted to check the center shaft on the rocket ship ride, the base of which was still Lakeside's original Circle Swing ride from 1908. The shaft was encased in cement, and the park had to use dynamite to get at it, essentially destroying the ride, only for investigators to find that the shaft was in excellent condition. The gleaming stainless steel rocket ship cars, described by the *Rocky Mountain News* as "vintage Flash Gordon," were removed and the ride never ran again. In 1985, insurance inspectors wanted to look at the center shaft on the still-popular Tumble Bug ride, which had been at the park since the 1920s. As with the rocket ship ride, the shaft on the Tumble Bug was buried in cement, and the park again had to resort to dynamite to expose it, only to find the shaft in perfect order. Rhoda Krasner, in a 2000 interview, mentioned the Tumble Bug as one of her favorite rides and losing it as one of her biggest disappointments at the park. Within three years Lakeside had lost two of its oldest rides, and as Krasner told Stuart Leuthner for his 1992 *American Heritage* article on Lakeside, "once you take a ride down, it never goes up again."[31]

Between necessary repairs and higher insurance costs (Elitch's, for example, had seen its insurance premiums balloon to over $1 million a year by 1986), the Fun House became an unsustainable attraction by 1985. In a 1987 interview with the *Rocky Mountain News*, Rhoda Krasner said "it was a real dilemma to let it go," but in the end it was the only choice that made sense. Laffing Sal went into storage, and the Fun House was torn down. The 1986 season saw the debut of a new steel roller coaster called the Dragon, so named because the train resembled a dragon, complete with head and tail, on the site of the Fun House. Krasner characterized the ride, which cost just under $1 million, as an intermediate coaster, giving the park something for those who were too big for the kiddy coaster but not ready or brave enough for the Cyclone. She also hoped the new coaster would help Lakeside better compete with Elitch's, letting people see it as something more than "Denver's 'other amusement park.'" Like her father, Krasner knew that as hard as it might be to let some of the old favorites go, it was necessary to do so if Lakeside wanted to stay in business.[32]

The eight years between Benjamin Krasner's death and the fire that destroyed the Swimming Pool building had been among the most tumultuous years Lakeside Amusement Park had ever endured. The once highly praised park saw its reputation in near ruins by 1973, in many ways a victim of its own longevity. In 1907 Lakeside's owners had decided to ignore the common amusement park practice of building structures that would soon decay and disappear and instead built permanent buildings at their park, buildings that would last long beyond the owners themselves. Zang and his associates had succeeded, and sixty-five years after Lakeside opened for the first time, most of its original buildings still stood. At a time when landmark buildings were disappearing throughout Denver, it seemed as if more than a few people would not have minded seeing a landmark amusement park disappear as well. But Lakeside had always proven itself resilient, and while the challenges posed might have been greater than ever before, it survived. The ballroom, Swimming Pool, and Fun House were lost in the end, but most of the park's historic structures were remodeled and still stood by the time the turmoil had settled. In the years after 1973, a few of the favorite rides and attractions disappeared from the park, but Rhoda Krasner took that in stride, repeatedly commenting that the park had to balance the old with the new. By 1979, wrote a reporter for the *Denver Post*, county officials were "openly" admiring improvements made at the park, and all inspections produced excellent results. Lakeside, however, still had one more threat to its survival with which to contend.[33]

CHAPTER 10

Lakeside, the Most Entertaining City in America

Like Lakeside Amusement Park's owners, Walt Disney watched nervously as less-than-desirable businesses crept in around Disneyland after it opened in 1955. Frustrated, Disney decided that at his next park he would make sure he controlled enough surrounding land to guarantee he could keep unwelcome neighbors away. In 1964 and 1965, agents for Disney purchased more than 27,000 acres of land outside Orlando, Florida, for construction of an East Coast version of Disneyland. In an extraordinary move, Florida granted Disney complete control over the property, allowing it to have its own laws, police force, hospital, maintenance department, and tax rates.[1]

Lakeside Amusement Park, however, had always had the kind of control Disney had in Florida, though on a smaller scale. In 1907 Marvin Adams, Lakeside's first mayor, had predicted that his grandson, the first baby born in the new town, would one day be the mayor of the great city of Lakeside. Adams's prediction never came true, as Lakeside remained a small town dominated by the amusement park and the shopping mall. The handful of people who called Lakeside home continued to live in the small houses along Sheridan Boulevard, and for most of the year the town was a relatively quiet place in which to live. But the amusement park and the shopping mall enabled it to do quite well financially. The mall's impressive financial impact (earnings ranged from $25 million in 1960 to $60 million in 1988) was a fact Lakeside's neighbors began to take special notice of in the 1970s and 1980s.

Lakeside's biggest neighbor was Denver, its onetime champion, whose boundaries with the town were Sheridan Boulevard and Forty-Eighth Avenue. For years, Denver had gobbled up its small neighbors as it rapidly grew in size and economic power. The town of Highlands, in north Denver, was founded by temperance advocate Horatio B. Pearce in 1871. It did not permit smelters or factories within its borders and discouraged bars from serving liquor by requiring a yearly $3,000 license fee for such establishments. By 1890 Highlands had seven streetcar lines and 5,000 residents and was Colorado's sixth largest city. Just three years later, however, Highlands was in such bad financial shape as a result of the economic depression plaguing the country that its residents accepted annexation to Denver in order to survive. The towns of Barnum, Harman, and South Denver also accepted annexation to Denver to survive the tough economic times. Nine years later, when the City and County of Denver was carved out of Arapahoe County, the towns of Elyria, Globeville, Montclair, Valverde, and Berkeley (across Sheridan from the future town of Lakeside) were also annexed. The additional land created a city of 59.25 square miles with a population of over 130,000 people.[2]

By 1902, nine of the dozen incorporated towns that had once ringed Denver had become part of the city. Other cities soon sprang up, including Aurora, Lakewood, Wheat Ridge, Mountain View, and Lakeside. The new cities managed to remain independent of Denver, although for some it was a close call. Voters in Lakewood, for example, rejected official incorporation of their town in 1947, 1956 (when backers proposed merging the town with Wheat Ridge), and 1961, when backers organized the election in the face of rumors that Denver was eager to annex the town. Voters finally approved incorporating Lakewood in 1969 following continued threats of annexation from Denver and concern that the town needed better law enforcement after a string of brutal rapes terrorized the community.[3]

During the post–World War II housing boom, builders constructed houses in several older, unoccupied areas of Denver, but new suburbs quickly grew up on the southwest edge of the city, including Brentwood and Harvey Park.

Denver moved quickly to annex those areas and continued to annex new areas into the 1960s, including the wealthier Bear Valley and Pinehurst neighborhoods. As land hungry as Denver appeared to be, when it came to its annexation activities, the city was no different from most other major cities in the United States. As political scientists Jered B. Carr and Richard C. Feiock note in their article on the subject, "Municipal annexation is the most widely used method of jurisdictional expansion, and its use has been central to the economic and political development of cities." Annexation, they write, is often promoted as giving residents of outlying areas needed services, such as a water supply and police protection, while giving the annexing city an enlarged tax base. Between 1950 and 1970, write sociologists Vivian Z. Klaff and Glen V. Fuguitt, annexation was one of the principal means by which metropolitan areas expanded their populations and tax bases.[4]

Denver's smaller neighbors annexed their share of surrounding land as well. Lakeside's neighbor, Arvada, annexed portions of the Rocky Flats Nuclear Weapons Plant for development in the 1990s, while both Arvada and Lakewood annexed parts of unincorporated Jefferson County. Smaller towns like Lakeside and neighboring Mountain View watched annexation activity nervously, "jealously" guarding their independence. The town of Lakeside became an especially attractive prospect for annexation after Lakeside Mall opened in 1956. With the exception of Arvada, which had rejected Gerri Von Frellich when he originally wanted to build the mall there, nearly every city around Lakeside at one time or another expressed interest in having the mall property. Many wondered what would happen to the rest of the town and the amusement park if another city did annex the mall property.[5]

Denver's land-grabbing days came to an abrupt halt in 1974 with passage of the Poundstone amendment to the Colorado State Constitution. Prior to the amendment's passage, only the voters living in the area subject to annexation had to approve it. Under the new law, voters in both the proposed annexed area and the county that would lose the land had to approve. While the new law applied to the entire state, it was specifically aimed at Denver, which throughout the 1960s and early 1970s had experienced serious racial problems, especially when it came to segregation in its public schools. Residential segregation, more than any official policy, accounted for the majority of segregation in Denver's schools, but the school board failed to address the issue satisfactorily and angry parents went to court. After a long battle, which made it all the way to the US Supreme Court, Federal District Judge William Doyle issued a ruling in April 1974 that rearranged school boundaries, created paired schools that would trade students during the day, and called for busing over 11,000 students to achieve racial integration. Earlier attempts at busing had caused many white families to flee Denver for the suburbs, and after Doyle's April 1974 order, families left the city in droves. Suburban residents overwhelmingly supported the Poundstone amendment, which passed with 58.4 percent of the vote statewide, because it severely limited the possibility that Denver could annex a neighboring town and its schools, which would then be brought under the busing order that many of them had left Denver to escape in the first place.[6]

The Poundstone amendment's passage did not stop cities from dreaming about annexing land, however and occasionally those dreams included Lakeside and its very successful shopping mall. The annexation bug first hit the town of Lakeside in 1958, two years after the mall opened. In March of that year, mall owner Gerri Von Frellich complained to Jefferson County commissioners that property taxes on the mall, which came to about $440,000 a year, were "grossly unfair and inconsistent" with comparable properties in the county. Von Frellich believed taxes would be $40,000 less if the mall was in Denver, and he instructed his attorneys to appeal the tax assessment and explore the possibility of annexing the mall property to Denver. Intrigued by the possibility of Denver getting the mall, the *Denver Post* sent a reporter to talk to Denver city attorney John Banks to get his opinion on the matter. After investigating, Banks determined that Denver could not annex the shopping center because the city's rules required that one-sixth of the total boundary line of a proposed annexation area be contiguous to Denver's boundaries. Unfortunately for Von Frellich, Lakeside Mall had Lakeside Amusement Park sitting between it and Denver.[7]

Banks may have determined that Denver could not annex the mall, but that was not the end of the issue as far as Von Frellich was concerned. Over the next two years the shopping center continued to expand to the north, which eventually brought it to the edge of Forty-Eighth Avenue, the northern boundary between Lakeside and Denver. Mall spokesman Joseph Schuller announced in May 1960 that Lakeside Mall was once again studying the financial benefits of leaving Lakeside and attaching itself to Denver. Although Schuller put forth the same argument Von Frellich had two years earlier about high property taxes being the reason for wanting to leave, *Rocky Mountain News* reporter Bill Miller revealed an even better reason why another city might want the mall: estimates suggested that the mall did between $25 million and $30 million in business each year, which with Denver's 1 percent sales tax would bring the city an additional $300,000 in tax revenue per year.[8]

Officials from both the town and the amusement park remained silent throughout the 1958 and 1960 de-annexation talks. Both the amusement park and the mall were important parts of the community for the revenue they brought, and town officials were surely not happy at the thought of losing one of them. As far as the amusement park was concerned, the mall had been good for attendance, but whether it was in Denver or Lakeside made little difference in that regard. Of greater concern was whether the town of Lakeside would continue to exist if it lost half its land to another city. In the end, the 1960 effort to have Denver annex the mall also failed, and Von Frellich sold the shopping center for $8 million in 1962. Other cities remained intrigued by the revenue potential Lakeside Mall presented but always ran up against the difficulty of getting the mall property away from the town of Lakeside. The best chance for that to happen would come in 1988, when Jefferson County attempted to abolish the small town of Lakeside altogether.[9]

Had the town of Lakeside become the exclusive playground for the well-to-do its first owners had hoped for, there certainly would not have been a Lakeside Mall, which was built on the land where Adolph Zang and his partners hoped mansions would one day rise. And there might not have been a Lakeside Amusement Park by the 1930s if Robert Speer's experience with Arlington Park in the 1890s and early 1900s was any indication. While the town did not become the thriving metropolis Mayor Marvin Adams had predicted in 1907, it had survived, although some did forget about it. After conducting its official count in 1970, the US Census Bureau issued a list of a dozen towns that had lost all of their population in the 1960s. Two in Colorado made the list, one of which was Lakeside, whose surprised residents objected to the ghost town designation. The *Denver Post*'s article on the mix-up was headlined "Lakeside Does So Have a Population," and the Census Bureau had to admit that it had indeed made a mistake in forgetting Lakeside's population of seventeen. To most, the Census Bureau's mistake was just a humorous incident, but it did arouse people's curiosity about the Denver area's smallest town.[10]

In 1979 the *Denver Post* began profiling several of the small communities around Denver, including Lakeside. The town's population had grown to twenty people by then, although only seventeen were registered voters. All city officials (the mayor, city council, and treasurer) worked for Lakeside Amusement Park. Among other amenities, the town had a twelve-man fire department (all residents) and two fire engines, with two more available if needed. The amusement park also had mutual protection agreements with the Denver, Wheat Ridge, Lakewood, and Arvada fire departments, as did the shopping center. The shopping center and adjoining office building relied on the Jefferson County Sheriff's Department for police protection, while a combination of security officers and town police were responsible for the residents and the park. Outside of issuing liquor licenses, the town's main responsibility was maintaining half of Forty-Fourth Avenue and half of Harlan Street on the western edge of the town, the only two streets in the town of Lakeside. Almost a decade after the *Post* profiled the town in 1979, the population had dropped to eight. Those eight, however, lived in what the *Rocky Mountain News* said "could well be the most entertaining city in America." According to the article, when the number of rides in the amusement park was divided by the number of residents, it came to five rides per person. Mall space was even more impressive—each resident had nearly 90,000 square feet of it, far greater than the amount available to residents of Aurora, where the Aurora Mall had recently opened. Lakeside was small, but its residents loved living in their "own little world."[11]

Because the amusement park owned all the houses in town and rented them to the occupants, residents paid no property taxes. Rent was also fairly reasonable: Carl Chadwick, who had been mayor in the 1960s and was again mayor in 1979, paid just $45 a month for his house. Unemployment in Lakeside was nonexistent, as the amusement park was always hiring residents to fill its needs. The size of the town gave everyone who lived there a chance to be part of the government as well, as residents essentially rotated the government positions among themselves every two years. In 1982, for example, Chadwick, who had worked for the park since the 1950s, returned to a seat on the city council after finishing another round of two terms as mayor, while former mayor George Thomas (who had been mayor during the events of 1973) returned to the top job. The amusement park office served as the town's polling place; it opened at 7:00 a.m. and closed when the last resident had voted or at 7:00 p.m., whichever came first.[12]

The lighthearted newspaper articles on the number of amusement rides per resident and the ease of the electoral process painted an amusing picture of the quirky town of Lakeside, but behind the scenes things were not as light as many residents wanted to believe. One scandal made headlines in March 1980 when Lakeside chief of police Roy Ray Duncan was arrested and charged with bribery and soliciting unlawful compensation for selling a Lakeside police commission to Morton Karman, a pimp who owned two escort agencies in Denver. Karman had originally applied for a job with the Lakeside Police Department because he needed extra money and because it would allow him to carry a concealed weapon. During his interview, Duncan told Karman that the commission would cost him $200. Disturbed by what he took to be the chief of police soliciting a bribe, Karman went to Jefferson County authorities with the story and agreed to help them bust Duncan. He wore a wire to his next meeting with Duncan, and after they agreed on a price of $150, county sheriffs arrested the chief. Authorities quickly began investigating how many other police commission cards Duncan may have sold in his four years as Lakeside's chief of police; eight months after his arrest, he pled guilty to official misconduct and received a much lighter punishment than he would have if convicted of the more serious charges.[13]

Lakeside mayor Carl Chadwick expressed dismay at the incident, telling a reporter from the *Rocky Mountain News* that "nothing like this has ever happened before in Lakeside." Still mindful of what had happened at the amusement park in 1973, the town moved quickly to try to contain the damage. In mid-June 1981 the town council called a meeting at which it ordered acting police chief Ray Russo to revoke all concealed weapons permits, to prevent officers from having sirens or flashing red lights on their personal vehicles, and to make sure to confine the police department's activities to Lakeside city limits. Russo objected to the new rules and resigned in response; along with four part-time city police officers, he walked out of the meeting. The protest was short-lived, however, as by that afternoon all the officers had returned to work, and city officials quickly replaced Russo. Lakeside officials dealt with the problem effectively, but other trouble was on the horizon.[14]

Rhoda Krasner had pointed to political issues over maintenance of Forty-Fourth Avenue as a possible motivation for the Wheat Ridge Fire Protection District not renewing its contracts with Lakeside and the amusement park in 1972, and it remained a problem seven years later. As late as 1979, Lakeside officials told the *Denver Post* that they typically let Jefferson County keep any of the highway use-tax funds that were designated for the town so the county could maintain Forty-Fourth. But Jefferson County was no longer interested in being responsible for Lakeside's half of the street or in administering the maintenance fund that existed for it. As a result, the road continued to deteriorate while the amount of money in the fund continued to grow, reaching a balance of over $167,000 by 1988. Town lawyer Harold Eisenhuth also pointed out that Lakeside had little interest in its share of Jefferson County's open space fund, which was just over $34,000, because there was no place in the town to build a park. Lakeside officials urged the county to take the road money and have its crew fix the street. County officials responded that they could not touch the money without approval from the town council, and by March 1988 they were in the process of writing an agreement to that effect.[15]

Ongoing maintenance proved to be the sticking point in reaching an agreement for Jefferson County to rebuild the road. The county had no problem repairing the road one time, but it did not want to be responsible for maintaining it. Both neighboring Mountain View and Wheat Ridge offered to take over Lakeside's maintenance responsibilities on Forty-Fourth Avenue but only if Lakeside gave them ownership of the entire road. Wheat Ridge's offer was further contingent on Lakeside repaving the road prior to the transfer of ownership. The town of Lakeside, through Eisenhuth, refused both offers, saying it made little sense for the town to give up one of its two streets. Jefferson County officials were unmoved by Lakeside's arguments, saying that county road crews had no enthusiasm for taking care of eight blocks of roadway for the town. Lakeside officials responded by offering to give the county 75 percent of its road and bridge money if it would take over construction and maintenance of both Forty-Fourth Avenue and Harlan Street.[16]

Lakeside's offer to let the county keep 75 percent of the money instead of all of it seemingly incensed Jefferson County officials, who lashed out at the town. County commissioner John Stone argued that it was simply not the county's responsibility to fix a city's roads and that the county was "at the end of our rope" when it came to dealing with Lakeside officials. Critics were so angry that they quickly invented their own history of the town of Lakeside, with Wheat Ridge city manager Mike Smith characterizing the Lakeside of 1907 as "a tent city of transients at the end of a trolley line from Denver" while Stone added that "it was a facade even back then." This was far different from the truth, which was that Lakeside had been a sparsely settled section of farmland in the Berkeley District of Jefferson County in 1907 with no trolley lines near it. Smith's and Stone's version of the story, however, worked well with the case they were trying to make against Lakeside. Stone's fellow county commissioners referred to Lakeside as "the uncity" and "a joke," and they asked the Colorado legislature for permission to abolish the town of Lakeside once and for all.[17]

An article in the *Rocky Mountain News* pointed out that if Jefferson County succeeded in disbanding the town, both the amusement park and the shopping mall "could find themselves eyed hungrily by Wheat Ridge and Mountain View." While the *News* included it as one of the prizes, the amusement park was nearly forgotten as cities dreamed of getting the mall. Wheat Ridge mayor Dan Wilde said his town had "more than a passing interest" in the property. With an estimated $60 million a year in sales, having the mall as part of Wheat Ridge would mean an extra $1.2 million a year in revenue for his city. Mayor Garfield "Bob" Johnson of Mountain View, which had a population of around 550, said his town might be interested as well. Denver also had its eye on the mall property, which had been the case for nearly thirty years. City planning director Bill Lamont told the *Rocky Mountain News* that with the Poundstone amendment in effect, however, it would be virtually impossible for the city to annex the land, since both Denver and Jefferson County voters would have to approve the change.[18]

While some people speculated about what would happen to the shopping mall if the town of Lakeside were eliminated, others saw one more chance to get rid of the amusement park. Critics alleged that the existence of the town of Lakeside allowed the amusement park to avoid tougher safety inspections, seemingly forgetting the events of 1973 when Jefferson County attempted to close the park. Since the park controlled the town, detractors said, it dictated to the town council what safety standards it should set for the park. Mayor Robert Gordanier refuted the charges, which were still tossed around in 1994, rightfully pointing out that the park's insurance company had a major financial stake in a safe operation and that insurance company inspectors would not approve insuring the park if unsafe conditions existed. The fact that it was insurance inspectors, not county officials, who had brought down the rocket ship ride and the Tumble Bug in the early 1980s added weight to Gordanier's arguments. Still, critics argued that the town only existed to protect the amusement park and that the situation needed to end. A lot had obviously changed since 1908, when supporters pointed to the existence of the town of Lakeside as a guarantee that Lakeside Amusement Park would enjoy a fine reputation and be unlike any other amusement park in the country.[19]

Lakeside's residents were understandably defensive of their town in the face of the county commissioners' threat to eradicate it, and they found support from Guy Kelly, a reporter with the *Rocky Mountain News*. Kelly urged in his January 15, 1989, column, "let's lighten up on Lakeside." In supporting the small, struggling town, Kelly pointed out that it had no unemployment issues, did not need a computer to handle election returns, had not had any scandals other than the debacle involving the chief of police in 1980, and got by on a budget of less than $100,000 a year. Despite so much that seemed to be in its favor, Kelly described Lakeside as "a Rodney Dangerfield kind of town" that got no respect from its neighbors. Granted, Kelly wrote, Lakeside had its issues, but contrary to what most believed, the town was at least surviving, if not thriving. All it seemed to want, Kelly said, was to be left alone, and he ended his column with the question "is that too much to ask?"[20]

Jefferson County's attempt to have Lakeside wiped off the map during the 1988 legislative session failed, but Commissioner John Stone was far from done. He continued his crusade against Lakeside, trying once again to have the town abolished during the 1993 legislative session. Stone argued that Lakeside Amusement Park and town officials refused to speak to the county, even if just to have informal talks about intergovernmental agreements or the possibility that the town might qualify for community grants. State representative Maryanne "Moe" Keller, whose house district included Lakeside, agreed with Stone's assertion that the town was a farce but told the *Denver Post* that no one had approached her about sponsoring any legislation that would strip the town of its status. The *Denver Post*'s editorial board joined Stone's fight, writing that "taxpayers ought to be annoyed that Lakeside enjoys the benefits of an incorporated town when in fact the 'town' of Lakeside really is little more than the amusement park of the same name." The editorial argued that Rhoda Krasner could remove the mayor or any of the town council members by simply evicting them from their homes, that the town could unfairly apply for federal Community Block Grants to improve the for-profit amusement park, and that the mall owners had no say in how the town was run because they did not live in the town of Lakeside. The *Post* concluded that "clearly, Lakeside should be dis-incorporated" and either annexed by Wheat Ridge or made part of unincorporated Jefferson County. It was quite a change for the newspaper Benjamin Krasner had once counted on for heavy publicity and support.[21]

Stone's second attempt to disband Lakeside failed as well. Representative Keller told the *Rocky Mountain News* that she had no plans to introduce legislation to de-certify Lakeside during the 1994 session, even though she agreed with Stone that the town had major problems. Stone was unmoved, referring to the town as a joke that existed only to serve the needs of the amusement park. Two defeats had deflated the move to abolish the town, however, and despite Stone's very public campaign against it, the town, like the amusement park from which it took its name, managed to survive. Stone still took every opportunity to criticize the town, however. In 1997 Lakeside asked its voters to approve the first-ever city sales, property, and occupational taxes. If approved, the taxes had the potential to raise as much as $3.2 million annually for the town, which city officials planned to use primarily for increased police services as Jefferson County sheriffs were no longer responsible for policing the mall. Stone criticized the city's police department, calling it a sham, and questioned the legality of its officers making arrests. Mayor and Police Chief Robert Gordanier and city attorney Richard Daly defended the proposed increases, saying the city needed the money to meet its obligations, especially with its police force patrolling the mall. There was no talk of trying to get rid of the town.[22]

Lakeside Mall, however, was not done trying to leave. By 1988 it had been sold, damaged by a fire in 1975 (which investigators blamed on an electrical short), remodeled twice, and the subject of an asbestos scare in 1987. In October 1988 Lakeside Mall's owners signed a tentative agreement with the city of Wheat Ridge to annex the mall property. Mall management took the Jefferson County commissioners' plan to de-certify the town seriously, and with no way of knowing that the plan would end in failure, they decided they needed to protect themselves by attaching the mall to another town. Mall officials also argued that Lakeside did not provide police protection and did not plow the center's parking lot after snowstorms. As the annexation battle loomed, the big question, reported the *Rocky Mountain News*, was what Lakeside Amusement Park owner Rhoda Krasner would do about the mall's plan to leave. John Stone argued that if the town approved the de-annexation of the mall, the only thing left would be the amusement park, leaving little reason for the town to exist. Stone further predicted that if Lakeside fought the mall's plan to leave it, the battle could very well land in court.[23]

In their study of municipal annexation, Klaff and Fuguitt write that in the years before World War II, rurally dominated state legislatures, including Colorado's, passed laws that made it harder to annex land in the face of political opposition to such a move. Lakeside decided to take advantage of those laws. At times, it looked dicey for Lakeside. Rhoda Krasner, for example, admitted in her deposition in the case that she prepared the town's budget and that, when the town needed money to operate, the amusement park simply paid another license fee, as it had been doing since 1908. But in February 1989 Jefferson County district judge Gaspar Perricone ruled that state law did not allow non-agricultural areas to disconnect from a town and that a town board could refuse to let a piece of land de-annex "if the move would be prejudicial to the town." The city council reviewed the mall's proposal and determined that, if the mall left, the town would lose 59 percent of the money it received for road maintenance and the sizable amount of cigarette tax revenue the mall generated. In addition, six Lakeside Mall merchants, including Montgomery Ward, the largest store in the mall after Denver Dry Goods closed in March 1987, had written letters to the Lakeside City Council opposing the plan, arguing that Wheat Ridge's higher tax rate would result in lost business. The potential for lost revenue and the merchants' objections led the council to reject the mall's bid to leave, saying "the financial impact would be too devastating." Lakeside Mall manager Tony Lemberger, surprised by the court ruling that had initially allowed the town to reject the de-annexation request, told the *Rocky Mountain News* that he did not know what further steps the mall's owners might take to get out of Lakeside. Commissioner John Stone expressed surprise that the court battle had not gone on longer. Less than a year later, the mall's owners defaulted on their loans, sending the mall into receivership. No further de-annexation efforts took place, and Lakeside Mall remained a part of the town of Lakeside until it closed in 2008.[24]

While the town of Lakeside fought for its survival, longtime rival Elitch's was dealing with its own serious problems. By the 1980s the park had run out of room to expand its operation, and new rides were literally built on top of older ones. As the park's renowned flower gardens continually gave way to new rides and attractions, owner Budd Gurtler grumbled that the park's name was Elitch Gardens and that asphalt should not replace the famous flowerbeds. Elitch's location, surrounded by houses at Thirty-Eighth Avenue and Tennyson Street, was also starting to work against it. People sometimes had a hard time finding the park if they did not know where to look, and the Gurtlers found that tourists, who were becoming important customers for Denver's amusement parks, were unwilling to take the time to search for it. Finally, Elitch's owners found that its family appeal was lost on crowds of thrill-seeking teenagers who wanted bigger and more exciting rides. Lakeside did not necessarily have more thrilling rides than Elitch's, but it did have a very different customer base. The Krasners had spent years building and perfecting the park's image as an inexpensive entertainment option for Denver's working class while also spending a great deal of time and money trying to keep the park fresh for its customers. Such an approach may not have given Lakeside the bigger number of annual visitors that Elitch's enjoyed, but it did create a fiercely loyal group of customers who helped protect the park from the kinds of problems its rival was facing.[25]

As far as the Gurtlers were concerned, the only way to create the beautiful state-of-the-art amusement park of which they dreamed was to move Elitch's. After investigating several options, Budd Gurtler announced on May 1, 1986, that, after ninety-six years in North Denver, Elitch's would move to the booming suburb of Highlands Ranch in Douglas County. Two months after he made the announcement, Gurtler and Rhoda Krasner agreed to a joint interview with newspaper columnist Bill Gallo for *Denver Magazine*. Krasner told Gallo the announcement of Elitch's move took her completely by surprise, saying "I had no idea, I really didn't." When Gallo suggested that the move, which would end the close rivalry that had existed between the two parks for nearly eighty years, would be beneficial to Lakeside, Gurtler expressed his pleasure that Gallo had said it and not him. Krasner responded that she and her staff had been too busy with the 1986 season to even think about what the move would mean for Lakeside, but some park employees speculated that they would definitely see more business when they no longer had to compete with a nearby Elitch's.[26]

Elitch's move to Highlands Ranch fell apart when residents of the area objected, but Budd Gurtler's son, Sandy, who had taken over as president of the park, found a new spot in 1989—a sixty-eight-acre former railroad yard in Denver's Central Platte Valley that the US Environmental Protection Agency had deemed a Superfund site because of the high amount of hazardous waste present. Denver voters had approved $14 million in bonds to pay for improvements to the area, where the city hoped to build a baseball stadium, a hockey and basketball arena, and an aquarium. Just as Lakeside had played a big part in Denver's City Beautiful program in 1908, Elitch's became a key part of Denver's vision for the Platte Valley, and the city pledged $21 million in public funds to help the Gurtlers with cleanup and construction costs. Sandy Gurtler had to form several partnerships to raise the $95 million it would cost to build the new park, but once he did so, construction proceeded rapidly and the new park opened in May 1995. During the first season the new Elitch Gardens was open, it rained nearly half of the total days the park was in operation, and the area was constantly threatened with flooding. Visitors put off passing judgment until the second season, but the higher admission prices and lack of old trees and flowers were too much. The park did not look or feel like the old Elitch's, and Denverites were not impressed or interested. As Gallo had written in his *Denver Magazine* article in 1986, Lakeside and Elitch's were "such a deep-rooted Denver tradition that they draw and draw through the generations," but with its move in 1995 Elitch's had seemingly broken that tradition. Sandy Gurtler's partners began to pressure him to repay their money, and he was forced to sell Elitch's to Premier Parks, Inc., in 1996. Two years later Premier purchased all of the Six Flags theme parks and renamed the Denver park Six Flags Elitch Gardens. The theme park had finally arrived in Denver.[27]

Under Benjamin Krasner's leadership, Lakeside had been able to hold its own against the bigger theme parks; with the arrival of Six Flags, the family-owned Lakeside had a chance to once again see how it would hold up against direct competition with one of the giants. Given the success its focus on working-class family entertainment had brought over the years, Lakeside saw little reason to change. Elitch's much higher admission price at the new park kept many visitors away, while others complained because they could no longer bring picnics—one of the great traditions at the old Elitch's—to the theme park, whose corporate owners wanted visitors to buy food at the park. Lakeside's steadfastness worked in its favor, and when the financially struggling Six Flags decided to sell Elitch's in 2006, Lakeside Amusement

Park was still going strong. With Elitch's on the market once again, many people speculated that Six Flags would sell the property to a developer and leave Lakeside as the only amusement park in Denver. Elitch's survived when a subsidiary of Parc Management LLC bought it and six other Six Flags parks, maintaining Denver's claim to two parks.[28]

On September 6, 1994, one fully loaded train on the Cyclone crashed into another fully loaded train that was ready to leave the loading platform. Two dozen people, about half the total number of passengers on the two trains at the time of the accident, were injured. They were treated for minor injuries at area hospitals and quickly released. The accident had occurred on the last day of the season, leading Lakeside spokeswoman Connie Schafer to comment later, "what a way to end it." Park officials were grateful that no one was seriously injured, but Colorado Department of Labor and Employment investigators arrived on the scene to look into the accident.[29]

In its coverage of the accident, the *Rocky Mountain News* parroted criticisms of the park that Jefferson County commissioner John Stone had been making for years, particularly that the amusement park controlled the town and therefore the safety codes. The newspaper pointed out that forty-seven personal injury lawsuits had been filed against Lakeside between 1975 and January 1994 while only twenty-seven were filed against Elitch's during that same period. The newspaper did not report how many of the lawsuits against either park were ultimately successful or dismissed. Not until thirteen paragraphs into the news story was there a mention of a similar accident that had occurred on Elitch's Twister coaster two weeks earlier. Also pushed to the end of the article was news of a mechanical malfunction on an unlicensed roller coaster at the Taste of Colorado celebration in downtown Denver that forced firefighters to rescue twenty-four very frightened people on the same day as the incident at Lakeside. Investigators quickly determined that human error was to blame for the accident on the Cyclone and stressed that there were no mechanical problems with the fifty-four-year-old ride.[30]

It had been an interesting ride for Lakeside Amusement Park and the tiny town to which it gave its name. The repeated attempts to get rid of both had been very public and had turned some longtime friends such as the *Denver Post* against them, but both had been able to stand up to bigger neighbors in order to preserve themselves. In fact, the existence of the town had prevented bigger cities from eliminating the park or taking the mall. Denverites fleeing court-ordered busing had helped the town survive when they passed the Poundstone amendment. But at times it seemed as if Lakeside Amusement Park was the only major institution interested in staying where it was, as the owners of Lakeside Mall begged nearly every city around it to annex the property and the owners of Elitch Gardens decided that it was necessary to leave North Denver after nearly a century. These were just the latest in a long line of battles, and for decades Lakeside Amusement Park had fought its way through them all, including the loss of Denver's backing during the City Beautiful era, bankruptcies, two world wars, the deaths of owners, and the rise of theme parks. After each battle, the park had successfully reinvented itself and moved forward. As it had every time in the past when the odds were against it, Lakeside Amusement Park had once again proven that it was indeed a survivor.

CONCLUSION

A Century of Fun at Lakeside Amusement Park

Municipal boosters said Denver needed Civic Center Park. Having the haven in the heart of downtown Denver, they said, was vital to residents' health and well-being. In addition, it offered an ideal place to hold important civic gatherings while also giving the city a "front yard." As part of the debate over Civic Center Park, many argued that Denver needed to decide whether Robert Speer's City Beautiful program had a role in its future as a pleasant and livable place. While debate raged over Civic Center Park, Denver also had to get ready for the Democrats, as the city was hosting the party's upcoming national convention. The convention, boosters argued, meant not only increased business revenue but also the chance to prove that Denver had become an important city. For residents and visitors seeking an escape from it all, there was a grand amusement park celebrating a rarely achieved milestone as it offered fun and games. While all of this could have been happening in Denver in 1908, it was in fact a century later.[1]

On July 18, 2008, Lakeside Amusement Park owner Rhoda Krasner hosted a dinner, a special tour of the park, and an ice cream social for invited guests, including members of the National Amusement Park Historical Association, who had come to celebrate the park's 100th anniversary. Coverage of the centennial made the front page of the *Rocky Mountain News*, the first time a story on the park had occupied that spot in many years. Billboards, posters, T-shirts, water bottles, and stickers reminded everyone in Denver that it had been a "Century of Fun" at Lakeside Amusement Park, one of only twenty-eight family-owned amusement parks in the United States to reach that milestone. That same summer, Denver hosted the 2008 Democratic National Convention, 100 years after it had first hosted the event. Denver city auditor Dennis Gallagher, speaking at the centennial dinner at the park, expressed his hope that some delegates might visit Lakeside, the place where Speer had hosted a dinner for delegates at the new Casino restaurant in 1908. A reporter for the *Colorado Independent* also commemorated the park's role in the first convention in a short article, but, snubbing history, Denver chose rival Elitch Gardens to host a media party for convention delegates, busing in over 9,000 people "for a night of gladhanding and libations." Lakeside did not let the slight ruin its celebration of the amazing achievement.[2]

Although a century had passed, if Adolph Zang had walked into Lakeside on July 18, 2008, there was much he would have recognized. The automobile entrance handled the majority of customers arriving at Lakeside, but the Tower of Jewels still marked the main entrance to the park. The covered parking spaces that had been on the north side of the Tower entrance since 1908 still stood, although they were now reserved for Lakeside employees instead of the park's automobile-owning customers. Close observers could still make out the words "Casino Theater" above the Sheridan Boulevard side of that building, which, although the upper floors had long been closed, still stood next to the Tower. Once inside the gates, visitors could stand in the area known as Central Park, though it had not divided the park's social and entertainment areas since 1912 when the Derby coaster went up. The wood and metal benches, with Lakeside Park and Denver stamped on the legs, still ringed the Art Deco fountain in the middle of Central Park. The space once occupied by the College Inn, on the north side of the main entrance, no longer offered dinner and dancing; games and pizza were the modern replacements. But the Art Deco sign *Billboard* praised so highly in 1937 still hung above the entrance. The Gayway Inn, on the south side of the entrance, had been renamed the Eatway Inn, but the impressive marble back bar Benjamin

Krasner had rescued from Denver's Union Station, the multicolored light that ran down the center of the restaurant's ceiling, and the Art Deco–style wooden booths and terrazzo floor were still in place.[3]

The lone reminder of the former social area was the foundation of the ballroom and entrance to the long-closed Riviera nightclub, which still stood across from the Wild Chipmunk. Disneyland's original Satellite ride (the second one in the country) had long been dismantled, but riders at Lakeside could still "Be a Pilot" on the first, and one of the few still operational, Satellite rides in the country. On the opposite side of the onetime social area of the park, the Scrambler, which Benjamin Krasner had purchased along with the Satellite in 1958, still delighted customers as it spun them around. Nearby, the Spider, which had replaced the park's original Octopus ride, still left customers dizzy. The silent structure of the Staride also still stood, waiting for the day when someone might restore it and once again let it run so "the lights on the Star, meet the stars in the sky."[4]

In the area of the park formerly dedicated solely to amusements, Avenues A and B still ran alongside the former Shoot-the-Chutes lagoon, where the captains of Skoota boats happily bumped into each other. No one called the avenues by their original names and they were no longer decorated with Greek statues, but, just as they had in 1908, they ended at a picnic area, now located on the edge of Kiddies Playland. The Whip, installed in 1914, still delighted customers, as did the Hurricane, Dragon coaster, Auto Skooters, Heart Flip, Matterhorn, and other rides, all of which had been at the park for decades. Scattered throughout the amusement area were many of the park's original light poles, most with the original globes on them.[5]

Although history was everywhere at Lakeside, the park had not lost its desire for the new. Innovation remained a constant at Lakeside in the years prior to its 100th anniversary, although the pace slowed considerably in the 1980s and 1990s. Among the permanent rides added to the park's lineup were a Flying Dutchman, new go-karts on the miniature racetrack next to the Satellite (which were again replaced in 2012), and a Frog Hopper in Kiddies Playland. Frequently returning temporary attractions included a Fun House, Gravitron, Wisdom Boomerang, Flying Carpet, Pirate Ship, and a Tea Cup ride. In 2007, the year before the centennial, Rhoda Krasner had a 140-foot drop tower called Zoom, manufactured by Texas-based ARM/Larson, installed near the park's Ferris wheel. Zoom's installation came at a time when rival Elitch's tower, 80 feet taller and named the Tower of Doom, was closed because of a freak accident on the similarly designed Tower of Power at Six Flags Kentucky Kingdom that resulted in a thirteen-year-old girl's feet being severed at the ankles. The Towers of Doom and Power were designed by Intamig AG, a Swiss company, and a spokeswoman for Lakeside assured the *Denver Post* that not only was Zoom built by a different company, but the tower's design was different from the other two towers and it was completely safe.[6]

On the southwest edge of the park, the long-closed Lakeside Speedway stood as a silent reminder of the very noisy races that had once taken place there. The men and women who raced at the track, along with fans, occasionally spoke of restoring the Speedway as a memorial to those who had died there, but most settled for telling stories in on-line forums or at weekly breakfast meetings during which they reminisced about the past. Twenty years had passed since the last race at the Speedway, but for those who had been there, the memories were very much alive. Some people talked of listing Lakeside on the National Register of Historic Places, but park owner Rhoda Krasner seemed reluctant, preferring to make sure the park remained the family-friendly destination it had been for decades. Just west of the Speedway was the empty field where Lakeside Mall, a onetime financial powerhouse, had once stood; the site had been cleared earlier that summer to await future redevelopment.[7]

As rich as Lakeside's history was as it celebrated its centennial, the park was proudest of two attractions that had been there since opening day. One was the original 1908 Parker Merry-Go-Round, whose horses and other animals were still galloping inside the building Benjamin Krasner had asked Richard Crowther to design for it in 1942. The ride's original band organ had quit working in the 1970s, but recorded music gave riders a hint of what it had sounded like in 1908. The other ride was the Lakeshore Railway, where the steam engines ran only on weekends while the diesel engine circled the lake the rest of the week. The train remained one of the most popular rides at the park, especially late at night when tired visitors wanted to relax. Always unique, Lakeside Amusement Park had managed to reinvent itself once again, and by the time of its 100th anniversary the park was a family-friendly, lower-cost alternative to the big corporate-owned theme parks that dominated the industry. A reporter covering the park's anniversary for *Intermountain Jewish News* wrote that Lakeside was a "confluence of architectural moods spanning the 20th century" and that "this conscious stylistic eclecticism—from Beaux Arts to art deco to contemporary—has made Lakeside unique among amusement parks." Photographers from historical and architectural magazines visited the park regularly, as did tourists from around the world. As park owner Rhoda Krasner said, "We're not vintage, we're different vintages." Lakeside's devoted fans loved it, as did the thousands of visitors who still screamed on the Cyclone or whooped as the train plunged into the dark tunnel near the end of its journey around Lake Rhoda.[8]

As proof of what a fixture Lakeside had become in the Denver community, a number of urban legends developed around the park, although none were true. Most of the stories focused on the park's roller coasters and supposed deaths on them. Passengers waiting in line for the Cyclone frequently told of the time when one of the coaster's fully loaded trains flew off the track and into the lake, sometimes drowning everyone onboard and sometimes not, the horror of the accident usually depending on how many young children were listening. Others told of the time one of the cars on the Wild Chipmunk fell off the edge of the track, killing its passengers. Some people insisted that Lakeside was the inspiration for the identically named haunted amusement park in the Silent Hill videogame series, which included a tower that marked the park's location. The legends were simply part of Lakeside's longevity.

The next year, as Lakeside entered its 101st season, a reporter for the *Denver Post* wondered if longtime rival Elitch's might finally have lost its hold as Denver's preeminent amusement park. Arguing that Elitch's failed to "match the quality and vibrance" of the cultural attractions around it, John Wenzel wrote that some saw the big park as simply an "interim" use of the land it occupied. Comparing it to Lakeside, he said the older park was a "smaller, more affordable place" full of "whiplash-inducing rides" such as the Wild Chipmunk and Tilt-a-Whirl. With its aging neon signs and the smell of hotdogs and popcorn seemingly embedded in the carousel animals, Wenzel wrote that Lakeside "oozes personality, while the modern Elitch's . . . sometimes feels like a second-rate corporate theme park." Wenzel argued that Denver surely could come up with a venue that mixed the thrill rides of Elitch's with the "relaxed family vibe" of Lakeside, but ultimately he called on Elitch's to either reinvent itself or get off the stage.[9]

As the park celebrated its 100th birthday, Rhoda Krasner told *Rocky Mountain News* reporter Janet Forgrieve that "Lakeside evolves, just as our lives do and our society as a whole . . . one thing leaves and another takes its place." Long gone, Krasner said, were the Saturday night dances at El Patio with men in suits and women in elegant gowns, replaced by a more casual clientele in a more casual time. As Jim Hillman, events coordinator for the National Amusement Park Historical Association, told the *News*, the small, family-owned amusement parks that survived did so "because they appeal to families, offering an affordable day of fun and a balance of thrilling new rides and timeless attractions." Krasner echoed those sentiments three years later as the park entered its 103rd season, telling the *Denver Post*, "My father's philosophy, and our philosophy, is that we want Lakeside to be affordable to everyone." That philosophy had guided Lakeside since the days when Adolph Zang's family first started to transform it into a typical working-class amusement park, proving the park's ability to evolve under circumstances most other parks would have found fatal.[10]

As Lakeside Amusement Park celebrated its 100th anniversary, interest in Denver's City Beautiful program revived yet again. The new conversation centered on Civic Center Park, which Mayor Robert Speer had viewed as the centerpiece of his City Beautiful plan. The park, one of the prime remaining examples of City Beautiful design in the country, had been listed on the National Register of Historic Places and was one of the few such listings to be rated a site of national significance. Two episodes initiated the new debate about the historic park. The first was a new design for Civic Center Park offered by architect Daniel Libeskind, who in 2006 had designed an addition to the Denver Art Museum. The Civic Center Conservancy, a private group that partnered with Denver to raise money for restoring and reviving the park, asked the architect to create a new design for it. Libeskind's plan for the park included replacing most of the flowerbeds and a large portion of the lawn with a six-inch-deep water feature, building a pedestrian bridge to connect the park to a nearby bus station, adding glass enclosures for restaurants and shops, and erecting a glass cover over the Greek Amphitheater.[11]

Reaction to Libeskind's plan was swift and highly critical, with most people arguing that the new design, if built, would destroy the park. Joanne Ditmer, a columnist for the *Denver Post*, wrote that the design was a great plan for a park anywhere other than Civic Center, where it would be "a frivolity superimposed on one of downtown's last green spaces." Michael Paglia, writing for *Westword*, referred to the members of the conservancy as "dim-witted, self-serving vandals" for approving the new design, which, he argued, would destroy the symmetry of the park's original design. Backers quickly shelved the almost universally hated design, but even its critics admitted that it had, at the very least, started people talking about Civic Center Park and the need to revive it. Much of the debate focused on what kind of park the space should be, whether quiet and dignified, as it always had been, or more active. One columnist for the *Denver Post* even argued that the city should stop using Civic Center as the focal point of all summer activities and move many of them to a new location, suggesting the "Elitch Gardens site if it ceases to be an amusement park" as one possible place.[12]

Opponents may have stopped the Libeskind plan for Civic Center Park, but the debate over the park's future was far from finished. The following year, History Colorado (then the Colorado Historical Society) was forced to begin searching for a new home after the state announced that it was going to build a new judicial complex that would require tearing down History Colorado's building at Thirteenth Avenue and Broadway. Several people suggested Civic Center Park as an ideal location for a new history museum, and the organization eventually proposed constructing a new four-story building on the south side of the park. The plan met with intense opposition, with the most vocal opponents arguing that giving a piece of the park to the state would rob the people of Denver of much-prized and badly needed green space. In words that echoed Speer and other City Beautiful advocates a century before, Carolyn and Don Etter, former co-directors of Denver's Parks Department, wrote in a column for the *Post* that the park gave Denverites "space for play and inspiration, room for civic gatherings."[13]

Supporters argued that the new History Colorado building was in fact compatible with Speer's City Beautiful ideas. Susan Barnes-Gelt, a former member of the Denver City Council, had opposed the Libeskind plan for the park but approved of History Colorado's relocation plan. In a column for the *Post*, she wrote that the plan gave the city a unique opportunity to partner with the state to transform the long-neglected park through restoration of the old Carnegie library building and a $100 million investment by the state that would have inspired private businesses to invest as well, all of which would have "generated regular, daily activity in a grossly underused public square." She used a quote from Speer, in which he said that a civic center without a city building was in fact a civic deformity and a sure sign that a city had lost its purpose, to defend the plan and argued that a new building on the south side of the park would complete Speer's master plan for Civic Center, which had called for such a building to balance the Carnegie library structure. History Colorado's supporters were no match for opponents, however, and the vigorous opposition eventually forced the organization to give up its plans for the new building. Denver offered to give History Colorado the Carnegie library and the option to build a smaller building on the south side of the park as a consolation prize, but it rejected that offer as well and decided to construct a new building at Twelfth Avenue and Broadway, a block south of its previous location. Critics were delighted, claiming they had once again saved the park from certain doom while calling for vigilance against any future threats.[14]

Never mentioned in the ongoing debate over Civic Center Park and its future was the fact that Lakeside Amusement Park had once been an integral part of Denver's City Beautiful movement. Both sides in the debate claimed to be the champions of Robert Speer's vision, but neither side had it quite right, as everyone forgot that the politically powerful and extremely realistic mayor had found room for an amusement park in his City Beautiful. Observers past and present argued that no amusement park could ever fit within the ideals behind the City Beautiful, but Speer, a former amusement park owner, thought otherwise. Whether Speer would have approved of the Libeskind plan or welcomed History Colorado to his beloved park is impossible to know, but his acceptance of an amusement park a century earlier showed that he was more flexible than his self-professed heirs when it came to what defined the City Beautiful.[15]

In 1901, Jerome Smiley had written extensively in his *History of Denver* that the city needed park space for the well-being of its residents. More than a century later, the debate over Civic Center Park showed that Denverites were as much in need of recreation space in 2008 as they had been at the beginning of the twentieth century. In fact, Denver had never stopped adding park space in the years since Speer's administration. Mayor Wellington Webb, like Speer, doubled the city's park acreage during his administration. At Red Rocks, which was part of Speer's Denver Mountain Parks system, the city purchased 193 acres of additional land to prevent ongoing development in the area from getting any closer to the park. Lakeside's once-celebrated role in fulfilling Denver's need for recreational space may have been long forgotten by the time it turned 100 years old, but the park was just as willing and able to provide entertainment for Denver's residents as it had been on the day it opened in 1908.[16]

For decades, Lakeside stood virtually alone in the unusual combination of factors that made it so different from other amusement parks. The closest comparable amusement resort, Blackpool, is more than 4,500 miles away in northwestern Great Britain and includes an amusement park, Pleasure Beach, which opened in 1897. Both Lakeside and Blackpool used lighting and technology to, as historians Gary Cross and John Walton write, give "adults permission to act like children." Blackpool's government was "master of its own municipal destiny," write Cross and Walton, and town officials worked closely with local businesses to ensure the town's survival. The leaders of Blackpool shared Marvin Adams's and other early Lakeside officials' dream of seeing their town grow and prosper. But while Lakeside remained a small town occasionally forgotten by the people of Denver, Blackpool grew into a thriving town that happened to be a major recreational area. Also like Lakeside, Blackpool found that to survive the arrival of a new customer base, it had to change. But while Lakeside went after the working-class customers who surrounded the park, Blackpool went after middle- and upper-class customers. Just as Adolph Zang and his associates expected Lakeside's design to attract only conservative amusement seekers, Blackpool's leaders sought to create "a spacious and civilized setting for crowds whose behavior was expected to improve in step with the environment." Blackpool's leaders extended the upscale areas of the resort in the 1920s and 1930s and even planned for City Beautiful–inspired improvements, including large flowerbeds and boulevards. Both parks looked to retail establishments to protect themselves, with the mall at Lakeside and the "world's greatest Woolworth's" at Blackpool.[17]

The new customer bases both Lakeside and Blackpool embraced in the 1920s remained relatively stable thereafter. Lakeside, with its vast picnic grounds and lower admission price, remained a favorite of its working-class customers. Described as "blue collar," "family friendly," and "affordable," Lakeside was a popular destination for birthday parties and school and church group outings, while Elitch's, especially after Six Flags took over in 1998, banned picnics and raised prices significantly. Blackpool managed to remain one of the few British seaside resorts left relatively untouched by

World War II, and people flocked to it during the twenty years after the war ended. The advent of paid vacations and continued rationing left British pleasure seekers with plenty of money to spend but limited ways in which to do so, leading Cross and Walton to write that the crowds at Blackpool became "more affluent than ever." Not until the 1960s did a new youth culture appear at Blackpool, but the new crowds still demonstrated a "persisting respectability." The rise of automobile ownership in England in the late 1950s and early 1960s (decades later than in the United States) allowed more working-class customers to visit Blackpool, but middle- and upper-class customers maintained a strong presence.[18]

Automobile parking set Lakeside apart from Blackpool and most other early amusement locations. Even though the Denver Tramway Company rushed to build a streetcar line to Lakeside, Zang and his fellow owners thought far enough ahead to include automobile parking at a time when few people in Denver owned automobiles. The rise of the car culture was often a sign of impending doom for amusement parks that lacked parking lots as part of their original designs and had trouble finding space for them when the need arose. Elitch's, for example, had to tear down the long-empty zoo enclosures to make room for a parking lot, while as late as the 1920s the owners of San Francisco's Playland at the Beach encouraged customers to take the streetcar to the park rather than drive. By that time, people wanted to drive to their amusement destinations rather than rely on public transportation. Many park owners were either stuck or out of touch when it came to the love affair with the automobile.[19]

Lack of parking space was not the only major challenge the car culture posed for amusement parks. The freedom the automobile provided, allowing people to go virtually anywhere they wanted instead of only where streetcars took them, was another. Owners built new resorts that catered almost exclusively to those who could afford the cars that were necessary to get to them (foreshadowing the rise of the theme park in the 1950s), leaving the once great amusement parks to those who still relied on mass transit. In New York, for example, the overpasses above the highways leading to the new resort areas were purposely built too low for buses to fit underneath, and requests for train connections were always dismissed, effectively preventing anyone who did not have a car from getting to the resorts. This meant that the poorer members of society congregated at the old Coney Island parks, which often led to increased social and racial tensions that in turn led to the demise of many of the parks.[20]

Lakeside, however, embraced the car. In 1938, thirty years after the park opened, the baseball field gave way to a parking lot that could hold 7,000 cars, in addition to those that could park under the covered parking area along Sheridan Boulevard, while the Tower of Jewels gave way to the automobile gate as the park's primary entrance. The automobile gate was never as grand as the Tower entrance; for many years it was a simple arched, stuccoed gate with lighted letters that spelled out "Lakeside Park." But the fact that a large paved lot and separate entrance gate existed at the amusement park at all was significant. The Speedway and the enormous crowds it attracted further represented the important role the automobile played at Lakeside Amusement Park. The park's acceptance of the car set it apart from nearly every other amusement park of its era.[21]

As Lakeside celebrated its centennial, many people were certain that Adolph Zang and his associates would have been surprised to see the park still in business 100 years after they opened it. But it was Zang, after all, who had decided to build the park to last with brick and wood construction instead of staff, something newspapers noted repeatedly during its construction and grand opening. Somewhat lost in the scathing results of the grand jury investigation of 1972 and 1973 was the astonishing fact that Lakeside's buildings still stood, sixty-five years after they were built. Visitors to the century-old park could still enter through the Tower of Jewels, for example, and walk down a staircase flanked by lion statues that had been there since opening day in 1908. The permanence of Lakeside's historic buildings began to work in its favor once it got past the sticky issues of the early 1970s.

Theme park builders and owners often planned their parks around the concepts of fantasy, history, and nostalgia. Disneyland's Main Street USA is a prime example, but the Six Flags parks, Busch Gardens, and California's Great America, among many others, followed the same design ideas. Closer to Lakeside, visitors at the new Elitch Gardens entered through an old-fashioned–looking streetscape designed to bring back memories of the original park. At Lakeside, however, the history was authentic: the Tower of Jewels, the merry-go-round, the Hurricane, the Satellite, and the trains, along with many other things, were all originals. Even the Cyclone, the nearly seventy-year-old coaster, was the real deal, and the American Coaster Enthusiasts

(ACE) named it an ACE Roller Coaster Landmark for both its historical significance and the fact that it was one of only a handful of pre–World War II coasters still in operation in the United States. In 2011 Jim Futrell, historian for the National Amusement Park Historical Association, told reporter Claire Martin of the *Denver Post* that Lakeside was indeed a classic, adding "what makes Lakeside special . . . is that it has so many original features." *Intermountain Jewish News* writer Andrea Jacobs observed that "at Lakeside, the past and future continually merge—inherently, and intentionally." In an industry that thrived on constant change and innovation, often at the expense of history, Lakeside had managed to adapt while keeping its past.[22]

The decision by Lakeside's first owners to use building materials that would last was one very important factor in why the park survived. Equally important was Zang's decision to incorporate the town of Lakeside as home to the park to escape Denver's harsh liquor laws. For a park to occupy its own town was almost unheard of in the amusement park industry and would not be matched until Walt Disney began to build his Florida theme park. In the short run, the town allowed Zang to serve beer at the park, but in the long run the town kept Lakeside from dealing with the interference that plagued many other amusement parks. The pages of *Billboard* are filled with stories of towns passing laws against amusement parks or the activities that went on inside them in an effort to drive them out of business. In New York, for example, parks and highway planner Robert Moses used his position to wage a personal crusade against the parks on Coney Island. He provided public transportation only to the beaches at Coney, rather than the new beaches he had opened on Long Island in 1924, to prevent people without cars from reaching the new beaches. He launched a personal attack against Coney's "raunchy frivolities" in the 1930s and later supported redevelopment of the area that destroyed most remnants of the once thriving amusement business. Events at Coney also worked in favor of Moses's crusade, as tension increased between poor whites and poor blacks, gang violence grew, and the public became more interested in redevelopment. At Lakeside, prior to the 1973 grand jury investigation, the only thing critics had been able to do to the park was prosecute the owners and employees on trumped-up charges of violating laws against serving liquor on Sundays more than sixty years earlier. The most serious threat to the park's survival was the lawsuit against it that came as a result of the grand jury's findings in 1973, but even then the park was given a chance to reinvent itself, which it did successfully. Later critics had to resort to attempts to abolish the town of Lakeside or annex parts of it to threaten the amusement park, all of which failed as the town and park survived.[23]

In addition to protecting it, Lakeside Amusement Park's location also helped insulate it from many of the problems that eventually brought down other amusement parks. As closely as it may have been linked to Denver throughout its first years in operation, Lakeside was located in a very suburban setting at a time when most amusement parks were in or near urban areas. Suburban residents eventually came to perceive urban amusement parks as crime-ridden havens for thugs or battlegrounds in the ongoing racial conflicts most cities faced in the second half of the twentieth century. More than a decade after Elitch's opened its new location in downtown Denver in 1995, *Denver Post* reporter John Wenzel found many of the same problems there, detailing one incident in which two rival groups of men shouted and flashed tattoos at each other. A security guard removed the man who appeared to be the ringleader from the park before a fight broke out, but the incident was disturbing to Wenzel, who wrote that Elitch's was just as safe as, if not safer than, any other place in downtown Denver, which was not necessarily a ringing endorsement. Lakeside's suburban location and the obvious presence of the town's police force and park security during the summer season spared it from the same types of problems many people identified in other amusement parks during the 1960s and 1970s. Those problems caused many of the parks that had survived economic downturns, war, and competition from theme parks to finally succumb.[24]

Just as important as the roles of design, location, and timing in Lakeside Amusement Park's long-term survival was the determination of the park's owners, the Zang and Krasner families, who simply refused to let the park die. After Adolph Zang built the park, the members of his family, especially his step-brother, William Buck, and nephew, Phillip Friederich, worked tirelessly to maintain the park and keep it going. Even after two bankruptcies, Buck and Friederich had a difficult time letting go of the park, although they were too close to the park and its past to make the full transition to a working-class park. That was not the case with Benjamin Krasner, and as hard as the Zang family worked for the park, Krasner worked even harder. He made choices that were sometimes tough but necessary, such as paving over the baseball field to create a parking lot in recognition of the fact that more customers were arriving at Lakeside in their own cars rather than on the aging streetcars. Krasner also started a program of constant innovation and renovation at the park that enabled it to survive. His daughter, Rhoda, successfully fought off several attacks in the 1970s, 1980s, and early 1990s that threatened the park with closure. Without owners committed to its survival and willing to adapt, Lakeside Amusement Park likely would have closed its gates long before its centennial.

As tenacious as the park's owners were, they also possessed very good business sense. Adolph Zang had a proven record of success when it came to his father's brewery and other businesses. Zang single-handedly transformed the family's grubstaking business into a successful bank, and his long-term plan to open outlets for Zang Beer also worked well. Building an amusement park was his biggest venture in that area, but it was one that was relatively certain to succeed based on the number of other brewers who did the same thing. William Buck and Phillip Friederich enjoyed great success in real estate investing outside of their joint association at Lakeside. Benjamin Krasner had a rare awareness of what the public wanted in an amusement park and had also made connections, especially with the *Denver Post*, that allowed him to promote the park effectively in the press. The Krasners' business skill and sense enabled them to do what was needed to allow the park to survive, from embracing the new car culture to constant innovation in rides and attractions to building the Speedway.

Benjamin Krasner's 1935 slogan for the park, "Denver Has Gone Lakeside," was perhaps more fitting than he had ever imagined, as the park essentially served as a mirror for Denver's search for its identity. In 1908 the park had reflected Denver's struggle to find its place on the national stage as it left behind the rough and unattractive appearance of its early days. The park's transition to working-class playground reflected Denver's suburban growth in the 1910s and 1920s, while the town's fight to survive in the 1970s reflected suburbanites' fears of Denver's power and racial problems. The construction of Lakeside Mall reflected both Denver's continued growth and changing trends in the way people lived. Denver's interstate highway construction, urban renewal, and political battles, among many other things, were also reflected in Lakeside. And throughout its history, Lakeside filled the needs of Denver's residents for recreation, relaxation, entertainment, and the ability to test Freddy Cannon's theory about the greatness of kisses while stopped at the top of a Ferris wheel.

Pioneer, survivor, and entertaining amusement park—all were labels Lakeside Amusement Park wore proudly as it became one of the rare amusement parks to reach its centennial. In 2009, as Lakeside embarked on its 101st season, the park adopted a new slogan: "Life's a Roller Coaster, Enjoy the Ride." Lakeside's story over the course of a century had indeed been a very wild roller coaster ride, but through good timing, adaptation, and determination, the park lived on. When Lakeside celebrated its 100th birthday in 2008, owner Rhoda Krasner said, "I think Lakeside will be here in another 100 years. This particular piece of geography was meant to entertain people. It's unique to our metro area." Only time will tell if she is correct, but a Century of Fun at Lakeside Amusement Park had proven that it was, undeniably, a very unique place.[25]

Notes

Abbreviations

CT—*Colorado Transcript*
DMF—*Denver Municipal Facts*
DP—*Denver Post*
RMN—*Rocky Mountain News*
WHGD—*Western History and Genealogy Department, Denver Public Library, Denver, CO*

Introduction: In Search of Blooming Gardens

1. "A Century of Thrills: Lakeside Reaches 100 with Formula for Family Fun," *RMN* (July 16, 2008): Business section, 2.
2. Thomas J. Schlereth, *Victorian America: Transformations in Everyday Life, 1876–1915* (New York: HarperPerennial, 1992), 238–39.
3. Duane A. Smith, Karen A. Vendl, and Mark A. Vendl, *Colorado Goes to the Fair: World's Columbian Exposition, Chicago, 1893* (Albuquerque: University of New Mexico Press, 2011), 91, 97; Biography of Carl Lammers, in *Portrait and Biographical Record:*

Denver and Vicinity, available at http://www.memoriallibrary.com/CO/1898Den verPB/pages/pbrd0494.htm, accessed March 31, 2012; David F. Burg, *Chicago's White City of 1893* (Lexington: University Press of Kentucky, 1976), 91, 284; Erik Larson, *Devil in the White City: Murder, Magic, and Madness at the Fair That Changed America* (New York: Vintage Books, 2003), 255; Robert W. Rydell, *All the World's a Fair: Visions of Empire at American International Expositions, 1876–1916* (Chicago: University of Chicago Press, 1987), 40; Thomas J. Noel and Barbara S. Norgren, *Denver: The City Beautiful* (Denver: Historic Denver, Inc., 1987), 1; Judith A. Adams, *The American Amusement Park Industry: A History of Technology and Thrills* (Boston: Twayne, 1991), 21–24, first quotation on p. 23, second quotation on p. 24.

4. Rydell, *All the World's a Fair*, 2, 235–36; Burg, *Chicago's White City of 1893*, 299.

5. Larson, *Devil in the White City*, 373–74.

6. Ibid., 374–75; quotation in Burg, *Chicago's White City of 1893*, 310.

7. Rydell, *All the World's a Fair*, 235–36; Gary S. Cross and John K. Walton, *The Playful Crowd: Pleasure Places in the Twentieth Century* (New York: Columbia University Press, 2005), 39–42; Adams, *American Amusement Park Industry*, 28–29.

8. William F. Mangels, *The Outdoor Amusement Industry: From Earliest Times to the Present* (New York: Vantage, 1952), preface: 3–13; "William F. Mangels Amusement Industry's 'First Historian,'" *NAPHA News* 30 (2008): 15; John F. Kasson, *Amusing the Million: Coney Island at the Turn of the Century* (New York: Hill and Wang, 1978), 30–33.

9. Mangels, *Outdoor Amusement Industry*, 13–14, 17–19.

10. Ibid., 19–25, 38 (quotation); Kasson, *Amusing the Million*, 3–4, 7, 41, 93–94; LeRoy Ashby, *With Amusement for All: A History of American Popular Culture since 1830* (Lexington: University Press of Kentucky, 2006), 140–41; Cross and Walton, *Playful Crowd*, 69–70.

11. Nell Irvin Painter, *Standing at Armageddon: The United States, 1877–1919* (New York: W. W. Norton, 1989), 171–73, 385; John Milton Cooper Jr., *Pivotal Decades: The United States, 1900–1920* (New York: W. W. Norton, 1990), 8; Robert H. Wiebe, *The Search for Order, 1877–1920* (New York: Hill and Wang, 1967), 111–12; Ashby, *With Amusement for All*, 143–75; Adams, *American Amusement Park Industry*, 53–55; Roy Rosenzweig, *Eight Hours for What We Will: Workers and Leisure in an Industrial City, 1870–1920* (Cambridge: Cambridge University Press, 1992), 127, 129, 140–41.

12. David Nasaw, *Going Out: The Rise and Fall of Public Amusements* (New York: Basic Books, 1993), 1–2, 5, 45, 65–66, 85–86, quotation on p. 85.

13. Adams, *American Amusement Park Industry*, 63–65; Schlereth, *Victorian America*, 239.

14. Any random issue of *Billboard* between about 1905 and 1960 provides ample evidence of the number of stories on amusement parks that appeared in that publication during those years. By 1960 the coverage was dropping off, and it had

disappeared from the magazine entirely by 1965. After that time, the amusement park industry was covered in a new magazine, *Amusement Business*, which ceased publication in 2006. Lyrics to "Palisades Park" as sung by Freddy "Boom Boom" Cannon available at http://www.stlyrics.com/lyrics/confessionsofadangerousmind/palisadespark.htm, accessed March 30, 2012; the description of the back story for "Rollercoaster" is available at http://www.imdb.com/title/tt0076636/trivia, accessed March 30, 2012.

15. "Another Immense Amusement Resort Planned for Suburb That Overlooks a Fine View of Farm Scenery," *Denver Republican* (September 1, 1907): 2; Noel and Norgren, *Denver*, 10.

16. Jim Prochaska, "The Bottoms Tour Notes," provided to the author, 2008.

17. Noel and Norgren, *Denver*, 1–2, 5.

18. Ibid., 9.

19. Ibid., 9–10.

20. Roy Rosenzweig and Elizabeth Blackmar, *The Park and the People: A History of Central Park* (New York: Cornell University Press, 1992), 18; Noel and Norgren, *Denver*, 9; Stephen J. Leonard and Thomas J. Noel, *Denver: Mining Camp to Metropolis* (Niwot: University Press of Colorado, 1990), 140–41; Jerome C. Smiley, *History of Denver: With Outlines of the Earlier History of the Rocky Mountain Country* (Evansville, IN: Unigraphic, Inc., 1971 [1901]), 972, 975–78, first quotation on p. 972, second quotation on p. 975.

21. Smiley, *History of Denver*, 645–46, 975, first quotation on p. 646, second quotation on p. 975; Noel and Norgren, *Denver*, 9; Noel and Leonard, *Denver*, 140–41.

22. Annette Stott, *Pioneer Cemeteries: Sculpture Gardens of the Old West* (Lincoln: University of Nebraska Press, 2008), 40, 42–44, 48–49, quotation on p. 51; Rosenzweig and Blackmar, *The Park and the People*, 5, 31.

23. William B. Vickers, *History of the City of Denver, Arapahoe County, and Colorado: Containing a History of the State of Colorado . . . a Condensed Sketch of Arapahoe County . . . a History of the City of Denver . . . Biographical Sketches . . .* (Chicago: O. L. Baskin, 1880), 291; "Another Immense Amusement Resort Planned for Suburb That Overlooks a Fine View of Farm Scenery," *Denver Republican* (September 1, 1907): 2; "Opened to the Public," *Denver Republican* (May 2, 1890): 3; Betty Lynne Hull, *Denver's Elitch Gardens: Spinning a Century of Dreams* (Boulder: Johnson Books, 2003), 3, 7–9.

24. Hull, *Denver's Elitch Gardens*, 22–30, 37–38.

25. "A City's Beauty Spot," *Denver Times* (May 13, 1891): 6; Gene Lowall, "Famous Resort at Sloan's Lake Leveled by Fire," *RMN* (February 18, 1940): sec. 2, 10.

26. "Catch the Quarters," *Denver Times* (April 8, 1891): 8; Lowall, "Famous Resort at Sloan's Lake Leveled by Fire," *RMN* (February 18, 1940): sec. 2, 10; "Elitch and

Manhattan," *Denver Republican* (July 24, 1892): 11; Hull, *Denver's Elitch Gardens*, 22, 36; "Terrorized," *RMN* (July 6, 1891): 1.

27. "'The Little Trooper' at Manhattan," *Denver Times* (June 8, 1902): 24.

28. "Amusements," *Denver Republican* (May 26, 1902): 8; "Manhattan Beach Opens Next Saturday in Brightest Array," *Denver Republican* (June 12, 1904): 11 (quotation); "Fine Little Theater for the New Amusement Resort at the Beach," *Denver Republican* (May 1, 1910): 7; Lowall, "Famous Resort at Sloan's Lake Leveled by Fire," *RMN* (February 18, 1940): sec. 2, 10.

29. "A New Amusement Resort," *Colorado Sun* (Denver) (February 28, 1892): 7; "Sure to Be a Park," *RMN* (July 1, 1891): 8.

30. "Sure to Be a Park," *RMN* (July 1, 1891): 8; "Denver's New Pleasure Park," *RMN* (December 19, 1897): 4; Jack Foster, "Arlington Park Entertainment Spot," *RMN* (February 19, 1956): 57; "Wiping out Pompeii," *Denver Republican* (July 4, 1892): 2.

31. "Denver's New Pleasure Park," *RMN* (December 19, 1897): 4; "Why M'Farland Is Glad He Is Alive," *Denver Times* (August 7, 1898): 8.

32. "Denver's New Pleasure Park," *RMN* (December 19, 1897): 4.

33. "Chutes Park to Make Room for City Streets," *Denver Times* (April 2, 1903): 9. A plaque at Alamo Placita Park in Denver, which describes the history of Arlington Park and the events that went on there, is the only memorial to the park that exists and is the only indication that a quiet Denver park was once a lively amusement park. "Chutes Park Is No More," *Denver Times* (January 22, 1901): 10; "It's a Great Day at Arlington Park," *Denver Times* (July 4, 1901): 1; "Again Arlington Park Grandstand Burns," *Denver Times* (June 5, 1902): 6; Jack Foster, "Arlington Park Entertainment Spot," *RMN* (February 19, 1956): 57.

34. "The Arlington Park Land and Improvement Company Prospectus," Denver Park Land and Improvement Company Papers, WHGD.

35. "The Tuileries," *Denver Republican* (July 29, 1906): 15; "The Tuileries," *RMN* (June 23, 1907): sec. 2, 8; Jack Foster, "What Became of Tuileries?" *RMN* (August 9, 1959): 21A; Leonard and Noel, *Denver*, 285.

36. "Opened to the Public," *Denver Republican* (May 2, 1890): 3; Leonard and Noel, *Denver*, 102–12.

37. Rosenzweig and Blackmar, *The Park and the People*, 7, 239, 241–42; Noel and Norgren, *Denver*, 19; *Rocky Mountain News* cited in Leonard and Noel, *Denver*, first quotation on p. 146, second quotation on p. 148; "Opening of Lakeside Drew Thousands to the New White City of the Dazzling Lights," *Denver Republican* (May 31, 1908): 7.

38. Noel and Norgren, *Denver*, 9–10, 12, 16–17, 22; Leonard and Noel, *Denver*, 148.

39. Schlereth, *Victorian America*, 240–41.

40. "A Century of Thrills: Lakeside Reaches 100 with Formula for Family Fun," *RMN* (July 16, 2008): Business section, 2.

Chapter 1: Lakeside, an Amusement Enterprise

1. Michele H. Bogart, "Barking Architecture: The Sculpture of Coney Island," *Smithsonian Studies in American Art* 2 (Winter 1988): 3–6, 8 (quotation), 11, 13; Smiley, *History of Denver*, 908–10.

2. Gertrude "Betty" Arnold, interview by the author, Denver, CO, July 22, 2011; "Death of Mrs. Philip Zang," *Denver Republican* (April 15, 1896): 8; "Peter Friederich, Banker, Brewer, Dead of Apoplexy," *Denver Times* (May 13, 1911): 1; "William Buck," *RMN* (July 11, 1949): 36.

3. Arnold interview; "Adolph J. Zang Succumbs to Diabetes after Sudden Attack at Cripple Creek," *DP* (September 28, 1916): 1; Philip Zang Family Plot, Block 7, Riverside Cemetery, Denver, CO; "Godfrey Schirmer, Head of Denver Bank, Dies," *DP* (November 15, 1928): 1, 8; "Peter Friederich, Banker, Brewer, Dead of Apoplexy," *Denver Times* (May 13, 1911): 1; "American National Bank Has 22 Years' Progress," *RMN* (May 23, 1927): 16.

4. Certificate of Incorporation of the Lakeside Realty and Amusement Company, Document 8539, Wyoming State Archives, Laramie; "The Local News," *CT* (April 18, 1907): 8.

5. Colorado Secretary of State, Plat and Map of Lakeside, April 24, 1907, City of Lakeside Incorporation Records, Incorporation of Cities and Towns 1800–1977, Julesburg to Lakewood Number 2, Roll 19, Colorado State Archives, Denver; Colorado Secretary of State, Petition for Incorporation, October 21, 1907, City of Lakeside Incorporation Records, Incorporation of Cities and Towns 1800–1977, Julesburg to Lakewood Number 2, Roll 19, Colorado State Archives, Denver; Colorado Secretary of State, Untitled Document—Election Results, October 21, 1907, City of Lakeside Incorporation Records, Incorporation of Cities and Towns 1800–1977, Julesburg to Lakewood Number 2, Roll 19, Colorado State Archives, Denver; "The Local News," *CT* (August 8, 1907): 8; "The Local News," *CT* (September 26, 1907): 8; "The Local News," *CT* (October 24, 1907): 8; "The Local News," *CT* (November 21, 1907): 8; "Youngest Town Holds Election," *CT* (December 12, 1907): 1.

6. Mangels, *Outdoor Amusement Industry*, 18, 20; 100th Anniversary Tour of Lakeside Amusement Park, July 18, 2008; "Colorado News Items," *CT* (December 19, 1907): 2; "The Local News," *CT* (August 8, 1907): 8; "Youngest Town Holds Election," *CT* (December 12, 1907): 1 (quotation); "Lakeside Town Officers Are Re-Nominated," *CT* (March 12, 1908): 8; "Adjourned Meeting of Lakeside Trustees," *CT* (February 27, 1908): 4.

7. "Youngest Town Holds Election," *CT* (December 12, 1907): 1.

8. Kasson, *Amusing the Million*, 63–65.

9. Ibid.; Hull, *Denver's Elitch Gardens*, 13, 53, 66, 96, 105; Nasaw, *Going Out*, 86.

10. "Another Immense Amusement Resort Planned for Suburb That Overlooks a Fine View of Farm Scenery," *Denver Republican* (September 1, 1907): 2; Lakeside Realty and Amusement Company, *Lakeside Realty and Amusement Company, Lakeside Park, the White City, Denver Colorado, Official Guide and Views* (Denver: Smith Books, 1908), 1–2.

11. "Lakeside Park Will Be a Maze of Lights," *CT* (February 20, 1908): 8; "The Local News," *CT* (May 28, 1908): 8; "Lakeside to Be Opened to the Public toward the Close of the Present Month," *Denver Republican* (May 17, 1908): sec. 2, 11.

12. Lakeside Realty and Amusement Company, *Lakeside Park, the White City*, 1–2; "Another Immense Amusement Resort Planned for Suburb That Overlooks a Fine View of Farm Scenery," *Denver Republican* (September 1, 1907): 2.

13. "Another Immense Amusement Resort Planned for Suburb That Overlooks a Fine View of Farm Scenery," *Denver Republican* (September 1, 1907): 2; *Lakeside Realty and Amusement Company, Lakeside Park, the White City*, 2; "A Glimpse of the Coney Island of the West: Lakeside the White City," Lakeside Amusement Park 1910 Brochure, File Folder 1, Lakeside Amusement Park Papers, Stephen H. Hart Library, History Colorado, Denver.

14. Thomas J. Noel, *Denver Landmarks and Historic Districts: A Pictorial Guide* (Niwot: University Press of Colorado, 1996), 16–17; *Lakeside Realty and Amusement Company, Lakeside Park, the White City*, 1–2; Pat Wilcox, "Memories of Lakeside: Amusement Mecca for Millions," *Arvada (CO) Citizen Sentinel* (August 16, 1973): 5; 100th Anniversary Tour of Lakeside Amusement Park, July 18, 2008; spare-tire cover in possession of the author.

15. "Adjourned Meeting of Lakeside Trustees," *CT* (February 27, 1908): 4; "Lakeside Town Officers Are Re-Nominated," *CT* (March 12, 1908): 8.

16. Beth J. Harpaz, "Trolley Parks Carry Visitors to a Simpler Time," *DP* (August 8, 2010): 1T; Don Robertson, Morris Cafky, and E. J. Haley, *Denver's Street Railways*, vol. 1: *1870–1900: Not an Automobile in Sight* (Denver: Sundance, 1999), 71–78; Smiley, *History of Denver*, 858–70, quotations on p. 870.

17. Hull, *Denver's Elitch Gardens*, 18, 29–30; "Elitch and Manhattan," *Denver Republican* (July 24, 1892): 11; "Sure to Be a Park," *RMN* (July 1, 1891): 8; "Denver's New Pleasure Park," *RMN* (December 19, 1897): 4; Don Robertson and W. Morris Cafky, *Denver's Street Railways*, vol. 2: *1901–1950: Reign of the Denver Tramway* (Denver: Sundance, 2004), 138–39.

18. "Lakeside to Be Opened to the Public toward the Close of the Present Month," *Denver Republican* (May 17, 1908): sec. 2, 8; Leonard and Noel, *Denver*, 55–56; "Adjourned Meeting of Lakeside Trustees," *CT* (February 27, 1908): 4; "Lakeside Town Officers Are Re-Nominated," *CT* (March 12, 1908): 8.

19. David Forsyth, "Eben Smith: Western Mining Man" (master's thesis, University of Colorado at Denver, 2003), 230; *1915 Denver Automobile Directory* (Denver:

Wahlgreen, 1915); Leonard and Noel, *Denver*, 481; car sales information taken from sign at 2011 Denver International Auto Show; James R. Smith, *San Francisco's Playland at the Beach: The Early Years* (Fresno: Craven Street Books, 2010), 13.

20. "Election Proclamation," *CT* (March 26, 1908): 1; "Lakeside News," *CT* (April 23, 1908): 5.

21. "A Bill for an Ordinance," *CT* (May 14, 1908): 5.

22. "Placing Finishing Touches on Big Lakeside Park," *CT* (April 30, 1908): 4; "Car Flies through Air; 15 Hurt," *RMN* (February 24, 1908): 1, 7; "Died," *RMN* (March 1, 1908): 6; "Serious Accident on Scenic Railway," *(Telluride, CO) Daily Journal* (February 24, 1908): 1; Frank Luther Mott, *American Journalism: A History: 1690–1960*, 3rd ed. (New York: Macmillan, 1962), 567–70.

23. "Placing Finishing Touches on Big Lakeside Park," *CT* (April 30, 1908): 4; "Lakeside Resort Nears Completion," *CT* (May 7, 1908): 5; "Lakeside to Be Opened to the Public toward the Close of the Present Month," *Denver Republican* (May 17, 1908): sec. 2, 11.

24. "Lakeside Denver's New Amusement Place to Open Its Numerous Attractions on Saturday," *Denver Republican* (May 24, 1908): sec. 2, 20.

25. 100th Anniversary Tour of Lakeside Amusement Park, July 18, 2008; "Lakeside Opens May 30," *DMF* (May 23, 1914): 16.

26. *Lakeside Realty and Amusement Company, Lakeside Park, the White City*, 1–2 (first quotation); "Many New Features at Big Amusement Park," *CT* (December 26, 1907): 1 (second quotation); Mangels, *Outdoor Amusement Industry*, 88–91 (last two quotations).

27. *Lakeside Realty and Amusement Company, Lakeside Park, the White City*, 1–2; "Many New Features at Big Amusement Park," *CT* (December 26, 1907): 1; "Lakeside, Denver's New Summer Resort Will Be the Coney Island of the West," *Denver Republican* (January 1, 1908): sec. 4, 8; "Lakeside Denver's New Amusement Place to Open Its Numerous Attractions on Saturday," *Denver Republican* (May 24, 1908): sec. 2, 20. Photographs of the White City (Lakeside Amusement Park) show the architecture and style of the park's grounds and buildings; Box 1, Colorado Snapshots Photograph Collection, WHGD.

28. Mangels, *Outdoor Amusement Industry*, 6–7.

29. Ibid., 139–40.

30. "A Glimpse of the Coney Island of the West: Lakeside the White City," Lakeside Amusement Park 1910 Brochure, File Folder 1, Lakeside Amusement Park Papers, Stephen H. Hart Library, History Colorado, Denver; Frances Melrose, "Doc's Carnival Show Nurtured Incubator Technology," *RMN* (July 28, 1991): Sunday magazine, 9M.

Chapter 2: Just Take a Trip Out to Jolly Lakeside

1. Elmore Lee, "Just Take a Trip Out to Lakeside" (Denver: Tolbert R. Ingram, 1908), available at University of Colorado at Boulder archives; "Opening of Lakeside Drew Thousands to the New White City of the Dazzling Lights," *Denver Republican* (May 31, 1908): 7; "Lakeside Park, Denver," *Fort Collins (CO) Weekly Courier* (July 1, 1908): 5.

2. "Opening of Lakeside Drew Thousands to the New White City of the Dazzling Lights," *Denver Republican* (May 31, 1908): 7; "Lakeside Department," *CT* (June 18, 1908): 5; "Lakeside Park, Denver," *Fort Collins (CO) Weekly Courier* (July 1, 1908): 5.

3. "Opening of Lakeside Drew Thousands to the New White City of the Dazzling Lights," *Denver Republican* (May 31, 1908): 7.

4. Ibid.

5. "Faces Death; Tells Experience," *CT* (August 6, 1908): 1; Anne Ryan, "The 'Army Surgeon' of Lakeside Amusement Park," *DP Empire Magazine* (March 27, 1977): 30–33.

6. "Opening of Lakeside Drew Thousands to the New White City of the Dazzling Lights," *Denver Republican* (May 31, 1908): 7; "A Glimpse of the Coney Island of the West: Lakeside the White City," Lakeside Amusement Park 1910 Brochure, File Folder 1, Lakeside Amusement Park Papers, Stephen H. Hart Library, History Colorado, Denver.

7. "Bold Pickpockets Quickly Nabbed," *CT* (June 25, 1908): 1.

8. Leonard and Noel, *Denver*, 144; "Lakeside," *CT* (July 2, 1908): 4; Mayor's Budget 1908, File Folder 22, Robert W. Speer Papers, WHGD.

9. "Pencil Pushers Entertained at the White City," *CT* (June 25, 1908): 1; "Choppers Picnic to Be Big Affair," *CT* (July 16, 1908): 1.

10. "Big Days for This County at Lakeside," *CT* (September 2, 1909): 1; "Three Day Corn Festival and Carnival at Lakeside," *Wray (CO) Rattler* (September 25, 1908): 1.

11. Julian Helber, "Lakeside," *Billboard* (June 27, 1908): 28; "Lakeside Park, Denver," *Billboard* (July 17, 1909): 29.

12. "Denver, Col.," *Billboard* (July 24, 1909): 10; "Denver, Col.," *Billboard* (August 21, 1909): 10; "Denver, Col.," *Billboard* (September 11, 1909): 23; untitled article on Albert Lewin in *Svensk Amerikanska Western (Denver)* (August 24, 1911): 7; "Denver's New Public Market Has a Few Choice Spaces Left," *Fort Collins (CO) Courier* (July 31, 1919): 7.

13. "The Local News," *CT* (April 29, 1909): 8; Certificate of Amendment to the Articles of Incorporation of the Lakeside Realty and Amusement Company, Document 10148, Wyoming State Archives, Cheyenne; "Ballot," *CT* (April 1, 1909):

5; "The Local News," *CT* (April 8, 1909): 8; "The Local News," *CT* (April 12, 1909): 8; "The Local News," *CT* (April 15, 1909): 8; "The Local News," *CT* (May 13, 1909): 8; "The Local News," *CT* (July 1, 1909): 7; "The Local News," *CT* (August 26, 1909): 6.

14. Untitled article, *CT* (July 30, 1908): 4.

15. "The Local News," *CT* (July 8, 1909): 8; "Tries to Save County Money and Loses Job," *CT* (July 8, 1909): 1; "Prosecution Assumes Air of Persecution," *CT* (August 5, 1909): 1.

16. "Millionaires Are Taken by Sheriff," *Fort Collins (CO) Weekly Courier* (July 28, 1909): 11; "Prosecution Assumes Air of Persecution," *CT* (August 5, 1909): 1; "Five Minutes to Clear Man of Murder Charge," *CT* (November 18, 1909): 1.

17. "Complains against Big Resort and Must Pay Costs," *CT* (August 12, 1909): 1; "White City Liquor Cases Are Suddenly Ended," *CT* (November 25, 1909): 1; "Jefferson Battle Ground in Expensive Contest," *CT* (August 19, 1909): 1.

18. "Five Minutes to Clear Man of Murder Charge," *CT* (November 18, 1909): 1; "White City Liquor Cases Are Suddenly Ended," *CT* (November 25, 1909): 1.

19. "White City Liquor Cases Are Suddenly Ended," *CT* (November 25, 1909): 1; "Five Minutes to Clear Man of Murder Charge," *CT* (November 18, 1909): 1; "Jefferson Battle Ground in Expensive Contest," *CT* (August 19, 1909): 1.

20. Phil Goodstein, *Robert Speer's Denver, 1904–1920: The Mile High City in the Progressive Era* (Denver: New Social Publications, 2004), 21, 38, 65–67, 104, 135, quotation on p. 67.

21. "Prosecution Assumes Air of Persecution," *CT* (August 5, 1909): 1.

22. "The Local News," *CT* (April 29, 1909): 8 (quotation); untitled article, *CT* (September 2, 1909): 4; "Sheriff Raids Gambling Joint," *CT* (October 17, 1907): 1.

23. "Lakeside," *RMN* (May 30, 1909): sec. 3, 3; "30,000 at Lakeside View Opening Attractions," *RMN* (May 31, 1909): 7.

24. "Farmers Taking Great Interest in County Fair," *CT* (August 26, 1909): 1 (first quotation and "bewitching fairyland" quote); "Big Days for This County at Lakeside," *CT* (September 2, 1909): 1 (third quotation).

25. "Farmers Taking Great Interest in County Fair," *CT* (August 16, 1909): 1; "Big Days for This County at Lakeside," *CT* (September 2, 1909): 1; "Boulevard Will Be Built between This City and Denver," *CT* (April 8, 1909): 1; "North Road Selected for Boulevard," *CT* (July 15, 1909): 1.

26. "Farmers Taking Great Interest in County Fair," *CT* (August 26, 1909): 1; "Substantial Aid to Golden-Denver Boulevard Fund," *CT* (August 26, 1909): 1; "Big Days for This County at Lakeside," *CT* (September 2, 1909): 1 (quotations); "Lakeside Receipts Nearly Complete Boulevard Fund," *CT* (September 16, 1909): 1; "Meeting to Decide on Boulevard," *CT* (February 24, 1910): 1; "Will Make Golden Cemetery a Beauty Spot," *CT* (February 16, 1911): 1.

27. "Will Be Big Advertisement for Jefferson County," *CT* (September 16, 1909): 1; Prize List (untitled), *CT* (September 23, 1909): 1; "Farmers Taking Great Interest in County Fair," *CT* (August 26, 1909): 1; "Supremacy of Jefferson as Agricultural Section Proved," *CT* (September 30, 1909): 1; "Get Ready for Lakeside Farmers' Day," *CT* (September 16, 1909): 9.

28. "Supremacy of Jefferson as Agricultural Section Proved," *CT* (September 30, 1909): 1; "Success of County Fair Now Assured," *CT* (February 17, 1910): 1; "County Fair Knocker Sadly Out of Joint," *CT* (March 24, 1910): 1.

29. "Many Changes at Lakeside Next Year," *CT* (October 7, 1909): 1.

30. Harry Johnson, "Lakeside News," *CT* (December 17, 1908): 5; "Lakeside News," *CT* (December 3, 1908): 5; Harry Johnson, "Lakeside News," *CT* (January 7, 1909): 5; US Bureau of the Census, *Thirteenth Census of the United States, 1910, Lakeside, Colorado*.

31. "Lakeside News," *CT* (August 13, 1908): 4; Harry Johnson, "Lakeside News," *CT* (January 28, 1909): 4; "Lakeside News," *CT* (December 3, 1908): 5; Harry Johnson, "Lakeside News," *CT* (January 7, 1909): 5.

32. "Untitled," *CT* (January 2, 1908): 4; Mayor's Budget 1909, 5, File Folder 22, Robert W. Speer Papers, WHGD (Speer quotation); Leonard and Noel, *Denver*, 135.

Chapter 3: Lakeside, the White City Beautiful

1. All four Denver amusement parks were written about in the July 30, 1910, July 6, 1912, and July 11, 1914, issues of *Denver Municipal Facts*. Lakeside, Elitch's, and Manhattan Beach were written about together in the June 18, 1910, and February 28, 1914, issues. Lakeside and Elitch's were written about together in the May 13, 1911, issue, while Lakeside and Manhattan Beach were written about in the June 17, 1911, issue. Elitch's and Manhattan Beach were written about together in the July 1 and August 5, 1911, issues. Lakeside received coverage alone in the August 29, 1908, January 8, August 20, August 27, and October 29, 1910, July 11, July 22, and August 11, 1911, May 17, June 14, and August 24, 1912, June 28 and July 12, 1913, and May 23 and July 25, 1914, issues. Elitch's received coverage alone in the June 24 and August 19, 1911, August 3, 1912, August 23, 1913, and March 28 and May 23, 1914, issues. Manhattan Beach/Luna Park received coverage alone in the July 23 and November 26, 1910, issues. Tuileries received coverage alone in the August 13, 1910, issue. The quote about the lights of Denver and Lakeside creating a brilliant spectacle is from "Three Beautiful Lakes in Sight," *DMF* 2 (October 29, 1910): 4.

2. "Denver and Colorado to Provide Royal Entertainment for Visitors to National Real Estate Convention," *DMF* 3 (July 17, 1911): 3–6.

3. "Denver's Four Pleasure Parks Show Great Variety of Amusements," *DMF* 4 (July 6, 1912): 3–5.

4. Ibid.; Arnold interview.

5. "Denver's Four Pleasure Parks Show Great Variety of Amusements," *DMF* 4 (July 6, 1912): 3–5.

6. "A Glimpse of the Coney Island of the West: Lakeside the White City," Lakeside Amusement Park 1910 Brochure, File Folder 1, Lakeside Amusement Park Papers, Stephen H. Hart Library, History Colorado, Denver; "Amusement Park News," *Billboard* 24 (April 27, 1912): 22; *Denver, the Convention City of America: The City of Hospitality, at the Base of the Rocky Mountains, Scintillating with Millions of Electric Lights* (Denver: Denver Convention League, 1910): 20, WHGD.

7. Cited in Smith, *San Francisco's Playland at the Beach*, 1–2, 6–8.

8. Derek Gee and Ralph Lopez, *Laugh Your Troubles Away: The Complete History of Riverview Park, Chicago, Illinois* (Livonia, MI: Sharpshooter Productions, 2000), 6–7, 25, 94–95.

9. David Francis and Diane Francis, *Cleveland Amusement Park Memories: A Nostalgic Look Back at Euclid Beach Park, Puritas Springs Park, Geauga Lake Park, and Other Classic Parks* (Cleveland: Gray, 2004), 9–10, 35, 40, 42–43, 56–57, 77–80.

10. "Many Changes at Lakeside Next Year," *CT* (October 7, 1909): 1 (management quotation); "Lakeside News," *CT* (December 3, 1908): 5; "Denver, Col.," *Billboard* 24 (March 26, 1910): 9; "Parks List," *Billboard* 23 (March 26, 1910): 54; "Lakeside Park, Denver, Col.," *Billboard* 24 (June 11, 1910): 14 (*Billboard* quotation); "Summer Park News, Denver Parks," *Billboard* 23 (May 7, 1910): 16.

11. Untitled article, *Denver Express* (March 26, 1910), Lakeside Amusement Park Clipping File 4, WHGD.

12. "Many New Features at Lakeside," *CT* (May 5, 1910): 1; "Denver's Coney Island to Open with New Theater," *CT* (May 26, 1910): 1; *Denver, the Convention City of America*, 20.

13. "Many Changes at Lakeside Next Year," *CT* (October 7, 1909): 1; Adams, *American Amusement Park Industry*, 52 (first quotation); Gee and Lopez, *Laugh Your Troubles Away*, 34; Steven A. Reiss, *City Games: The Evolution of American Urban Society and the Rise of Sports* (Urbana: University of Illinois Press, 1989), 66–67, 70–71, 149.

14. "Big Town Amusement News in Brief" for Denver, CO, *Billboard* 23 (July 16, 1910): 10; "Big Town Amusement News in Brief" for Denver, CO, *Billboard* 23 (July 23, 1910): 11.

15. "Denver Canceling Attractions," *Billboard* 24 (August 13, 1910): 16; "This Is 'Railroad Day,'" *DMF* 2 (August 20, 1910): 13; "'Railroad Day' a Success," *DMF* 2 (August 27, 1910): 13; Julian Helber, "Big Town Amusement News in Brief" for Denver, CO, *Billboard* 23 (September 3, 1910): 11; "Park Notes," *Billboard* 24 (May 6, 1911): 23; "Peter Friederich, Banker, Brewer, Dead of Apoplexy," *Denver Times* (May 13, 1911): 1; "Funeral Notices, Friederich," *RMN* (May 17, 1911): 12.

16. "Gov. Shafroth Opens Season at Lakeside," *RMN* (May 29, 1911): sec. 1, 5; "Chamber of Commerce Carnival at Lakeside Next Week," *DMF* 3 (June 17, 1911): 10.

17. Julian Helber, "Resume of the Week's Important Amusement Events in Big American Cities" for Denver, CO, *Billboard* 23 (June 10, 1911): 18; "Resume of the Week's Important Amusement Events in Big American Cities" for Denver, CO, *Billboard* 23 (June 17, 1911): 19; "Active Plans for Poynter," *Billboard* 23 (July 15, 1911): 7.

18. "Resume of the Week's Important Amusement Events in Big American Cities" for Denver, CO, *Billboard* 23 (June 17, 1911): 19; "Resume of the Week's Important Amusement Events in Big American Cities" for Denver, CO, *Billboard* 23 (July 8, 1911): 19; "Resume of the Week's Important Amusement Events in Big American Cities" for Denver, CO, *Billboard* 23 (July 15, 1911): 18; "Resume of the Week's Important Amusement Events in Big American Cities" for Denver, CO, *Billboard* 23 (September 9, 1911): 60; Julian Helber, "Resume of the Week's Important Amusement Events in Big American Cities" for Denver, CO, *Billboard* 23 (September 2, 1911): 21.

19. "White City Has $20,000 Fire Loss," *CT* (November 16, 1911): 1.

20. Noel and Norgren, *Denver*, 22–26 (newspaper citations); Goodstein, *Robert Speer's Denver*, 491, 496–97.

21. Leonard and Noel, *Denver*, 120–22, 151–52; Smiley, *History of Denver*, 977–78.

22. Leonard and Noel, *Denver*, 307–8, 310–11, 321.

23. Robertson, Cafky, and Haley, *Denver's Street Railways*, 71; Smiley, *History of Denver*, 870.

24. "Lakeside Park Celebrates 100 Years," *NAPHA News* 30 (2008): 5; untitled article, *Billboard* (March 24, 1928): 4, Lakeside Amusement Park Clipping File 1, WHGD.

25. "Western League Baseball Schedule" (Denver: Lakeside Realty and Amusement Company, 1912), WHGD.

26. "Amusement Park News," *Billboard* 24 (April 27, 1912): 22; "Resume of the Week's Important Amusement Events in Big American Cities" for Denver, CO, *Billboard* 23 (June 10, 1911): 18; "Lakeside Theater Program," June 9, June 26, July 14, July 28, and August 4, 1912, all in Lakeside Theater File Folder, Box 11, Colorado Theater Program Collection, WHGD. The theater programs, without notations by patrons, are also available in Lakeside Amusement Park Clipping File 4, WHGD.

27. "Amusement Park News," *Billboard* 24 (April 27, 1912): 22; "Park Notes," *Billboard* 24 (June 15, 1912): 20; "'Gator Joe' Bereft; Mrs. Joe Hits Trail," *RMN* (May 30, 1912): 3.

28. "'Dry' at Lakeside; Bartenders Strike," *RMN* (May 31, 1912): 4.

29. Certificate of Incorporation of Colorado Realty and Amusement Company, Document 14724, Wyoming State Archives; "Big-Time Bands Business Boon to

Denver's Lakeside El Patio," *Billboard* 43 (November 14, 1931): 34; Arnold interview.

30. "City Entertains Thousands during Bundes Turnfest," *DMF* 1 (June 28, 1913): 3; "Lakeside Park," *DP* (August 5, 1913): 5.

31. "Lakeside Park," *DP* (August 5, 1913): 5; "Breezy, Noisy Play and Immense Crowd at Lakeside Casino," *Denver Republican* (June 17, 1913), Lakeside Amusement Park Clipping File 1, WHGD; programs for the twelve Cavallo Symphony Orchestra concerts are in Lakeside Theater File Folder, Box 11, Colorado Theater Program Collection, WHGD.

32. "Ad for Lakeside: The White City," *Billboard* (August 17, 1912): 20; "Lakeside Park Celebrates 100 Years," *NAPHA News* 30 (2008): 5; Mangels, *Outdoor Amusement Industry*, 133–34; untitled article, *Billboard* (March 13, 1915): 19, Lakeside Amusement Park Clipping File 1, WHGD; "Lakeside Theater to Remain Open All Season," *DP* (July 8, 1915), Lakeside Amusement Park Clipping File 4, WHGD.

33. "Lakeside Park Celebrates 100 Years," *NAPHA News* 30 (2008): 8–9.

34. "Lakeside Opens May 30," *DMF* (May 23, 1914): 16; "Program for the Elks' Convention," *DMF* 2 (July 11, 1914): 15.

35. "Lakeside Park Throws Open Gates for Season, Panorama of Panama Canal Leads New Attractions," *RMN* (May 31, 1914): sec. 2, 3.

36. Leonard and Noel, *Denver*, 158.

37. Ibid., 159; "Adolph J. Zang Succumbs to Diabetes after Sudden Attack at Cripple Creek," *DP* (September 28, 1916): 1; Arnold interview.

38. "Casino Theater Program," June 26 and July 3, 1916, also 1915, all in Lakeside Theater File Folder, Box 11, Colorado Theater Program Collection, WHGD; "Company at Lakeside Sings Charming Opera," *RMN* (June 12, 1916), Lakeside Amusement Park Clipping File 1, WHGD; "Amusements," *RMN* (May 27, 1916): 5; David Meyers, "Buildering: The Art of Climbing . . . Skyscrapers," at http://www.google.com/url?sa=t&rct=j&q=&esrc=s&source=web&cd=14&ved=0CCkQFjADOApqFQoTCK3ortey-scCFdGLkgodrYoOFw&url=http%3A%2F%2Fwww.davidmeyercreations.com%2Fmysteries-of-history%2Fbuildering-the-art-of-climbing-skyscrapers%2F&usg=AFQjCNGFmfueak8-8D_Ui1nfkmuWJdKMhA, accessed September 15, 2015.

39. "Death amidst Gayety," *CT* (June 16, 1910): 2; "Two Are Drowned in White City Lake," *CT* (July 6, 1916): 2; "Complain of Lakeside Noise," *CT* (June 22, 1916): 4.

40. Robin Chotzinoff, "For Your Amusement: It's Been a Great Ride at Lakeside," *Westword* (Denver) (June 22, 2000), at http://www.westword.com/2000-06-22/news/for-your-amusement/, accessed January 5, 2012.

41. Noel and Norgren, *Denver*, 51.

Chapter 4: Keeping Lakeside's Bright Lights Shining

1. Adams, *American Amusement Park Industry*, 66, 158; Cross and Walton, *Playful Crowd*, 136.

2. "White City Sold for $42,750," *CT* (February 15, 1917): 1.

3. Certificate of Incorporation of Denver Park and Amusement Company, Document 20546, Wyoming State Archives; "Little Colorado Items," *Wray (CO) Rattler* (October 24, 1912): 6; "Park Notes," *Billboard* 30 (March 11, 1918): 47; *Denver Park and Amusement Company v. Francis J. Kirchoff, et al.*, Case Number 12234 in the Supreme Court of Colorado, Abstract of Record and Assignment of Error, Filed December 17, 1928, Folios 1366–70, Colorado State Archives, Denver.

4. Schlereth, *Victorian America*, 295–97.

5. Phil Goodstein, *In the Shadow of the Klan: When the KKK Ruled Denver, 1920–1926* (Denver: New Social Publications, 2006), 4, 17–19, 59, quotation on p. 17; Carl Abbott, Stephen J. Leonard, and David McComb, *Colorado: A History of the Centennial State*, 3rd ed. (Niwot: University Press of Colorado, 1992), 277.

6. Hull, *Denver's Elitch Gardens*, 53, 55–57.

7. Leonard and Noel, *Denver*, 146–48.

8. "Lakeside Lights Shine Again for Summer Season," *RMN* (May 27, 1917): sec. 2, 1.

9. Ibid.; "Will Open under Receiver," *Billboard* (April 29, 1933), Lakeside Amusement Park Clipping File 2, WHGD; "Lakeside Park Celebrates 100 Years," *NAPHA News* 30 (2008): 7; "Lakeside, Denver, Colo., Week-End Season Starts," *Billboard* 43 (April 25, 1931): 56; "Benjamin Krasner: Lakeside Park Manager Dies," *DP* (August 8, 1965): 2F.

10. "Pheasant Puts Town in Darkness," *CT* (August 16, 1917): 2; "Improvements at Denver Park," *Billboard* 30 (June 15, 1918): 29; "Lakeside Park Celebrates 100 Years," *NAPHA News* 30 (2008): 7.

11. "Circle Swings Changed to Captive Aeroplanes," *Billboard* (March 22, 1919), Lakeside Amusement Park Clipping File 3, WHGD; "Denver Parks Ready," *Billboard* 31 (June 7, 1919): 52; "Revue at Denver's Lakeside," *Billboard* (July 3, 1920), Lakeside Amusement Park Clipping File 1, WHGD; "Thirteenth Season of Denver Park Begins," *Billboard* 32 (June 12, 1920): 60; "Lakeside Park Open an Extra Week," *Billboard* 32 (September 18, 1920): 60.

12. "Denver's Lakeside Opens," *Billboard* 33 (May 28, 1921): 71 (quotations); "Lakeside, Denver," *Billboard* 33 (June 18, 1921): 70; "Free at Lakeside," *Billboard* 33 (July 23, 1921): 66.

13. "Lakeside Park Will Feature Sunset Dinners," *Billboard* 34 (June 24, 1922): 56.

14. "Denver Mid-Summer Carnival," *Billboard* 35 (August 25, 1923): 85.

15. "Lakeside Park Celebrates 100 Years," *NAPHA News* 30 (2008): 7; "Lakeside, Denver, Opens," *Billboard* 39 (May 21, 1927): 64; "Denver's Lakeside Ready for May 18," *Billboard* (May 18, 1929), Lakeside Amusement Park Clipping File 1, WHGD; Rhoda Krasner, interview by the author, Lakeside, CO, July 12, 2012; "Color Scheme of Lakeside Casino Tower Is Changed," *Billboard* 43 (May 23, 1931): 41.

16. Robertson and Cafky, *Denver's Street Railways*, 526; Leonard Mosley, *Disney's World* (Lanham, MD: Scarborough House, 1992), 282–83; "Lakeside Is Leased for Movie Studio, Work Starts May 17," *RMN* (April 29, 1920): 1, 8; Tim Dirks, "1920s Film History," at http://www.filmsites.org/20sintro4.html, accessed October 22, 2011.

17. Michael E. Parrish, *Anxious Decades: America in Prosperity and Depression, 1920–1941* (New York: W. W. Norton, 1992), 147–49; "A Flapper Described," *Estes Park (CO) Trail* (October 28, 1921): 2; "Save Flappers' Souls," *Ouray (CO) Herald* (June 8, 1922): 3.

18. "Flappers in Contest Show Pretty Styles," *Daily Journal* (Telluride, CO) (July 19, 1922): 1.

19. "Lakeside Park Celebrates 100 Years," *NAPHA News* 30 (2008): 6–7; Hull, *Denver's Elitch Gardens*, 60; "Amusement Devices," unknown source and date, and "Denver's Lakeside Ready for May 18," *Billboard* (May 18, 1929), Lakeside Amusement Park Clipping File 1, WHGD.

20. "Lakeside Park, Denver, Stepping Right Along," *Billboard* 38 (July 10, 1926): 64; "Lakeside Park, Denver, Stepping Right Along," *Billboard* (July 10, 1929), Lakeside Amusement Park Clipping File 2, WHGD; Photo Call Number X-27619, "Joe Mann's Orchestra at Jail at Lakeside," Western History and Genealogy Photo Collection, WHGD; Frances Melrose, "'The Jail' at Lakeside Made Habitués Prisoners of Pleasure," *RMN* (September 3, 1995): 72A; Lakeside Casino china and Lakeside Jail tin cup in possession of the author; Mary Frances Berry, *The Pig Farmer's Daughter and Other Tales of American Justice: Episodes of Racism and Sexism in the Courts from 1865 to the Present* (New York: Alfred A. Knopf, 1999), 180, 191–92, 194; Nasaw, *Going Out*, 12–13.

21. "Lakeside Park, Denver, Stepping Right Along," *Billboard* (July 10, 1929), Lakeside Amusement Park Clipping File 2, WHGD; Menu for the Plantation restaurant, 1926, in possession of the author; M. M. Manring, *Slave in a Box: The Strange Career of Aunt Jemima* (Charlottesville: University Press of Virginia, 1998), 11–12, 23, 96.

22. *Clason's Denver Map Guide* (Denver: Clason Map Co., 1925), 27; Hull, *Denver's Elitch Gardens*, 60, 65–66; Jack Gurtler Oral History, WHGD; Robertson and Cafky, *Denver's Street Railways*, 526; Robin Chotzinoff, "For Your Amusement: It's Been a Great Ride at Lakeside," *Westword* (Denver) (June 22, 2000), at http://www.westword.com/2000-06-22/news/for-your-amusement/, accessed January 5, 2012.

23. *Denver Park and Amusement Company v. Francis J. Kirchoff, et al.*, Folios 4–5, 7, 10, 12, 16, 19–20, 25, 747, 1033–53, 1354.

24. Ibid., Folios 4–5, 7, 10, 12, 16, 19–20, 25, 33, 78; "Denver's Lakeside Ready for May 18," *Billboard* (May 18, 1929), Lakeside Amusement Park Clipping File 1, WHGD; "Godfrey Schirmer, Head of Denver Bank, Dies," *DP* (November 15, 1928): 1, 8; "Will Open under Receiver," *Billboard* (April 29, 1933), Lakeside Amusement Park Clipping File 2, WHGD.

25. "Denver's Lakeside Ready for May 18," *Billboard* 41 (May 18, 1929): 68; "Business Good for Denver Parks," *Billboard* 42 (June 14, 1930): 85; Leonard and Noel, *Denver*, 204–5; Adams, *American Amusement Park Industry*, 66–67; Cross and Walton, *Playful Crowd*, 137–38.

26. "Denver Parks Adding New Riding Devices," *Billboard* 42 (April 26, 1930): 78; "Closed Canadian Parks, Ontario," at http://cec.chebucto.org/ClosPark/ErieBech.html, accessed October 29, 2011; "Business Good for Denver Parks," *Billboard* 42 (June 14, 1930): 85 (quotation); "Lakeside Park, Denver, Has Pre-Season Opening," *Billboard* 42 (May 10, 1930): 60.

27. "George Morrison," at http://www.denvergov.org/Portals/633/documents/George%20Morrison.doc (page no longer available), accessed October 26, 2011.

28. "Business Good for Denver Parks," *Billboard* 42 (June 14, 1930): 85; "Good Season for Lakeside," *Billboard* 42 (November 29, 1930): 66.

29. "Bands Boost Denver Spot," *Billboard* 43 (October 3, 1931): 36; "Big-Time Bands Business Boon to Denver's Lakeside El Patio," *Billboard* 43 (November 14, 1931): 34; *Denver Park and Amusement Company v. Francis J. Kirchoff, et al.*, Folio 732.

30. "Big-Time Bands Business Boon to Denver's Lakeside El Patio," *Billboard* 43 (November 14, 1931): 34 (quotation); "Denver Trying Low Prices," *Billboard* 44 (August 6, 1932): 37; "Managers Keep up on Toes in Denver," *Billboard* 44 (August 20, 1932): 36; "May Open Early in Denver," *Billboard* 45 (February 25, 1933): 30; "Denver Lakeside Drawing," *Billboard* 45 (August 5, 1933): 32; "Biz Not So Bad in Denver," *Billboard* 45 (September 2, 1933): 36.

31. "Will Open under Receiver," *Billboard* (April 29, 1933), Lakeside Amusement Park Clipping File 2, WHGD.

32. "Lakeside Ready for Fresh Start," *Billboard* 46 (May 19, 1934): 38; "Tourists Help in Denver," *Billboard* 46 (June 30, 1934): 52; "Denver Lakeside More than Doubles Play of Last Year," *Billboard* 46 (August 4, 1934): 38; "Denver Lakeside Bought," *Billboard* 47 (March 2, 1935): 42.

33. "Business Good for Denver Parks," *Billboard* 42 (June 14, 1930): 85; Colorado Writer's Program of the Works Project Administration, *Life in Denver Part VII*, 1942, 32, WHGD.

Chapter 5: Benjamin Krasner and Lakeside's New Setup

1. Nasaw, *Going Out*, 242.
2. Ernest Anderson, "Circulation," *Billboard* 47 (March 2, 1935): 42.
3. Stuart Leuthner, "Lake Side: An Art Deco Masterpiece Struggles to Survive," *American Heritage* 43 (July-August 1992), at http://www.americanheritage.com /content/lake-side?page=show, accessed September 15, 2015; "Denver Lakeside Bought," *Billboard* 47 (March 2, 1935); 42. The price Krasner paid for the park is based on figures in Robert J. Olson, "Lakeside Is the Place! A History of the Lakeside Amusement Park," *Historically Jeffco* 19 (2006): 36. Also see US Bureau of the Census, *Sixteenth Census of the United States, 1940, Lakeside Town, Colorado*.
4. Ashby, *With Amusement for All*, 233–38; Nasaw, *Going Out*, 116–18; *Ned Stout, an Infant, by Emory L. O'Connell, His Next Friend v. Denver Park and Amusement Company*, Case number 12262 in the Supreme Court of Colorado, Filed 1928, Folios 59–60, Colorado State Archives, Denver.
5. "Lakeside's New Setup by Krasner in Denver Has Big Public Appeal," *Billboard* 47 (September 21, 1935): 38; "About Kay Kyser," at www.kaykyser.net, accessed December 9, 2011. Photos X-27613, X-27403, X-27401, X-27617, WHGD, show Kyser and his band at Lakeside as well as billboards advertising the park and Kyser; see also "Duke Ellington El Patio Denver 1942," Big Band Serenade Podcast by Humphrey Camardella Productions, first podcast September 12, 2011, available on iTunes. This podcast is Ellington's performance at El Patio on July 6, 1942, originally broadcast on KLZ radio, and includes the reference to Paul Whiteman and his band performing after Ellington's final performance the next night. See also Rhoda Krasner, interview by the author, Lakeside, CO, July 5, 2012.
6. "Denver Lakeside Bought," *Billboard* 47 (March 2, 1935): 42; "Lakeside's New Setup by Krasner in Denver Has Big Public Appeal," *Billboard* 47 (September 21, 1935): 38; "Tourists Aid in Excellent Season in Denver Environs," *Billboard* 47 (September 14, 1935): 34.
7. "Denver Lakeside Bought," *Billboard* 47 (March 2, 1935): 42; Leuthner, "Lake Side"; "Lakeside Park Celebrates 100 Years," *NAPHA News* 30 (2008): 11.
8. Bevis Hillier and Stephen Escritt, *Art Deco Style* (London: Phaidon, 1997), 19, 21–23, 72, 76–77, 87, first quotation on p. 21, second quotation on p. 19, last quotation on p. 87.
9. Leuthner, "Lake Side."
10. Ibid.; "Many Improvements at Lakeside, Denver," *Billboard* 54 (May 16, 1942): 52; "Colorado Coastin'," unknown source and date, Lakeside Amusement Park Clipping File 2, WHGD (first quotation); "Origin of Lakeside's Famous Carousel Is Lost," *DP Roundup* (August 5, 1962): 9.

11. "Denver Lakeside Puts out $60,000," *Billboard* 49 (May 22, 1937): 46; "Outlay Big for Elitch's," *Billboard* 49 (May 15, 1937): 43, 47; "30% Upturn for Lakeside," *Billboard* 49 (September 11, 1937): 46 (quotation), 49.

12. "Lakeside's New Setup by Krasner in Denver Has Big Public Appeal," *Billboard* 47 (September 21, 1935): 38; "30% Upturn for Lakeside," *Billboard* 49 (September 11, 1937): 46, 49 (quotation); "Denver's Lakeside Is Augmented for Its 30th Anniversary Season," *Billboard* 50 (April 16, 1938): 40, 45; "Gleanings from the Field," *Billboard* 50 (July 23, 1938): 40; "Lakeside's Take up 12% over '40," *Billboard* 53 (July 19, 1941): 50; Smith, *San Francisco's Playland at the Beach*, 38.

13. "Novel Ideas in New Devices," *Billboard* 50 (March 5, 1938): 42; "Krasner Has Best in Denver Lakeside Spot," *Billboard* 51 (November 18, 1939): 36; "Krasner in Best Year," *Billboard* 51 (December 30, 1939): 113; "Denver Lakeside to Step out with Outlay of $95,000," *Billboard* 52 (April 20, 1940): 38; "Lakeside up 14% in Denver," *Billboard* 52 (July 27, 1940): 48, 50; "Octopus for Denver Spot," *Billboard* 50 (January 22, 1938): 47; "Lakeside Park Celebrates 100 Years," *NAPHA News* 30 (2008): 11; "The Tumble Bug," at www.ridezone.com/rides/tumblebug/index.htm, accessed December 9, 2011. Denver Public Library Western History Photograph X-27622 shows that the Chutes was torn down by the time the greyhound track was built in 1927, and a ticket stub for a jewelry drawing in 1941 in the possession of the author shows that the Chutes ride pool was filled in and referred to as the Sunken Gardens by 1941.

14. ACE Landmark Sign for the Cyclone Roller Coaster at Lakeside Amusement Park; "Lakeside Park Celebrates 100 Years," *NAPHA News* 30 (2008): 9; Irene Clurman, "Classic Coaster Ride Still Tops in Thrills," *RMN* (July 14, 1974): 3 (quotations).

15. 100th Anniversary Tour of Lakeside Amusement Park, July 18, 2008; "Lakeside up 14% in Denver," *Billboard* 52 (July 27, 1940): 48, 50; "Colorado Coastin'"; "Lakeside Park Celebrates 100 Years," *NAPHA News* 30 (2008): 9; Bill Gallo, "Life Is a Carousel and a Rollercoaster," *Denver Magazine* 16 (July 1986): 27.

16. "Healthy Denver Lakeside Period Riding to Promotional Climax," *Billboard* 52 (September 7, 1940): 35; "Krasner Foresees Good Denver Period," *Billboard* 52 (November 30, 1940): 41; "Lakeside's Take up 12% over '40," *Billboard* 53 (July 19, 1941): 50; "Many Improvements at Lakeside, Denver," *Billboard* 54 (May 16, 1942): 52.

17. "Negroes Barred," *Colorado Statesman* (August 23, 1940): 1; Leonard and Noel, *Denver*, 190–92; 100th Anniversary Tour of Lakeside Amusement Park, July 18, 2008; "Lakeside Park Celebrates 100 Years," *NAPHA News* 30 (2008): 7.

18. Wayne Arner, interview by the author, Denver, CO, December 29, 2011; Bob Campbell, interview 1 by the author, Denver, CO, December 29, 2011; Bill Hill, *Decades of Daring: Midget Racing in the Rocky Mountains* (North Little Rock, AK: Bill Hill Productions, 2001), 42.

19. Gurtler, Oral History; Nasaw, *Going Out*, 253–54. Elitch's theater was desegregated in 1947, thanks in part to Denver librarian Pauline Robinson. She is mistakenly credited by some sources with desegregating Lakeside, but as detailed in Steve Jackson's article "By the Book," for the September 6–12, 1995, issue of *Westword*, it was actually Elitch's. Victoria W. Wolcott, in *Race, Riots, and Roller Coasters: The Struggle over Segregated Recreation in America* (Philadelphia: University of Pennsylvania Press, 2012), cites a 1952 letter from the Urban League of Denver noting that both Lakeside and Elitch's were integrated at that point with the exception of Lakeside's Swimming Pool (p. 262n76). In 1955, eight black customers unsuccessfully sued Lakeside over the segregated Swimming Pool; *Opal Doris Jernigan et al. v. Lakeside Park Company et al.*, Civil Action 9939, Case Number 18080, Colorado Supreme Court, filed August 17, 1955, Colorado State Archives, Denver.

20. Hull, *Denver's Elitch Gardens*, 77–79, 81. Betty Hull discussed the Glenn Miller situation in an e-mail to the author, June 7, 2010.

21. "Lakeside Park Celebrates 100 Years," *NAPHA News* 30 (2008): 9; "Phil Harris Band at Lakeside Monday Eve," *DP* (July 19, 1937): 8; "Phil Harris Band at Lakeside Friday Eve," *DP* (July 20, 1939): 20; Hull, *Denver's Elitch Gardens*, 86; Gallo, "Life Is a Carousel and a Rollercoaster," 27.

22. Julian Bamberger, "Problem of Present Day: Public to Stay Amusement Conscious?" *Billboard* 53 (January 11, 1941): 41, 55.

23. "Krasner Married in Denver," *Billboard* 53 (February 22, 1941): 46; "Lakeside Park Celebrates 100 Years," *NAPHA News* 30 (2008): 10; Ashby, *With Amusement for All*, 270.

24. "Lakeside Park Celebrates 100 Years," *NAPHA News* 30 (2008): 10; Lakeside Amusement Park ad for experienced superintendent, *Billboard* (April 4, 1942): 90, Lakeside Amusement Park Clipping File 2, WHGD; "Many Improvements at Lakeside, Denver," *Billboard* 54 (May 16, 1942): 52.

25. Leonard and Noel, *Denver*, 220–25.

26. Hull, *Denver's Elitch Gardens*, 90; "2 Denver Spots Foresee Big Biz; Plug Name Orks," *Billboard* 55 (May 22, 1943): 44; "Krasner Lights Tower in Snow; Spot Glistens," *Billboard* 58 (June 1, 1946): 75.

27. "Duke Ellington El Patio Denver 1942." The podcast includes the "For Fun in '42" tagline. See also "Lakeside Park Celebrates 100 Years," *NAPHA News* 30 (2008): 10; "Girl Is Killed on Coaster at Lakeside Park," *DP* (June 26, 1944): 1, 5; "Girl, 18, Killed, 7 Hurt When Roller-Coaster Crashes at Lakeside," *RMN* (June 26, 1944): 5.

28. Hull, *Denver's Elitch Gardens*, 90–91.

29. "Pastor's Band Will Open at Lakeside Friday Night," *DP* (August 2, 1945): 19; "Pastor Polishes off First Week," *DP* (August 9, 1945): 15; "Denver's Lakeside Has Lush Fourth," *Billboard* 57 (July 21, 1945): 48.

30. Hill, *Decades of Daring*, 67; "Krasner Lights Tower in Snow; Spot Glistens," *Billboard* 58 (June 1, 1946): 75; Leonard and Noel, *Denver*, 234–35, 243–46, 481, first quotation on p. 235, second quotation on p. 246.

31. Leonard and Noel, *Denver*, 247.

32. "Philip Friederich," *RMN* (January 11, 1947): 8; "William Buck," *RMN* (July 11, 1949): 36; "Krasner Lights Tower in Snow; Spot Glistens," *Billboard* 58 (June 1, 1946): 75.

33. "Krasner Lights Tower in Snow; Spot Glistens," *Billboard* 58 (June 1, 1946): 75; "New Boating Thrill Imported from England," *DP* (July 11, 1948): 23.

34. "Krasner Lights Tower in Snow; Spot Glistens," *Billboard* 58 (June 1, 1946): 75; "Day-Glo Signs and Brochure Help Flack Elitch Gardens," *Billboard* 61 (June 18, 1949): 63.

35. Nasaw, *Going Out*, 40, 252–55, first two quotations on p. 40, final quotation on p. 254.

Chapter 6: Lakeside Speedway and the Roaring Bugs of Speed

1. Wayne Arner, telephone interview by the author, Denver, CO, December 19, 2011.

2. Jack C. Fox, *The Mighty Midgets: The Illustrated History of Midget Auto Racing* (Speedway, IN: Carl Hungness, 1978), 7–9, 14–15, 17, 21–23, 31, 38, 42.

3. Louisa Ward Arps, *Denver in Slices: A Historical Guide to the City* (Athens, OH: Swallow, 1998), 182–89.

4. Ibid.; Allan E. Brown, *The History of the American Speedway: Past and Present* (Marne, MI: Slideways, 1985), 99–102.

5. Hill, *Decades of Daring*, 1–3; "Midget Autos Race at Park," *RMN* (June 20, 1935): 4B.

6. Hill, *Decades of Daring*, 1–3; Chester "Red" Nelson, "Midget Auto Races Thrill at Lakeside," *RMN* (June 22, 1935): 4B (first three quotations); "Tiny Speedsters," *RMN* (July 12, 1935): 21.

7. "Midget Auto Races Return to Lakeside Park Thursday Night," *RMN* (July 18, 1935): 16; "Cunningham Victor as Driver Crashes," *RMN* (July 19, 1935): 22; advertisement for Lakeside Speedway, *DP* (August 16, 1938): 20; Rebecca Cantwell, "Safety at Auto Track Questioned after Death," *RMN* (July 26, 1988): 7; Scott Stocker, "Races to Resume in Wake of Death," *RMN* (July 26, 1988): 50; Hill, *Decades of Daring*, 1–3. The following articles appeared covering baseball and softball games at Lakeside during the same period in July in which the midget races were running (all are from the *RMN*): "Lakeside Results" (July 17, 1935): 13; "Lakeside Softball" (July 20, 1935): 12; "Lakeside Batting Averages" (July 21, 1935): Sports 2; "Schnabal Bats Wards to

Lakeside Victory" (July 21, 1935): Sports 4; "City Park All-Stars to Face Lakeside's Best Sunday Night" (July 26, 1935): 20; "Lakeside Games" (July 28, 1935): Sports 3; "Lakeside Schedule" (July 29, 1935): 13.

8. Hill, *Decades of Daring*, 5; Jerry Brown, interview by the author, Denver, CO, December 29, 2011; Sonny Coleman, interview 2 by the author, Denver, CO, January 20, 2012.

9. Bill Peratt, "Lakeside Speedway—Denver, Colorado," at http://autoracing-memories.com/forums/showthread.php?t=15, accessed January 23, 2012; Photograph 81A, Lakeside Amusement Park, Box 1, Otto Roach Photograph Collection, WHGD. Popular history holds that the Speedway was built on the site of the old baseball field at Lakeside, but this photograph shows that the baseball field was directly behind the row of houses that still stands on Sheridan Boulevard on the east side of the park property while the Speedway is to the west of it. Also, as the article "Denver Lakeside to Step out with Outlay of $95,000" (*Billboard* 52 [April 20, 1940]: 38) makes clear, the baseball field was not paved over for a parking lot until 1940, two years after the Speedway opened. The photograph of the Bundes Turnfest stadium from "City Entertains Thousands during Bundes Turnfest" (*DMF* [June 28, 1913]: 3) shows that the Speedway occupied the land from the stadium.

10. Bob Olds, interview by the author, Denver, CO, December 29, 2011; Coleman, interview 2; Leroy Byers, interview by the author, Denver, CO, December 29, 2011; Charles Gottschalck, interview by the author, Denver, CO, December 29, 2011; Gene Pastor, interview by the author, Denver, CO, December 29, 2011; Arner, interview; Irv Moss, "The Lure and Lore of Lakeside Track," *DP* (June 27, 2011): 1B, 6B.

11. Hill, *Decades of Daring*, 23, 30–34; advertisement for Lakeside Speedway, *DP* (August 16, 1938): 20

12. Hill, *Decades of Daring*, 43–44.

13. Hill, *Decades of Daring*, 34, 43, 55; Campbell, interview 1; Arner, interview; Byers, interview; Pastor, interview.

14. Arner, phone interview; Arner, interview; Byers, interview; Sonny Coleman, interview 1 by the author, Denver, CO, December 29, 2011; Hill, *Decades of Daring*, 72–73. The James cars and their consecutive numbering by ten were especially famous in the midget racing world, and their appearance at the track, including their numbers, was a very notable event for the racing community.

15. Pastor, interview; Arner, interview; Byers, interview; Coleman, interview 1.

16. Olds, interview; Byers, interview; Coleman, interview 2; Arner, interview.

17. Hill, *Decades of Daring*, 62–63.

18. Ibid.; Moss, "Lure and Lore of Lakeside Track."

19. Hill, *Decades of Daring*, 67, 77.

20. Ibid., 78; Arner, interview; Coleman, interview 2.

21. Rhoda Krasner and driver Marv Slusser, both quoted in Moss, "Lure and Lore of Lakeside Track," 6B.

22. Ibid.; Coleman, interview 2; Hill, *Decades of Daring*, 49–50, 55, 59–61; Jerry Miller, interview by the author, Denver, CO, July 19, 2012.

23. Vera Hawks, Scrapbook, Leon and Vera Hawks Papers, WHGD (this scrapbook is filled with stories of drivers killed on the track); Coleman, interview 2; Cantwell, "Safety at Auto Track Questioned after Death"; Hector Gutierrez, "Lakeside Speedway Ends Racing," *RMN* (September 2, 1988): 49.

24. Hill, *Decades of Daring*, 67; Moss, "Lure and Lore of Lakeside Track"; "Lakeside, Denver, Installs Wrestling as Arena Feature," *Billboard* 54 (July 11, 1942): 40.

25. Mark S. Foster, *A Nation on Wheels: The Automobile Culture in America since 1945* (Belmont, CA: Thomson, Wadsworth, 2003), 9–11, 21–25, 29, 31, 36–37, 42.

26. Ibid., 67–68, 73–74; Byers, interview; Olds, interview; Gottschalck, interview; Coleman, interview 2; Irv Moss, "Denver: A Baseball Town," *DP* (October 14, 2007), at http://www.denverpost.com/rockies/ci_7166267, accessed March 12, 2012; Mark S. Foster, *The Denver Bears: From Sandlots to Sellouts* (Boulder: Pruett, 1983), 56. According to Foster (51), during the Bears' 1941 season, after the season opener attendance rarely exceeded 1,000 people.

27. Coleman, interview 1; Coleman, interview 2.

28. Hill, *Decades of Daring*, 65, 101, 103, 121, 127–28; Miller, interview.

29. Hill, *Decades of Daring*, 133; Olds, interview; Gottschalck, interview; Coleman, interview 2; Foster, *Denver Bears*, 57–58.

30. Hill, *Decades of Daring*, 133–35; Brown, *History of the American Speedway*, 50; Olds, interview; Gottschalck, interview; Coleman, interview 2; Frank Jamison, interview by the author, Lakewood, CO, April 2, 2012.

31. Hill, *Decades of Daring*, 133, 147; "Lakeside Gate Nudges 1949 Score but Ride, Races, Dance Spending Falls Short of Mark," *Billboard* 62 (September 2, 1950): 66.

32. Hill, *Decades of Daring*, 147, 150, 159; Brown, *History of the American Speedway*, 50; Moss, "Lure and Lore of Lakeside Track"; Arner, interview; Byers, interview; Coleman, interview 1.

Chapter 7: The Wild Chipmunk versus the Mouse

1. "Lakeside Gate Nudges 1949 Score but Ride, Races, Dance Spending Falls Short of Mark," *Billboard* 62 (September 2, 1950): 66, 68; Nasaw, *Going Out*, 252–55.

2. "Lakeside Owner, Wife Kidnapped; $5566 Stolen," *RMN* (August 20, 1951): 1, 5; "Krasners Lose 5½ G in Holdup," *Billboard* 63 (September 1, 1951): 48; "Lakeside Bandits Flee with $36,484," *RMN* (September 9, 1964): 5.

3. "Krasners Lose 5½ G in Holdup," *Billboard* 63 (September 1, 1951): 48; Pat Wilcox, "Memories of Lakeside: Amusement Mecca for Millions," *Arvada (CO) Citizen Sentinel* (August 16, 1973): 5.

4. "Lowry Airman Falls to Death from Speeding Roller Coaster," *DP* (June 19, 1954): 1, 3 (quotation); "Lowry Airman, 19, Killed on Roller Coaster," *DP* (June 16, 1962): 1.

5. "Lakeside Park Upheld in Thrill Ride Injury," *DP* (April 4, 1960): 3.

6. Krasner interview cited in Robin Chotzinoff, "For Your Amusement," *Westword* (Denver) (June 22, 2000), at http://www.westword.com/content/printVersion/214580/, accessed January 5, 2012; "Trains Roll at Lakeside," *DP* (August 3, 1950): 25; "Denver Op Bows Miniature Diesel," *Billboard* 62 (August 12, 1950): 63; "Lakeside Gate Nudges 1949 Score but Ride, Races, Dance Spending Falls Short of Mark," *Billboard* 62 (September 2, 1950): 66, 68; New 'Prospector' Gets Test Run," *DP* (May 7, 1953): 39; Gallo, "Life Is a Carousel and a Rollercoaster," 27.

7. "Lakeside Gate Nudges 1949 Score but Ride, Races, Dance Spending Falls Short of Mark," *Billboard* 62 (September 2, 1950): 66, 68.

8. Advertisement for Lakeside's Kiddies Playland in the *RMN* (May 13, 1951): 3A; "New Attractions at Lakeside," *DP* (May 26, 1960): 40; "Origin of Lakeside's Famous Carousel Is Lost," *DP Roundup* (August 5, 1962): 9; Hull, *Denver's Elitch Gardens*, 92–94. According to an interview with Rhoda Krasner by the author on September 7, 2014, the Kiddies Playland rides also included a Turtle, Star Fighter, Horse and Buggy ride, and a Fire Truck. The Flying Tigers was the first of the kid rides and was located near the pony track in 1950.

9. "Denver Meeting Plans Carry Western Brand," *Billboard* 64 (June 28, 1952): 74; "NAAPPB's Denver Session Pulls Strong Turnout," *Billboard* 64 (August 16, 1952): 68.

10. James J. Farrell, *One Nation under Goods: Malls and the Seductions of American Shopping* (Washington, DC: Smithsonian Books, 2010), 4–6.

11. Bill Miller, "$12 Million Shopping Center Planned Here," *RMN* (September 12, 1954): 5, 12; Leonard and Noel, *Denver*, 308–9.

12. Miller, "$12 Million Shopping Center Planned Here," 5, 12; "3-Day Fete to Mark Opening of Lakeside Mall," *RMN* (April 29, 1956): 26; "Lakeside Center to Include Seven-Story Medical Building," *DP* (March 6, 1955): 22A. The shopping center also included a seven-story office building, which still stood on the site as of 2016.

13. Miller, "$12 Million Shopping Center Planned Here," 5, 12; "3-Day Fete to Mark Opening of Lakeside Mall," *RMN* (April 29, 1956): 26; "Statistics Show Immensity of New Lakeside Mall," *RMN* (August 12, 1956): 19, "New Center Called Boon to Economy of Lakewood Area," *RMN* (August 9, 1956): 25.

14. "Gala Opening Planned at Lakeside Center," *RMN* (August 23, 1956); 14; "25,000 Jam Lakeside Stores as Giant Shopping Mart Opens," *DP* (August 30, 1956): 2; "50,000 Flock to Opening of Lakeside Mall," *RMN* (August 31, 1956): 5 (last quotation).

15. "Lakeside Center Borrows $4.7 Million," *RMN* (December 28, 1956): 25; "Lakeside Center Boasts 41 Merchants," "Center's Stores Entirely under One Roof" (first quotation), "Lakeside Offers Variety of Goods, Many Services," and "Colorado Welcomes First White Store," all in *DP Roundup* (August 25, 1957): 16L–18L; "Lakeside Ward Store 1st in a Center," *DP* (August 12, 1958): 25 (second quotation); "Wards New Lakeside Store Opens," *DP* (August 13, 1958): 3; "Lakeside Bank Opens," *RMN* (June 16, 1959): 58; "Lakeside's Fifth Birthday Celebration Is Now in Progress . . . with Low Prices . . . Big Prizes," *RMN* (August 24, 1961): 49; "Lakeside a Shopper's Dream," *RMN* (February 28, 1962): 36; "Shopping Center Sold for $8 Million," *DP* (August 22, 1962): 1.

16. "Krasner Spot Extends Run, Garners Biz," *Billboard* (September 22, 1956), Lakeside Amusement Park Clipping File 1, WHGD.

17. Ibid.; "Denver Spots Score; Movie Crew at Elitch," *Billboard* 65 (August 1, 1953): 62; "Bands, Filmers Pull Denverites to 2 Funspots," *Billboard* 65 (August 8, 1953): 60 (quotation); "Denver Spot Quits Names; Tries House Band, Talent," *Billboard* 66 (June 12, 1954): 60; "2 Denver Parks Start Season, Use Big Bands," *Billboard* 67 (May 21, 1955): 76; "Lakeside Pushes Bargain Rates for Denverites," *Billboard* 66 (July 10, 1954): 57.

18. "Supermarkets Outings Jam Denver's Lakeside Funspot," *Billboard* 67 (September 10, 1955): 61; Frank and Joyce Jamison, interview by the author, Lakewood, CO, April 2, 2012.

19. "Stocks Pull Well for Denver Park; Rotor Top Ride," *Billboard* 67 (July 2, 1955): 57; "Bands, Racing Attract Crowds at Denver Spot," *Billboard* 67 (August 6, 1955): 77; "Denver Funspot Clicks with Auto Thriller," *Billboard* 67 (August 27, 1955): 69; Richard L. Crowther, Architectural Drawings for the Wild Chipmunk, FFC 16, Richard L. Crowther Manuscript Collection, WHGD; *DP* quoted in Wilcox, "Memories of Lakeside," 5.

20. Adams, *American Amusement Park Industry*, 93.

21. Ibid., 93–101, 107; Wilcox, "Memories of Lakeside," 5.

22. Adams, *American Amusement Park Industry*, 96, 107–9; Hull, *Denver's Elitch Gardens*, 96.

23. "Magic Mountain Offering Circular," 1958, WHGD; Richard J. Gardner, "Magic Mountain: The Lost Heritage of Heritage Square," at http://goldenlandmarks.com/museum/magicmountain/, accessed April 2, 2011.

24. Gardner, "Magic Mountain" (first quotation); Adams, *American Amusement Park Industry*, 105.

25. David Forsyth, "Spares and Splashes: Walt Disney's Celebrity Sports Center," *Colorado Heritage* (Autumn 2007): 32–47.

26. Ibid.

27. Ashby, *With Amusement for All*, 291–92; Watts quoted in Ashby, *With Amusement for All*, 291; "New Attractions at Lakeside," *DP* (May 26, 1960): 40; "Lakeside Ballroom Has Colorful History," *RMN* (May 4, 1974): 65.

28. "Lakeside Ballroom Has Colorful History," *RMN* (May 4, 1974): 65. The first page of this article is missing from the microfilm copy of the newspaper. It is difficult to read but is apparently page 25 or 26, but in either case it is missing. Given the subject matter of the second page, however, it is easy to infer that the article is related to a May 1974 inspection of the park and the demolition of the ballroom at that time. Untitled article, *Billboard* (February 10, 1958), Lakeside Amusement Park Clipping File 1, WHGD; "2 New Rides Spark Lakeside Business," *Billboard* 70 (June 2, 1958): 61; "Lakeside Park to Open Friday," *RMN* (May 8, 1958): 71; "Holter Animals Mark Denver's Lakeside Bow," *Billboard* 68 (June 9, 1956): 54.

29. "Bull Fighter Injured in Lakeside Exhibition," *RMN* (July 16, 1955): 17; "Bands, Racing Attract Crowds at Denver Spot," *Billboard* 67 (August 6, 1955): 77; "Holter Animals Mark Denver's Lakeside Bow," *Billboard* 68 (June 9, 1956): 54; "Lakeside Builds Good Crowds at Midget, Stock Car Races," *Billboard* 68 (June 16, 1956): 54; "Ballrooms Build Denver Business," *Billboard* 68 (August 4, 1956): 86; "2 New Rides Spark Lakeside Business," *Billboard* 70 (June 2, 1958): 61.

30. "Lakeside Park to Open Friday," *RMN* (May 8, 1958): 71; "2 New Rides Spark Lakeside Business," *Billboard* 70 (June 2, 1958): 61. Tickets from many of the companies that held their annual picnics at Lakeside are in the Lakeside Amusement Park Papers, Stephen H. Hart Library, History Colorado, Denver.

31. "Accident at Lakeside Injures Four Persons," *RMN* (September 14, 1959): 29; "Lakeside Amusement Park Ride Crash Sunday Injures 4 Patrons, 2 Hospitalized," *DP* (September 14, 1959): 17.

32. Notice from *Amusement Business* that Lakeside was selling the Lindy Loop ride in Lakeside Amusement Park Clipping File 2, WHGD; "Himalaya's Debut at Lakeside Park Scheduled Again This Weekend," *DP Roundup* (June 21, 1964): 9. Drawings for the proposed ballroom and Staride ticket booths, along with two versions of the new Satellite sign, are in FFC 16, Richard L. Crowther Manuscript Collection, WHGD;

33. "Himalaya's Debut at Lakeside Park Scheduled Again This Weekend," *DP Roundup* (June 21, 1964): 9; "Lakeside Bandits Flee with $36,484," *RMN* (September 9, 1964): 5; "$36,484 Taken from Lakeside," *DP* (September 9, 1964): 3; "Lakeside Starts Out with Record Crowd," *DP Roundup* (May 16, 1965): 7; "Lakeside Has Capacity for 10,000 Riders an Hour," *DP Roundup* (June 6, 1965): 34; Devil's Joy Ride ad, copy from unknown magazine, in author's possession.

34. "Origin of Lakeside's Famous Carousel Is Lost," *DP Roundup* (August 5, 1962): 9; "90 Years of Know-How," *DP Empire Magazine* (July 29, 1962): 26–27.

Chapter 8: The Stockers Take over at Lakeside Speedway

1. Tom Wolfe, *The Kandy-Kolored Tangerine-Flake Streamline Baby* (New York: Farrar, Straus, and Giroux, 1965), xv–xvi, 78.
2. Brown, *History of the American Speedway*, 60–61; Leon Mandel, *American Cars* (New York: Stewart, Tabori and Chang, 1982), 297–99.
3. Brown, *History of the American Speedway*, 59–60.
4. Johnny Cribbs, "It Started atop Table Mountain," *Speed Age* (July 1948), at https://modcoupes.com/Stories.html, accessed September 21, 2015. The website www.modcoupes.com is the official website of the Colorado Automobile Racing Club (CARC).
5. Cribbs, "It Started atop Table Mountain."
6. Ibid.; Hill, *Decades of Daring*, 133–35.
7. Hill, *Decades of Daring*, 147, 150–51, 159–62, 195.
8. Marv Slusser, interview by the author, Denver, CO, February 16, 2012.
9. Ibid.; Bob Land, interview by the author, Denver, CO, December 29, 2011; Coleman, interview 2; Sheri Thurman Graham, interview by the author, Arvada, CO, April 7, 2012.
10. Coleman, interview 2.
11. Gottschalck, interview; Coleman, interview 2; Slusser, interview; Land, interview; Campbell, interview 1; Graham, interview; Blu Plemons, interview by the author, Denver, CO, February 16, 2012; Bob Campbell, interview 2 by the author, Denver, CO, February 16, 2012.
12. Coleman, interview 2; Cambell, interview 1.
13. "Ben Krasner's Lakeside Speedway," at http://www.bigwestracing.com/forums/showthread.php?t=20322, accessed April 9, 2012; "Pegi Plue Induction Speech," at http://www.modcoupes.com/carc/other/carc-history/stories?start=5 (page no longer available), accessed April 9, 2012; Graham, interview; Coleman, interview 1; Slusser, interview; Miller, interview; Arner, interview; Campbell, interview 1.
14. Lois Barr, "Powder Puff Gals Take Auto Races in Stride," *DP* (June 17, 1968): 21; Coleman, interview 2; "Audrey Bolyard," at http://autoracingmemories.com/forums/showthread.php?t=470, accessed April 9, 2012; Graham, interview.
15. Graham, interview; "The Memories Flood!!" by Nostalgic Mike, at http://www.bigwestracing.com/forums/showthread.php?t=12499&page=4, accessed April 9, 2012.
16. Barr, "Powder Puff Gals Take Auto Races in Stride"; Graham, interview.
17. Graham, interview.
18. Ibid.; Barr, "Powder Puff Gals Take Auto Races in Stride."

19. Barr, "Powder Puff Gals Take Auto Races in Stride"; Graham, interview.

20. Graham, interview; Gottschalck, interview; Coleman, interview 2; Slusser, interview; Land, interview; Campbell, interview 2; Miller, interview.

21. "Denver Spots Score; Movie Crew at Elitch," *Billboard* 65 (August 1, 1953): 62; "Denver Spot Quits Names; Tries House Band, Talent," *Billboard* 66 (June 12, 1954): 60; "'Johnny Dark,' a Racing Story, Is at Palace," *New York Times* (June 26, 1954), at http://movies.nytimes.com/movie/review?res=9C02E2DD103EE53BBC4E51DFB066838F649EDE, accessed April 9, 2012; Geoffrey Hacker, "Collectibles from the Movie 'Johnny Dark'—Lobby Cards," at http://www.forgottenfiberglass.com/?p=9071, accessed April 9, 2012.

22. "Bands, Racing Attract Crowds at Denver Spot," *Billboard* 67 (August 6, 1955): 77; "Denver Funspot Clicks with Auto Thriller," *Billboard* 67 (August 27, 1955): 69; "Sport: Joie Chitwood's Indianapolis Thrill Show," at http://canadiannews1.com/archive/StuntDriver1/stuntdriver1.com/history/Joie-Chitwoods-Indianapolis-Thrill-Show.html, accessed April 9, 2012; "'Little 500' Races Draw at Lakeside," *Billboard* 69 (June 18, 1957): 82; "2 New Rides Spark Lakeside Business," *Billboard* 70 (June 2, 1958): 61.

23. "2 Denver Parks Start Season, Use Big Bands," *Billboard* 67 (May 21, 1955): 76; "Stocks Pull Well for Denver Park; Rotor Top Ride," *Billboard* 67 (July 2, 1955): 57; "Ben Krasner's Lakeside Speedway."

24. "Stocks Pull Well for Denver Park; Rotor Top Ride," *Billboard* 67 (July 2, 1955): 57; "Bands, Racing Attract Crowds at Denver Spot," *Billboard* 67 (August 6, 1955): 77; "Lakeside Builds Good Crowds at Midget, Stock Car Races," *Billboard* 68 (June 16, 1956): 54; "Re: Lakeside, the Shrine," at http://www.bigwestracing.com/forums/showthread.php?t=12499&page=4, accessed April 9, 2012; "2 Denver Parks Stay Open for Mid-September Profits," *Billboard* (October 7, 1957), Lakeside Amusement Park Clipping File 1, WHGD.

25. "Lakeside Compacts/Late Models," at http://autoracingmemories.com/forums/showthread.php?t=809, accessed April 9, 2012; "Gentlemen, Start Your Stock Cars," *DP* (April 25, 1975): 71; Slusser, interview; "Ken Tandolini—the Two Minute Interview," at http://autoracingmemories.com/forums/showthread.php?t=157, accessed April 14, 2012.

26. Regina Quackenbush, e-mail to David Forsyth, March 7, 2012. In this e-mail she discusses a conversation she had with Rhoda Krasner when she worked at the park in which Krasner explained how she used the demolition derby to keep people in their seats until the end of the races.

27. Slusser, interview; Plemons, interview; Graham, interview.

28. Irv Moss, "The Lure and Lore of Lakeside Track," *DP* (June 28, 2011): 6B; Scott Stocker, "Anniversary Races Tonight at Lakeside," *RMN* (July 27, 1988): 78;

Scott Stocker, "Oregon Racer Wins Lakeside Feature," *RMN* (July 28, 1988): 81; Rebecca Cantwell, "Safety at Auto Track Questioned after Death," *RMN* (July 26, 1988): 7; Scott Stocker, "Races to Resume in Wake of Death," *RMN* (July 26, 1988): 50; "Midget Pioneer Recalls His Lakeside Inaugural," *RMN* (July 28, 1988): 81.

29. Cantwell, "Safety at Auto Track Questioned after Death"; Stocker, "Races to Resume in Wake of Death."

30. Graham, interview.

31. Cantwell, "Safety at Auto Track Questioned after Death"; Stocker, "Races to Resume in Wake of Death"; Slusser, interview; Land, interview; Graham, interview; 100th Anniversary Tour of Lakeside Amusement Park, July 18, 2008.

32. Stocker, "Anniversary Races Tonight at Lakeside"; Scott Stocker, "Oregon Racer Wins Lakeside Feature," *RMN* (July 28, 1988): 81B; Graham, interview.

33. Slusser, interview; Hector Gutierrez, "Lakeside Speedway Ends Racing," *RMN* (September 2, 1988): 49.

34. Search results for "Lakeside Speedway" at coloradomotorsportshalloffame.com. This lists inductees dating back to 1979 who raced at Lakeside Speedway and have since been inducted into the Colorado Motorsports Hall of Fame. "Jim Malloy—Lakeside to Indy," at http://www.bigwestracing.com/forums/showthread.php?t=16914, accessed April 9, 2012.

35. "Ben and Rhoda Krasner" biographies listed under the 2006 Colorado Motorsports Hall of Fame inductees at http://coloradomotorsportshalloffame.com/2015/03/colorado-motorsports-hall-of-fame-inductees-2006/, accessed April 9, 2012; Justin Zoch, "Ben Krasner," National Sprint Car Hall of Fame Induction Biography, at http://www.sprintcarhof.com/Pages/Inductees under the 2010 list of inductees, accessed March 15, 2012; Gordon Eliot White, *Lost Race Tracks: Treasures of Automobile Racing* (Hudson, WI: Iconografix, 2002), 126. Details of the fan's experiences can be found at "Re: Lakeside, the Shrine."

Chapter 9: Lakeside Amusement Park, Public Nuisance?

1. Adams, *American Amusement Park Industry*, 164–66; Gallo, "Life Is a Carousel and a Rollercoaster," 28.

2. Leonard and Noel, *Denver*, 448–50.

3. Pat Wilcox, "Memories of Lakeside: Amusement Mecca for Millions," *Arvada (CO) Citizen Sentinel* (August 16, 1973): 5; Robin Chotzinoff, "For Your Amusement," *Westword* (Denver) (June 22, 2000), at http://www.westword.com/content/printVersion/214580/, accessed January 5, 2012.

4. "Lakeside Park Manager Dies," *DP* (August 9, 1965): 2F; "Lakeside Park General Manager Dies," *RMN* (August 9, 1965): 89; Wilcox, "Memories of Lakeside," 5.

5. Janet Forgrieve, "A Century of Thrills," *RMN* (July 16, 2008): Business section, 1; Wilcox, "Memories of Lakeside," 5 (first quotation); Claire Martin, "Nostalgia Rides on at Lakeside," *DP* (July 2, 2011): 1D, 8D; Chotzinoff, "For Your Amusement"; Gallo, "Life Is a Carousel and a Rollercoaster," 26, 28.

6. Leuthner, "Lake Side"; Andrea Jacobs, "Lakeside Marks 100th Anniversary," *Intermountain Jewish News* (July 3, 2008), at http://ijn.com/features/ijn-features/210-lakeside-marks-anniversary, accessed September 23, 2015; "Lakeside Park Celebrates 100 Years," *NAPHA News* 30 (2008): 11; Wilcox, "Memories of Lakeside," 5.

7. Colorado Department of Transportation, "The History of I-70 in Colorado," http://www.coloradodot.info/about/50th-anniversary/interstate-70, accessed February 8, 2012; Colorado Department of Transportation, "Construction Timeline," at http://www.coloradodot.info/about/50th-anniversary/interstate-70/construction-timeline.html, accessed February 8, 2012. A security guard was also murdered at Lakeside in October 1966, as detailed in the stories "3 Plead Guilty in Murder" and "Brotherly Love Sends Man to Jail," both from *DP* (January 10, 1967): 2.

8. The account of Count Basie's Band appearing at Lakeside is from an issue of *Amusement Business* and is in Lakeside Amusement Park Clipping File 2, WHGD; Gallo, "Life Is a Carousel and a Rollercoaster," 27; "Huge Display at Lakeside," *RMN* (July 3, 1971): 101; Hull, *Denver's Elitch Gardens*, 108–9.

9. "2 Safety Units Investigate Lakeside Park Conditions," *DP* (May 24, 1972): 32; John Toohey, "Operator 'Mystified' by Park-Closure Effort," *DP* (June 27, 1973): 3.

10. "4 Hurt in Rollercoaster Crash at Lakeside Park," *RMN* (May 15, 1972): 8; "Coaster-Accident Cause Eludes Probe," *DP* (May 17, 1972): 34.

11. "2 Safety Units Investigate Lakeside Park Conditions," *DP* (May 24, 1972): 32.

12. John Toohey, "Jeffco DA Will Seek Injunction to Close Lakeside Park," *DP* (June 26, 1973): 3; "Body of Fireman Killed Fighting Blaze Is Recovered," *RMN* (October 22, 1972): 5.

13. "Town of Lakeside Sued for $131,800 in Bar Fire," *RMN* (March 23, 1973): 40.

14. Wilcox, "Memories of Lakeside," 5; Toohey, "Jeffco DA Will Seek Injunction to Close Lakeside Park"; John F. McLaughlin, "Jeffco Sets Plans to Close Lakeside Amusement Park," *RMN* (June 27, 1973): 3; Toohey, "Operator 'Mystified' by Park-Closure Effort"; "The Local News," *CT* (May 28, 1908): 8; "Prosecution Assumes Air of Persecution," *CT* (August 5, 1909): 1. According to the Jefferson County Court, the grand jury report is still considered a confidential document and is therefore not available for public inspection without filing a Freedom of Information lawsuit. However, the Denver newspapers gave fairly good descriptions of the overall findings without going into specific details that might be available in the report itself.

15. Toohey, "Jeffco DA Will Seek Injunction to Close Lakeside Park"; Toohey, "Operator 'Mystified' by Park-Closure Effort"; Rhoda Krasner, interview by the author, Lakeside, CO, July 31, 2014.

16. "Lakeside Park Complying with Safety Requirements," *DP* (July 25, 1973): 55; John Toohey, "Pact Keeps Lakeside Open," *DP* (July 31, 1973): 21; "Lakeside Safety Case Settled in Golden Court," *RMN* (July 31, 1973): 8.

17. Wilcox, "Memories of Lakeside," 5; "Miss Colorado Plies Waves at Lakeside," *DP Roundup* (August 19, 1973): 11; Jack Olsen Jr., "Proud 'Lady' Stuck in Water and Nobody Wants Her," *RMN* (June 11, 1976): 8.

18. "Fire Destroys Shops at Amusement Park," *DP* (December 11, 1973): 3; Christopher Smith, "Lakeside Damaged in Spectacular Fire," *RMN* (December 12, 1973): 5, 36.

19. "Lakeside Safety Case Settled in Golden Court," *RMN* (July 31, 1973): 8; 100th Anniversary Tour of Lakeside Amusement Park, July 18, 2008.

20. "Fire Destroys Shops at Amusement Park," *DP* (December 11, 1973): 3; Smith, "Lakeside Damaged in Spectacular Fire"; 100th Anniversary Tour of Lakeside Amusement Park, July 18, 2008.

21. "Fire Destroys Shops at Amusement Park," *DP* (December 11, 1973): 3; Smith, "Lakeside Damaged in Spectacular Fire"; Chris Whitbeck, "Inspection Approves Reopening of Lakeside Park," *DP* (May 10, 1974): 31.

22. Whitbeck, "Inspection Approves Reopening of Lakeside Park."

23. Ibid.; Claire Martin, "Nostalgia Rides on at Lakeside," *DP* (July 2, 2011): 1D, 8D; 100th Anniversary Tour of Lakeside Amusement Park, July 18, 2008.

24. Whitbeck, "Inspection Approves Reopening of Lakeside Park."

25. Irene Clurman, "Classic Coaster Ride Still Tops in Thrills," *RMN* (July 14, 1974): "Now" 3.

26. Barry Morrison, "Fun House Gives Laughs Again," *DP* (June 3, 1975): 12.

27. "Lakeside Opens Season," *RMN* (May 7, 1975): 80; Edward Osborn, "Off with Old, on with New at Elitch, Lakeside," *RMN* (April 22, 1981): 58 (last quotation).

28. Rykken Johnson, "They're Always Busy at Lakeside," *DP Contemporary Magazine* (May 6, 1979): 42–44; Andrew Schlesinger, "'Coaster Freaks' Find Denver Parks Rich in Thrills," *RMN* (July 18, 1977): 8; Osborn, "Off with Old, on with New at Elitch, Lakeside."

29. Johnson, "They're Always Busy at Lakeside."

30. Osborn, "Off with Old, on with New at Elitch, Lakeside"; "Fun Parks to Open Friday," *RMN* (May 3, 1985): 9W; Tracy Seipel, "Pale Riders," *RMN* (July 4, 1985): lifestyles 12S–14S; Rebecca Jones, "Lakeside Park Tries to Blend Past, Future," *RMN* (March 8, 1987): 16.

31. "Lakeside Park Celebrates 100 Years," *NAPHA News* 30 (2008): 13; Chotzinoff, "For Your Amusement"; Leuthner, "Lake Side."

32. Jones, "Lakeside Park Tries to Blend Past, Future"; Gallo, "Life Is a Carousel and a Rollercoaster," 26; 100th Anniversary Tour of Lakeside Amusement Park, July 18, 2008; "Lakeside Park Celebrates 100 Years," *NAPHA News* 30 (2008): 14.

33. Jones, "Lakeside Park Tries to Blend Past, Future"; John Head, "Lakeside a City? Right, since 1907 Incorporation," *DP* (June 11, 1979): 17B.

CHAPTER 10: LAKESIDE, THE MOST ENTERTAINING CITY IN AMERICA

1. Mosley, *Disney's World*, 280–83; Adams, *American Amusement Park Industry*, 137–38.
2. Leonard and Noel, *Denver*, 61, 129.
3. Ibid., 304–5.
4. Sharon R. Catlett, *Farmlands, Forts, and Country Life: The Story of Southwest Denver* (Boulder: Westcliffe, 2007), 158, 162, 192, 196; Jered B. Carr and Richard C. Feiock, "State Annexation 'Constraints' and the Frequency of Municipal Annexation," *Political Research Quarterly* 54 (June 2001): 459–60; Vivian Z. Klaff and Glenn V. Fuguitt, "Annexation as a Factor in the Growth of U.S. Cities, 1950–1960 and 1960–1970," *Demography* 15, no. 1 (February 1978): 1.
5. Leonard and Noel, *Denver*, 321.
6. Ibid., 293, 374–79. The vote totals for passage of the Poundstone amendment are at http://www.leg.state.co.us/lcs/ballothistory.nsf/835d2ada8de735e787256ffe0 074333d/41b277f58ce305f187256ffd006a4949?OpenDocument, accessed March 12, 2012.
7. "Shop Area Can't Be Annexed," *DP* (March 11, 1958): 19.
8. Bill Miller, "Lakeside Considers Annexing to Denver," *RMN* (May 28, 1960): 5.
9. Bill Myers, "Shopping Center Sold for $8 Million," *DP* (August 22, 1962): 1; Rebecca Cantwell, "Lakeside Mall Seeks Annexation to Wheat Ridge," *RMN* (October 7, 1988): 7.
10. Ken Pearce, "Lakeside Does So Have a Population," *DP* (August 30, 1971): 1.
11. John Head, "Lakeside a City? Right, since 1907 Incorporation," *DP* (June 11, 1979): 17B; Rebecca Jones, "Lakeside's 8 Residents Love Their 'Own Little World,'" *RMN* (March 8, 1987): 22.
12. Jones, "Lakeside's 8 Residents Love Their 'Own Little World,'" 22; Marlys Duran, "Elections Simple in a Town of 15," *RMN* (October 31, 1982): 8.
13. John Baron, "Lakeside Police Chief Is Arrested," *RMN* (March 7, 1980): 6; Philip Reed, "Lakeside Chief Pleads Guilty," *RMN* (November 6, 1980): 16.
14. Baron, "Lakeside Police Chief Is Arrested," 6; "Police-Council Dispute Results in Added Officer," *RMN* (June 16, 1981): 7.
15. John Head, "Lakeside a City? Right, since 1907 Incorporation," *DP* (June 11, 1979): 17B; Marlys Duran, "Lakeside Shirks Repair of West 44th," *RMN* (March 24, 1988): 38.

16. Duran, "Lakeside Shirks Repair of West 44th," 38; Marlys Duran, "Jeffco Wants to Abolish Lakeside Government," *RMN* (July 13, 1988): 13.

17. Duran, "Jeffco Wants to Abolish Lakeside Government," 13.

18. Ibid. Population figures for Mountain View from "Mountain View, CO," at http://www.usbeacon.com/Colorado/Mountain-View.html, accessed May 2, 2012.

19. Angel Hernandez, "Lakeside: Town of 15 Is Metro Area's Smallest—and Most Curious—Community," *RMN* (January 30, 1994): 24A–25A.

20. Guy Kelly, "Lakeside: Small Town Asks a Little Respect, to Be Left Alone," *RMN* (January 15, 1989): 30.

21. Steve Garnaas, "Lakeside Doesn't Amuse Officials," *DP* (June 21, 1993): 1A; "Legislature Should Revoke Lakeside's Municipal Status," *DP* (June 22, 1993): 6B.

22. Hernandez, "Lakeside: Town of 15 Is Metro Area's Smallest—and Most Curious—Community," 24A–25A; Kieran Nicholson, "Lakeside Looking at Taxes for a Life," *DP* (October 29, 1997): B1.

23. "Fire Damages Lakeside Mall Store," *RMN* (January 16, 1975): 5; "Fire Erupts in Lakeside Mall," *DP* (January 16, 1975): 22; Peter G. Chronis, "Remodeling Slated at Lakeside Mall," *RMN* (July 14, 1976): 66; "Lakeside Mall Details Face Lift with Price Tag of $1.6 Million," *RMN* (July 14, 1983): 98; Mike Anton, "Lakeside Mall Asbestos Hazard Unknown," *RMN* (August 30, 1987): 8, 22; Cantwell, "Lakeside Mall Seeks Annexation to Wheat Ridge," 7; Garnaas, "Lakeside Doesn't Amuse Officials," 1A.

24. Klaff and Fuguitt, "Annexation as a Factor in the Growth of U.S. Cities," 2; Cantwell, "Lakeside Mall Seeks Annexation to Wheat Ridge," 7; "Lakeside Rejects Mall's Bid to Leave," *RMN* (February 7, 1989): 90 (first quotation); Garnaas, "Lakeside Doesn't Amuse Officials," 1A; Kathryn Nielson, "Receiver Appointed at Lakeside," *RMN* (March 2, 1990): 65.

25. Hull, *Denver's Elitch Gardens*, 116–17.

26. Ibid., 117; Gallo, "Life Is a Carousel and a Rollercoaster," 24, 26, 28.

27. Hull, *Denver's Elitch Gardens*, 117–25; Gallo, "Life Is a Carousel and a Rollercoaster," 28.

28. Margaret Jackson, "Florida Firm to Buy Elitch's, 6 Other Six Flags Parks," *DP* (January 12, 2007): 1C.

29. Natalie Soto, "Roller Coaster Accident Injures 24 at Lakeside," *RMN* (September 6, 1994): 5A, 8A; Lynn Bartels, "Roller Coaster Accident Blamed on Human Error," *RMN* (September 7, 1994): 6A.

30. Natalie Soto, "Roller Coaster Accident Injures 24 at Lakeside," *RMN* (September 6, 1994): 5A, 8A; Lynn Bartels, "Roller Coaster Accident Blamed on Human Error," *RMN* (September 7, 1994): 6A.

Conclusion: A Century of Fun at Lakeside Amusement Park

1. Susan Barnes-Gelt, "A Failure of Mayoral Leadership," *DP* (February 17, 2008): 3E.
2. Janet Forgrieve, "A Century of Thrills," *RMN* (July 16, 2008): Business section, 1–2; Naomi Zeveloff, "Lakeside, a 1908 Democratic Convention Attraction, Turns 100," *Colorado Independent* (July 16, 2008), at http://coloradoindependent.com/4526/lakeside-a-1908-democratic-convention-attraction-turns-100, accessed April 27, 2012; 100th Anniversary Tour of Lakeside Amusement Park, July 18, 2008; John Wenzel, "Has Elitch's Run Its Race as Denver's Main Event?" *DP* (July 12, 2009): 8E. Elitch's is also on the list of century-old amusement parks, although in the opinion of many people the true Elitch's ceased to exist when it moved to the Platte Valley, and the new theme park is simply a park that has its name.
3. "30% Upturn for Lakeside," *Billboard* 49 (September 11, 1937): 46, 49.
4. Dave Smith, Walt Disney Company Archivist, Letter to David Forsyth, April 7, 2012; "Lakeside Park Celebrates 100 Years," *NAPHA News* 30 (2008): 8.
5. 100th Anniversary Tour of Lakeside Amusement Park, July 18, 2008. The original globes on lights were pointed out repeatedly during this tour.
6. "Lakeside Park Celebrates 100 Years," *NAPHA News* 30 (2008): 13–14; Simona Gallegos, "Ky. Accident Won't Delay Lakeside's New Drop Ride Zoom, Which Is Made by a Different Company," *DP* (June 24, 2007): 1C.
7. Irv Moss, "The Lure and Lore of Lakeside Track," *DP* (June 27, 2011): 6B; Development Agreement for Lakeside Center, December 16, 2009, at http://d.scribd.com/ScribdViewer.swf?document_id=38661033&access_key=key-1ptrl4uy7z55x4pace1s&page=1&version=1&viewMode=, accessed January 16, 2016 (a copy of the agreement is in the author's possession). In early 2012, Walmart began construction of a new store on the Lakeside Mall site, which opened in late 2012. Prior to that, it was rumored that King Soopers would close its existing store at Thirty-Eighth Avenue and Sheridan and build a new store in Lakeside. The building was later replaced with a new Key Bank near the newer building that houses the Town of Lakeside municipal offices. Several other businesses have moved into the site since the Walmart opened.
8. The last time the band organ on the carousel is mentioned as working is in "Lakeside Features Old Merry-Go-Round," *RMN* (August 16, 1970): 5. Jacobs, "Lakeside Marks 100th Anniversary."
9. Wenzel, "Has Elitch's Run Its Race as Denver's Main Event?"
10. Forgrieve, "Century of Thrills"; Claire Martin, "Nostalgia Rides on at Lakeside," *DP* (July 2, 2011): 1D, 8D.
11. "The Civic Center Conservancy," at http://www.civiccenterconservancy.org/about-us.html, accessed April 26, 2012; Michael Paglia, "Park and Wreck," *Westword*

(Denver) (September 14, 2006), at http://www.westword.com/2006-09-14/culture/park-and-wreck/full, accessed April 26, 2012; Joanne Ditmer, "Too Much of a Good Thing," *DP* (September 3, 2006), at http://www.denverpost.com/search/ci_4274787, accessed April 26, 2012.

12. Ditmer, "Too Much of a Good Thing"; Paglia, "Park and Wreck"; Kyle MacMillan, "A New Civic Center," *DP* (December 24, 2006), at http://www.denverpost.com/entertainment/ci_4881622, accessed April 26, 2012.

13. Caroline and Don Etter, "Open Space or Public Space?" *DP* (October 21, 2007): 1E; Mike McPhee, "Mayor Presents Civic Fix to House Museum," *DP* (December 5, 2007): 1B.

14. Barnes-Gelt, "Failure of Mayoral Leadership"; Kyle MacMillan, "Mayor Won't Rule Out Future Construction in Civic Center," *DP* (February 10, 2008): 2E.

15. As noted in chapter 2, Michele Bogart argues that no amusement park could be connected to the City Beautiful movement in her article "Barking Architecture: The Sculpture of Coney Island."

16. As noted in chapter 1, Jerome Smiley, in his 1901 *History of Denver*, repeatedly called for Denver to establish a viable park system. See also Tom Noel, "The City Beautiful Revisited," *Historic Denver News* (Spring 2012): 3.

17. Cross and Walton, *Playful Crowd*, 12–13, 16, 131–32, 140–41, 143–45, 153, last two quotations on p. 141; Gary Cross, "Crowds and Leisure: Thinking Comparatively across the 20th Century," *Journal of Social History* (Spring 2006): 633, 639.

18. Lakeside is described as blue collar in Robin Chotzinoff, "For Your Amusement: It's Been a Great Ride at Lakeside," *Westword* (Denver) (June 22, 2000), at http://www.westword.com/2000-06-22/news/for-your-amusement/, accessed April 28, 2012; as family friendly in Wenzel, "Has Elitch's Run Its Race as Denver's Main Event"; and as affordable in Martin, "Nostalgia Rides on at Lakeside"; Cross and Walton, *Playful Crowd*, 152–53, 156–57, 160, 162–63.

19. Hull, *Denver's Elitch Gardens*, 65; Smith, *San Francisco's Playland at the Beach*, 13.

20. Cross, "Crowds and Leisure," 639.

21. Picture of Lakeside Park Automobile Entrance Gate, File Folder 9, Photo Box 6, Richard L. Crowther Papers, WHGD; Cross and Walton, *Playful Crowd*, 160–61.

22. Cross, "Crowds and Leisure," 635; Michael DeAngelis, "Orchestrated (Dis)orientation: Roller Coasters, Theme Parks, and Postmodernism," *Cultural Critique* 37, no. 37 (Autumn 1997): 111; ACE Landmark Sign for the Cyclone Roller Coaster near the exit ramp of the Cyclone platform at Lakeside Amusement Park, presented to Lakeside by ACE, August 2003; Claire Tregeser, "Thrill Idle at Lakeside," *DP* (June 25, 2009): 1B; Martin, "Nostalgia Rides on at Lakeside"; Jacobs, "Lakeside Marks 100th Anniversary."

23. There are numerous examples of governments working against amusement parks in the pages of *Billboard* from the early 1900s to the mid-1960s when the magazine stopped publishing amusement park news. Examples include "Trouble over Sunday Dancing," *Billboard* 43 (May 23, 1931): 41; "A.C. Protest Arousing Hope," *Billboard* 49 (August 20, 1932): 36. The issue as it played out in Kansas City is mentioned in Adams, *American Amusement Park Industry*, 65–66; Cross, "Crowds and Leisure," 638–39.

24. DeAngelis, "Orchestrated (Dis)orientation," 109; Wenzel, "Has Elitch's Run Its Race as Denver's Main Event."

25. Jacobs, "Lakeside Marks 100th Anniversary."

Bibliography

I. PRIMARY SOURCES

A. Manuscript Collections

Colorado Theater Program Collection. Western History and Genealogy Department. Denver Public Library, Denver, CO.

Crowther, Richard L., Manuscript Collection. Western History and Genealogy Department. Denver Public Library, Denver, CO.

Denver Park Land and Improvement Company Papers. Western History and Genealogy Department. Denver Public Library, Denver, CO.

Hawks, Leon and Vera. Scrapbook. Western History and Genealogy Department. Denver Public Library, Denver, CO.

Lakeside Amusement Park. Clipping Files. Western History and Genealogy Department. Denver Public Library, Denver, CO.

Lakeside Amusement Park Papers. Stephen H. Hart Library. History Colorado, Denver.

"Magic Mountain Offering Circular." 1958. Western History and Genealogy Department. Denver Public Library, Denver, CO.

Speer, Robert W., Papers. Western History and Genealogy Department. Denver Public Library, Denver, CO.

B. Photographs

Colorado Snapshots Photograph Collection. Western History and Genealogy Department. Denver Public Library, Denver, CO.

"Joe Mann's Orchestra at Jail at Lakeside." Photo Call number X-27619. Western History and Genealogy Department. Denver Public Library, Denver, CO.

"Kay Kyser and His Orchestra at El Patio Ballroom, Lakeside Amusement Park." Photo Call number X-27613. Western History and Genealogy Department. Denver Public Library, Denver, CO.

"Lakeside Billboard." Photo Call number X-27403. Western History and Genealogy Department. Denver Public Library, Denver, CO.

"Lakeside Park—Kay Keyser [sic]." Photo Call number X-27401. Western History and Genealogy Department. Denver Public Library, Denver, CO.

"Lakeside Park Entrance, Union Pacific Decoration." Photo Call number X-27617. Western History and Genealogy Department. Denver Public Library, Denver, CO.

Roach, Otto. Photograph Collection. Western History and Genealogy Department. Denver Public Library, Denver, CO.

C. Government Documents

City of Lakeside Incorporation Records. Incorporation of Cities and Towns 1800–1977, Julesburg to Lakewood number 2. Microfilm. Roll 19. Colorado State Archives, Denver.

Colorado Realty and Amusement Company. Incorporation Papers. File 14724. Wyoming State Archives, Cheyenne.

Colorado Department of Transportation. "Construction Timeline," 1961–75. At http://www.coloradodot.info/about/50th-anniversary/interstate-70/construction-timeline.html, accessed February 8, 2012.

Colorado Department of Transportation. "The History of I-70 in Colorado," 1944–56. At http://www.coloradodot.info/about/50th-anniversary/interstate-70, accessed February 8, 2012.

Denver Park and Amusement Company. Incorporation Papers. File 20546. Wyoming State Archives, Cheyenne.

Development Agreement for Lakeside Center. December 16, 2009. At http://d.scribd.com/ScribdViewer.swf?document_id=38661033&access_key=key-1ptrl4uy7z55x4paceis&page=1&version=1&viewMode=, accessed January 16, 2016. Copy also in the author's possession.

Lakeside Realty and Amusement Company. Incorporation Papers. File 8539. Wyoming State Archives, Cheyenne.

US Bureau of the Census. *Twelfth Census of the United States, 1900*. Washington, DC.

US Bureau of the Census. *Thirteenth Census of the United States, 1910*. Washington, DC.

US Bureau of the Census. *Fourteenth Census of the United States, 1920*. Washington, DC.

US Bureau of the Census. *Fifteenth Census of the United States, 1930*. Washington, DC.

US Bureau of the Census. *Sixteenth Census of the United States, 1940*. Washington, DC.

D. Court Cases

Denver Park and Amusement Company v. Francis J. Kirchoff, et al. Case number 12234. Supreme Court of Colorado. Colorado State Archives, Denver.

Ned Stout, an Infant, by Emory L. O'Connell, His Next Friend v. Denver Park and Amusement Company. Case number 12262. Supreme Court of Colorado. Colorado State Archives, Denver.

Opal Doris Jernigan et al v. Lakeside Park Company et al. Civil Action 9939. Case number 18080. Supreme Court of Colorado. Colorado State Archives, Denver.

E. Books

Clason's Denver Map Guide. Denver: Clason Map Co., 1925.

Colorado Writer's Program of the Works Project Administration. *Life in Denver Part VII.* Published in 1942. Copy available at Western History and Genealogy Department, Denver Public Library, Denver, CO.

Denver, the Convention City of America: The City of Hospitality, at the Base of the Rocky Mountains, Scintillating with Millions of Electric Lights. Denver: Denver Convention League, 1910.

Lakeside Realty and Amusement Company. *Lakeside Realty and Amusement Company, Lakeside Park, the White City, Denver Colorado, Official Guide and Views*. Denver: Smith Books, 1908.

1915 Denver Automobile Directory. Denver: Wahlgreen, 1915.

Smiley, Jerome C. *History of Denver: With Outlines of the Earlier History of the Rocky Mountain Country*. Evansville, IN: Unigraphic, Inc., 1971 [1901].

Vickers, William B. *History of the City of Denver, Arapahoe County, and Colorado: Containing a History of the State of Colorado . . . A Condensed Sketch of Arapahoe County . . . A History of the City of Denver . . . Biographical Sketches*. Chicago: O. L. Baskin, 1880.

Wolfe, Tom. *The Kandy-Kolored Tangerine-Flake Streamline Baby*. New York: Farrar, Straus, and Giroux, 1965.

F. Articles

"Ben Krasner's Lakeside Speedway." At http://www.bigwestracing.com/forums/showthread.php?t=20322, accessed April 9, 2012.

Cribbs, Johnny. "It Started atop Table Mountain." *Speed Age* (July 1948). At https://modcoupes.com/Stories.html, accessed September 21, 2015.

Gallo, Bill. "Life Is a Carousel and a Rollercoaster." *Denver Magazine* 16 (July 1986): 22–28.

Hacker, Geoffrey. "Collectibles from the Movie 'Johnny Dark'—Lobby Cards." At http://www.forgottenfiberglass.com/?p=9071, accessed April 9, 2012.

Jacobs, Andrea. "Lakeside Marks 100th Anniversary." *Intermountain Jewish News* (July 3, 2008). At www.inj.com/features/210-lakeside-marks-anniversary, accessed April 26, 2012.

"Lakeside Compacts/Late Models." At http://autoracingmemories.com/forums/showthread.php?t=809, accessed April 9, 2012.

Leuthner, Stuart. "Lake Side: An Art Deco Masterpiece Struggles to Survive." *American Heritage* 43 (July-August 1992). At http://www.americanheritage.com/content/lake-side?page=show, accessed September 15, 2015.

"The Memories Flood!!" by Nostalgic Mike. At http://www.bigwestracing.com/forums/showthread.php?t=12499&page=4, accessed April 9, 2012.

Peratt, Bill. "Lakeside Speedway—Denver, Colorado." At http://autoracingmemories.com/forums/showthread.php?t=15, accessed January 23, 2012.

G. Newspapers

Arvada (CO) Citizen Sentinel

Colorado Statesman (Denver)

Colorado Sun (Denver)

Colorado Transcript (Golden)

Daily Journal (Telluride, CO)

Denver Express

Denver Post

Denver Republican

Denver Times

Estes Park (CO) Trail

Fort Collins (CO) Courier

Fort Collins (CO) Weekly Courier

New York Times

Ouray (CO) Herald

Rocky Mountain News (Denver)

Svensk Amerikanska Western (Denver)

Westword (Denver)

Wray (CO) Rattler

H. Periodicals

Amusement Business

Billboard

Denver Municipal Facts

I. Interviews

Arner, Wayne. Telephone interview by the author. Denver, CO. December 19, 2011.

Arner, Wayne. Interview by the author. Denver, CO. December 29, 2011.

Arnold, Gertrude "Betty." Interview by the author. Denver, CO. July 22, 2011.

Brown, Jerry. Interview by the author. Denver, CO. December 29, 2011.

Byers, Leroy. Interview by the author. Denver, CO. December 29, 2011.

Campbell, Bob. Interview 1 by the author. Denver, CO. December 29, 2011.

Campbell, Bob. Interview 2 by the author. Denver, CO. February 16, 2012.

Coleman, Sonny. Interview 1 by the author. Denver, CO. December 29, 2011.

Coleman, Sonny. Interview 2 by the author. Denver, CO. January 20, 2012.

Gottschalck, Charles. Interview by the author. Denver, CO. December 29, 2011.

Graham, Sheri Thurman. Interview by the author. Arvada, CO. April 7, 2012.

Jamison, Frank. Interview by the author. Lakewood, CO. April 2, 2012.

Jamison, Joyce. Interview by the author. Lakewood, CO. April 2, 2012.

Krasner, Rhoda. Interview by the author. Lakeside, CO. July 5, 2012.

Krasner, Rhoda. Interview by the author. Lakeside, CO. July 12, 2012.

Krasner, Rhoda. Interview by the author. Lakeside, CO. July 31, 2014.

Krasner, Rhoda. Interview by the author. Lakeside, CO. September 7, 2014.

Land, Bob. Interview by the author. Denver, CO. December 29, 2011.

Miller, Jerry. Interview by the author. Denver, CO. July 19, 2012.

Olds, Bob. Interview by the author. Denver, CO. December 29, 2011.

Pastor, Gene. Interview by the author. Denver, CO. December 29, 2011.

Plemons, Blu. Interview by the author. Denver, CO. February 16, 2012.

Slusser, Marv. Interview by the author. Denver, CO. February 16, 2012.

Tandolini, Ken. "Ken Tandolini—the Two Minute Interview." At http://autoracingmemories.com/forums/showthread.php?t=157, accessed April 14, 2012.

J. Other

ACE Landmark Sign for the Cyclone Roller Coaster. Lakeside Amusement Park. Lakeside, CO.

"Audrey Bolyard." At http://autoracingmemories.com/forums/showthread.php?t=470, accessed April 9, 2012.

"Ballot History" for the Poundstone Amendment to the Colorado State Constitution. At http://www.leg.state.co.us/lcs/ballothistory.nsf/835d2ada8de735e787256ffe0074333d/41b277f58ce305f187256ffd006a4949?OpenDocument, accessed March 12, 2012.

"Duke Ellington El Patio Denver 1942." Big Band Serenade Podcast. Humphrey Camardella Productions. First podcast September 12, 2011. Available on iTunes.

Gurtler, Jack. Oral History. Western History and Genealogy Department. Denver Public Library, Denver, CO.

Lee, Elmore. "Just Take a Trip Out to Lakeside." Sheet music. Denver: Tolbert R. Ingram, 1908. Available at University of Colorado at Boulder archives.

100th Anniversary Tour of Lakeside Amusement Park. July 18, 2008.

"Palisades Park" performed by Freddy "Boom Boom" Cannon. Lyrics. At http://www.stlyrics.com/lyrics/confessionsofadangerousmind/palisadespark.htm, accessed March 30, 2012.

"Pegi Plue Induction Speech." At http://www.modcoupes.com/carc/other/carc-history/stories?start=5 (page no longer available), accessed April 9, 2012.

"Re: Lakeside, the Shrine." At http://www.bigwestracing.com/forums/showthread.php?t=12499&page=4, accessed April 9, 2012.

"Trivia for Rollercoaster." http://www.imdb.com/title/tt0076636/trivia, accessed March 30, 2012.

"Western League Baseball Schedule." Denver: Lakeside Realty and Amusement Company, 1912. Copy available at Western History and Genealogy Department, Denver Public Library, Denver, CO.

Zang, Philip. Family plot. Block 7. Riverside Cemetery. Denver, CO.

II. Secondary Sources

A. Books

Abbott, Carl, Stephen J. Leonard, and David McComb. *Colorado: A History of the Centennial State*, 3rd ed. Niwot: University Press of Colorado, 1992.

Adams, Judith A. *The American Amusement Park Industry: A History of Technology and Thrills*. Boston: Twayne, 1991.

Arps, Louisa Ward. *Denver in Slices: A Historical Guide to the City*. Athens, OH: Swallow, 1998.

Ashby, LeRoy. *With Amusement for All: A History of American Popular Culture since 1830*. Lexington: University Press of Kentucky, 2006.

Berry, Mary Frances. *The Pig Farmer's Daughter and Other Tales of American Justice: Episodes of Racism and Sexism in the Courts from 1865 to the Present.* New York: Alfred A. Knopf, 1999.

Brown, Allan E. *The History of the American Speedway: Past and Present.* Marne, MI: Slideways, 1985.

Bunker, Nancy A. *Tuileries Amusement Park: A Short History.* Englewood, CO: Englewood Public Library, 1991.

Burg, David F. *Chicago's White City of 1893.* Lexington: University Press of Kentucky, 1976.

Cartmell, Robert. *The Incredible Scream Machine: A History of the Roller Coaster.* Fairview Park, OH: Amusement Park Books, 1987.

Catlett, Sharon R. *Farmlands, Forts, and Country Life: The Story of Southwest Denver.* Boulder: Westcliffe, 2007.

Cooper, John Milton, Jr. *Pivotal Decades: The United States, 1900–1920.* New York: W. W. Norton, 1990.

Cross, Gary S., and John K. Walton. *The Playful Crowd: Pleasure Places in the Twentieth Century.* New York: Columbia University Press, 2005.

Farrell, James J. *One Nation under Goods: Malls and the Seductions of American Shopping.* Washington, DC: Smithsonian Books, 2010.

Foster, Mark S. *The Denver Bears: From Sandlots to Sellouts.* Boulder: Pruett, 1983.

Foster, Mark S. *A Nation on Wheels: The Automobile Culture in America since 1945.* Belmont, CA: Thomson, Wadsworth, 2003.

Fox, Jack C. *The Mighty Midgets: The Illustrated History of Midget Auto Racing.* Speedway, IN: Carl Hungness, 1978.

Francis, David, and Diane Francis. *Cleveland Amusement Park Memories: A Nostalgic Look Back at Euclid Beach Park, Puritas Springs Park, Geauga Lake Park, and Other Classic Parks.* Cleveland: Gray, 2004.

Gargiulo, Vince. *Palisades Amusement Park: A Century of Fond Memories.* New Brunswick: Rutgers University Press, 1995.

Gee, Derek, and Ralph Lopez. *Laugh Your Troubles Away: The Complete History of Riverview Park, Chicago, Illinois.* Livonia, MI: Sharpshooter Productions, 2000.

Goodstein, Phil. *In the Shadow of the Klan: When the KKK Ruled Denver, 1920–1926.* Denver: New Social Publications, 2006.

Goodstein, Phil. *Robert Speer's Denver, 1904–1920: The Mile High City in the Progressive Era.* Denver: New Social Publications, 2004.

Hill, Bill. *Decades of Daring: Midget Racing in the Rocky Mountains.* North Little Rock, AK: Bill Hill Productions, 2001.

Hillier, Bevis, and Stephen Escritt. *Art Deco Style.* London: Phaidon, 1997.

Hull, Betty Lynne. *Denver's Elitch Gardens: Spinning a Century of Dreams.* Boulder: Johnson Books, 2003.

Kasson, John F. *Amusing the Million: Coney Island at the Turn of the Century.* New York: Hill and Wang, 1978.

Larson, Erik. *Devil in the White City: Murder, Magic, and Madness at the Fair That Changed America*. New York: Vintage Books, 2003.
Leonard, Stephen J., and Thomas J. Noel. *Denver: Mining Camp to Metropolis*. Niwot: University Press of Colorado, 1990.
Mandel, Leon. *American Cars*. New York: Stewart, Tabori and Chang, 1982.
Mangels, William F. *The Outdoor Amusement Industry: From Earliest Times to the Present*. New York: Vantage, 1952.
Manring, M. M. *Slave in a Box: The Strange Career of Aunt Jemima*. Charlottesville: University Press of Virginia, 1998.
Mosley, Leonard. *Disney's World*. Lanham, MD: Scarborough House, 1992.
Mott, Frank Luther. *American Journalism: A History, 1690–1960*, 3rd ed. New York: Macmillan, 1962.
Nasaw, David. *Going Out: The Rise and Fall of Public Amusements*. New York: Basic Books, 1993.
Noel, Thomas J. *Denver Landmarks and Historic Districts: A Pictorial Guide*. Niwot: University Press of Colorado, 1996.
Noel, Thomas J., and Barbara S. Norgren. *Denver: The City Beautiful*. Denver: Historic Denver, Inc., 1987.
Painter, Nell Irvin. *Standing at Armageddon: The United States, 1877–1919*. New York: W. W. Norton, 1989.
Parrish, Michael E. *Anxious Decades: America in Prosperity and Depression, 1920–1941*. New York: W. W. Norton, 1992.
Peiss, Kathy. *Cheap Amusements: Working Women and Leisure in Turn-of-the-Century New York*. Philadelphia: Temple University Press, 1986.
Reiss, Steven A. *City Games: The Evolution of American Urban Society and the Rise of Sports*. Urbana: University of Illinois Press, 1989.
Robertson, Don, and W. Morris Cafky. *Denver's Street Railways, vol. 2: 1901–1950: Reign of the Denver Tramway*. Denver: Sundance, 2004.
Robertson, Don, Morris Cafky, and E. J. Haley. *Denver's Street Railways, vol. 1: 1870–1900: Not an Automobile in Sight*. Denver: Sundance, 1999.
Rosenzweig, Roy. *Eight Hours for What We Will: Workers and Leisure in an Industrial City, 1870–1920*. Cambridge: Cambridge University Press, 1992.
Rosenzweig, Roy, and Elizabeth Blackmar. *The Park and the People: A History of Central Park*. New York: Cornell University Press, 1992.
Rydell, Robert W. *All the World's a Fair: Visions of Empire at American International Expositions, 1876–1916*. Chicago: University of Chicago Press, 1987.
Schlereth, Thomas J. *Victorian America: Transformations in Everyday Life, 1876–1915*. New York: HarperPerennial, 1992.
Smith, Duane A., Karen A. Vendl, and Mark A. Vendl. *Colorado Goes to the Fair: World's Columbian Exposition, Chicago, 1893*. Albuquerque: University of New Mexico Press, 2011.

Smith, James R. *San Francisco's Playland at the Beach: The Early Years*. Fresno, CA: Craven Street Books, 2010.

Stott, Annette. *Pioneer Cemeteries: Sculpture Gardens of the Old West*. Lincoln: University of Nebraska Press, 2008.

Underhill, Paco. *The Call of the Mall: A Walking Tour through the Crossroads of Our Shopping Culture*. New York: Simon and Schuster, 2004.

White, Gordon Eliot. *Lost Race Tracks: Treasures of Automobile Racing*. Hudson, WI: Iconografix, 2002.

Wiebe, Robert H. *The Search for Order, 1877–1920*. New York: Hill and Wang, 1967.

Wilson, William H. *The City Beautiful Movement*. Baltimore: Johns Hopkins University Press, 1989.

Wolcott, Victoria W. *Race, Riots, and Roller Coasters*. Philadelphia: University of Pennsylvania Press, 2012.

B. Articles

"About Kay Kyser." At www.kaykyser.net, accessed December 9, 2011.

Bogart, Michele H. "Barking Architecture: The Sculpture of Coney Island." *Smithsonian Studies in American Art* 2 (Winter 1988): 3–17.

Carr, Jered B., and Richard C. Feiock. "State Annexation 'Constraints' and the Frequency of Municipal Annexation." *Political Research Quarterly* 54 (June 2001): 459–70.

"Closed Canadian Parks, Ontario." At http://cec.chebucto.org/ClosPark/ErieBech.html, accessed October 29, 2011.

Cross, Gary. "Crowds and Leisure: Thinking Comparatively across the 20th Century." *Journal of Social History* 39 (Spring 2006): 632–50.

Davis, J. Tait. "Middle Class Housing in the Central City." *Economic Geography* 41, no. 3 (July 1965): 238–51. http://dx.doi.org/10.2307/141901.

DeAngelis, Michael. "Orchestrated (Dis)orientation: Roller Coasters, Theme Parks, and Postmodernism." *Cultural Critique* 37, no. 37 (Autumn 1997): 107–29. http://dx.doi.org/10.2307/1354542.

Dirks, Tim. "1920s Film History." At http://www.filmsites.org/20sintro4.html, accessed October 22, 2011.

Forsyth, David. "Spares and Splashes: Walt Disney's Celebrity Sports Center." *Colorado Heritage* (Autumn 2007): 32–47.

Gardner, Richard J. "Magic Mountain: The Lost Heritage of Heritage Square." At http://goldenlandmarks.com/museum/magicmountain/, accessed April 2, 2011.

"George Morrison." At http://www.denvergov.org/Portals/633/documents/George%20Morrison.doc, accessed October 26, 2011.

Goldman, Robert. "'We Make Weekends': Leisure and the Commodity Form." *Social Text* 8, no. 8 (Winter 1983–84): 84–103. http://dx.doi.org/10.2307/466324.

Jackson, Kenneth T. "All the World's a Mall: Reflections on the Social and Economic Consequences of the American Shopping Center." *American Historical Review* 101, no. 4 (October 1996): 1111–21. http://dx.doi.org/10.2307/2169636.

"Jim Malloy—Lakeside to Indy." At http://www.bigwestracing.com/forums/showthread.php?t=16914, accessed April 9, 2012.

Klaff, Vivian Z., and Glenn V. Fuguitt. "Annexation as a Factor in the Growth of U.S. Cities, 1950–1960 and 1960–1970." *Demography* 15, no. 1 (February 1978): 1–12. http://dx.doi.org/10.2307/2060487.

Kovak, Richard M. "Urban Renewal Controversies." *Public Administration Review* 32, no. 4 (July-August 1972): 359–72. http://dx.doi.org/10.2307/975000.

"Lakeside Park Celebrates 100 Years." *NAPHA News* 30 (2008): 3–14.

Meyers, David. "Buildering: The Art of Climbing . . . Skyscrapers." At http://www.google.com/url?sa=t&rct=j&q=&esrc=s&source=web&cd=14&ved=0CCkQFjADOApqFQoTCK3ortey-scCFdGLkgodrYoOFw&url=http%3A%2F%2Fwww.davidmeyercreations.com%2Fmysteries-of-history%2Fbuildering-the-art-of-climbing-skyscrapers%2F&usg=AFQjCNGFmfueak8-8D_UiinfkmuWJdKMhA, accessed September 15, 2015.

Olson, Robert J. "Lakeside Is the Place! A History of the Lakeside Amusement Park." *Historically Jeffco* 19 (2006): 35–39.

"Sport: Joie Chitwood's Indianapolis Thrill Show." At http://canadiannews1.com/archive/StuntDriver1/stuntdriver1.com/history/Joie-Chitwoods-Indianapolis-Thrill-Show.html, accessed April 9, 2012.

"The Tumble Bug." At www.ridezone.com/rides/tumblebug/index.htm, accessed December 9, 2011.

"William F. Mangels Amusement Industry's 'First Historian.'" *NAPHA News* 30 (2008): 15.

Wright, Gwendolyn. "Urban Spaces and Cultural Settings." *Journal of Architectural Education* 41, no. 3 (Spring 1988): 10–14. http://dx.doi.org/10.1080/10464883.1988.10758482.

Zoch, Justin. "Ben Krasner." National Sprint Car Hall of Fame Induction Biography. At http://www.sprintcarhof.com/Pages/Inductees under the 2010 list of inductees, accessed March 15, 2012.

C. Manuscripts

Forsyth, David. "Eben Smith: Western Mining Man." Master's thesis, University of Colorado at Denver, 2003.

D. Websites

Colorado Motorsports Hall of Fame. www.coloradomotorsportshalloffame.com.

Index

Acosta, Ostobina (matador), 82
Adams, Judith, 5, 9, 89; on Disneyland, 157; on Magic Mountain (Golden), 159
Adams, Kate, 26, 30, 33, 55
Adams, Marvin, 25–27, 45, 78, 197, 209, 213; first mayor of Lakeside, 33, 54, 55; opening day of Lakeside Amusement Park, 39–40
Airship (ride), 36, 62
Alfrey, Naomi, 51
Allen, Charlie (driver), 140
Allen, Elmer, 26
Allen, Ernest, 26
Allen, Gracie, 160
Alligator Joe. *See* Frazee, William
Allison, June, 115
American Automobile Association (AAA), 137, 145, 168, 170
Amole, Gene, 115
amusement park, 3, 6–8, 9–10, 23, 89–90, 101, 105–6, 147, 157, 191, 236, 237; admission fee, 8; architecture at, 27; attractions, 36, 37, 101, 114; corporate ownership of, 158, 191; during World War II, 114–15, 116; family-owned, 158, 191; Ferris wheels, 4, 9; gates, 27–28; Glen Echo Park (MD), 8; Kennywood (PA), 8; merry-go-round, 7, 8, 36; Parker's Grove (OH), 8; in popular culture, 10; roller coasters, 9; transportation to, 32, 33, 158, 234; trolley parks, 31. *See also individual attraction names; individual park names;* theme parks
Anderson, Ernest, 106
annexation, 210, 211, 220
Anti–Saloon League attack on Lakeside, 45–48; statewide prohibition, 85
Arlington Park (Denver), 17–18, 20, 23, 32, 48, 87, 162, 213, 244n33
Arlington Park Land and Improvement Company, 18–19
ARM/Larson, 227
Arner, Wayne (driver), 114, 131, 136, 138, 139, 141
Arnold, Betty, 24, 69, 82
Arnold, Henry (mayor of Denver), 77
Arps, Louisa Ward, 132

Art Deco style 1925 Paris Exhibition, 108–9; at Lakeside Amusement Park, 109–10; moderne, 109; zig-zag, 109
Arvada (Colorado), 77, 78, 93, 153, 200, 211, 214; annexes part of Rocky Flats Nuclear Weapons Plant, 211
Asay, Bill (promoter), 145–46
Ashby, LeRoy, 161
Atkins, Johnny (promoter), 142
automobile ownership, 33, 89, 143, 234
automobile racing (Denver): Bandimere Speedway (Morrison), 182; Barney Oldfield races at Overland Park, 132; Billy Betteridge stages midget race, 133; Brighton Speedway, 169; DuPont Speedway (Commerce City), 133, 140; Colorado National Speedway (Erie), 182; Englewood Speedway, 140, 143, 144, 146, 169, 175, 182; Higley Airport, 133; Merchant's Park (Denver), 134–35, 137, 140; Overland Park (Denver), 132–33; School of Mines 133. *See also* Lakeside Speedway; *individual sanctioning bodies*
Auto Skooters (ride), 161–62, 227
Avila, Jose (matador), 82
Axel, Lloyd (driver), 136, 139, 140, 141; forms Rocky Mountain Midget Racing Association, 137; leads defection to Lakeside Speedway, 135; leads defection to Englewood Speedway, 144; and Pikes Peak Auto Hill Climb, 140, 186

Bailey, Kent (band), 154
Balater, Al (band), 154
Baldwin, Ivy balloon ascensions at Elitch Gardens, 15; at Overland Park, 132
Banks, John, 212
Barber, Mr. and Mrs. Robert, 113
Barnes, J. W., 47
Barnes, W. H., 17
Barnes-Gelt, Susan (columnist), 231
Barnum, P. T., 14–15
Barr, John, 155
Barr, Lois (reporter), 175–76
Bartlett, Charles, 96. *See also* Yellowstone Pictures
Bates, Joseph C. (mayor of Denver), 13
Beall, Kate Walker (doctor), 41
Bellows, Walter Clarke (theater director), 72
Beneke, Tex (singer), 150
Benny, Jack, 160

Berry, Mary Frances, 98
Billboard magazine, 10, 83, 89, 236, 242–43n14; Lakeside Amusement Park described in, 44
Blackpool (Great Britain), 233–34; Pleasure Beach, 233
Bloedt, Arnold, 81, 90
Boat House (building), 30, 35, 60
Bogart, Michele, 23, 274n15
Bohn, Eddie (sponsor), 145
Bolyard, Audrey (driver), 173
Bonfils, Frederick, 76–7; and Sells-Floto Circus, 92
Boston Marine Band, 80
Bowe, Roy (driver), 145
Boyer, Chuck, 133
Boyton, Paul, 7, 8
Bozo the Clown, 154
Bray, Francis W., 34
Brown, Allan, 146, 168
Brown, Harry, 197
Brown, Jerry (driver), 135
Brown, Les (musician), 150
Brown, Nolan (district attorney), 197, 201, 202
Buchtel, Henry (governor of Colorado), 48
Buck, William, 24, 81, 90, 120, 237, 238
Buell, Temple, 153
Buford, Frank (Lakeside Speedway employee), 114
Burbank, R. C. (matador), 82
Burg, David, 5
Burlew, Harry, 82
Burnham, Daniel, 5, 6
Burns, George, 160
Burt, Frank, 44–45, 46, 47, 50, 54, 74–76, 83, 90
Burton, Gary (driver), 180, 182
Byers, Leroy (photographer), 136, 138–39, 143, 146

Campbell, Bob (driver), 114, 137, 172
Campbell, Foster (driver), 114, 137
Cannon, Freddy "Boom Boom," 10, 239
Carle, Frankie (pianist), 121
Carlson, Kristy, 180
Carlson, Ronald, 181–82
Carr, Jered B., 211
Carter, Allen (actor), 73
Casa Mañana, 111
Casino (building), 29–30, 35; College Inn opens in, 110; Fountain Room opens in, 94–95;

Tango Lair opens in, 84, 127; preserved, 201, 226
Casino Theater, 72–73, 74, 75–76, 82–83, 85, 226; closure, 93; Fealy-Durkin Stock Company at, 79–80, 82; Lakeside Stock Company at, 75–76
Cassidy, Hopalong, 151
Cavallo, Raffaelo, 82; Cavallo Symphony Orchestra, 82, 253n31
Celebrity Sports Center (Denver), 159–60, 161
cemeteries (Denver): Fairmount Cemetery, 14, 19–20; Riverside Cemetery, 14, 19–20
Central Park (New York City), 12–13, 20
Chadwick, Carl (mayor of Lakeside), 214, 215
Childers, Jerry, 204
Christian, John, 204–5
Christiansen, Don, 163
Christiansen, Jim, 163
Chutes Park (Denver). *See* Arlington Park
Circle Swing (ride), 94; monoplanes on 97; seaplanes on 112; rocket ships on 129, 206
City Beautiful movement, 6, 87; and amusement parks 23, 70–72, 233; William Stead role in 6
Clark, Lou, 156
Clifton, Alice (actress), 73
Cline, Hugh, 42
Clow, Dad, 55
Clurman, Irene (reporter), 203
Cobb, Walter F., 158–59. *See also* Magic Mountain (Golden)
Cohen, Louis (mayor of Fairplay), 54
Coleman, Dan, 149
Coleman, Sonny (driver), 135, 136, 139, 142, 143–44, 145, 146, 171, 172, 173, 176
Colorado (state), 220; Department of Labor and Employment, 223; Department of Transportation (formerly Department of Highways), 194; Division of Labor, 195–96; economy, 91; History Colorado (Colorado Historical Society), 231–232; state prohibition and effect on breweries, 85
Colorado Automobile Racing Club (CARC), 143, 146, 168–69, 170, 172, 181, 182; and Powder Puff racers, 173, 175
Colorado Realty and Amusement Company, 81, 90
Columbian Exposition (Chicago), 4–5, 23; architecture at, 5, 6, 27; Court of Honor, 6–7; referred to as White City, 5

Coney Island, 27, 105–06, 116, 234–35, 236; Dreamland, 7, 27–28, 54, 73; Luna Park, 7, 37; Sea Lion Park, 7, 8; Steeplechase, 7, 8, 28
Conkle, J. A., 81
Conklin, William, 54
Connor, Cecil R. (Western Resources Publicity Service), 3, 76
Cooley, Earl (lieutenant governor), 97
Coon-Sanders Orchestra, 102
Corcoran, John (postmaster of Denver), 17
Couney, Martin (doctor), 37–38
Crawford, Mattie (evangelist), 97
Creation (ride) at Lakeside Amusement Park, 73–74; at Riverview Park (Chicago) 8
Creatore (band), 80
Cross, Gary, 6–7, 89, 233–34
Crowell, Palmer (driver), 181
Crowther, Richard, 157, 163; Art Deco makeover of Lakeside Amusement park, 108–10
Cullen, Cynthia, 155
Cunningham, Pat (driver), 133–34
Curtis, Tony (actor), 177
Cyclone roller coaster (ride), 156, 162, 192, 205; accidents on, 195–96, 223; construction of, 112–13, 118, 149; image, 126; named ACE Roller Coaster Landmark, 235–36; named to top ten list, 203; ticket booth, 209, *126*

Daly, Don (driver), 180
Daly, Richard, 219
Dante's Italian Band, 30, 40, 44
Dean, Arthur (actor), 73
Democratic National Convention in Denver, 12, 42–43, 226; Thomas Taggert and, 43
Denney, Bob (driver), 180
Denver (city and county of), 3–4, 11, 14, 68, 69, 225, 229, 238; annexation activities of, 210–11, 212, 217; Board of Public Works, 11; Career Service Authority, 119; Denver Art Museum, 120, 230; Denver General Hospital, 119; Denver Public Library, 120; Denver Urban Renewal Authority (DURA), 192, 198; during Great Depression, 100–101, 102; during World War I, 92; during World War II, 117–18; formation of, 12; Platte Valley redevelopment, 222; politics of, 67, 77, 91, 119; population of, 33, 119, 210; post–World War II, 119–20, 210–11; race and, 113, 211–12;

vice in, 48–49, 91. *See also* Denver City Beautiful Movement; Denver neighborhoods; Denver parks

Denver Bears, 143, 144–45, 169; Bears Stadium (later Mile High Stadium), 143

Denver City Beautiful Movement, 3–4, 12, 67, 77, 87, 90, 92, 119–20, 225; Art Commission role in, 12; bathhouse built, 12; Civic Center Park controversy and, 230–32; Denver Mountain Parks, 77, 232; *Denver Municipal Facts*, 55 67–70, 82, 84, 87, 205n1; Municipal Auditorium, 10–11, 12, 42; parks, 12–13, 77, 232; Robert Speer's definition of, 20–21, 48–49; *See also* Lakeside Amusement Park and City Beautiful connection; City Beautiful movement

Denver Midget Racing Club, 146, 170

Denver neighborhoods, 31, 78–79, 91; Berkeley, 77–78, 210; Bonnie Brae, 91; Capitol Hill, 77; Cherry Hills, 91; Denver Country Club, 77; Denver Polo Club, 77; North Denver, 113, 137

Denver Park and Amusement Company, 90, 99–100, 104

Denver parks, 12–13, 19, 20–21, 232–33; Alamo Placita Park, 18, 244n32; Berkeley, 21; City, 13, 68, 199; Chaffee, 13; Civic Center, 21, 77, 119–20, 225, 230–32; Congress, 13; Curtis, 13; Dunham, 13; Fuller, 13; Highland, 13; Inspiration Point, 21, 68, 77, 154; Jefferson, 13; Lincoln, 13; Mountain Park system, 77, 232; Park Avenue, 13; Platt, 13; Red Rocks, 151, 232; Sloan's Lake, 21; Washington, 13; Wellington Webb and, 232

Denver radio stations: KLZ 150; KOA 115; KYMR 115

Denver television stations: KBTV 178; KLZ-TV 176

Denver Tramway Company, 31, 32, 121; line to Lakeside Amusement Park, 30–31, 32, 42, 83, 121

Derby coaster (ride), 79, 83, 84, 97, 107, 110, 122

Devil's Joy Ride, 164

Devil's Palace (attraction), 36

Disney, Walt, 157, 158, 161, 209, 236. *See also* Disneyland; Celebrity Sports Center; Walt Disney World

Disneyland, 10, 147, 157–58, 209, 235; and Lakeside Amusement Park, 161, 227

Ditmer, Joanne (reporter), 230

Dixon, Edward, 42

Doherty, Hugh, 47

Dong Fung Gu (dancer), 84

Dorsey, Jimmy, 150, 155

Douglas, Purlie, 118

Doyle, William (judge), 212

Dragon coaster (ride), 206, 227, 189

Dragoo, Red, 46

Drumm, August, 104

Dumbauld, Ted (driver), 134

Duncan, Roy Ray (chief of police), 215

Dunham, Frederick (actor), 93

Dunham, Sonny (musician), 121

Dunn, Roy, 196

Durkin, James (actor), 80

Dye, Emma, 86–87

Earent Williams (band), 80

Easter, Roy, 102

Eaton, George W., 15–16

Eatwell, John (driver), 180

Eisenhuth, Harold, 216

Elitch, John, 14–15, 20, 31, 69

Elitch, Mary (Mary Elitch Long), 14–15, 69, 91–92, 99

Elitch Gardens, 8, 14–15, 20, 28, 99, 110, 229, 230–31; amusement rides, 15, 227–28; attendance figures, 205; automobile parking at, 99, 234; deaths at, 118; during World War II, 118; financial difficulties, 91–92, 222; gardens, 20, 114–15; *The Glenn Miller Story* filmed at, 115; Gurtler family as owners, 114–15; in *Denver Municipal Facts*, 68, 69–70; John Mulvihill buys, 92; KiddieLand, 151; lawsuit against, 223; moves to Platte Valley, 220–22, 235, 237; proposed move to Highlands Ranch, 221; relationship with Denver, 222, 226; rivalry with Lakeside, 87, 103, 107, 114, 121, 162, 177–78, 206, 222–23; segregation at, 101–2, 114, 259n19; sold to Parc Management LLC, 223; sold to Premier Parks, Inc., 222; sold to Six Flags, 222, 233; streetcar service to, 31–32, 117; theater, 24, 69, 72, 73, 80, 82, 104; Trocadero ballroom, 99, 102–3, 115, 194 (demolition); Twister roller coaster, 113, 156, 223; Wildcat roller coaster, 99; Woodward Gardens San Francisco as inspiration for, 14; *See also individual owner names*

Ellington, Duke, 107

El Patio Ballroom, 30, 35, 74, 94–95, 96, 101–2, 197, 227; name band policy, 102–3, 107, 156, 162; radio broadcasts from, 115, 122; renamed Moonlight Gardens 162; Riviera Club opens 150; closure 194; demolition 202, 60; *See also* individual band names
Erwin, Lou (driver), 133
Escritt, Stephen, 109
Espy, J. Reimer, 104
Etter, Carolyn, 231
Etter, Don, 231
Euclid Beach Park (Cleveland), 71–72
Evans, Tom (driver), 180
Ezekiel, Albert, 26–27

Fahrney, Dan, 198
Farrell, James, 152
Fashi, John, 26
Fealy, Maude (actress), 80, 82
Feiock, Richard C., 211
Felt, Vic (driver), 135, 140
Fishman, Brenda, 190
Flohr, John, 95–96, 106, 119, 147
Flying Carpet (ride), 227
Flying Dutchman (ride), 227
Flying Tigers (ride), 151, 263n8
Forcellato, Dante, 30. *See also* Dante's Italian band
Forgrieve, Janet (reporter), 229
Foster, Allan K. (director), 73
Four Lads (vocal group), 162
Fouts, Rosemary, 38
Fox, Jack, 132
Franz, Albert, 149
Frazee, William ("Alligator Joe"), 75, 80–81
Fredericks, T. A., 46
Friederich, Elizabeth Buck, 24
Friederich, Patricia Campion, 25
Friederich, Peter, 24, 25, 75
Friederich, Phillip, 24, 25, 75, 81, 90, 94, 99, 103, 120, 237, 238; death, 120
Friedle, John, 70–71. *See also* Playland at the Beach (San Francisco)
Fritz, E. P., 46
Frog Hopper (ride), 227
Fuguitt, Glen V., 211, 220
Fulkerson, Lyle, 201
Fun House, 83, 111, 118, 197, 202, 227; demolished, 206; Hilarity Hall, 97; House of Troubles, 97; remodeled, 203–4; Third Degree (original fun house), 30, 36, 97, *188*
Furlong, Harry, 46–47
Futrell, Jim, 236

Galante, Al (ballroom), 162
Gallagher, Dennis (Denver city auditor), 3, 226
Gallo, Bill (reporter), 221, 222
Ganz, Rudolph (orchestra), 99
Gardiner, Harry (the Human Fly), 86
Gates Rubber Company, 150, 156
Gayway Inn (restaurant), 111, 197; back bar from Denver Union Station in, 111; renamed Eatway Inn, 226–27
George Morrison and His Rigadooners, 101–2. *See also* Morrison, George
Gene Holter Wild Animal Show, 162
Gessell, Ernie (driver), 138
Gillpatrick, William, 19. *See also* Tuileries Park (Englewood)
Giovanni, Pete, 150
Gordanier, Robert (mayor of Lakeside), 217, 219
Gottschalck, Charlie (driver), 136, 145, 171
Graf, Bob, 102
Graham, Sheri Thurman (driver), 171, 172, 173–76, 179, 180
Gravitron (a ride), 227
Greene, Frank, 47
Gumpertz, Samuel W., 54
Gurtler, Arnold, 114–15, 118, 151.
Gurtler, Budd, 151, 221.
Gurtler, Jack, 114, 121, 143, 151.
Gurtler, Sandy, 221–22.
Gustafson, Anna, 54
Gustafson, Lillie, 54
Gustafson, Mable, 54
Guth, Anna, 50, 53; owner of Pete's Place (later Northwestern Park), 50

Haffner, William, 118
Hall, Frank, 149
Haney, Linden K., 103–4
Hardigan, H. D., 93–94
Harris, Clarence, 42
Harris, Phil (musician), 115
Harry's Club Forty-Four (Lakeside), 196–97
Hart, Toney (actor), 73
Harvey, Georgia (actress), 73
Hazard, J. W., 47

Heart Flip (ride), 204, 227
Helber, Julian (reporter), 44
Hemberger, Theodore (driver), 133
Hemminger, Spec (driver), 133
Henry Busse (band), 117
Heritage Square (Golden). *See* Magic Mountain (Golden)
Herman, Woody (band), 155
Herrmann, Al, Jr. (district attorney), 196
Hewitt, Earl (Denver Fire and Police Board), 42
Hicks, Bonnie, 118
Hill, Bill, 114, 140, 170
Hillier, Bevis, 109
Hillman, Jim, 230
Hines, Issac, 47
Hogen, Henry, 42
Holden, Tom, 135, 137. *See also* automobile racing (Denver), Merchant's Park (Denver)
Hook, Flora, 149
Hook, Irving, 149
Horano, Roberto H. (matador), 82
Hoxsey, Arch (driver), 132
Hull, Betty, 118, 259n20
Hurricane (ride), 112, 205, 227, 235; ticket booth 109

Interstate, 70, 193–94
Irving Aaronson and His Commanders (band), 102
Ivers, Walter C., 29
Ives, Burl, 160

Jackson, Cowboy (driver), 171
Jacobs, Andrea, 236
Jail (restaurant), 98, 123, 124
Jamison, Frank, 145
Jan Garba's Band, 102
Jefferson County (Colorado), 10, 45, 46, 49, 51, 211; Berkeley area of, 25; economic impact of Lakeside Amusement Park on, 49; economic impact of Lakeside Mall on, 154, 212, 217; Fair Association, 52–53; Fire Safety Committee, 196; grand jury, 196–97, 198–99, 202, 269n14; and town of Lakeside, 195, 215–17, 218–19, 220
Jernigan, Opal Doris, 259n19
Joe Mann's Orchestra, 123
Johnson, Albert W., 106
Johnson, Edwin (US senator), 194

Johnson, Garfield "Bob" (mayor of Mountain View), 217
Johnson, Rykken (reporter), 204
Johnson, Samuel (judge), 103
Jones, Spike, 160
Jurgens, Dick (band), 121

Karman, Morton, 215
Kasson, John, 8, 27
Kaynor, Carl (actor), 73
Keefe, John A., 25, 46, 81, 90
Keller, Maryanne "Moe" (state representative), 218, 219
Kelly, Carroll (driver), 141
Kelly, Guy (reporter), 218
Kelly, Lew (actor), 73
Kendell, Lothe (actor), 73
Kennywood (PA), 8, 105, 121
Kessler, George, 21
King, Wayne (band), 102
Kingsland, Ambrose (mayor of New York City), 12–13
King Soopers, 156; at Lakeside Mall, 153, 273n7
Kirchoff, Frank, 81, 90, 100, 202
Klaff, Vivian Z., 211, 220
Kline, Eddie, 83
Koch, Clarence, 154
Koch, Karl, 104
Krasner, Benjamin: arrives at Lakeside, 104, 106–7; buys Lakeside Amusement Park, 257n3; as conservative man, 108; daughter born, 116; 192; early life, 93; inducted into Colorado Motorsports Hall of Fame, 182; inducted into National Sprint Car Hall of Fame, 182; kidnapped and robbed, 149–50; Lakeside Speedway, 136, 137, 138, 139, 144, 145, 169, 170, 174, 177–78, 182; marriage, 116; passion for Lakeside, 192–93, 237–38; passion for trains, 149–50, 165, 125
Krasner, Miriam Caplan, 116, 148, 151, 174
Krasner, Rhoda, 11, 150, 228–29; 65th anniversary of Lakeside Amusement Park, 199; 100th anniversary of Lakeside Amusement Park, 225–26, 229–30, 239; birth, 6; and El Patio Ballroom, 194; fights for Lakeside Amusement Park, 201–2, 238; and grand jury investigation, 197–98, 203; growing up at Lakeside Amusement Park, 193; inducted into Colorado Motorsports Hall of Fame,

Index   295

182; inherits Lakeside Amusement Park, 193; on Kiddies Playland, 263n8; and Lakeside (town), 195, 218, 219–20; on Lakeside Speedway, 141, 173, 181, 267n26; on rides and attractions at Lakeside Amusement Park, 204–5, 206, 227; rivalry with Elitch Gardens, 221, 190

Kurtz, Maxine, 120

Kyser, Kay, 107, 257n5; *Kay Kyser's Kollege of Musical Knowledge* (radio series), 107

Labb, W. H., 35, 36

LaCouvre, Maybelle (actress), 93

Laffing Sal, 111, 141, 204; put in storage, 206

Lake Rhoda, 116, 161, 195, 229; Chris Craft and Dodge speedboats on, 110; *Miss Colorado* on, 199. *See also* Sylvan Lake

Lakeshore Railroad, 35, 110, 112; California Zephyr added, 149–50; Denver, Rio Grande, and Western railroad and, 150, 127; Prospector steam engine added, 150; Puffing Billie (steam engine), 150; station, 30; Whistling Tom (steam engine), 150

Lakeside (town of), 25–26, 34–35, 45, 54–55, 78, 209–10, 214, 218, 236; decertification attempts, 216–17, 218–19; fire department, 76, 195, 197, 214; government, 33, 45, 214; jail, 26, 202; police, 26–27, 42, 214, 215, 237; population, 54, 213; relationship to Lakeside Amusement Park, 217–18, 223–24; road maintenance, 215–16; streetcar line, 30–31, 32

Lakeside Amusement Park, 18, 227–28, 238–39; 100th anniversary, 3, 225–26, 229–30, 235; 1972 Grand Jury investigation of, 196–99, 200–1, 202, 206–07, 236–37; advertising, 107–8; American National Bank role in, 24–25, 90, 99, 100, 103, 104; Art Deco makeover, 108–10, 119; attendance figures, 40, 43, 44, 50, 51, 53, 75, 83, 97, 102, 108, 113, 119, 158, 160, 205; automobile parking, 32–33, 111–12, 120, 234, 235; baseball at, 43, 50, 79, 74, 82, 103, 111–12, 134, 260–61n7; Benjamin Krasner buys, 106–7; Central Park area of, 35, 226; Children's Days, 51, 102; City Beautiful connection, 4, 21–22, 42–43, 48–49, 55, 67–69, 70, 72, 74–75, 76, 147, 149, 232; City Beautiful connection unravels, 76–77, 79, 82–84, 85–86, 87; community relations, 51–52; comparison to Blackpool (Great Britain), 233–34; competition with Elitch Gardens, 115, 151, 221, 222–23; deaths at, 34, 86–87, 118, 269n7; development and construction, 4, 10, 24, 27, 28, 30, 34; family friendly, 162–63; financial difficulties, 90, 99–100, 103–4; fires at, 76, 199–200; fireworks displays, 108, 194–95; grand opening, 20, 39–40, 41; Great Depression and, 102, 103; greyhound track, 99–100, 124, 125; Hibernia Bank and Trust purchases, 90; hospital, 41; identity as historic park, 164–65, 199, 204, 228–29, 236; Interstate 70 construction and, 193–94; Kiddies Playland, 151, 263n8; Ku Klux Klan at, 113–14; Lakeside Museum, 84; lawsuits, 149, 223; lighting, 29–30, 40, 93, 109, 110; newspaper and magazine coverage of, 35, 40–41, 43, 44, 49, 50, 70, 72–73, 84–85, 92–93; original layout, 35–36, 44–45; outlasts Magic Mountain and Celebrity Sports Center, 161; picnics, 43, 102, 108, 111, 120, 150, 156, 163; referred to as White City, 39, 42, 45, 50, 53, 67, 70, 86, 94, reinvention as working class park, 90–91, 93–94, 95–96, 104; restaurants, 93, 95; rides and attractions, 35–36, 36–37, 50, 54, 81, 83–85 (song in praise of), 94, 97–98, 100, 101, 110, 120, 161–62, 163–64, 197, 205, 227; robbery, 42, 164; segregation at, 113–14; special events and celebrations at, 43–44, 51, 52–53, 75, 76, 80, 83, 86, 95, 96–97, 103, 113, 162; unions and, 72–73, 81, 102–3, 163; working class identity of, 115–16, 121; World War II, 116, 117–8, 118–19. *See also individual building names; owner names; individual restaurant names; individual ride names*

Lakeside Mall: compared to Cherry Creek Shopping Center, 153; construction of, 153–54; deannexation talks, 211, 212–13, 217, 219–20; demolition, 228; Denver Dry Good Store at, 153, 154, 220, 184; financial impact of, 210, 220; grand opening, 154; Krasner sells land for, 152, 153; Lakeside National Bank opens, 155; list of stores at, 153; Markets, Inc. and, 152–53; Montgomery Ward store opens, 155; relationship to Lakeside Amusement Park, 155–56, 184; Walmart built on site, 273n7

Lakeside Park Company, 106, 197, 259n19

Lakeside Realty and Amusement Company, 10, 25, 45

Lakeside Shopping Center. *See* Lakeside Mall
Lakeside Speedway, 131, 228; 50th anniversary season, 180; attendance, 136–37, 141–42, 143, 144, 176, 177–78; Bill McGaw's Tournament of Thrills appearance at, 177; closure, 181–82; and Colorado Motorsports Hall of Fame, 181, 182, 268n34; compact class, 178–79; competition between midgets and stock cars, 169–70, 172; competition with other tracks, 137, 143, 182; construction, 135; demolition derby at, 179; driver deaths, 141–42; family involvement with races, 173–74; fan death, 180; Hooligan race, 171; Jimmie James Team at, 138; Johnny Dark Race at, 177; Joie Chitwood Thrill Show appearance at, 177; Late Model class, 179; layout of track, 136, 138, 179; legacy, 182–83; midget racers, 131–32 (history of), 133–34 (first attempt at Lakeside), 135, 136–37, 145–46; Offenhauser engines at, 133, 137, 139, 140, 144, 183; Powder Puff drivers, 172–73, 174–76; racing circuit, 143, 144 ; relationship with Lakeside Amusement Park, 138, 139, 146, 170; reputation, 137–38; Rocky Mountain Classic, 139; stock cars, 145 (first appearance at), 167–68 (history of), 168–69 (in Colorado), 169–70, 171, 171–72 (accidents in), 176; television broadcasts from, 176, 178; V8 engines at, 179; V8-60 engines at, 144, 183, 184, 186, 187. *See also individual driver names; race sanctioning bodies*
Lakeside Village. *See* Lakeside Mall
Lammers, Carl, 4
Lamont, Bill, 217
Land, Bob (driver), 170–71, 181
Lane, Milo, 185
Larson, Erik, 5–6
Laurie, Piper, 177
Lauterback, E. J., 97
Lee, Elmore, 39
Lemberger, Tony, 220
Leslie, Roy (sponsor), 141, 144
Leuthner, Stuart (writer), 108, 110, 193, 206
Lewin, Albert, 25, 29, 34, 43, 44
Libeskind, Daniel, 230–31
Lilly, Gib (driver), 169
Lindsey, Barry, 149
Lindsey, Benjamin (judge), 97
Lindsey, John (sheriff), 27, 42, 73

Lindstrom, Flora, 54
Lindy Loop (ride), 101, 163
Linkletter, Art, 160
Livesay, John (lawyer), 46
Londoner, Wolf (mayor of Denver), 20
Loof, Arthur, 70–71. *See also* Playland at the Beach (San Francisco)
Loop-O-Plane (ride), 112, 149, 150
Lorrea, Rafael (matador), 162
Luchenback, H. L., 104

Magic Mountain (Golden), 158–59, 161; Marco Engineering role in, 158–59
Mandel, Leon, 168
Mangels, William F., 7–9, 36, 37, 83, 151
Manhattan Beach (Denver), 15–17, 20, 91, 132, 162; Aero Coaster at, 16; *Denver Municipal Facts* and, 68, 69–70, 250n1; Jerome Smiley on, 23; Sloan's Lake and, 15; streetcars and, 31
Manring, M. M., 98–99
Mapelli, Herman, 140
Mapelli Meat Company, 140
Marks, Fred, 46
Martell, Larry (driver), 187
Martin, Claire, 236
Matterhorn (ride), 163, 227
Matthews, G. C., 46
Maynard, Dorothy (actress), 86
McCabe, Albert, 55
McCarthy, Wilson, 150
McDaniel, Hattie, 101
McFarland, William, 17–18
McFarland, W. W., 16
McGee, H. M., 148
McLaughlin, Cyrus H., 11
McLaughlin, E. E., 46
McNeese, Burt (driver), 186
McWilliams, Charles, 201
McWilliams, George, 201
McWilliams, Paul, 200, 201
Means, Rice, 113
Melvin Anthony Jazz Orchestra, 95
Merry-go-round (ride), 35, 36–37, 83, 164, 228, 235; in Kiddies Playland, 151, 188; new building for, 110
Michael, Henry W., 17
midget racing: Gilmore Stadium (CA), 132; "Hap" Woodman and, 132; Ken Brenneman

and, 132; Oakland Speedway (CA), 132; Santa Ana Municipal Stadium (CA), 132. *See also individual driver names*; Lakeside Speedway; race sanctioning bodies
Mile High Greyhound Park (Commerce City), 121, 143
Mile High Racing Association (MHRA, later Colorado Midget Racing Association), 140, 143
Miles, Tim (CARC), 181
Miller, Bill, 213
Miller, Glenn, 107, 115, 259n20
Miller, Jerry (racing photographer), 141, 173, 176
Miller, Johnny, 84
Miller, J. W., 81, 95
Mills, W. B., 86
Miniature golf course (attraction), 101
Moffett, Jim, 204, 205
Moore, Joseph, 54, 101, 103
Moorman, Edwin H., 28
Morgan, W. M. (district attorney), 46
Morley, Clarence (governor of Colorado), 113
Morris, J. M., 104
Morrison, Barry (reporter), 203–4
Morrison, George (band), 101–2, 114
Moses, Robert, 236
Mott, Frank Luther, 34
Mountain View (Colorado), 50, 77, 78, 195, 210, 211, 216; Lakeside Mall and, 217
Moyer, Cliff (driver), 133
Mullen, Robert R., 106
Mulvihill, John, 99, 114; buys Elitch Gardens, 92
Music Corporation of America (MCA), 106–7, 108, 115
Musick, Morris (driver), 169
Music Plaza (area in Lakeside), 30, 35

Nasaw, David, 9, 28, 105, 121
National Amusement Park Historical Association (NAPHA), 112, 225–26, 230, 236
National Association of Amusement Parks, Pools, and Beaches (NAAPPB), 115–16, 151–52; Julian Bamberger and, 115–16
Na Vassar Ladies Band, 80
Naylin, Robert, 196
Neice, Ira, 47
Newton, Quigg (mayor of Denver), 119
Nichols, Marjorie, 97
Nicholson, Will (mayor of Denver), 154

Noel, Thomas J., 12, 13
Nollenberger, Theodore, 16
Norgren, Barbara, 12, 13

O'Connell, Hugh, 26
Octopus (ride), 112
Old Mill (ride): at Elitch Gardens, 118; at Lakeside Amusement Park, 83, 97; at Sea Lion Park (Coney Island), 8. *See also* Tunnel of Love (ride)
Olds, Bob (driver), 136, 139, 145
Olinger, George, 78
Olmsted, Frederick Law, Jr., 77
Olmsted, Frederick Law, Sr., 14, 21; Columbian Exposition, 5
Olson, George (musician), 102

Pachello, Dick (CARC), 181
Paglia, Michael, 230–31
Parrish, Michael, 97
Parsons, Johnnie (driver), 138
Pastor, Gene (driver), 136, 138
Pastor, Tony, 118–19
Payne, John (actor), 160
Pearce, Fred, 79, 97. *See also* Derby coaster (ride)
Pearce, Horatio B., 210
Pearce, Josiah, 79, 97. *See also* Derby coaster (ride)
Pedroza, Romey (driver), 133
Perkins, Percy, 164–65
Permitt's Male Quartet, 95
Perricone, Gaspar (judge), 220
Peterson, Leo, 154
Philippina, Don (band), 74
Philip Zang Brewing Company. *See* Zang Brewing Company
Pickup, Judd (driver), 137
Pirate Ship (ride), 227
Plantation (restaurant), 98–99, 123
Playland at the Beach (San Francisco), 33, 70–71, 234
Plemons, Blu (driver), 172, 179
Pony track (attraction), 36
Poundstone amendment to the Colorado State Constitution, 211–12; town of Lakeside and, 217, 223–24
Poynter, Beulah (actress), 75–76
Proctor, Juanita, 195

298   INDEX

Progressive era working class reforms 9, 21, 40
Public Service Company of Colorado, 156, 163

Quinn, Bob, 201

race-sanctioning bodies. *See* American Automobile Association (AAA); Denver Midget Racing Club; Colorado Automobile Racing Club (CARC); Rocky Mountain Midget Racing Association (RMMRA)
Read, Henry (artist), 12
Reiss, Charles, 54
Reiss, Steven A., 74
Ribbet, George, 30
Rivas, Antonio (matador), 82
River Front Park (Denver), 11. *See also* Walker, John Brisbane
Riverview Park (Chicago), 71
Roberts, Blanche, 54–55
Roberts, Jim (driver), 133
Roberts, Randy (driver), 180
Robertson, William, 108
Robins, Jimmy (driver), 133
Robinson, Pauline, 259n19
Rock-O-Plane (ride), 112, 150
Rocky Mountain Midget Racing Association (RMMRA), 114, 140, 141, 143, 144–45, 180, 181; formation, 137; ceases to function, 146, 170; revival, 170
Rodriguis, Jose (matador), 82
Rogers, Byron, 154
Rogers, Eddy, 156
Roll-O-Plane (ride), 112
Ross, "Bud" (actor), 73
Rotor (ride), 156
Round-Up (ride), 156, 205
Ruhl, Capt. Ernest, 84
Russo, Ray, 215
Ruth, Joseph, 150
Ruttner, Jennie, 106
Ruttner, Martie, 106, 164, 193

Satellite (ride), 161, 162, 205, 227, 235, 265n32
Saxon, Don, 163
Scenic Railway (ride), 34, 36, 40, 76, 62, 63
Schafer, Connie, 223
Schey, Vic (driver), 141–42. *See also* Shay, Buddy
Schirmer, Godfrey, 25, 46, 48, 81, 90, 99; death, 100

Schneider, Emil, 154
Schuller, Joseph, 212
Scrambler (ride), 161, 162, 227
Scripps, Edward W., 55, 72
Sedlemeyer, Frank, 41
Shafroth, John (governor of Colorado), 75
Shaw, Artie, 119
Shay, Buddy (driver), 141–42. *See also* Schey, Vic
Shoot-the-Chutes (ride), 36, 41, 74; demolished, 112, 258n13
shopping malls, 152
Simpson, William, 19. *See also* Tuileries Park (Englewood)
Skating Rink (building), 30, 35, 60, 74
Skoota Boats (ride), 120, 164, 227
Slusser, Marv (driver), 170, 172, 173, 176, 179, 180
Smiley, Jerome: amusement parks and, 23–24; Denver park space and, 13, 232, 274n16; streetcars and, 31, 78–79; tuberculosis and, 78
Smith, Eben, 32
Smith, Mike, 216
Snyder, Ben (judge), 47
Snyder, Chas, 27
Sopris, Richard (mayor of Denver), 13
Speer, Robert W. (mayor of Denver), 3, 4, 11–13, 17–19, 92; Arlington Park, 20–21, 38; and Elitch Gardens, 120, 225; and Lakeside Amusement Park, 40, 42, 48–49; legacy, 230, 231–32; and parks, 24, 32; and vice, 55. *See also* Denver City Beautiful Movement
Spickler, Burton (driver), 140
Spickler, Miles (driver), 139
Spider (ride), 227. *See also* Octopus (ride)
Sports Car Club of America, 177
Sproul, Derby, 108
Stapleton, Benjamin: Elitch Gardens and, 113; mayor of Denver, 77, 119
Staride (ride), 83, 163, 200, 227, 265n32; 66
Stewart, James (Jimmy), 115
Stickrod, Albert W., 148
stock car racing: Automotive Racing Club of America, 168; Darling Raceway (SC), 168; Central State Racing Association, 168; Long Island Stock Car Classic, 168; Midwest Auto Racing Club, 168; National Association for Stock Car Auto Racing (NASCAR), 168; Oakland Speedway (CA), 168; Tom Wolfe on, 167. *See also individual driver names*; Lakeside Speedway; *race sanctioning bodies*

Stone, John (Jefferson County commissioner), 216–17, 218, 219, 220
Stout, Ned, 107
streetcar companies (Denver): Denver amusement parks, 31–32; Denver Circle Railroad, 132; Denver City Railway Company, 31; and West End Electric Car Company, 31. *See also* Denver Tramway Company
Sutherland, Ann (actress), 80
Sutton, Daniel (mayor of Englewood), 54
Sutton, John Calvin, 158. *See also* Magic Mountain (Golden)
Swanson, Don, 199
Swimming Pool (Natatorium), 30, 100, 102, 111, 197; destroyed in fire, 199–200
Sylvan Lake, 10, 25; *See also* Lake Rhoda

Taft, Al (driver), 187
Tammen, Harry, 15; owner of Sells-Floto Circus, 15
Tate, Beth (actress), 73
Taylor, William A., 86
Tea Cup (ride), 227
theme parks, 10, 121, 147, 158, 191; in Denver, 191, 222–23
Thomas, George (mayor of Lakeside), 196, 197, 214
Thompson, Frederic, 27
Thompson, Jack, 200
Thompson, LaMarcus A., 36; Thompson Scenic Railways, 36
Thompson, William "Big Bill" (mayor of Chicago), 71
Thornsberry, Harry, 150
Throckmorton, Lusion Gibson, 99, 100; Denver Greyhound Racing Association, 99
Thurman, Don (driver), 173, 175, 180
Tickler (ride), 7, 37, 64
Tilt-a-Whirl (ride), 150, 229
Tolan, Johnny (driver), 140–41, 182, *186*
Tower of Jewels (building), 27–28, 40, 95–96, 111, 226, 235, *55*
Trabant (ride), 164
True, Walter, 154
Tuileries Park (Englewood), 19, 20, 91; *Denver Municipal Facts* and, 68, 69–70, 250n11; streetcar line and, 32
Tumble Bug (ride), 112, 206, *128*
Tunnel of Love (ride), 81, 97

Underwood, James, 195–96

Van Dyke, Jerry (driver), 181
Van Rosen, Agnes (Tournament of Thrills), 162
Velvet Coaster (ride), 30, 35–36, 40; destroyed in fire, 76, *63*
Vettel, Edward, 112; Zephyr coaster (New Orleans), 112. *See also* Cyclone (ride)
Vichiola, Hans, 205. *See also* Cyclone (ride)
Vickers, William B., 14
Vivian, John, 39
Von Frellich, Gerri, 152–53, 211, 212–13. *See also* Lakeside Mall
Vorbeck, Bob (driver), 137

Walker, John Brisbane, 11. *See also* River Front Park (Denver)
Walt Disney World, 155, 158; Celebrity Sports Center and 160
Walton, John, 6–7, 89, 233–34
Waltz Trip (ride), 81
Ware, Bob, 145
Watkins, K. C., 164
Watts, Steven, 161
Weber, Harry L., 16, 28
Welk, Lawrence, 121
Wenquist, Chester, 26
Wenzel, John, 229, 237,
Werner, Bill (driver), 133
Wheat Ridge (Colorado), 77, 78, 153, 195, 200, 210, 216; Lakeside Mall and, 217, 219–20; Wheat Ridge Fire Protection District, 195, 196, 214
Whip (ride), 7, 83, 205, 227; in Kiddies Playland, 151; ticket booth, 109
White, J. F., 50, 53
Whiteman, Paul, 107, 257n5
Wild Chipmunk (ride), 156–57, 163, 205, 229
Wilde, Dan (mayor of Wheat Ridge), 217
Williams, Swede (driver), 133
Wilson, Dempsey (driver), 139
Wisdom Boomerang (ride), 227
Wise, Myrle, 200
Wolvington, Winston (judge), 199, 202
Wood, Cornelius Vanderbilt (C. V.) Jr., 158–59
Woodard, Aaron (driver), 138
World's Fairs, 5; Century of Progress International Exposition, 103; Midway

Plaisance at, 6–7; Panama–Pacific International Exposition, 90–91. *See also* Columbian Exposition
Wright, Loyd Sr., 159

Yaeger, John P., 26, 45
Yellowstone Pictures, 96

Zang, Adolph, 4, 24, 25, 238; arrested for violating liquor laws, 46, 47–48; builds Lakeside Amusement Park, 10, 26, 69, 77, 235; builds Oxford Hotel (Denver), 85; death, 85; sells Lakeside Amusement Park, 81; Zang Mansion (Denver), 85
Zang, Anna Buck, 24
Zang, Gertrude, 40
Zang, Minnie, 24
Zang, Philip, 24
Zang Brewing Company, 24, 85
Zang Beer 4, 25, 81, 238
Zeckendorf, William, 159
Zimmerhackel, Harry, 103, 104
Zoch, Justin, 182
Zoom (ride), 227–28

www.ingramcontent.com/pod-product-compliance
Lightning Source LLC
Chambersburg PA
CBHW020354080526
44584CB00014B/1013